T0302261

"This is a seminal work simplifying and clarifying the complex web of payments. Payments has gone from being boring to the boardroom, and *Understanding Payments* shines a light on the intricacies and actors within the payments ecosystem. It's a must-read to help decode what has been a poorly understood subject."

Sir Ron Kalifa, *Author of* The Kalifa Review of UK Fintech

"A must-read for anyone interested in payments or fintech. I wish I had this book when building Monzo."

Tom Blomfield, *Founder of Monzo and GoCardless, Y Combinator Partner*

"*Understanding Payments* will gain a significant place in the payments industry, being both an extremely good educational tool and an ongoing reference book. Anyone entering the complex world of payments will benefit from this book from day one. It's an easy read and covers all areas of the payments value chain based on Neira's considerable knowledge and experience. She set out to demystify payments and has certainly achieved that objective. I particularly liked the detailed analysis of payments regulations and licences; the former are often viewed as a mundane area, but adherence is essential in any business operating in the payments industry. This is one of Neira's main areas of focus and will be a key reference chapter for many of us. The glossary is amazing. Probably a decent subject for Mastermind and clearly worth having with you at all times! Already recognised as an industry expert, Neira's first book will, I am sure, not be her last, and I look forward to the second volume."

Roger Alexander, *NED Portfolio*

"It's very hard to find all you need to know about payments in one place. This is the place."

Chris Skinner, *CEO, TheFinanser.com*

"This indispensable guide to the payments industry will become one of the most well-thumbed books in my study, I have no doubt whatsoever."

Dave Birch, *Author, Advisor and Commentator on Digital Financial Services*

"*Understanding Payments* is a tour de force in depth and scope, and it's a likely candidate to become the first authoritative source of knowledge and reference for payments professionals, those aspiring to join the ranks of payments professionals, investors, regulators, academic research and education. There is a common saying in the payments industry: 'Payments are easy as long as they work'. Neira Jones very expertly lays out how and why different payment types, cards, open banking, crypto, actually work and how they depend on technology, collaboration, private enterprise, regulation, and innovation. Neira Jones's grasp of the interdependence of technology, business models and trust gives *Understanding Payments* additional relevance to all professional communities that depend on getting paid – or paying someone else."

Stanley Skoglund, *Partner, Minerva Partnership Consultancy*

"Neira's book is a much-needed guide to the complex and diverse world of payments. It is also a highly entertaining guide to that world – I particularly love her cartoons!"

Jim Wadsworth, *EVP, Konsentus; Formerly at Mastercard, Vocalink, and JPMorgan*

"*Understanding Payments* serves as a comfortable digest of the complex and many-faceted world of payments. For the average merchant, the organizations that enable electronic payments probably seem like a secret society complete with clandestine meetings where world-changing decisions are made and whose black-robed members expect merchants to be grateful for only having to pay a few percentage points for the privilege of having access to the fringes of the system. Neira Jones has done a wonderful job of peeling back the covers and providing down-to-earth explanations and illustrations that help to dispel these myths and fears and to peel away the complexities. Kudos for the research and shared experience."

Gary Yamamura, *President, Edept LLC*

"Neira has brought her wealth of experience together and produced the go-to resource tool for providers, users and advisers operating in the incessant payments ecosystem. *Understanding Payments* guides the reader, using plain English and intuitive graphics, through all the details essential to understanding and demystifying the world of payments and is essential reading for those who are new to the industry as well as more seasoned professionals."

Stuart Campbell, *Head of Payments at TLT LLP*

"A fascinating summary covering cards, interbank payments and open banking at a comprehensive but accessible level of detail. I keep dipping in and reading sections, with clear explanations, industry context and Neira's distilled words of wisdom on every page. No matter your level of experience, there is great learning content and concise explanations, making it valuable to all levels of reader."

Simon Burrows, *Payments Partner, EY LLP*

"Neira shines clarity and gives light to the complex world of payments. This is the payments bible and is a great accompaniment to Neira's lifelong purpose of educating the payments industry. Every payment professional should read it, and every business should have it as a reference point."

Angela Yore, *Co-founder, SkyParlour*

"*Understanding Payments* is a must-read for anyone in the business – be they a payment geek or a non-geek. The book demystifies the complex worlds of card and non-card payments in an entertaining and highly accessible way. An internationally recognised expert in payments, Neira Jones has written an authoritative work that bridges the gap between complex financial systems and everyday life. Her deep knowledge of and passion for the subject matter shine through every page. With her engaging writing style, she guides readers through the landscape of both established payment systems and emerging technologies, and highlights the increasingly 'blurred lines' we now live and work with. *Understanding Payments* is an exceptional work that is poised to become a definitive reference in the field of payments. I wish I'd had this book when I started out in payments!"

Jeremy Nicholds, Managing Director, Judo

"I've been in payments now for over 20 years and have always tried to resist the label of 'expert'; and how vindicated (and humble) do I feel when reading Neira's invaluable and comprehensive text on all things payments. Here is the expert! This will certainly become my go-to reference for all the things I thought I knew, should have known or never really got to the bottom of! I've been leading payments teams for a while and have been an advocate of the need to create some recognition of the specialist and the critical nature of the knowledge required – this book is a huge step forward in illustrating the crucial nature of the payments industry. Nothing moves without the value transaction to support it, and Neira's eloquent and easy-to-navigate explanations and illustrations will ensure we can continue to underpin that vital service with a foundation of knowledge for practitioners old and new. We all owe a huge thank you to Neira for the commitment to create such an important body of work."

Paul Horlock, Chief Payments Officer, Payments Centre of Excellence, Chief Operating Office, Santander

"A superb enlightening journey through the world of payments! This book masterfully navigates decoding complex concepts into digestible form, making the payments industry, for the first time, accessible to readers across a wide audience. From traditional methods to cutting-edge digital innovations, the book covers it, sparking a newfound appreciation for the payments ecosystem under constant evolution. The author's engaging prose effortlessly bridges all the moving parts. A must-read for anyone curious about the mechanics of payments, this book leaves you empowered with knowledge and a positive outlook on the limitless opportunities within payments."

Adrian Hausser, CEO, PayX Group

"This is the book that needed to be written. To dissolve the myths. To get us all to the same level of understanding. To fill in the gaps. Equipped with the insights from Neira's clear, unambiguous and thorough book, we can now align, resolve, plan and direct our resources towards a better future through payments. Underlying this excellent book is something that reveals the difference that payments makes to the world around us – removing friction and cost, reducing risk, enhancing convenience and increasing trust in a low-trust world. *Understanding Payments* helps us achieve our goal of democratising payments, removing the knowledge elites and opening up the industry to everyone. After reading this book, there will be no more exclusion through ignorance. I commend it to anyone who wants to understand the part our industry plays in making the world work and enhancing their role in it."

Tony Craddock, *Director General, The Payments Association*

"*Understanding Payments* is the book we have been waiting years to be written. Neira Jones, a highly respected industry practitioner, helps explain the many different payment types available today, how payments are actually made, introduces us to the multitude of stakeholders, showing where they fit in the value chains, covers the economic models involved and presents the current regulatory environment in which they operate. In this easy-to-digest book, she demystifies the abbreviations and buzzwords bandied around, using a light-hearted writing style and original hand-drawn illustrations. *Understanding Payments* will appeal to all those holding responsibility for payments, newcomers to the industry, as well as those with an inquiring mind. The payments industry is highly complex and experiencing rapid change. Thanks to this comprehensive and up-to-date book, readers will be better equipped to take sensible decisions."

Mark McMurtrie, *Director, Payments Consultancy Ltd and Ambassador, The Payments Association*

"Neira Jones' *Understanding Payments* is a well-crafted, researched and detailed review of the card payments industry and is a significant and weighty tome that will help both those in the industry and those wishing to understand its depth and complexity. The structure and fresh approach made the subject easy to follow and will enhance the knowledge of those who consume its goodness. I particularly enjoyed the illustrations by Neira's hand; they are clear, well-presented, and will add significant value to anyone with a card payments curiosity. The book is beyond compare; I know no other author with the depth of knowledge and understanding of this complex subject."

Soteris Vasili, *Chairman, Vasili Advisory*

"I had the pleasure of reviewing Neira's book or rather handbook or even bible. Neira is a long-time expert and practitioner in our industry, and it shows in the way she has approached the topic. It is a hugely detailed and useful guide that caters to everyone: whether you are a payments industry professional, an entrepreneur, a technology enthusiast, or simply curious about payments, this book caters to readers of all backgrounds. Whether you seek to upgrade your knowledge of payments or simply wish to comprehend the intricate mechanisms that underpin our daily financial interactions, this book promises to be an enlightening and enjoyable read. It's written in an easy-to-read, not too serious manner but with sufficient depth to satisfy those who really want to gain a thorough understanding of the area. Having reviewed the first four chapters on payment mechanics, economics, non-card-based mechanics and regulations and licences including KYC AML and a review of crypto standards, I can wholeheartedly recommend the book, which is engaging and informative, leaving no stone unturned in its exploration of the fascinating world of payments. Its well-structured content, insightful analysis, and real-world examples make it an invaluable resource."

Janusz Diemko, *CEO Xelopay, Angel Investor Mentor, Industry Enthusiast and Consultant*

"Simply … superb! Written by somebody who has clearly had 'a life in and around payments' and decades of experience, it is very clearly and concisely referenced and covers each and every facet of the complexity that surrounds banking, payments, technology and their respective, inexorable interfaces and intersections. Additionally, it cross-references key components whilst avoiding the inevitable Jargonese that typically surrounds intricate ecosystems in an 'unputdownable' manner. This book is a must-read and re-read for anybody that even remotely or deeply touches payments or who needs to learn real quick!"

Ken Lipton, *Chairman, Paycross*

"Neira has produced a comprehensive overview of payments that is both informative and very readable. Comparing the local and global systems and using up-to-date examples of systems and players make this book an ideal and, indeed, unique 'go-to' source for novices and payment geeks alike!"

Alison Donnelly, *Director, fscom*

"As a so-called 'payments veteran' having spent most of my career in payments companies, I found myself finally linking all the roles of the participants together, why they exist and what their value is to end users. If this bible of payments existed when I was entering the industry 30 years ago, it would have transformed my career, enabling a fast demystification of what can be experienced as a complex market, and encouraged innovative ideas and entrepreneurial actions for the good of myself and the industry at large. I encourage anyone that has payments experience or those considering entering this fascinating and rewarding industry to consume this book, revisit it regularly and help contribute new ideas as they emerge in this highly disruptive period which can only continue to accelerate in terms of change. Investors, start-ups, banks, regulators and anyone involved in the payments industry should read this book. You will finally be able to piece together the ecosystem delivered in such a concise and well-written way. This book should be mandatory for every employee in a company that contributes to the payments industry.

Understanding the respective roles and responsibilities of all payments players along with clear views on the economic drivers of those parties can only drive efficiency and value in the payments ecosystem. Having a global perspective enables the reader to relate to the challenges of international payment acceptance and articulates the solutions to overcome these. Finally, being able to easily consume material around the world of digital payments, crypto and blockchain and to relate this to our legacy payment systems and methods will help the reader to tackle this new world with confidence rather than worry about not being relevant anymore."

Andy McDonald, CEO Cloudapps, Advisor to Truevo Payments Ltd, Business Coach; Formerly at ACI Worldwide, Retail Decisions, Moneybox, and NCR

"Neira Jones has great timing. There is so much changing in payments in 2023, and along comes Neira's book on 'payments everything'. It is up to date with the new Payment Systems Regulator (PSR) proposed regulations in the UK. She has a discussion on the proposed PSD3 regulations in the EU, and she talks about the new real-time payments in the US. She covers cards, digital wallets and online payments, along with the regulatory issues of the day. I spend my time in online security, but this will be a really good reference for payments."

Ken Palla, Retired Director, MUFG Union Bank and Consultant at Palla Consulting

"This book is a must for anyone within the cyber security professional who is offering consultancy to the finance sector. Having a sound understanding on how the payment ecosystem works is critical if you are to assist with securing it."

Charles White, CEO, The Cyber Scheme

"A book to read and to have for everybody who works and is interested in the payment industry and beyond! A masterpiece combining a clear explanation of the complex payment ecosystem with a valuable perspective on future developments and opportunities! Brava Neira."

Flavia Alzetta, CEO, NED, Advisor

"In a field where jargon often clouds understanding, *Understanding Payments* by Neira Jones stands as a lighthouse of clarity. Neira masterfully deciphers the complexity of payments and fintech, offering invaluable insights for both seasoned experts and novices alike. I was particularly captivated by her detailed yet accessible breakdowns of open banking, interbank systems, cross-border, and emerging technologies. The book's perfect blend of depth, real-world examples, and clear language makes it an essential resource that you'll want to keep within arm's reach, whether you're in the C-suite or just entering the industry. Just like AI, you'll survive without it, for now, but with it you will go further and faster."

John Davies, CTO/Co-founder of Velo Payments

"On behalf of all payment professionals and enthusiasts, we extend our heart-felt gratitude for Neira's selfless dedication to publishing a book on payments that isn't boring. Her efforts are poised to establish an enduring educational legacy, a sentiment succinctly encapsulated by the words of political scientist Kalu Ndukwe Kalu: 'The things you do for yourself are gone when you are gone, but the things you do for others remain as your legacy'. In this luminous context, Neira's accomplishment shines through as she presents a book about payments that masterfully engages readers without succumbing to monotony. This book not only caters to those seeking to revisit or comprehend unfamiliar facets of the industry, but also warmly welcomes newcomers to the intricate world of payments. With bated anticipation, we eagerly await the forthcoming release of the second volume!"

Dr Mark Goldspink, *Payments Professional*

UNDERSTANDING PAYMENTS

This is the book for professionals in the payments industry. Written in an engaging and accessible style, it enables new and experienced payments practitioners alike to understand the fundamentals of the various payment ecosystems, and to quickly get up to speed on developments in the industry.

From cards to bank and alternative payments, the jargon is debunked and myths are busted. For each ecosystem, a simple framework is used: mechanics, economics, risks, and future outlook, enabling comparison and the evaluation of the best applications in different scenarios. The book also provides an overview of the global regulatory landscape. Drawing on real examples throughout, it weaves together the underpinning ecosystem principles, legislation, and key stakeholders. It offers readers practical advice regarding, and insights into, the key disciplines and equips them with an understanding of the key issues and opportunities. Also including an extensive and comprehensive glossary of terms – the first of its kind in the payments industry – this book will be used as an essential reference for years to come.

Understanding Payments will enable payments practitioners, private sector corporations, and regulators to keep up with a fast-evolving and extremely competitive industry. It can be used across businesses to help train staff and as part of continuing professional development, and will be useful to those involved in mergers and acquisitions, investors wanting to understand the industry, professional services firms, law firms and consultants, and policy makers.

Neira Jones advises organisations of all sizes on payments, fintech, regtech, cybercrime, information security, fraud, and regulations. As a strategic board advisor and non-executive director, she takes great pride in working with innovative companies and contributing to their growth. She is an independent panel member for the Payment Systems Regulator, and has previously worked for Barclaycard, Santander, Abbey National, Oracle Corp., and Unisys.

UNDERSTANDING PAYMENTS

A Whistle-Stop Tour into What You Thought You Knew

Neira Jones

Routledge
Taylor & Francis Group

LONDON AND NEW YORK

Designed cover image: © Getty Images / ipopba

First published 2024
by Routledge
4 Park Square, Milton Park, Abingdon, Oxon OX14 4RN

and by Routledge
605 Third Avenue, New York, NY 10158

Routledge is an imprint of the Taylor & Francis Group, an informa business

British Library Cataloguing-in-Publication Data
A catalogue record for this book is available from the British Library

Library of Congress Cataloging-in-Publication Data
Names: Jones, Neira, author.
Title: Understanding payments: a whistle-stop tour into what you thought you
knew / Neira Jones.
Description: Abingdon, Oxon; New York, NY: Routledge, 2024.
Identifiers: LCCN 2023044471 (print) | LCCN 2023044472 (ebook) |
ISBN 9781032631363 (hardback) | ISBN 9781032631349 (paperback) |
ISBN 9781032631394 (ebook)
Subjects: LCSH: Electronic funds transfers.
Classification: LCC HG1710 .J66 2024 (print) | LCC HG1710 (ebook) |
DDC 332.1/78—dc23/eng/20230926
LC record available at https://lccn.loc.gov/2023044471
LC ebook record available at https://lccn.loc.gov/2023044472

ISBN: 978-1-032-63136-3 (hbk)
ISBN: 978-1-032-63134-9 (pbk)
ISBN: 978-1-032-63139-4 (ebk)

DOI: 10.4324/9781032631394

Typeset in Joanna
by codeMantra

CONTENTS

ABOUT THE AUTHOR

With more than 25 years in financial services and technology, Neira believes in change through innovation and partnerships, and always strives to demystify the hype surrounding current issues. She advises organisations of all sizes on payments, fintech, regtech, cybercrime, information security, fraud, and regulations. As a strategic board adviser and non-executive director, she takes great pride in working with innovative companies and contributing to their growth. Her coaching and training services include the popular live Payments 101, Regulations 101, and Payments 102 courses and her e-learning platform at neirajones.thinkific.com. She also provides payment security expert witness services and helps with mergers and acquisitions, as well as cybersecurity due diligence. She likes engaging on social media and as a professional speaker regularly addresses global audiences in person and virtually. She is an independent panel member for the Payment Systems Regulator, and has previously worked for Barclaycard, Santander, Abbey National, Oracle Corp., and Unisys. Her clients span industry sectors, including financial services, fintech, retail, legal, consulting, information security, and technology.

INTRODUCTION

Payments are pervasive

A Google search on the word "payments" returns about 9.8 trillion results. A further search on "what are payments?" reduces this number by two thirds. If you narrow it down to "payments training courses", you get about 140 million results including sponsored entries, each focussing on the piece of the payments puzzle that is relevant or commercially important. Evidently, payments are complicated and confusing, because the word means different things to different people.

As a cardholder or bank account holder, we don't really need to understand payments, we just want to send money, buy things, or use services. At some point, a payment will take place, but this is only secondary to the primary goal, and therefore, as consumers, we object to jumping through seemingly unnecessary hurdles ... And we want reassurance that our money is safe with those to whom it has been entrusted. When we tap our mobile phone on a card reader to buy our morning coffee, we don't need to know that data could have travelled from our favourite coffee shop, through

DOI: 10.4324/9781032631394-1

multiple entities and networks in the value chain, eventually reaching our bank or card provider, and then coming all the way back before we see the "transaction approved" message only a few milliseconds later. When our offspring needs an emergency financial top-up because budgeting is not their strong point, we use online banking, or our mobile banking app if we're tech savvy, and expect the money to be there straight away. We don't need to know how it works, because we just trust that it works.

Payments evolve fast

Fifteen years ago – at least in the UK, one of the most advanced markets in the world – we wouldn't have dreamt of payments being so convenient, instantaneous, and ubiquitous. We thought nothing of bank payments taking three days or more to process. We still had cheque books and much cash in our wallets. Today, we may still have a cheque book somewhere, just in case, probably a few years old, and we may carry some cash to pay the window cleaner. But increasingly, even the window cleaner may carry one of those devices enabling them to take card payments, or even just use an app on their own mobile phone. Payments have evolved to fulfil a consumer need driven by technology, especially mobile phones.

Payments are complicated

In 1958, Bank of America launched BankAmericard, now recognised as the first modern credit card. Barclaycard launched the first UK consumer credit card in 1966. In 2008, the UK introduced the first 24 hours/day, 365 days/year real-time payments scheme, the Faster Payment System. Do consumers know, when they pay with a credit or debit card, that they will have different protections and different processes to those applicable to online banking payments? Do they know that they will use completely different infrastructures? Probably not. Do they need to know? In some cases, maybe.

During the recent COVID-19 pandemic, it took two editors at Martin Lewis' MoneySavingExpert[1] to explain how cardholders could get their money back on previously purchased airline tickets they could no longer use due to lockdown, bringing the infamous – and well-established – chargeback process into public consciousness.

Let's pause for a second and consider how much innovation and technological advancements were deployed over the past 60 years. Imagine the investments made in payments infrastructures and processes over that period. Consider how Big Tech players, such as Apple, Google, and Facebook, inserted themselves into traditionally closed payments ecosystems, forcing incumbent players to interact with them due to consumer demand (Apple Pay anyone?). Spare a thought for regulators and standards bodies which had to evolve to cope with this moving feast, forcing established players to open their infrastructures and new entrants to face increasing regulation.

And that's the nub of it.

For consumers to be able to do what they do in the way they want to do it, and to continue to trust the system without really having to know how things work, there is an awful lot that needs to happen in the background.

 Be like a duck. Ducks look calm as they glide along the surface of the water, but they're paddling like hell underneath.
(Michael Caine)[2]

Technology suppliers, payments services providers, retailers, regulators, standards bodies, amongst others, are the ducks.

These ecosystems players not only need to understand the part they play in their piece of the puzzle, but they also must remain relevant in a fast-evolving and extremely competitive industry.

Market pressures have forced a blurring of boundaries between traditionally segregated infrastructures (i.e. card payments and bank payments). Ongoing market consolidation and growing innovation have only added to the confusion. Long gone are the days where you could unequivocally describe what a PSP is and does. Now we have "payment orchestration", "Payment-as-a-Service", "Third Party PSPs", BaaS, MSP, ACH, and an almost endless supply of confusing terms. The payments industry loves acronyms and can be very precious about terminology. Casually wielding four- or five-letter abbreviations makes us feel like insiders of an exclusive community. But even within that special, multifaceted community, stakeholders invariably find it tough to keep up with constant change. They may be experts in one or several area(s) of payments, but will they understand the relevance of other parts of the various ecosystems and take advantage of the opportunities available to them?

Today, getting this knowledge is not only desirable but necessary. The pandemic accelerated the need for all things digital, including payments. Sourcing the relevant knowledge is tough. Whilst several publications, YouTube videos, and other online resources are available, they generally cover specific and limited aspects (e.g. "mobile payments", "acquiring card payments", "settlement systems", etc.), and you'd have a hard job putting together all the pieces of this ever-evolving puzzle. Knowledge is difficult to obtain.

Payments made simple and accessible

The payments industry has never been as fascinating as it is right now, from traditional financial services institutions jumping on the digital transformation bandwagon to innovators and new entrants creating new business models and capitalising on new technologies, to regulators trying to cope with it all and maintain some sort of integrity whilst fostering innovation in increasingly complex ecosystems that facilitate the exchange of value.

This book will take readers through the fundamentals of the various payments ecosystems. From cards to bank and alternative payments, jargon will be debunked and myths will be busted. For each ecosystem, simple frameworks will be used, enabling comparison – mechanics, economics, risks, and future outlook – all the while drawing on real-life examples. It will also take the readers through an overview of the global regulatory landscape.

This book weaves together the underpinning ecosystem principles, legislation, and key stakeholders. It offers readers practical advice and insights into the key disciplines, and equips them with an understanding of the key issues and opportunities. It may not answer all the questions – after all, this industry is vast – but readers will be able to ask the right questions and know where to find the answers, as well as look up terms in what I believe to be the first comprehensive and practical glossary in the payments industry.

Why I wrote this book

The payments industry is fascinating, why make a book about it boring? This book is not a textbook; it is written in plain English in a style accessible to all with clear illustrations and an abundance of references. I would have wanted this book when I first started in payments, but it didn't exist, and I learnt on the job. I wanted to write something that would appeal not only to those payments professionals needing a refresher or wanting to understand parts of the industry with which they are unfamiliar, but also to those new to the industry wanting to "get into payments".

In an effort to democratise payments knowledge, I wrote this book primarily for the ducks, as it should help them remain calm on the surface whilst maximising the value of the paddling underneath. However, this book is not just for payments professionals, it's also for hiring companies giving induction to new hires, those involved in mergers and acquisitions, and investors wanting to understand the industry, professional services firms, law firms, and consultants, as well as policy makers.

Points of particular interest to professionals and things to remember will be highlighted by a duck icon. I have also produced an extensive and comprehensive glossary (Chapter 7), which I believe is a first in this space.

I also wrote this book for the inquisitive minds with a casual interest in payments. These are the people who want to know why they can't pay someone on Cash App from their PayPal account, or why their bank is not allowing them to transfer money to a crypto exchange, or those who wonder why it sometimes takes a few days to receive a payment and why sometimes it's instantaneous. I hope I have succeeded in my endeavour.

That said, let me take you on this whistle-stop journey into the fascinating world of payments. I promise it won't be boring.

LET'S GO!

Notes

1 Petar Lekarski and Emily White, "Coronavirus travel rights: Latest on UK and overseas travel rules, plus refunds and insurance help", MoneySaving-Expert, 21 December 2022. Available at: https://www.moneysavingexpert.com/news/2020/02/coronavirus-travel-help-and-your-rights/#booked (Accessed 29 July 2023).
2 Michael Caine *Blowing the Bloody Doors Off*, Hodder and Stoughton, London, 2018. ©Michael Caine, 2018. Quote reproduced with permission of the Licensor through PLSclear.

1

CARD PAYMENTS MECHANICS

Overview and jargon buster (making sense of it all)

The payments industry loves acronyms and can be very precious about terminology. Casually wielding four- or five-letter abbreviations makes us feel like insiders of an exclusive community. In that special, multifaceted community, professionals may find it tough to keep up with the constant change. Evidently, "payments" are complicated and confusing, because common terms may mean different things to different people. Limiting ourselves to the world of card payments doesn't make the task of understanding any easier, or shorter. Long gone are the days where you could unequivocally describe what a PSP is and does. Now, we have an almost endless supply of confusing terms.

And what do we do when we try to make sense of things? We try to organise them in logical order by slotting them into recognisable boxes – a framework if you will. Luckily, in centralised payments ecosystems, such as card payments, we already have this framework. It's called "regulations". Centralised payments ecosystems are heavily regulated, and if you want to

DOI: 10.4324/9781032631394-2

regulate something, it must be clearly defined. Lack of clarity and consist-ency in regulations leads to varying interpretations at best and unforeseen loopholes at worst, making the regulations difficult to enforce. Regulatory vagueness keeps lawyers in jobs. But largely, regulations give us consistency of terminology. Fortunately, in Europe since 2018, the **Second Payment Services Directive (PSD2)**,[1] whilst it introduced new acronyms, gave us that reference framework. For the rest of this book, we will use the PSD2 terminology and map it to more familiar terms throughout. For those not in Europe, the definitions will be simple enough to draw parallels in any geography.

And as familiarity goes, I have good news! The PSD2 specifically mentions PSPs, a term we've all heard. But there is also not so good news: PSD2 defines a **Payment Service Provider (PSP)** as any ecosystem actor that supplies a payment service or serves a function in the pay-ments ecosystem. Also, because I can't find any clear usage rule, I will use the terms "payment" and "payments" interchangeably (e.g. pay-ment ecosystem/payments ecosystem). Vagueness right there. Fear not! We still can classify card payment ecosystem actors into a few simple categories.

Main card ecosystem actors

- The actor who provides the centralised payments infrastructure and operating rules: the PSD2 term is **Payment Scheme**. This entity pro-vides and manages the required technical infrastructure and the set of rules that ecosystem participants must follow. We sometimes refer to it as a **Payment System**. The card world refers to this entity as a **Card Scheme**, **Card Network**, or **Card Brand**. Card schemes have different names for their network infrastructure: for example, Visa has **VisaNet**, and Mastercard has **Banknet**.
- The actor who uses payment services: the PSD2 term for this is **Payment Service User**, or **PSU**. There are two types:
  - The actor who pays with a card: the PSD2 term is **Payer**. In the card world, this is a **Cardholder**.
  - The actor who gets paid by card: the PSD2 term is **Payee**. In the card world, this is a **Merchant** (e.g. a retailer).

For merchants, the process of taking payments by card is known as **Payment Acceptance** or **Card Acceptance**.

- The actors who provide payment services to payees: these can be different PSPs depending on the role they play, and can be:
  - Those that enable a payee (i.e. merchant) to accept card payments through the provision of technology. The PSD2 term for these is **Payee's PSPs**. In the card world, they can supply physical technology (e.g. card terminal providers), or virtual facilities (e.g. e-commerce payment gateways). In the card world, we refer to this PSP as the **Merchant's PSP**.
  - Those that enable a payee (i.e. merchant) to connect to a payment scheme. The PSD2 term for these is **Acquiring PSPs**. In the card world, several other terms can be used: **Acquirer**, **Acquiring Bank**, **Processor**. An Acquiring PSP is sometimes referred to as a **Merchant Services Provider**, or **Merchant Acquirer**. The payee (e.g. merchant) will connect to the acquiring PSP through their payee's PSP technology (e.g. payment gateway or card terminal).

Nowadays, very few banks providing merchant services have their own acquiring infrastructure. For example, in the UK Royal Bank of Scotland (RBS) sold Worldpay to Advent & Bain in 2010.[2] Before then, RBS was one of the two banks with their own acquiring infrastructure, the other one being Barclays (with Barclaycard). Today, Barclays and NatWest are the only UK banks to do so, whilst Lloyds (with Cardnet) has a joint venture with First Data (Fiserv). In the US, Bank of America had a long-standing partnership with Fiserv, but the contract came to an end in 2020[3] and wasn't renewed, and Bank of America is now building its own acquiring infrastructure. When referring to acquiring services providers, the term "processor" is more commonly used in the United States and refers to non-bank acquirers such as Fiserv, Global Payments, and Worldpay (FIS), as it is common practice for banks to form partnerships or joint ventures with pure processors, where the bank is responsible for merchant engagement and the processor provides the acquiring infrastructure and processing.

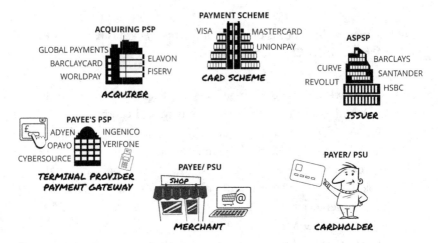

Figure 1.1 Card payments ecosystem actors.

Source: drawing by the author.

- The actor who manages the payer's payment account: the PSD2 term is **Account Servicing PSP (ASPSP)**. For card payments, this could be a bank or a non-bank financial institution that provides payers (cardholders) with cards (e.g. a Visa card). The ASPSP's role is to manage the payer's account (i.e. cardholder card account) throughout its lifecycle. In the card world, we commonly refer to the ASPSP as an **Issuer** or **Issuing Bank**. In theory, the ASPSP is the **Payer's PSP**, but this term is not often used in practice.

Confused? A picture speaks a thousand words. See Figure 1.1 for a visual summary.

New card ecosystem actors

Payments ecosystems evolve fast, and this is especially true for the card world. Over the years, new entrants and innovators inserted themselves into this well-established operation. You may be familiar with some of them: Apple Pay, Google Wallet, etc. In Europe, PSPs of this type became regulated when PSD2 came into force (this is not necessarily the case in other geographies, and probably why Venmo is only available in the US at the time of writing). These PSPs were given their own category: **Third Party PSPs (TPPs)**. TPPs come in three main types:

- A TPP that initiates a payment on behalf of a payer: the PSD2 term is **Payment Initiation Service Provider (PISP)**. For card payments, this could be a technology provider that supplies payers (cardholders) with a hardware-tied payment facility (e.g. Apple Pay, Samsung Pay), or a software facility (e.g. Google Wallet, Venmo when funded by a card).
- A TPP that accesses payment account information on behalf of a payer (on a read-only basis): the PSD2 term is **Account Information Service Provider (AISP)**. In theory, an AISP would enable payers (e.g. cardholders) to check their card account (e.g. balance, last payment, transaction history, etc.), but I can't find any pure play examples on the market at the time of writing, although existing PISPs will enable account holders to check some transaction history.

Let's complete our visual summary, which Figure 1.2 provides.

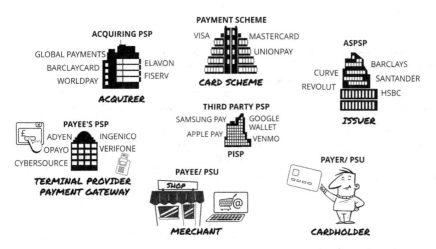

Figure 1.2 Card payments ecosystem actors including TPPs.

Source: drawing by the author.

You may have heard of payments ecosystems referred to as rails. We often refer to the card payments ecosystem as the **Card Rails** or **Card Scheme Rails**.

A new type of TPP is emerging:

- A **Card-Based Payment Instrument Issuer** (**CBPII**). A TPP that issues card-based payment instruments (physical or virtual) that can be used to initiate a payment transaction from a payment account (e.g. a bank account) held with a PSP other than the issuer. Essentially, a CBPII is a combination of an AISP, a PISP, an issuer, and **Money Remittance** (a payment service by which funds are sent by a payer to a payee where no payment account needs to be opened in the name of either the payer or payee).

Terminology mapping

For future reference, Table 1.1 provides a tabular summary with examples.

Table 1.1 shows how regulatory terminology has introduced clarity into this complex ecosystem. You may wonder why some actors with which you may be familiar don't appear in this section. Table 1.2 lists examples of stakeholders.

Table 1.1 Terminology mapping for card payments ecosystem actors.

PSD2 terminology	Common terminology for the card rails	Examples for the card rails
Payment Scheme	Card scheme, card brand, card network	Visa, Mastercard, UnionPay
Payee's PSP	Card terminal manufacturer, payment gateway	Ingenico, Verifone Adyen, CyberSource
Acquiring PSP	Acquirer, acquiring bank, merchant services provider (MSP), merchant acquirer, processor, merchant bank (US)	Worldpay (FIS), Fiserv, Elavon, Barclaycard
Payment Service User (PSU) Payer	Cardholder	Anyone with a card account
Payment Service User (PSU) Payee	Any entity that accepts card payments, such as a retailer, an airline, or a subscription service; merchant	Tesco, Walmart, British Airways, Netflix
Account Servicing PSP (ASPSP)	Issuing bank, issuer; issuers can also be referred to as processors	Barclays, HSBC Curve, Revolut

Table 1.1 (Continued)

PSD2 terminology	Common terminology for the card rails	Examples for the card rails
Third Party Payment Service Provider (TPPs) Payment Initiation Service Provider (PISP)	Third Party Payment Service Provider (TPPs)	Amazon Pay, Samsung Pay, Google Wallet, Venmo
Third Party PSP (TPP) Account Information Service Provider (AISP)	No pure play examples at the time of writing	No examples at the time of writing, although PISPs may enable cardholders to see some transaction history, thus providing an account information service.

Table 1.2 The card payments ecosystem today (not an exhaustive list, June 2023).

Card ecosystem actors	Examples
Acquirers	Worldpay (FIS), Barclays, Crédit Mutuel, Sberbank, Nexi, Crédit Agricole, Dojo, BPCE, Elavon, Worldline, Fiserv, JPMorgan Chase, Global Payments, Paysafe, Adyen, checkout.com
Card networks	Visa, Mastercard, American Express, Discover, JCB, UnionPay, MIR, Carte Bancaire, Girocard, Bancomat, Dankort, BankAxept, Bancontact, Maestro, Diners Club
Issuers	Barclays, HSBC, Santander, Wells Fargo, Bank of America, American Express, Marqeta, Capital One, Curve, Monzo, Starling Bank, N26, Citi, Revolut, Wise, Paysafe, checkout.com
Gateways, Payment Facilitators (Payfacs), and other PSPs	Adyen, ACI Worldwide, Stripe, PayPal, Block, Barclays, Worldpay (FIS), CyberSource, Opayo, Ingenico, Verifone
ISOs, MSPs, VARs, and other ISVs	PayPoint, eMerchantPay, Global Blue, Fexco, Corefy, 365 Business Finance, iwoca, Liberis, Bibby Financial Services, Epsilon, Comarch, Kobie, Klarna, Cardinal Commerce, Signifyd, Riskified, Kount, Feedzai, Fireblocks

Table 1.2 will become rapidly obsolete, or of historical interest, depending on the way you look at it. This is further evidence of the complexity of this ecosystem, which is continuously worsened by market consolidation[4]

and new partnerships. For example, Worldline acquired Ingenico in 2020, but sold its "terminals, solutions and services" business line only two years later to private equity fund manager Apollo Funds. Another example is Maestro, a debit card scheme launched in 1991 by Mastercard and now being retired after 30 years[5] perhaps due to the fact that it can only be used in face-to-face environments (nowadays, who needs a card that can't be used online?).

> You will notice that some companies appear in several rows. On the card rails, stakeholders can play multiple roles depending on the services they offer (e.g. Adyen is both a payment gateway and an acquirer, and so is Barclays; Paysafe, Barclays, and checkout.com are both acquirers and issuers). It is never sufficient to mention just a company name because the function an actor performs in the value chain dictates several factors: economic, contractual, liability, etc. This is explained in Chapter 2 'Costs and value chain'.

Further actors (e.g. payfacs, ISOs, MSPs, VARs, and other ISVs) will be introduced at the right time throughout this book, but for now the card ecosystem players introduced so far are sufficient to understand the basic mechanics.

Ecosystem actors and models (who's zoomin who?)

The Four Party Model

The model where the acquirer, issuer, merchant, and cardholder participate in a scheme is known as the **Four Party Model**. Obviously, there are more than four parties in this configuration (more than those usually shown),[6] but only the four parties circled in Figure 1.3 take part in an economic model which reflects the contractual relationships for processing card payment transactions:

- A merchant has a contract with an acquirer.
- An acquirer has a contract with a card scheme.
- An issuer has a contract with a card scheme.
- A cardholder has a contract with an issuer.

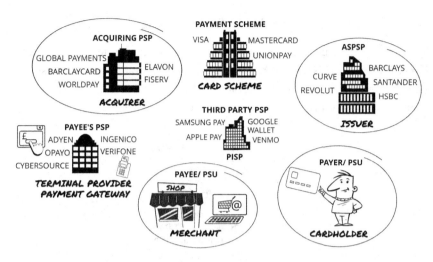

Figure 1.3 The Four Party Model.

Source: drawing by the author.

In the Four Party Model, there is clear separation between acquiring and is-suing. This is a two-sided economic model: the consumer side (cardholder and issuer) and the merchant side (merchant and acquirer). A card scheme enables any qualifying issuer or acquirer to join (see Chapter 2, *Scheme mem-berships*). Consumers are free to choose between multiple card providers for that card scheme (e.g. a Visa card from Santander or Halifax). Simi-larly, merchants can choose between multiple acquirers. Consequently, this model promotes competition on both sides of the market. As shown in Table 1.2, there are more than four parties involved in the end-to-end pro-cessing of card payments. But we must remember that only the four parties circled in Table 1.2 are economic participants in the end-to-end card pay-ment transaction value chain (see Chapter 2, *Costs and value chain*).

Because it promotes open competition in the card payment value chain, the Four Party Model is referred to as **Open Loop**. Visa, Mastercard, and UnionPay operate on this model. Cards issued by issuers on the Four Party Model are referred to as **Open Loop Cards**.

The Four Party Model is the predominant economic model[7] in the card industry. Predictably, it would be too easy if we didn't have variations from the norm.

The Three Party Model

The next model, used by other well-known card schemes, is the **Three Party Model**. In this configuration, there is no separation between issuing and acquiring. In fact, the three roles of the card scheme, acquirer, and issuer are performed by a single entity, as per Figure 1.4.

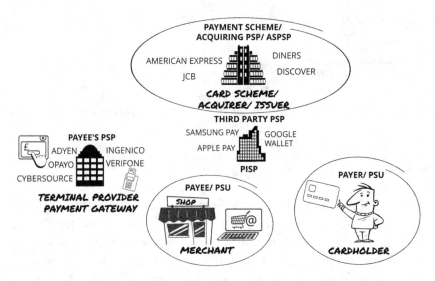

Figure 1.4 The Three Party Model.
Source: drawing by the author.

American Express, Diners Club, Discover, and JCB operate on this model. Other than the economic implications of this model (see Chapter 2, *Merchant models and contract types*), the processes for transactional payments and services are like those in the Four Party Model (and we will henceforth use the Four Party Model to explain the various concepts in this book).

In the Three Party Model, the card scheme – being also an issuer and an acquirer – has contractual relationships with both merchants and cardholders. From a practical perspective, Three Party Model cards are more expensive to process for merchants, which is why small to medium businesses are usually reluctant to accept them (see Chapter 2, *Charges and fees*). They are also generally more expensive to hold for cardholders, but they offer enough added benefits (e.g. reward programmes and other value-added services) to keep these customers loyal. In addition, larger merchants are usually more interested in accepting Three Party Model cards as cardholder spending levels are higher.

The Two Party Model (closed loop)

For completeness purposes, I must also mention the **Two Party Model**, which is where a merchant is both the issuer and the acquirer. Cardholders for these schemes can only use the card for payments at the issuer, which in this case is the merchant itself. Examples include some store cards (e.g. Target REDcard™ Debit), some fuel cards (e.g. Shell Fuel Card), some public transport cards (e.g. Oyster for Transport for London), and gift cards. These are true **Closed Loop** networks.

Confusingly, the Three Party Model is often described as closed loop, even by American Express themselves[8] and other parties, even though these cards are widely accepted. In my opinion, three-party schemes are not, strictly speaking, closed loop networks as they are still two-sided economic models, with the characteristic of one entity serving both sides. Conversely, store cards may be open loop and can be issued in collaboration with a card scheme (e.g. the John Lewis Partnership Card with Mastercard). This type of store card is called a **Co-branded Card**. Other types of co-branded cards include airline cards, which are very popular in the US (e.g. Southwest Rapid Rewards®, Delta SkyMiles® Gold, United[SM] Explorer) but not so in France, or Europe in general.

Market dynamics (round and round it goes)

We complete the picture by looking at the market, the evolution of which is a testimony to the fast pace of change in payments.

The acquiring market

Acquiring in Europe

The Nilson Report,[9] an essential publication in the cards industry, listed the top acquirers in Europe for 2013[10] and 2021,[11] and Table 1.3 compares the ranks.

Table 1.3 Europe's top merchant acquirers, 2013 and 2021.

Rank	2013		2021	
	Acquirer	**Transactions (billion)**	**Acquirer**	**Transactions (billion)**
1	Worldpay	5.67	Sberbank	37.9
2	Barclays	3.62	Nexi	14.2
3	Crédit Mutuel	2.75	Worldpay	9.0
4	Sberbank	2.39	Worldline	8.7
5	Crédit Agricole	2.23	Barclays	7.1
6	Swedbank	1.77	Fiserv	6.8
7	BPCE	1.27	Adyen	6.3
	TOTAL	19.7	TOTAL	90

Nilson Report, Issues 1042 and 1219. Figures include global network cards (Visa, Mastercard, American Express, UnionPay, Diners Club, and JCB) and domestic schemes (e.g. MIR, Bancomat, Girocard, etc. See *Domestic card schemes*).

Table 1.3 is amazing on many fronts. First, the total number of transactions for the top seven acquirers in Europe has increased by a huge 357% over just eight years! Notwithstanding the height of the pandemic in 2020–2021, which led to a massive usage increase in all things digital and virtual (including payments), 357% is an astounding figure.

Second, Nexi jumped to second place, seemingly out of nowhere. Well, not out of nowhere: Nexi went on an acquisition rampage in 2020 and bagged two major players, Sia and Nets, relegating Worldpay, top-ranked for many years, to third place. In August 2023, Nexi acquired a 30% stake in Computop,[12] a German payments processor. Market dynamics can be remarkably interesting. And Adyen, only founded in 2006 as an e-commerce gateway, and a relatively new player in the space (acquiring licence obtained in 2017),[13] is now seriously challenging incumbents.

Third, you may find it confusing that Sberbank, a Russian bank founded in 1841, finds itself at the top of a European chart ... Let me introduce you to one of the quirks of card payments: the world classification according to **EMVCo**.[14]

Box 1.1 WHAT IS EMVCO?

EMVCo is a consortium controlled equally by Visa, Mastercard, American Express, UnionPay, and Discover. EMVCo is responsible for developing and maintaining **EMV** card standards (see *Card payments data and 3D Secure*). EMV takes its initials from **E**uropay, **M**astercard and **V**isa, the original founders in 1999. In 2002, Mastercard merged with Europay International SA, the owners of the Eurocard brand. Whilst the Europay name disappeared, the EMV name remains.

EMVCo regularly produces EMV adoption statistics,[15] and for that purpose they split the world into regions:

- Africa and the Middle East;
- Asia;
- Canada, Latin America, and The Caribbean;
- Europe Zone 1 (Western Europe, including Turkey);
- Europe Zone 2 (Central Europe, including Russia); and
- The United States.

Generally, published card payments statistics with a geographical dimension will use the EMVCo regional split, which itself aligns with the United Nations classification, although global statistics will usually bundle Zone 1 and Zone 2 together. The Nilson Report is one example, and this is why Sberbank appears on a European chart. But that's not why we're interested in Sberbank.

The fact that it appears at the top of the chart for 2021, way ahead of its competitors, shows market dynamics at play. You may argue that we've had a pandemic and that consumers turned to cards and other digital payments. Of course, this is one of the drivers, but that happened worldwide, not just in Russia, and it doesn't explain the non-uniform growth globally.

You may also argue that demographics were a driver; after all, there are a lot of people in Russia, and, yes, this was a contributing factor.

Contactless payments

The main driver was the adoption of **Contactless Payments**, especially during the pandemic, as no one wanted to handle cash or touch card terminals. But on their own, contactless payments couldn't have driven these growth figures, unless there was a deliberate government push.

To drive any change in consumer behaviour, there must be a platform that fosters rapid consumer adoption. For contactless payments, that platform is usually public transport. As soon as a region deploys open loop contactless payments, digital payments adoption grows substantially. We saw this in the UK with Transport for London (TfL). In 2014, TfL deployed open loop contactless payments for their wider network (Tube, tram, DLR, London Overground, and some National Rail services) — they had been available on busses since 2012 — challenging the closed loop Oyster card. The rest is history, and you can see the effect this had on Oyster card usage in Figure 1.5a.

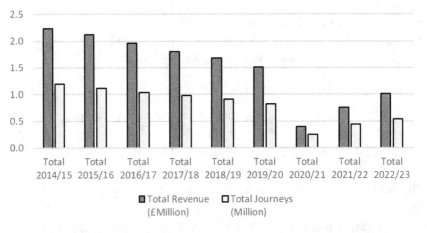

Figure 1.5a TfL Oyster card adoption statistics. Yearly figures from April to March (2014 to 2023).

Source: Transport for London, Analysis of Oyster pay as you go journeys.[16]

You can see that both volume and value decreased by about half since launch.

Conversely, Figure 1.5b shows that the number of journeys made using open loop contactless cards, whilst experiencing a dip in 2020, grew

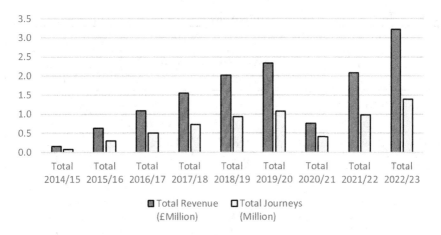

Figure 1.5b TfL Contactless card adoption statistics. Yearly figures from April to March (2014 to 2023).

Source: Transport for London, Analysis of contactless pay as you go journeys.[17]

steadily since and reached about 2.5 million in 2023, almost the reverse trend of the Oyster card.

This has not just happened in the UK. We can see this movement world-wide, from New York,[18] to Costa Rica,[19] Malaysia,[20] the Netherlands,[21] and, of course, Russia, starting with St Petersburg[22] and Moscow.[23] Moscow has a population of about 13 million, not including its metropolitan area (which could be about 20 million) and St Petersburg has about 5.5 million people. I'll let you do the maths with relation to employment rates and workforce concentration in Russia (this is not an economics textbook). But you get the gist: lots of payments. Adoption of contactless cards was further fuelled by the global increases in contactless limits in 2020,[24] facilitating even more contactless purchases. Russia doubled theirs from ₽1,000 to ₽5,000. In the UK, we increased our limit from £45 to £100 in October 2021.[25] The tech-nical term for the contactless purchase limit is the **Cardholder Verification Method (CVM) Limit**.

Acquiring worldwide

To complete our overview, we must look at global figures, not just Euro-pean ones, as shown in Table 1.4. Transaction volumes across the top seven players increased by 210% between 2013 and 2021.

Table 1.4 Top merchant acquirers worldwide, 2013[26] and 2021.[27]

Rank	2013		2021	
	Acquirer	Transactions (billion)	Acquirer	Transactions (billion)
1	Bank of America	14.1	FIS (Worldpay)	42.5
2	Vantiv	12.1	JPMorgan Chase	40.2
3	Chase Paymentech	10.2	Sberbank	37.9
4	First Data	10.0	Fiserv	27.6
5	Citi	6.5	Global Payments	18.1
6	Worldpay	5.7	Nexi	14.2
7	Barclays	3.6	China UnionPay	12.6
	TOTAL	62.2	TOTAL	193.1

Source: Nilson Report, Issues 1049 and 1229.

It's like a trip down memory lane, isn't it? Vantiv was founded in the 1970s, although the name Vantiv didn't exist until 2011. It acquired Worldpay in 2018,[28] and changed its name to Worldpay, Inc. before it was acquired by FIS in 2019.[29] Fiserv bought First Data in 2019, and I'm sure you can spot some more movement in the table. Interestingly, sometimes, what goes around comes around, and as of February 2023 there were talks of FIS selling Worldpay,[30] and the sale was agreed in July 2023.[31]

Card schemes

International card schemes

Now that you have an appreciation of the acquiring space, let's look at the dynamics of card brands. Table 1.5 gives us a view of the market share for the top five card brands globally in 2013 and 2022.

Again, market dynamics are at play: Visa is not as dominant a player as it was ten years ago. UnionPay has shown dramatic growth over the years, driven by economic improvements in China enabling millions of people to use debit and credit cards, as well as growing acceptance of UnionPay cards in other geographies.

If we look at Europe more specifically, Table 1.6 will show that Visa and Mastercard are very much still the dominant players, although the difference in market share between them is not as pronounced as it was a few years ago.

Table 1.5 Global brand card networks, 2013[32] and 2022.[33]

Rank	2013		2022	
	Card brand	Market share (%) transactions	Card brand	Market share (%) transactions
1	Visa	60.5	Visa	39
2	Mastercard	26.9	UnionPay	34
3	UnionPay	7.7	Mastercard	24
4	American Express	3.8	American Express	1.6
5	JCB	1.1	JCB	0.9

Source: Nilson Report, Issues 1037 and 1241.

Table 1.6 European card brand networks, 2015[34] and 2021.[35]

Rank	2015		2021	
	Card brand	Market share (%) transactions	Card brand	Market share (%) transactions
1	Visa	68	Visa	57
2	Mastercard	29	Mastercard	43
3	American Express	3	American Express	0.4
4	Diners Club	0.02	Diners Club/ Discover	0.02

Source: Nilson Report, Issues 1088 and 1221.

This is why we often talk about the "Visa/Mastercard duopoly" in Europe. Table 1.6 also shows how active Mastercard has been, increasing its market share by 14 percentage points over just six years. Also, Discover acquired Diners Club from Citi in July 2008[36] (I guess it takes a bit of time for the Nilson Report to consolidate figures).

BOX 1.2 MARKETS EVOLVE

In the card industry, the pace of change is relentless. Many actors evolve into other roles and obtain new permissions. New processes are developed. New mergers, acquisitions, and partnerships alter the dynamics. Environmental and geopolitical movements, as well as regulatory factors, alter the landscape. Technological innovation generates new opportunities. To understand this market, the trick is to keep up to date.

Domestic card schemes

Domestic schemes only operate in the national geography (unless co-branded). In some geographies, these schemes are the predominant method of payment, way ahead of international card schemes, as shown in Table 1.7.

Table 1.7 Domestic card schemes market share compared with other card schemes in Europe.

Country	Domestic scheme	Visa	Mastercard	Other
France	Carte Bancaire 85%	3%	5%	4%
Belgium	Bancontact 81%	6%	13%	1%
Germany	Girocard 71%	13%	11%	1%
Denmark	Dankort 69%	14%	17%	–
Norway	BankAxept 62%	6%	11%	21%
Italy	Bancomat 45%	34%	20%	1%
United Kingdom	–	82%	17%	1%

Source: Statista, June 2023, Market share of international and domestic payment card schemes in 14 countries in Europe in 2021.[37]

The UK has been added to Table 1.7 for comparison purposes, as this market, like the US, is card-dominated, and the UK has no domestic card scheme.

Elsewhere, UnionPay is the dominant card scheme in China (although not a domestic scheme), whilst Visa has a slightly higher share than Mastercard in that market. In Canada, Interac Debit (domestic card scheme) is the dominant card scheme. In Asia Pacific, UnionPay has a market share of 75%, followed by Visa (13%), Mastercard (9%), and JCB (2%), whilst JCB holds a 40% market share in Japan. In Russia, MIR (domestic card scheme) is gaining market share and catching up with Visa and Mastercard (which can still be used for domestic transactions).

The issuing market

Traditionally, issuers have been banks, and banks are hampered with legacy systems. Antony Jenkins, ex-Barclays boss, said in June 2023: "Banks are becoming museums of technology".[38] It is therefore no wonder to see that this traditional market is also being disrupted. With the advent of cloud technology, APIs, and a multitude of "as-a-platform" or "as-a-service" solutions, the issuing market is getting an overhaul.

Technology-driven third parties aimed to fill the technology gap for issuers, and a new type of player emerged: the **Issuer Processor**. The issuer processor is not a bank, or an issuer, and their aim in life is to connect issuers to card schemes. Think of it as the issuer outsourcing the processes of authorisation, clearing, and settlement (see the next section) in the same way a bank wants to provide acquiring services and outsources the process to a non-bank acquirer (hence the term "processor" being used in the US for these entities). Issuer processors are an important part of the ecosystem, and they have facilitated quick time to market for many fintechs and new entrants, as well as for incumbent issuers plagued by old technology. Prominent players in this space are Bancorp, Carta Worldwide, Marqeta, Paymentology, Thredd (formerly Global Processing Services), Tribe Payments, and many more. If you look again at Table 1.2, you will find that many of the existing players (the modern ones at least) now also offer what they call "full stack" platforms. For example, checkout.com also offers issuer processing in addition to acquiring services.

Where next?

Undeniably, there is more choice for everyone, especially for consumers. New consumer behaviours are driven by technology. Whilst the concept appeared a couple of decades ago, the **Internet of Things** (**IoT**) is now part of our lives, and this was largely driven by the mass adoption of smart phones. Apple seized this opportunity by launching Apple Pay in 2014. Now, paying with a phone, or indeed a wearable device, is part of life, and home assistants (e.g. Amazon Echo, Google Home) are commonplace.

Today, social media is as essential to us as fixed phones or email were only a decade ago. The use of social media for e-commerce has grown at an unparalleled pace,[39] and the global worldwide revenue for social commerce is set to grow from US$724 billion in 2022 to US$6 trillion by 2030. In Asia, over 80% of the population in Thailand, India, and China shop on social media.

Artificial Intelligence (**AI**), whilst not new, and already used extensively in the payments space (e.g. fraud prevention, customer analytics, customer experience), came into mass consciousness with the controversy surrounding Open AI's ChatGPT and similar technologies. The implications are fascinating and frightening at the same time.

The relentless push to deliver seamless, invisible payment experiences whilst ensuring consumers are safe and secure is an ongoing challenge. Businesses and policy makers alike have their work cut out for them (see Chapter 5, *Artificial Intelligence*).

And this is all very nice. But payments on centralised systems, regardless of technological advancements and business innovations of all kinds, must run on established mechanisms.

Authorisation, clearing, and settlement (show me the money!)

Yikes! Sounds horrible, doesn't it? Fear not, it's simple mechanics. Any payment ecosystem has processes for moving value from one party to the other. At the detailed level, these processes will vary, but fundamentally they will always follow these three broad steps:

1. Is the payer genuine and allowed to make the payment transaction? This is the **Authorisation** process.
2. Do all stakeholders involved in the payment process agree on a single truth of payment transaction information? This is the **Clearing** process.
3. Has the value moved from the payer to the payee? This is the **Settlement** process.

On centralised systems, payment ecosystem actors will perform specific functions to ensure these three steps are completed following the rules set by the payment scheme and within the applicable regulations. On the card rails, the combination of authorisation, clearing, and settlement describes how value gets from the payer (e.g. cardholder) to the payee (e.g. merchant).

Authorisation

Is the payer genuine and allowed to make the payment transaction?

Authorisation is a question-and-answer process. The merchant asks the issuer (ASPSP) to verify that the payment transaction is genuine before it is allowed to progress to the next stage. The issuer gives their answer, either authorising or declining the transaction. This process takes place in any payment ecosystem. The ASPSP, being the entity which manages the payment account, is the only entity able to answer the question as they hold and maintain all the information for that account: on the card rails, this is the issuer, as they provide card accounts to cardholders – although there is one exception (see Box 1.3)

BOX 1.3 WHAT IS STAND-IN PROCESSING?

Stand-in-Processing (STIP) is a process by which a card scheme would step in on behalf of an issuer when that issuer is unable to provide a real-time response during the authorisation process. An issuer may face this situation during planned or unplanned outages or network problems. The card scheme would "stand in" on behalf of the issuer to approve or decline a transaction using pre-defined rules set by the issuer. Whilst this type of service has long been established, card schemes continue to innovate by incorporating new technologies, such as AI or deep-learning models, into the STIP mechanism.[40]

The card authorisation process has two stages: authorisation request and authorisation decision.

Authorisation request

The **Authorisation Request** is a question and is described in Figure 1.6.

Step 1. The cardholder uses a card to purchase items either in person or remotely.

Physically, the cardholder interacts with the technology deployed in the merchant environment (e.g. a card terminal). This technology is supplied by the Card Terminal Provider (the merchant's PSP). This is a face-to-face interaction, as the cardholder is physically present.

Virtually, the cardholder interacts with the technology deployed in the merchant environment (e.g. an online **Payment Page** within the merchant

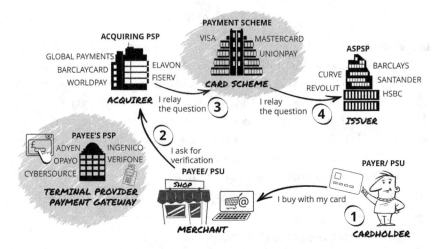

Figure 1.6 The authorisation request.

Source: drawing by the author.

website). This technology is supplied by the **Payment Gateway** (the merchant's PSP). This is a remote interaction, as the cardholder is not physically present (e.g. e-commerce, online shopping).

The payee's PSP (e.g. terminal provider, payment gateway) is greyed out in Figure 1.6, because they provide enabling technology as a background function to this process.

Step 2. The merchant asks for verification.

As the merchant takes the card payment (card acceptance), they need to verify that the transaction is genuine before parting with goods or supplying services. The technology supplied through the merchant's PSP (e.g. payment terminal or payment page) will relay the necessary information to the acquirer.

Step 3. The acquirer relays the question to the card scheme.

The acquirer will take the transaction information (card acquiring) and relay the information and question to the applicable card scheme (e.g. Visa for a Visa card presented).

Step 4. The card scheme routes the question to the issuer.

The card scheme is greyed out in Figure 1.6, because they provide a background switching function: they route information from the merchant side (acquirer) to the cardholder side (issuer) by relaying the card transaction information to the relevant issuer (e.g. a Visa card issued by HSBC).

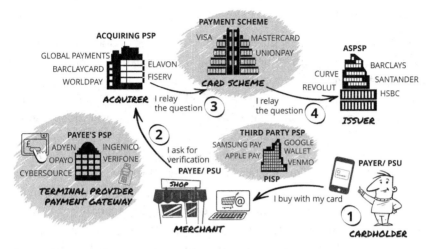

Figure 1.7 The authorisation request with TPP payment initiation.

Source: drawing by the author.

In recent years, consumers have moved to more convenient ways to pay. Buying things using mobile phones (iPhone with Apple Pay) or wearable devices (McClear ring, MuchBetter key fob) is commonplace. Yet, the authorisation request process is still the same. Ultimately, regardless of the underlying technology used, the cardholder is still making a purchase with a card. This is shown in Figure 1.7.

The PISP (TPP) is greyed out in Figure 1.7, because they provide a background function: they enable a cardholder to initiate a card payment through their technology. You can say that it is an overlay service on top of the card infrastructure which "wraps" a card to present it in a different way.

BOX 1.4 INNOVATORS CAN'T BYPASS AUTHORISATION, CLEARING, AND SETTLEMENT

Technology innovations are exciting in the card industry. Consumers love convenience, and this drives the adoption of new ways to pay. It may look like underlying processes have been simplified. They haven't. These technologies simply introduce a layer of abstraction on top of existing infrastructures for the convenience of consumers. Whether you use a plastic card, a wearable device, or a phone to initiate a payment, the *form factor is irrelevant* and the *authorisation process is the same*. Underneath, the ducks still paddle in the same way.

OPEN LOOP CBPII

The Card-Based Payment Instrument Issuer or CBPII is a TPP that issues card-based payment instruments (physical or virtual) that can be used to initiate a payment transaction from a payment account (e.g. a bank account) held with a payment service provider other than the issuer. Essentially, a CBPII is a combination of an AISP, a PISP, an issuer, and money remittance. A CBPII offers a type of decoupled debit (see Chapter 2, *Decoupled debit*), where the CBPII requests a **Confirmation of Funds (CoF)** from the ASPSP (bank), which must immediately return a Yes/No answer. The open loop CBPII, shown in Figure 1.8, is a special case of open loop card, where the authorisation request is slightly different from the standard process described earlier. An example of a player in this space is Currensea.

In the open loop CBPII model, you will see that the authorisation process is mostly the same as for standard open loop cards, the only difference being that the authorisation stage will have extra steps (5a, 5b, 5c) between the CBPII and the ASPSP (i.e. the cardholder's bank). Of course, for this to happen, and for the CBPII to remain usable, those extra steps need to be fast and transparent to the cardholder. This is why ASPSPs (banks) are required to give their Yes/No answer "immediately", and therefore the underlying bank payment scheme must be a **Real-Time Payment System**

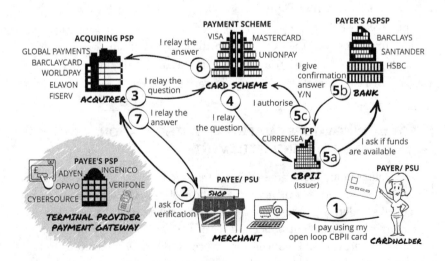

Figure 1.8 Open loop CBPII.

Source: drawing by the author.

(see Chapter 3). For an example of national API specification for CBPII, UK Open Banking has a good website.[41] For merchants, these cards will attract debit interchange.

For the remainder of this chapter, we will assume the open loop CBPII process is understood, and we will omit it from the descriptions.

Authorisation decision

Once this first step is completed, the issuer will give the **Authorisation Decision**, as shown in Figure 1.9.

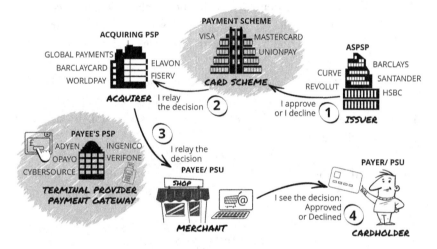

Figure 1.9 The authorisation decision.

Source: drawing by the author.

Step 1. The issuer verifies the cardholder and the transaction.

Issuers will have sophisticated fraud prevention mechanisms to do this. Fundamentally, they will authenticate the cardholder, assess their risk (e.g. is this cardholder blocked?), verify that there are sufficient funds, etc. According to their risk appetite, they will either accept or decline the transaction and relay that decision to the card scheme.

Step 2. The card scheme routes the answer to the acquirer.

The card scheme is greyed out in Figure 1.9, because they provide a background switching function: they route information from the cardholder side (issuer) to the merchant side (acquirer) by relaying the authorisation decision from the issuer to the relevant acquirer (e.g. Worldpay).

Step 3. The acquirer relays the decision to the merchant.

The acquirer will relay the issuer decision (e.g. accept, decline) to the merchant payment facility provided by the terminal provider or payment gateway (merchant's PSP).

Step 4. The cardholder sees the authorisation decision.

Depending on which mode of interaction the cardholder chose to make the card payment, they will receive the authorisation decision through that facility. The message may be "Approved" or "OK" on a card terminal, or it could be "Your order is confirmed" for an online shopping site, or even a call centre agent telling you that "your payment went through" if you ordered over the phone. Essentially, at this point, the merchant has a committed purchase and will let go of the goods or services, and the cardholder has either taken possession of their purchase (physical) or has an order confirmation (remote).

As per the authorisation request, the authorisation decision process remains the same if the cardholder is using a PISP. This is shown in Figure 1.10. The only difference is that the confirmation in Step 4 will be delivered through the PISP facility.

That's it! Two stages, four steps each, with data travelling across various networks and infrastructures through various stakeholders. We take this process for granted; we may not realise how fast the payment messages

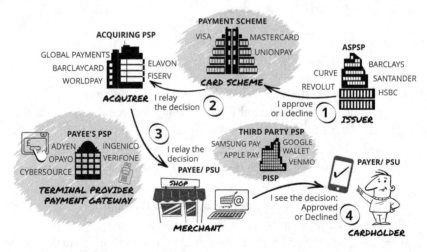

Figure 1.10 The authorisation decision with TPP payment initiation.

Source: drawing by the author.

must travel when we pay by card. We'd probably be disgruntled if the "Transaction Approved" message took more than a few milliseconds to appear on the card terminal. As a cardholder, by the time we have our physical or virtual purchases, we may be forgiven for thinking this is the end. But at this point, no money has changed sides. Underneath, the ducks must paddle.

 Professionals should remember:

- **There are industry-approved standards for authentication** during the authorisation process (see *Card payments data and 3D Secure*).
- In some geographies, **there may also be regulatory requirements for authentication** (e.g. Strong Customer Authentication for PSD2 in Europe).
- **Card schemes will charge a fee** (e.g. about £0.02 to £0.03 in the UK at the time of writing, but the fee amount will depend on the geography) for orchestrating the authorisation process. This is an example of a **Card Scheme Fee** (see Chapter 2, *Charges and fees*).

The stakeholders (issuers, acquirers, merchants) trust that this centralised ecosystem will make sure that the exchange of value will take place safely and correctly, at some point. And that's exactly what happens next.

Clearing

Clearing is commonly defined as the non-monetary exchange of transaction information. In any financial ecosystem, this is a reconciliation process.

On the card rails, clearing is the process by which card transactions are reconciled between acquirers (the merchant side) and issuers (the cardholder side).

This **centralised reconciliation function** is orchestrated by the card scheme with participation from both acquirers and issuers. This is described in Figure 1.11.

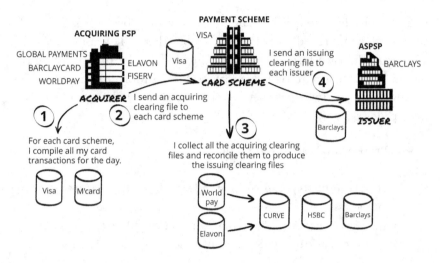

Figure 1.11 The clearing process.

Source: drawing by the author.

The clearing process is quite simple, albeit old-fashioned.

Step 1. The acquirer will, at the end of each day, produce their **Acquiring Clearing Files**. These files contain all their card transactions for that day. Each acquirer will produce as many acquiring clearing files as the number of card schemes (multiple clearing files during the day according to the acquirer clearing cycle) of which they are members (e.g. one for Visa, one for Mastercard, etc.). This is a batch process that usually takes place overnight.

Step 2. The **Acquirer** sends an acquiring clearing file to a card scheme, and this must align with the card scheme's clearing and settlement processes as specified in their **Operating Regulations**[42, 43] (i.e. the rules).

Step 3. The **Card Scheme** collects all the acquiring clearing files from their acquiring members for that day, in line with their clearing and settlement processes. Next, they collate and reconcile the files to produce the **Issuing Clearing Files**. A card scheme will produce as many issuing clearing files as there are issuing members for that scheme.

Step 4. The card scheme will send an issuing clearing file to each of their issuing members.

And that's it, job done. Transaction information has now been exchanged between both sides of this economic model.

Still, no exchange of value has taken place, and for this to happen we must look at the next stage.

Settlement

Simply put, **Settlement** is the last step in the transfer of value from a payer to a payee. This involves the exchange of funds between the parties and brings finality to the process. After settlement, **the obligations of all the parties are fulfilled and the transaction is considered complete.**

At a high level, like clearing, the settlement process is quite simple, albeit old-fashioned.

On the card rails, settlement is the process by which an exchange of value will take place between the merchant side and the cardholder side in two stages: interbank settlement and merchant settlement.

Interbank settlement

Interbank Settlement is a centralised function coordinated by the card scheme, with participation from both acquirers and issuers. Its purpose is to exchange value between acquirers and issuers. At a high level, this is described in Figure 1.12.

At the interbank settlement stage, the first exchange of value takes place between the issuer and the acquirer, orchestrated by the card scheme and supported by a new actor, the **Settlement Agent**.

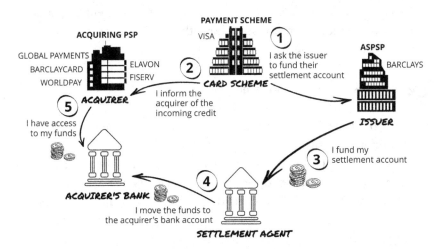

Figure 1.12 The interbank settlement process.

Source: drawing by the author.

Because not all settlement accounts are held at the same banks, when a cardholder makes a card payment to a merchant, the cardholder's issuer owes the merchant's acquirer the value of the payment. This creates a level of risk which dictates that a card scheme must use a trusted intermediary (the settlement agent) for the final settlement of funds between acquirers and issuers. The settlement agent holds accounts for acquirers and issuers, which are used to settle funds moved between them. On the card rails, **the settlement agent is generally a commercial bank**, which may be **chosen by the card scheme** for its size, reputation, geographical coverage, etc. However, in some geographies in Asia and Africa the settlement agent could be a central bank, as is the case with Nigeria.[44] Accordingly, card schemes may use several settlement agents.

The movement of funds typically happens on the same day for domestic transactions (i.e. cardholder and merchant in the same geography), or a few days later for cross-border transactions (i.e. merchant and cardholder in different geographies).

Step 1. The card scheme asks the issuer to fund their settlement account.

Step 2. The card scheme informs the acquirer of the incoming credit.

Step 3. The issuer funds their settlement account.

Step 4. The **Settlement Agent** moves the funds to the acquirer's bank account.

Step 5. The acquirer now has access to their funds.

This is a high-level explanation, and this book won't cover the intricacies of interbank settlement processes. I leave that to the economists, and you can always look at some references[45] ... BUT ...

 Professionals should remember:

- **Interbank settlement is done per scheme**: each scheme is a separate commercial entity.
- **The settlement agent is a commercial bank** (usually not a central bank).
- **Card schemes may choose settlement agents for their members** (e.g. issuers) to use. The selection criteria will include size, reputation, and geographical coverage. This is specified in the operating regulations.
- **Acquirers and issuers may have bilateral agreements** to settle between themselves, which is allowed by the card schemes, but members must inform them of the arrangement.

- **Interbank settlement is conducted on the bank rails** (see Chapter 3, *Interbank settlement*). It doesn't use the card scheme's infrastructure, which is only used for card transactions.
- And that's it for interbank settlement fundamentals. But we're not done yet: the merchant still hasn't received any money, and for this to happen, we must look at the next stage.

Merchant settlement

Merchant Settlement is a centralised function performed by the acquirer. We covered earlier in this chapter the relationships between the economic participants in the Four Party Model. You already know that the acquirer has a contract with the merchant. Therefore, merchant settlement terms will depend on this contractual arrangement. It is the process by which the acquirer will credit the merchant's bank account, which is illustrated in Figure 1.13:

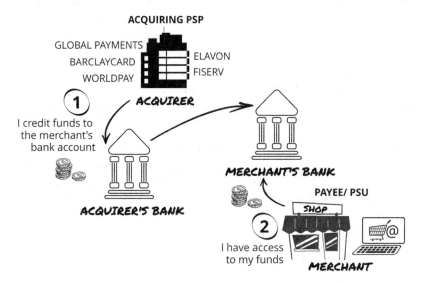

Figure 1.13 The merchant settlement process.
Source: drawing by the author.

Merchant settlement is a straightforward process and generally happens after interbank settlement. Of course, as for interbank settlement, this is a high-level explanation (for more details, see Chapter 2, *Merchant models and contract types*).

Professionals should remember:

- **Merchant settlement is done per merchant**: merchants and acquirers are separate commercial entities.
- **It is a bilateral agreement between the acquirer and the merchant**, the terms of which are specified in their contract.
- **Merchant settlement is conducted on the bank rails** (see Chapter 3, *Retail settlement*). It doesn't use the card scheme's infrastructure, which is only used for card transactions.

BOX 1.5 MERCHANT SETTLEMENT?

How fast does a merchant get settled? Well, how long is a piece of string? Short answer: it depends on the contract the merchant has with the acquirer. The cynic in me will tell you that the larger the merchant, the faster they will get settled, because they have more negotiating power in a competitive market. The more balanced me will tell you that several factors are at play: what risk vs value ratio does this merchant present for the acquirer? What commercial benefits are at play? What regulatory obligations does the acquirer have in that geography? And other economic factors. I'll let you decide, but you can always examine acquirer websites, or look at Chapter 2, *Costs and value chain*.

For some industry sectors (e.g. furniture retailers, travel, hospitality) which involve large ticket items and delayed delivery, the acquirer may decide to defer the settlement in line with the delivery to manage risk. This is called **Deferred Settlement**.

BOX 1.6 WHAT ABOUT CARDHOLDER SETTLEMENT?

For completeness purposes, I should also mention this. **Cardholder Settlement** is part of the commercial arrangement between the cardholder and the issuer. With debit cards, this is a "banking" arrangement. With credit cards, it is a "lending" arrangement. I will cover payments related to "banking" in Chapter 3, but I must draw the line somewhere, and so I won't cover consumer banking or lending processes in this payments book. There are plenty of references on this topic though.[46, 47]

And that's the gist of it. You now understand, at a high level, authorisation, clearing, and settlement on the card rails. I told you at the beginning: simple mechanics.

One must note, however, that what I described thus far is the "happy flow" of a purchase transaction. Once settlement is complete, we don't need to go back: the cardholder is happy with their purchase, the merchant has received their funds. And this is what happens most of the time. But sometimes, we *do* need to go back.

Exceptions and disputes (you need to calm down)

Settlement doesn't always mean finality. Exceptions exist to help us when something outside of the "happy flow" happens after the transaction has settled, which makes us go back. In this section, we will cover the main exception processes:

*   Retrieval (aka request for information);
*   Refund; and
*   Chargeback.

Retrieval

We've all done it. You look at your credit card statement, and you see a transaction that you don't recognise. This may be because the description of the transaction is obscure (e.g. it may show the registered name of a merchant instead of its trading name), or because you don't recognise the amount. You're unsure as to whether you've made that transaction, and the first thing you do is call your card provider. This happens more often than you think.

Rule number one for card issuers: the cardholder is (almost) always right. Therefore, it is unlikely that they will question the validity of the cardholder's request, and so they will initiate a **Retrieval Request** (sometimes called **Request for Information**).

This process can be invoked by cardholders, but issuers can initiate the process independently without the involvement of a cardholder (i.e. if their fraud prevention systems highlight that the transaction needs further investigation but is not necessarily flagged as fraudulent). The process shown in Figure 1.14 is for cardholder-initiated requests, but it is the same for issuer-initiated requests (just omit the cardholder).

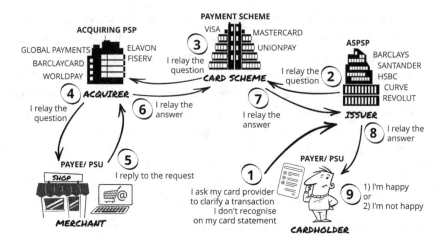

Figure 1.14 Retrieval request process.
Source: drawing by the author.

Retrieval requests, whilst seemingly *innocuous*, often end up morphing into a *chargeback*. Chargebacks are very painful for merchants (more on that later). So much so, that, in 2020, Mastercard tried to encourage merchants to load up their logos to a website[48] managed by fraud prevention platform Ethoca (Mastercard acquired Ethoca in 2019). The aim of this initiative was to give more clarity to consumers by showing logos on card statements, thus minimising disputes (this is not a new concept: neo-banks such as Starling Bank and Monzo have been doing it for their customers from the start ... but it's new to cards).

The retrieval request process is widely used, although card schemes are trying to replace it with more modern products such as Visa Order Insight[49] and Mastercard Mastercom.[50]

 Professionals should remember:

- **Whilst a retrieval request is not a dispute, it could result in one if not handled promptly.**
- **Merchant failure to reply to a retrieval request within the set time limit may result in a chargeback.**
- **Time limits vary by card scheme.** These are specified in their operating regulations – usually a couple of weeks or slightly longer.

- **Card schemes will charge a fee** (e.g. about £0.20 in the UK at the time of writing, but this may be higher in other geographies) for orchestrating retrieval requests. This is an example of a card scheme fee (see Chapter 2, *Charges and fees*).

Refund

The **Refund** process is simple: it is a purchase in reverse and will follow the same steps as in Figures 1.6 and 1.7 (authorisation request) and Figures 1.9 and 1.10 (authorisation decision). The only difference is that the transaction amount will be a credit to the cardholder account instead of a debit. I have included refunds in this section because if not handled properly they may result in a dispute; otherwise, they are perfectly legitimate transactions.

Because there is an exchange of value, a refund transaction will go through the clearing and settlement processes just like a purchase. After merchant settlement, the cardholder account will be credited for the refund amount and a corresponding debit will be applied to the merchant's bank account.

As a testimony to evolution, additional rules (*card scheme operating regulations*) are added from time to time. Here are two of them:

- **A refund must always be made to the card used for the original purchase.**
- **A refund must never be made, unless there was an original purchase on the card.** A merchant in breach of this rule may have their payment facility altogether withdrawn.

Whilst obvious, these rules didn't exist in the early days of card payments. This is because when new ecosystems emerge, how processes will work (or not) in practice is not immediately apparent. Fraudsters and criminals study ecosystems and their processes thoroughly, especially in the payments space, and are particularly adept at finding loopholes – the equivalent of a zero-day attack in the software world, if you will. When this happens, usually after critical mass is reached to make it worthwhile for criminals, those in charge of preserving the integrity of the ecosystem must plug the hole. And the operating regulations get updated.

Of course, there are always exceptions, even for simple rules such as the two I just mentioned (e.g. gambling). I'll let you explore that for yourself in the operating regulations.

Refunds are subject to abuse. The 2023 Ravelin Fraud Report[58] identifies refund (and returns) abuse as one of the top three fraud risks for 51% of UK businesses. The report defines this type of crime as either **First Party Fraud**, where genuine cardholders would try their luck during challenging economic conditions, or as outright fraud committed by organised crime gangs where "professional refunders" use social media to offer their services to legitimate customers looking for a bargain. Refund abuse is listed as the fastest-growing fraud threat after online payment fraud. Globally, 56% of businesses have seen refund abuse increase (17%) or significantly increase (39%). In recent years, the pandemic was a contributing factor to this increase as consumers felt the economic pinch.

 Professionals should remember:

- **Whilst a refund is not a dispute, failure, or refusal to process, one could result in a dispute** if the cardholder is unsatisfied.
- **Time limits vary by card scheme**, and they are specified in their operating regulations – usually between three days to a week, depending on the merchant and the issuer. Most merchants will process a refund immediately, but some may take a few more days. Each issuer will have their own process before the refund is applied to the card account.
- **Refunds are subject to abuse**, either through first party fraud, or through organised crime. Good customer service and a good refund policy will alleviate the former, whilst good fraud prevention will help with the latter.
- **Card schemes will charge a fee** (e.g. between £0.20 and £1 in the UK at the time of writing) for a refund, and the amount can vary widely across geographies. This is an example of a card scheme fee (see Chapter 2, *Charges and fees*).

Chargeback

A **Chargeback** is a process which can be invoked by a cardholder through their issuer to get the transaction amount back from the merchant for a disputed purchase, or it can be invoked directly by the card issuer when they suspect fraud. For merchants, the chargeback is the most painful of the exceptions. It is generally triggered by fraudulent activity, but not always.

The chargeback strikes fear in the hearts of merchants. But it is one of the features of card payments that has led cardholders to trust that little piece of plastic.

Chargebacks are good for cardholders; they were designed to protect consumers from fraud and merchant abuse. This is a mature process, and you can compare it with the processes available for bank payments in Chapter 3, *Bank payments risks*.

The result of a successful chargeback will be the same as a refund: the cardholder's account will be credited with the applicable amount, and the merchant's bank account will be debited accordingly, alongside applicable fees. But there are fundamental differences between refunds and chargebacks.

A refund request doesn't necessarily originate from a breach of the "sales contract" between the merchant and the cardholder. For example, the fact that the customer changed their mind about the colour or size of a jumper is not the merchant's fault.

By contrast, with a chargeback something more serious happened. It may be that the purchase transaction was not authorised by the cardholder, which generally points to fraud. It could be that the goods purchased didn't conform to their description or arrived damaged and the merchant refused to give a refund (a good returns policy generally avoids the process degenerating into a customer dispute). Or it may be that the transaction amount was charged twice.

Chargeback process

The process for a chargeback is explained in Figure 1.15, taking the example of a fraudulent transaction.

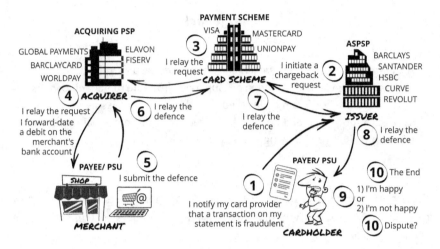

Figure 1.15 Chargeback process.

Source: drawing by the author.

The chargeback process is painful for merchants (and even more so for small merchants).

At Step 4, the acquirer will not only relay the **Chargeback Request** to the merchant, but they will also apply a debit to the merchant's bank account and put the debit on hold for the time period specified in the card scheme rules for that type of chargeback.

At Step 5, the merchant will gather the necessary information and provide a **Chargeback Defence** to their acquirer. They will have between 30 and 120 days to submit their defence, depending on the card scheme and type of chargeback. If a merchant fails to defend a chargeback within the specified time period, their bank account will automatically be debited (as the debit was applied and put on hold by the acquirer at the start). The industry often refers to the chargeback defence process as **Chargeback Representment**, and this is the only way for merchants to recover funds.

At Step 9, the cardholder may agree with the defence, or they may disagree, regardless of whether the anticipated outcome is to recover the funds. Sometimes it's clear cut: the transaction was clearly authorised (e.g. chip and PIN). Sometimes it's not, and the cardholder may decide to appeal a chargeback defence that looks successful. In such cases, issuers and card schemes are the arbiters.

Of course, this is but an overview of a complex process, and card scheme rules vary.

BOX 1.7 DO CHARGEBACKS ONLY APPLY TO CREDIT CARDS?

Contrary to popular belief, chargebacks apply to both credit and debit cards. In the UK, the confusion may have arisen due to the existence of chargebacks (card scheme rules) and Section 75 of the Consumer Credit Act[52] (regulation), which only applies to credit card purchases. Section 75 allows credit-card holders to raise a claim against the issuer if they paid some (or all) of the cost of the purchase by credit card or with a point of sale loan. Chargebacks and Section 75 are different processes.

Chargeback categories and reason codes

The classification of chargebacks is complex: for each card scheme, there are numerous chargeback types, and they are called **Chargeback Reason Codes**. A chargeback reason code is a description that must be provided as part of the chargeback request to help the merchant provide the correct information in defence. For clarity (!), the industry classifies these reason codes into a small number of chargeback categories, which will also vary per card scheme. Visa[60] and Mastercard[54] have four categories, whilst American Express (Amex)[55] and Discover have a few more. Good news: the industry is generally moving towards a maximum of four categories:

- Authorisation;
- Fraud;
- Consumer disputes; and
- Processing errors.

Just to show you how horrible these things are, Table 1.8 gives a comparison of a couple of chargeback reason codes between card schemes.

Table 1.8 Examples of chargeback reason codes.

Chargeback category	Visa	Mastercard	Amex	Discover
Authorisation	11.2 Declined Authorization	4808 Authorisation-Related Chargeback	A02 No Valid Authorisation	AT Authorisation Noncompliance
Fraud	10.3 Fraud – Card-Present Environment	4849 Questionable Merchant Activity	F24 No Card Member Authorisation	UA05 Fraud – Chip Counterfeit Transaction
Consumer disputes	13.2 Cancelled Recurring	4841 Cancelled Recurring or Digital Goods Transactions	C04 Goods/Services Returned or Refused	AA Does Not Recognise
Processing errors	12.1 Late Presentment	4834 Point-of-Interaction Error	P01 Unassigned Card Number	IN Invalid Card Number

Sources: Visa, Mastercard, Amex, Discover.

Chargeback monitoring

Chargebacks are often related to fraud or negligence; this is why the industry is trying to stamp them down. And when trying to control something, you must be able to measure it; consequently, the industry assesses chargebacks using the **Chargeback Ratio**, which represents the number of chargebacks filed against a merchant in a given month against their total number of transactions in a given month.

And because each card scheme has their own operating regulations, there is a different chargeback ratio for each scheme (you must be used to this by now!). The chargeback ratio is calculated per merchant and is shown in Table 1.9 for Visa and Mastercard.

Table 1.9 Chargeback ratio.

Card scheme	Chargeback ratio
Visa	$\dfrac{\text{current month Visa transactions}}{\text{current month chargebacks (on Visa)}}$
Mastercard	$\dfrac{\text{current month Mastercard transactions}}{\text{previous month chargebacks (on Mastercard)}}$

Acquirers generally consider the card scheme thresholds for the chargeback ratio (0.9% Visa, 1% Mastercard at the time or writing) to be critical but are free to impose stricter rules on their merchants. In general, anything above 0.65% is considered an early warning, and a chargeback ratio greater than 1.5% is considered excessive.

In 2021, according to Midigator,[56] the global average chargeback ratio across all industries was 1.52%, which is well above the card scheme limits, but it decreased by 21.6% between 2020 and 2021 (and by 59.6% since 2017). **There is direct correlation between chargebacks and merchant revenue**: in 2021, the global average percentage of merchant revenue lost to chargebacks was 2.31%; this also decreased by 1.5% from 2020 (and by 5.28% since 2017), fortunately moving in the right direction (according to Midigator). The industry must be doing something right, and the rules must be working.

But, whilst global statistics are interesting, they are of limited value to the practitioner who must understand a particular market, industry sector, or card brand. In addition, there isn't a single source of truth, and data is difficult to obtain: one source may indicate an increase, and another may indicate a decrease for the same aspect of chargeback management. These sources have their own data samples and are almost always commercial service providers. There are many ways to massage statistics, and I won't bore you by giving you some more!

As you may imagine, card schemes keep an eye on chargebacks through **Merchant Monitoring Programmes** with strict conditions. Here are two examples:

- **Visa Dispute Monitoring Program** (**VDMP**); and
- Mastercard **Excessive Chargebacks Program** (**ECP**).

> **Are disputes and chargebacks the same thing?** Well, good question. In 2019, Visa changed its terminology from "chargeback" to "dispute" in all their publications. Hence, the Visa Chargeback Monitoring Program (VCMP) became the Visa Dispute Monitoring Program (VDMP). The card industry, however, didn't follow suit. Today, we use both terms almost interchangeably.

In general, merchants may be included in a card scheme chargeback-monitoring programme if their chargeback ratio exceeds the card scheme limit (0.9% for Visa, 1% for Mastercard at the time of writing). Merchants on the programme will incur monthly fees for breaking the rules (these fees are levied by the card scheme on the acquirer, who recovers them from the merchant), and they will only be released from them once they remain below the card scheme limit for three consecutive months. The acquirer is responsible for helping their merchant reduce their chargeback ratio to an acceptable level and may even place a hold on the merchant's funds if they deem the ratio excessive, which may severely restrict a merchant's cash flow. In extreme cases, if a merchant is unable to remediate the situation and lower the ratio, they may have their card payment facility altogether removed for that card scheme (e.g. no longer be able to accept cards for that scheme). A serious issue indeed!

Chargeback abuse

Chargebacks are prone to abuse, just like refunds. This evolves as time goes by and depends on several factors. For example, the pandemic particularly affected airlines, as customers generated more chargebacks due to carriers refusing to refund flights. This was also the case for the hospitality and entertainment industries. The cost-of-living crisis is another driver for chargebacks, where cardholders might abuse the process and commit **Friendly Fraud** (i.e. first party fraud, where the cardholder tries to get money back on a purchase they made. There is nothing friendly about it, and it is sometimes called "cyber-shoplifting"). **Chargeback Activism** is another example of first party fraud where activists raise chargebacks to punish a company for ideological differences or disagreements.[57] The same behaviour can also be observed with the **General Data Protection Regulation** (**GDPR**) where disgruntled customers use **Data Subject Access Requests** (**DSARs**) to punish businesses for poor customer service.[58] Or when people use the description field available when making a bank payment to send abuse to the recipient: apparently, this was so much of a problem in Australia that banks and the police had to step in to curb the abuse.[59] These are perfect examples of processes being used for a purpose for which they weren't intended: in all cases, the facilities were designed for the benefit of consumers and were instead weaponised.

Consequently, if we agree that it is always in the best interest of the merchant to defend chargebacks promptly (if defensible, of course), I find it surprising that merchants surveyed in various papers only defend about half of their chargebacks. According to the Ravelin Fraud Report mentioned earlier, the 2022 global average percentage of chargebacks defended is 44%, with the UK at 40%, the US at 44%, and Australia and Brazil both at 49%. The success rate of chargeback defences is 60% globally. This may be due to lack of knowledge or resources. For larger merchants, it may be an economic decision, as they recognise that the effort required to defend a chargeback is often higher than the combined cost of the returned payment and chargeback fee (some even have policies by which chargebacks below a certain threshold won't be defended).

The chargeback ratio is an important risk indicator for acquirers, and card scheme thresholds form part of the monitoring activities. Some merchants in industries prone to high levels of chargebacks may abuse the process by sourcing acquiring services from multiple acquirers. This may result in their chargeback ratio being lowered as it would be split between acquirers, for example 0.6% for Visa and 0.7% for Mastercard across acquirers. The real chargeback ratio would be 1.3%, which is well above the limit, and may remain under the radar for a while. This practice is called **Load Balancing**, and merchants shouldn't engage in it, as they will in time be found out. This may result in the merchant being blacklisted and their payment facility being removed altogether. Of course, engaging in load balancing is not always a dubious practice, as merchants may legitimately want to spread the load across acquirers in an attempt not to put all their acquiring eggs in one basket, but this process can be perverted.

Chargeback industry

The chargeback process is resource-intensive and expensive. When a gap appears in an ecosystem, businesses will try to fill it. This happened with the chargeback process. To help stakeholders manage chargebacks effectively, a whole new industry emerged a few years ago, starting in the US: **Chargeback Process Outsourcing**. You may have heard of a few companies in that space: Midigator, Chargeback911, chargebackops, and chargehounds. These businesses take the burden of chargeback management away from merchants and other PSPs, and some have even evolved into full-blown fraud prevention services providers.

 Professionals should remember:

- Some **industries** are more prone to chargebacks than others: the software industry and the financial services industry generally experience higher chargeback levels, followed by media, retail (including e-commerce), and travel. Some industries are classified as high risk.
- Some **channels** are more prone to chargebacks than others: for example, physical retail is less affected than e-commerce.
- Some **products** are more prone to chargebacks than others: digital goods are more affected than physical goods.

- Some **sales models** are more prone to chargebacks: subscription services, and Software-as-a-Service (SaaS) products in general (where cardholders change their mind at the end of the free trial) are more prone to chargebacks than other models (e.g. single purchase).
- Some **geographies** are more prone to chargebacks than others: according to the Midigator report mentioned earlier, Western Europe has the lowest chargeback ratio at 0.46%, compared to Canada (3.57%), North America (1.5%), and Latin America and the Caribbean (1.8%).
- **Emerging payments services** are not immune: **Buy-Now-Pay-Later (BNPL)** and cryptocurrency (i.e. fiat-to-crypto transactions) are increasingly ending up in chargebacks.[60]
- **Acquirers are responsible for their merchants**: if a card scheme instructs an acquirer to include a merchant in a monitoring programme, the acquirer is responsible for taking the merchant out of it (as is the case for any breach of card scheme rules).
- **Merchants incur fees**: a fee is applied for chargeback requests (about £20 to £30 at the time of writing), another example of a card scheme fee. Fees (read "penalties") are also applied if the merchant is on a monitoring programme.
- **Card schemes have different rules**: time limits, thresholds, ratio calculations, chargeback codes, vocabulary, monitoring programmes, etc. (Hey, what did you expect?). For example, a merchant could be compliant with the chargeback ratio limit for one card scheme, and in breach for another card scheme. Anyone involved with chargebacks must understand the card scheme rules in detail.
- **The process is labour-intensive for merchants**: especially small merchants, who can hardly afford the labour cost, let alone the penalties and loss of revenue.
- **Effective fraud prevention mechanisms help minimise chargebacks**: multi-factor authentication, address verification, 3D Secure, and other technologies help minimise chargebacks (see later sections in this chapter).
- **Some processes can be perverted, but those engaging in these practices will eventually be found out** (e.g. load balancing).
- **Risk management is crucial and an understanding of AML/KYC obligations when onboarding merchants is a fundamental requirement** (see Chapter 5, *Customer Due Diligence*).

BOX 1.8 WHAT ARE HIGH-RISK SECTORS?

When an industry or business sector experiences higher levels of charge-backs or fraud, the card schemes tend to classify them as "high risk". These will include travel, online pharmaceuticals, adult entertainment, dating, gaming, health and wellness, gambling, jewellery, and legal services. They can be subject to additional rules and/or permissions (see Chapter 2, *Contracting and underwriting*).

And that's the end of our whistle-stop tour of the world of charge-backs, which completes our high-level overview of transactional and post-settlement processes.

Card payments data (too much information)

Now equipped with the knowledge of the main processes on the card rails, we need to complete the picture by understanding the data used as part of these processes.

Data will be present:

• As part of the card transaction; and
• As part of the card itself.

What's in a card transaction?

When looking at card transactions, you intuitively know three of the data elements required: the transaction amount, the transaction date, and the merchant's identification, but there are many more data elements available depending on the level of transaction-processing, and there are three levels.

Level 1

Consumer transactions – those associated with **Business-to-Consumer (B2C)** interactions – represent the majority of transactions on the card rails. Merchants are only required to transmit the three data elements when accepting these payments. Additional information – such as cardholder information, and transaction date and time – is automatically recorded by the issuer but isn't explicitly transmitted by the merchant processing the transaction. This type of transaction is referred to as a **Level 1** transaction. All merchants will be able to accept these transactions, physically or virtually, and all cards (e.g. consumer, commercial, corporate, government) can be accepted that way.

Level 2

Business-to-Business (B2B) and **Business-to-Government (B2G)** entities as well as **corporations** may benefit from making more data available when processing card transactions. This includes all Level 1 data, more merchant identification data, tax information, and additional customer information. These are called **Level 2** transactions and are associated with **government**, **corporate**, or **industrial buying**. Commercial, corporate, purchasing, and government cards are eligible for Level 2 processing, but not consumer cards (which can only be processed at Level 1). Historically, the amount of extra data transmitted in a card transaction by a merchant has been limited only by the capabilities of most hardware **Point of Sale (POS)** terminals, and Level 2 data was specified accordingly. Therefore, in theory, any merchant could transmit Level 2 data in a card transaction. In practice, this is not the case because:

- Some card schemes have annual transaction thresholds below which merchants are not allowed to process Level 2 transactions.
- The payment facility provided by the merchant's PSP (e.g. payment gateway or POS terminal) is not configured for it.
- The merchant doesn't know about it.

Level 3

The data elements in **Level 3** transactions include all Level 2 data and items such as invoice information, product information, quantity, unit of measure, postal code, VAT, and freight amount. This amount of data is equivalent to what you would find on an **itemised invoice**. Logically, this is associated with **B2B and supplier payments**, and the cards eligible for Level 2 processing are also eligible here.

Historically, these transactions could only be accepted virtually (i.e. through a payment gateway) and often integrated with enterprise resource planning (ERP) platforms such as SAP or Oracle NetSuite. This is because they were beyond the capabilities of traditional hardware POS terminals (as many of the data elements require text input and standard card terminals have basic numeric keypads).

Increasingly, modern card payment terminals offer Level 3 capability through touchscreen technology. These card terminals are called **Smart POS** and support standard card payments as well as a range of applications supporting a merchant's business. These modern terminals are usually cloud-based and based on open operating systems such as Android (making them much more flexible), but they are still proprietary to their manufacturers (see Chapter 2, *Value chain*).

Transaction level vs risk

In summary, the higher the level, the more data is processed and transmitted to the issuer as part of the card transaction.

Now that you understand the card transaction data levels, you're probably wondering why a merchant should care. After all, accepting Level 2 and Level 3 cards means that the merchant has to explicitly input more data at the point of interaction (through their PSP).

The answer is: it's all about **risk** (and cost). The greater the amount of data that is transmitted to the issuer, the more able they are to make better risk decisions. And minimising risk means minimising costs. If a merchant is able to process Level 2 or Level 3 transactions, they may benefit from better rates (see Chapter 2, *Charges and fees*).

But it's not all plain sailing.

 Professionals should remember:

• **Not all merchants will benefit from processing Level 2 or Level 3 data even if they could.** The shop in my little village in the middle of nowhere will likely not benefit from this. They will see very few eligible cards (e.g. commercial, business), because it's a sleepy village. That same shop in the middle of Canary Wharf in London (very much a corporate district) will, by comparison, see many commercial cards, and that same-size shop may very well benefit from processing higher data levels. These have different merchant profiles. You have to know your market.

- Whilst I tried to give a description of the various data elements for each level, you may have noticed that it was more illustrative than exhaustive. This is because the **data elements included in each level will vary depending on the card scheme** (what did you expect?). Generally, there will be 15 to 20 data elements available. You need to know what you're doing.
- **Whilst Visa and Mastercard are able to accommodate all data levels, not all schemes do.** For example, American Express doesn't process Level 3 transactions (the cynic in me would say "why would they?" – processing Level 3 transactions would mean discounting rates for merchants when they don't have to since they operate on the Three Party Model ... but then again, they might).[61]
- Processing Level 2 and Level 3 data – once confined to a small part of the ecosystem – is, in my opinion, set to grow. This is because **B2B payments now constitute a growth market** in the card space.[62]
- Merchants' PSPs are best placed to advise them on how they can optimise their payment acceptance fees. Several consultancies also specialise in this field, known as **Payments Optimisation**, or **Card Optimisation**.

And that's all, folks!

What's in a card? (PAN, BIN, EMV, etc.)

The card, in its many forms, is a fascinating piece of kit. It has a lot of data which is either visible on the card or contained in the card. For the data that is visible on the card (front and back), I list all *possible* data elements, as in modern days, not all of the listed data elements will be found on cards.

The front of the card

Data visible on the front of the card is shown in Figure 1.16.

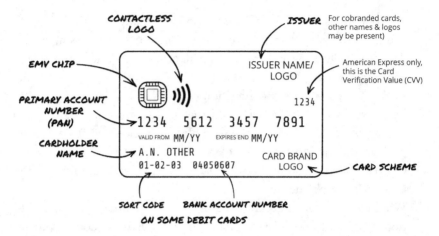

Figure 1.16 The front of a card.

Source: drawing by the author.

The issuer decides what data is shown on their cards, and therefore **not all data elements** shown in Figure 1.16 **will be present on all cards**.

EMBOSSED ELEMENTS

On some cards, the following elements, where present, can be **embossed** (i.e. slightly raised from the surface of the card):

- Primary Account Number (PAN);
- Start and expiry dates;
- Cardholder name; and
- Bank sort code and account number (where present).

The embossed elements are only needed if the card is to be used for payments using a **Card Imprinting Machine** (also known as a **Zip-Zap Machine** because of the noise they make when taking a card imprint, and sometimes called **Knuckle-Busters** for obvious reasons). How does the authorisation process take place? It was much simpler then. As there was no way of verifying the cardholder digitally, the merchant would manually check against a deny list of fraudulent card numbers sent by the issuer regularly.

Increasingly, modern payment cards don't have any embossed fields (e.g. Apple, Revolut, Starling Bank, N26). Some don't even show the cardholder's name or the PAN on the front of the card. This is due to the increase in contactless and digital payments (and the inevitable disappearance of the zip-zap machine, although you can still buy them on eBay if you're feeling nostalgic and find them in cash-dominated geographies): **none of the embossed or printed data elements are needed in a digital POS transaction**.

PRIMARY ACCOUNT NUMBER (PAN)

The **Primary Account Number** (**PAN**) is an interesting data element, and, unlike many other things in the card world, everyone agrees on how this should be constructed. The PAN follows the **ISO/IEC 7812** standard (identification cards), an international standard which dictates the structure shown in Table 1.10.

Table 1.10 Primary Account Number structure

Issuer Identification Number (IIN), aka Bank Identification Number (BIN)		Cardholder Account Number	Checksum
1	23456	123456789	1
Major Industry Identifier (MII)			

Essentially, a card using the ISO/IEC 7812 standard can be read in a card terminal. It's not just for payment cards (e.g. loyalty cards such as Boots Advantage or MyWaitrose, or government benefit cards), but in this book, we'll concentrate on payment cards.

BANK IDENTIFICATION NUMBER (BIN)

The first six digits represent the issuer. The modern term is **Issuer Identification Number** (**IIN**), which was supposed to replace the original term of **Bank Identification Number** (**BIN**) to reflect the fact that issuers don't have to be banks (e.g. eMoney institutions). But the term BIN is so well established that the industry still sticks with it. The BIN is used to identify the card scheme (not the cardholder).

The first digit in the BIN is called the **Major Industry Identifier** (**MII**) and identifies the industry or type of card. This is shown in Table 1.11.

Table 1.11 Major Industry Identifier (MII).

MII value	Issuer category
1	Airline cards
2	Airline cards and future assignments (New range for Mastercard since 2017)
3	Travel and entertainment cards (This is where American Express and Diners Club are)
4	Banking and financial cards (This is where Visa is)
5	Banking and financial cards (This is where Mastercard is)
6	Merchandising and financial cards (This is where Discover and UnionPay are)
7	Petroleum industry and future assignments (e.g. Shell)
8	Telecommunications, healthcare, and future assignments (You may find loyalty cards here)

As MIIs can be shared by several entities, you need further digits in the BIN to identify the organisation, for example:

- American Express: 34, 37;
- Discover: 6011, 622126 to 622925, 624000 to 626999, 628200 to 628899, 64, 65;
- Mastercard: 2221 to 2720, 51 to 55; and
- Visa: 4.

The BIN (first six or eight digits) enables you to identify a number of elements, including the card scheme (e.g. Visa), the issuer (e.g. Santander), the type of card (e.g. credit, debit, purchasing), and the country (e.g. UK).

BOX 1.9 WHAT IS BIN SPONSORSHIP?

Box 1.10 this term. It describes the process by which **BIN Sponsors**, which can be acquirers and issuers (See Chapter 2, *Scheme membership*), enable other eligible organisations to issue cards by allowing them to use BIN ranges that they control (this is sometimes described as **BIN Rental**).

> Working with a principal scheme member allows these eligible organisations to issue cards and adhere to the card scheme rules and regulatory requirements, giving them quick time to market. This is traditionally associated with the prepaid and eMoney markets. Anecdotally, all the digital challenger banks that readers will be familiar with (e.g. Monzo, Starling Bank, N26, etc.) started life through BIN sponsorship agreements as eMoney institutions (not banks). Some of these digital banks went on to acquire the relevant banking permissions and became banks.

In April 2022, BINs expanded from six to eight digits (ISO/ISE 7812-2). The PAN length remains the same. Both six- and eight-digit BINs will co-exist for a few years still, and issuers are not mandated to use eight-digit BINs (although they are encouraged to do so), but acquirers must be able to process eight-digit BINs. This gives more scope to the market[63] as each six-digit BIN encompasses 100 eight-digit BINs (more cards!). The structure of a PAN with an eight-digit BIN is shown in Table 1.12.

Table 1.12 Eight-digit BIN Primary Account Number.

Issuer Identification Number (IIN), aka Bank Identification Number (BIN)		Cardholder Account Number	Checksum
1	2345678	1234567	1
Major Industry Identifier (MII)			

CARDHOLDER ACCOUNT NUMBER

This identifies the cardholder (on most cards, nine digits for six-digit BINs, and seven digits for eight-digit BINs – but card numbers can have as many as 19 digits). In the past, you may have come across cards where this number was all zeros: these were anonymous prepaid cards, which have been banned in most geographies according to Anti-Money Laundering regulations.

CHECKSUM

The last digit in the PAN is calculated by applying a mathematical formula called the **Luhn algorithm** (aka Modulus 10) to the BIN and **Cardholder**

Account Number. The checksum is not part of the account number itself but is essential for validation of card numbers (e.g. typos, missed digits, etc.). I'm sure you've encountered this, perhaps without even realising it: when you shop online and mistype your card number, the page recognises that the account is not valid. Also, whilst the Luhn algorithm validates that a card number is valid, it doesn't know whether the card number actually exists (i.e. that the issuer has issued that card). It's still smooth on the surface, but the ducks are still paddling underneath!

And that's it for the PAN. I can't believe I spent so much time talking about a few digits!

EMV CHIP

And now, you're in for a treat! The **EMV Chip** is an integrated circuit consisting of a microprocessor and a memory. Again here, we have standards: **ISO/IEC 7816** (contact) and **ISO/IEC 14443** (contactless). The chip contains the data required for EMV transactions at the POS. The data on the chip will be read when:

- the card is inserted into the card terminal (contact transaction); or
- the card is held close to the card terminal (contactless transaction).

We will examine the data contained in the chip a bit later in conjunction with the data held in the magnetic stripe, or magstripe.

In **Chip and PIN** deployments (e.g. UK, Europe, Canada), a **Personal Identification Number** (**PIN**) – a four-digit code selected and managed by the cardholder – is used to authenticate face-to-face transactions at the physical POS.

In **Chip and Signature** deployments (e.g. US), a **signature** is used to authenticate face-to-face transactions at the physical POS.

In the early days, a **Chip Card** was often called a **Smart Card**, but this term is now rarely used. The first chip card, "la Carte à Puce" (*puce* is "microchip" in French), was introduced in France in 1986 using their own standard, but it has since migrated to the EMV chip standard. At the time of the original EMV deployments in Europe and elsewhere, electronic communications were extremely expensive, which meant that obtaining an online authorisation from the issuer was difficult and costly. Therefore, merchants were allowed to establish "floor limits" under which any card payment would be accepted by the issuers, consequently generating an unacceptable level of fraud. EMV chip was designed to address this issue (see *The data*). Online authorisation had been the standard in the US well before the introduction of EMV, and nowadays all major chip payment cards are EMV chip cards.

A couple of decades ago, the media was rife with massive data breaches at US brick-and-mortar retailers. Once example was Target's in 2013, then dubbed the biggest breach in history. It was so amazing that, in 2015, I was compelled to produce a YouTube video[64] about the events leading to it and about the post-breach impact. When I watch it now, the format is a bit dated, but it's still interesting to see the implications (sometimes unexpected) of not securing payments infrastructures. Watch it if you have time. Since then, we have seen many similar data breaches in the US, especially in retail and hospitality. All have one point in common: the breached entity, in the aftermath, vows to deploy EMV chip technology. However, the horse has bolted.

We introduced EMVCo earlier for the world geographical zones. They also regularly produce EMV chip[65] deployment statistics[66] on their website. These show a global EMV chip adoption rate of 91.94% as a percentage of all Card Present transactions, confirming it as a mature standard. But you must also look at regional variations. For example, Europe Zone 1 is at 99.58%, Canada, Latin America, and The Caribbean are at 97.94%, whilst the US and Asia lag behind at 84.84% and 82.80%, respectively. Countries that have deployed EMV chip have seen a massive reduction in face-to-face card fraud, which is why the regional discrepancies appear puzzling: for example, why is the US percentage so low, despite having started their EMV chip migration from magnetic stripe in 2015? Or does Asia have a similar face-to-face card fraud profile to the United States, their deployment percentages being similar?

I can't answer the first question with cast-iron data; therefore, I will offer my opinion: maybe it was a case of "not invented here"? Or perhaps because the deployment was chip and signature instead of chip and PIN, making the customer experience marginally worse than magstripe, forcing EMV-enabled retailers to create separate checkout queues, magnetic stripe transactions being much faster? Was it too difficult/expensive for issuers to produce new cards for their customers (because EMV terminals allow for both chip and PIN and chip and signature deployments)? Or would they lose out on interchange (see Chapter 2, *Charges and fees*)? Were merchants not convinced that the value of replacing their POS terminals to EMV-capable models was worth the cost? Was there enough knowledge in the ecosystem to deploy it? Or it could have been that consumers just didn't like it. Consumer preferences play a significant role in the payments industry. I'll let you decide, but I found an interesting post on Quora:[67] "Why are US credit card companies introducing 'chip and signature' cards instead of 'Chip and PIN'?".

As for the second question, Asia is a totally different market. The Asian market is so digitally enabled that they have, for all intents and purposes, leapfrogged EMV chip. The Asian market is the birthplace of Super Apps. WeChat launched in China in 2011 (~1.7 billion active users in June 2023), and Gojek launched in Southeast Asia in 2010 (~39 million users in 2020). And we have Paytm (90 million active users in January 2023), Tata Neu, and Reliance in India. That's a lot of people, and a lot of payments. And they don't use physical cards, so no wonder EMV chip deployment figures are lower. Consumer preferences again. **QR Code** payments were available in Asia long before anyone in the Western world thought they were "cool". Even beggars use QR codes in India.[68] For digital adoption, look East. Since then, the pandemic has driven the adoption of QR codes everywhere: signage, restaurant menus, marketing, ordering at table, etc. More and more merchants are offering the convenience of QR code payment options, and they may partner with ISVs who offer these solutions. EMVCo even has a standard for them.[69] According to Deloitte,[70] 4% of global consumer transactions used QR codes in 2022, and that number is predicted to increase at a Compound Annual Growth Rate (CAGR) of 16.1% by 2030.

The back of the card

The back of a card is no less interesting than the front, and it is shown in Figure 1.17.

MAGNETIC STRIPE

The first thing that catches our attention is the black band, which is the **Magnetic Stripe** (also called **Magstripe**), constructed in accordance with

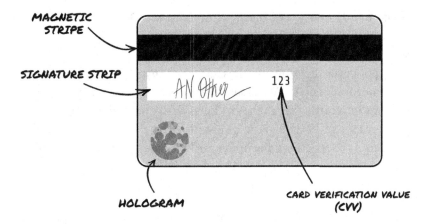

Figure 1.17 The back of a card.

Source: drawing by the author.

ISO/IEC 7813. For card payments, two magnetic tracks are used for data storage: **Track 1** and **Track 2**. We'll examine the data contained in these tracks in conjunction with EMV chip data below. **Card Swipe** is the term used for a card payment transaction using the magstripe. Increasingly, modern cards don't include a magstripe, and Mastercard signed off on its removal in 2021.[71] From 2024, most newly-issued Mastercard credit and debit cards won't be required to have a magstripe, and by 2029 no new Mastercard credit or debit cards will be issued with a magnetic stripe, which is expected to disappear by 2033. This leaves a long runway for the implementation of chip-enabled payment terminals.

HOLOGRAM

The **Hologram** may appear on the back of the card or on the front. It is a security feature originally designed to prevent fraudsters from cloning cards, as it is difficult to reproduce. This has often puzzled me. Imagine a fraudster cloning a magnetic stripe card and loosely including a hologram that resembles Visa's (a dove), or even something completely different (say a triangle), or even not including a hologram at all. Now, the fraudster goes to buy something with their newly cloned card, they pay with the card, the merchant gives them the receipt, and the fraudster signs it. What do you think happens next? Well, in my experience, merchants (in signature markets) hardly ever check the signature anyway. Do you think they will verify a hologram and even know what to check, let alone recognise the absence of one (in fact, most merchants allow the cardholder to use the card without ever showing it to the clerk, thus any visual verification is difficult, if not impossible)? Yet, issuers have spent much money embedding holograms into cards over the years. I personally put it down as a "marketing expense" … The hologram is now slowly being abandoned, but you can still find the specifications in the card scheme operating regulations.

SIGNATURE PANEL

The **Signature Panel**, sometimes called the **Signature Strip**, contains two elements: the cardholder's signature and a printed three-digit code. On some modern cards, you may also find the whole PAN printed on the signature strip, just before the three-digit code. This acts as a visual reminder for the cardholder when the PAN is not present on the front of the card. The cardholder's signature is used to authenticate the cardholder for face-to-face transactions in chip and signature or non-EMV markets. Increasingly on modern cards, the signature panel is not present, and since April 2019 Mastercard issuers are not required to include a signature panel on the back of Mastercard products.[72]

CARD VERIFICATION VALUE (CVV)

The three-digit code is the **CVV** for most cards (e.g. Visa, Mastercard), but the CVV for American Express has four digits and is printed on the front of the card (see Figure 1.16). The CVV is used to authenticate remote transactions (e.g. e-commerce or telephone) by verifying that the cardholder has the card in their possession. The technical term, as defined in the standard, is **CVV2**, and it is intended for the cardholder's eyes only (i.e. not machine-readable). Whilst there are other card verification values (see CVV1, CVV3), the term "CVV" in day-to-day life refers to the CVV2 because this is what cardholders see. Let the ducks deal with the other CVVs.

The CVV can be called many things: Card Verification Code (CVC) for Mastercard, Card Identification Number (CID) for American Express, Card Authorisation Value (CAV) for JCB, Card Security Code (CSC), and a few other things.

Now that we understand the various data elements visible on a card, we must look at the data inside. We must remember that the data contained in the EMV chip, or the magnetic stripe, is all that is needed for a digital POS transaction. Whether the data is contained in a plastic card, a watch, a mobile phone, a ring, a key fob – or another weird and wonderful form factor – doesn't matter as long as the form factor complies with the standards. Consequently, for the next few pages let's bear in mind that the data remains the same regardless of the "wrapper" (e.g. smart watch) you put around a card.

The data

There are five basic elements for the data contained in the card, as shown in Table 1.13.

Table 1.13 Data contained in a card.

Data element	Track 1	Track 2	Chip	Size
PAN	✓	✓	✓	Up to 19 characters
Name	✓	✗	✗	Up to 26 characters
Expiry date	✓	✓	✓	MM/YY
Service code	✓	✓	✓	3 digits
Discretionary data	✓	✓	✓	Balance of digits available: 79 characters on Track 1 40 characters on Track 2 and the chip

We have already covered the PAN, and the cardholder's name and expiry date are self-explanatory.

SERVICE CODE

The **Service Code** is used by issuers to tell merchants how the card can and can't be used. For example, whether the card is for international use or domestic use only, or if a PIN is required for all transactions, or if it's only to be used at ATMs and the applicable interchange (see Chapter 2, *Charges and fees*). Good news: everyone agrees on how service codes should be codified (e.g. card scheme, issuers). Table 1.14 shows examples of most commonly used service codes.

Table 1.14 Most commonly used service codes.

Service code	Definition
121	International magstripe card (1) Authorisation by issuer online (2) No terminal restrictions (1)
201	International chip card (2) Normal authorisation processing (0) No terminal restrictions (1)
206	International chip card (2) Normal authorisation processing (0) No terminal restrictions. Prompt for PIN if PIN pad present (6)
220	International chip card (2) Authorisation by issuer online (2) No terminal restrictions. PIN required (0)
221	International chip card (2) Authorisation by issuer online (2) No terminal restrictions (1)
520	National (domestic only) magstripe card (5) Authorisation by issuer online (2) No terminal restrictions. PIN required (0)
621	National (domestic only) chip card (6) Authorisation by issuer online (2) No terminal restrictions (1)
623	National (domestic only) chip card (6) Authorisation by issuer online (2) ATM only. PIN required (3)
702	Private (7) Normal authorisation processing (0) Goods and services only (2)

In summary, the service code gives the card its basic characteristics. Issuers also use the service code in conjunction with other card data elements (e.g. PAN, expiry date) when performing cardholder validation during the authorisation process.

DISCRETIONARY DATA

The **Discretionary Data** is used by issuers pretty much as they see fit. Table 1.13 shows that the chip and Track 2 have a similar structure. However, the constituents of the discretionary data will be different for Track 1, Track 2, and the chip. Issuers may use the discretionary data to create new card products with specific characteristics (e.g. a student card).

Importantly, **the discretionary data is used for security**. On Tracks 1 and 2, it may include PIN verification elements and a card verification value called the **CVV1**. The CVV1 is used to authenticate magstripe transactions (this process takes place between the magstripe, the card reader, and the issuer during the authorisation process).

CARD CLONING, FRAUD, AND CVVS

The chip doesn't contain the same card verification value as the magstripe, but an alternative value: the **iCVV** (**Integrated Chip Card Verification Value**, also known as **CVV3**). The iCVV is generated by the chip and the card reader for each transaction (i.e. it is dynamic) using a different calculation from that used for the CVV1 on the magstripe. Issuers use the iCVV to identify fraudulent use of chip cards in magstripe-read transactions.

In other terms, if a fraudster were to clone the magstripe present in an EMV chip card using a **Skimmer** and then use the counterfeit card to make a purchase through a magstripe terminal (e.g. UK-issued cloned card used in a swipe transaction), the card might be authorised by the issuer, depending on the market where the card is used (see EMV deployment figures shown earlier) and the card type, but it would be unusable in the UK.

If a fraudster compromised a chip card using a **Shimmer** planted in a card terminal, used the data to re-create the magstripe on a counterfeit card, and tried to make a swipe purchase, the same applies. BUT. The fraudster has to manipulate the data found on the chip so that the resulting counterfeit card magstripe shows a service code relating to a non-chip-enabled card, potentially allowing a swipe transaction to be authorised. This second attack is more complex, and fraudsters have to develop the shimmer, install it in the relevant geography, and understand what they're doing. Fraudsters also have to make sure that they deploy the devices where there is enough volume to make it worth their while. Why bother when you can easily compromise an insecure e-commerce website from the comfort of your armchair (literally)?

BOX 1.10 WHAT ARE CARD SKIMMERS AND SHIMMERS?

A skimmer is a device used by fraudsters to read information from the magstripe. Skimmers are most often found at ATMs and petrol stations and other unattended terminals, but shops and restaurants are not immune (although more difficult to compromise, unless the merchant colludes with the fraudster or is negligent). Skimmers are devices **over-layed on top** of the card terminals, and sometimes combined with small cameras to capture cardholder PINs. Skimmers can be bought cheaply on eBay and other platforms and can be spotted visually. A shimmer (aka "shim") is a device used to capture data from the EMV chip. A shimmer **fits inside** the card terminal, unattended payment terminal, or ATM, directly between the card and the reader, and is therefore difficult to detect (and needs to be less than 0.1 mm thick to enable the card reader to accommodate a card).

In summary, both CVV1 (magstripe) and CVV2 (printed on card) are static data elements (i.e. they remain valid for the life of the card). The iCVV is dynamic and can't be used twice.

CONTACT AND CONTACTLESS

In addition, I mentioned earlier that there are two standards for EMV chip, one for contact and one for contactless transactions. The security measures introduced earlier are the same for contact and contactless transactions, in as much as the iCVV will work in the same way (i.e. dynamic, generated each time). The only difference is that the card will not be inserted in the terminal, thereby preventing both skimming and shimming attacks. Criminals understand this, however, and can use devices equipped with a contactless interface (**NFC – Near Field Communication**, as defined in **ISO/IEC 18092** and **ISO/IEC 21481**) to try and collect card data from cardholders using that interface. Of course, you need to be uncomfortably close to the cardholder to do this (say, at a crowded concert). But what does that achieve? The fraudster would be able to get data that they will only be able to use once (because of the dynamic iCVV). Still, fraudsters can make multiple readings, and re-encode a new counterfeit card each time before a purchase. They must then use it in a magstripe market. That's a lot of effort! (Let's just hack an e-commerce website.)

All of these factors, combined with the contactless limits (which some issuers allow their customers to change for a lower value), the transaction count after which a PIN is needed, and the paranoia that made insulated wallets somewhat popular (although of questionable usefulness), make this attack of limited appeal to fraudsters.

However, the criminal mind never ceases to amaze me. I thought skimming and shimming was as far as this was going to go, when, in January 2023, I came across a new type of attack where fraudsters re-purposed Prilex, an ancient piece of malware first used to compromise ATMs in 2014.[73] The Prilex modifications block a consumer's ability to make contactless payments, forcing them to insert their card in the ter-minal (and then we're back to the start of this story). Conclusion: if criminals are trying to block contactless payments, forcing cardholders into contact transactions, the industry must be doing something right, wouldn't you say?

In addition, let's not forget that these attacks target physical cards. With the global increase in popularity of other digital payment means (e.g. Apple Pay, Google Wallet, Venmo), a minor problem becomes even smaller.

FRAUD MUSINGS

Fraudsters never give up, because **fraud is like a balloon: if you squeeze it in one area, it bulges out in another**. Consequently, criminals return to good old-fashioned methods: stealing the cards or the card data (i.e. credentials stolen after data breaches, enabling criminals to open card accounts – account takeover – or apply for card accounts – third-party ap-plication fraud). Industry fraud statistics seem to confirm this: Table 1.15 shows the UK card fraud losses in 2021–2022.

Of course, **the biggest fraud area remains Card Not Present (CNP)** (let's just hack an e-commerce website), but **theft of physical cards is in second position** (i.e. "lost or stolen" and "card non-receipt" where the card is stolen whilst in transit to the cardholder when issued), represent-ing 15% of all card fraud in 2022, an increase of more than 20% over the previous year. This makes even more sense when we consider that nearly half of burglaries in 30,100 neighbourhoods across England and Wales re-mained unsolved by UK Police between 2020 and 2023[74]: there are real-life consequences.

Table 1.15 UK card fraud losses in 2021–2022.

Fraud type	2021				2022				Percentage change 2021 vs 2022	
	Value (£ million)	% total	Volume (million)	% total	Value (£ million)	% total	Volume (million)	% total	Value	Volume
Card Not Present	412.5	78.65	2.42	85.85	395.7	71.13	2.22	81.27	–4%	–8%
Lost or stolen	77.2	14.72	0.32	11.53	100.2	18.01	0.40	14.69	+30%	+23%
Card ID theft	26.3	5.01	0.04	1.43	51.7	9.29	0.08	3	+97%	+105%
Counterfeit	4.7	0.89	0.02	0.88	4.7	0.84	0.02	0.72	+1%	–21%
Card non-receipt	3.9	0.74	0.009	0.32	4.0	0.72	0.009	0.32	+1%	–1%
TOTAL	524.5		2.8		556.3		2.7		6%	–3%

Source: UK Finance, Annual Fraud Report 2023

It is also interesting to note that whilst the percentage of counterfeit card fraud decreased by 21% in volume, it increased by 1% in value: fewer attacks, greater fraud losses. Fraudsters seemed to concentrate their efforts on higher-value targets, and this is true of overall card fraud (more "bang for the buck"). The UK Finance Annual Fraud Report also highlights that whilst contactless represented 57% of all card transactions in 2022, contactless fraud accounted for only 6% of overall card fraud losses: I think I've proved my point.

To all the EMV chip detractors: **EMV chip is, and continues to be, successful in fighting face-to-face card fraud.** Skimming and shimming attacks mentioned earlier are designed to bypass EMV chip controls, and yet EMV contactless attacks are not an issue. Of course, EMV chip doesn't do anything for Card-Not-Present fraud (see *3D Secure*), but that's another matter. If you don't agree, show me your data; I've shown you mine.

DYNAMIC CVV (dCVV)

The card payments industry never stands still. Some enhancements to the verification process have been attempted. One example is the **Dynamic CVV**, or **dCVV**. This is where the issuer supplies the cardholder with a little device as well as a card. The little device calculates a dCVV each time a remote transaction is initiated by the cardholder, and this the three-digit number that the cardholder would use on an e-commerce website or over the telephone (essentially a dynamic CVV2). This can also be achieved through the card itself, where a small electronic screen is embedded directly into the back of the card to perform the same function. The cost of production of these cards is such that they are quite rare, although some private banks offer the facility.

Card payments authentication (I am what I am)

Now that you understand the data in card transactions and cards, we can complete the picture through a summary of card authentication for the diverse types of cardholder interactions.

Face-to-face environments, also known as Card Present (CP)

- A PIN or signature are used to authenticate transaction in face-to-face environments (e.g. a card payment terminal). These elements are known by the cardholder.

- A static card verification value, the CVV1, is also used in conjunction with PIN or signature to authenticate magstripe transactions. Cardholders don't need to be aware of the CVV1.
- A dynamic iCVV (CVV3) is also used in conjunction with PIN or signature to authenticate EMV chip card transactions. Cardholders don't need to be aware of the CVV3.

But payments evolve fast, and so too does authentication. For example, the adoption of biometric cards – equipped with fingerprint sensors that work in conjunction with the chip – is set to grow substantially.[75]

Remote environments, also known as Card Not Present (CNP)

- The PAN, cardholder name, and expiry date must be supplied by the cardholder to make a remote card payment transaction (e.g. an e-commerce site).
- A different, static card verification value, the CVV2 (printed on the card), is used to authenticate remote transactions such as e-commerce or telephone payments. This is the only card verification value that cardholders know and is there to demonstrate to the issuer that the card is in possession of the cardholder.
- Merchants may elect to use additional security services. For example, an e-commerce payment page may verify that the billing address supplied by the cardholder matches that which the issuer has on record for that card. This is referred to as the **Address Verification Service** (**AVS**). The issuer will return a single letter code to the merchant (e.g. full match, partial match, etc.). This doesn't change the issuer's authorisation decision coming back as part of the authorisation process. Regardless of the code, the merchant ultimately decides, in line with their risk appetite, to proceed with or reject the transaction. Merchants would use this facility as part of a **multi-layered fraud prevention strategy**, as it helps minimise chargebacks. Finally, whilst the letter codes are agreed within the industry, their interpretation slightly varies per card scheme, and some codes may apply to one card scheme and not another (what did you expect?). The merchant's PSP is best placed to advise on this. The AVS process is invisible to cardholders (it's only for the ducks). In some geographies (e.g. the US), the AVS may be used in **Card Present** (**CP**)

environments, including at **Unattended Payment Terminals (UPT)** such as those used at petrol stations.

- Whilst the CVV2 is supplied by the cardholder to enable the issuer to authenticate a remote transaction, the process by which this is accomplished may require additional functionality, which is visible to cardholders. When a cardholder supplies their CVV2 at the checkout of an e-commerce purchase, they may, depending on their card issuer, see a pop-up box asking them for further authentication elements (e.g. supply a one-time code sent to them as a text message). This must follow another EMV standard: 3D Secure.

3D Secure

3D Secure is to e-commerce transactions what EMV chip is to face-to-face transactions. Visa launched this functionality in 2001 under the name "Verified by Visa", and this is commonly known as "3D Secure version 1". Other card schemes introduced functionality based on this protocol: Mastercard SecureCode (older versions) and Identity Check (newer versions), American Express SafeKey, Discover ProtectBuy, JCB J/Secure, etc. In 2019, Visa rebranded "Verified by Visa" to "Visa Secure".

3D Secure stands for "3 Domain Secure" and refers to the three ecosystem domains involved in the process: the **acquirer domain** (acquirer and merchant), the **issuer domain**, and the **interoperability domain** (the card scheme). In 2016, EMVCo launched 3D Secure version 2.1, version 2.2 in 2018, and version 2.3 in August 2022 (with newer subversions in 2023).

You already understand the high-level flow for transaction authorisation where the CVV2 is required as part of the authorisation request to the issuer. With 3D Secure authentication, this flow changes slightly, as **additional steps** may be introduced involving, for example, a pop-up box presented to the cardholder's screen asking for further authentication (e.g. a code, memorable word). This enables the issuer to further ascertain that the genuine cardholder is performing the transaction (although, this is not a fool-proof mechanism). It also **helps merchants reduce chargebacks**.

3D Secure is another example of a payment industry standard that moves on with the times, as shown in Table 1.16.

Table 1.16 Differences between 3D Secure versions.

3D Secure v1 − 2001	3D Secure v2.1 − 2016	3D Secure v2.2 − 2018
Little flexibility, clunky	The "Customer Experience" version	The "Customer Experience+" version
Lack of availability on mobile and IoT devices. One-time passwords supported, but not biometrics.	Greatly improved customer experience, especially on mobile devices. Allows for merchants to verify accounts and wallets without cardholder intervention (but not for payments). Biometrics supported.	Allows for whitelisting. Allows merchants to authenticate payments without customer intervention (e.g. recurring and subscription payments). Allows for **Decoupled Authentication** (e.g. deferred for a period of time), which can take place even if the cardholder is offline. Allows for **Delegated Authentication** (i.e. when the authentication is performed by an eligible third party other than the issuer). This could be a merchant, an acquirer, or a digital wallet provider.
A few extra data elements provided to the issuer.	Much more data provided to the issuer.	Yet more data provided to the issuer (some say ten times more data).
No support for exemptions to PSD2 Strong Customer Authentication (SCA) (see Chapter 5).	A little bit more support for SCA exemptions.	Supports SCA exemptions.

As e-commerce continues to evolve, so too does 3D Secure. New versions are aiming to future-proof technology investment on all sides of the market, enabling merchants to deliver the seamless checkout experiences their customers expect. As a picture speaks a thousand words, Figure 1.18 gives a quick comparison.

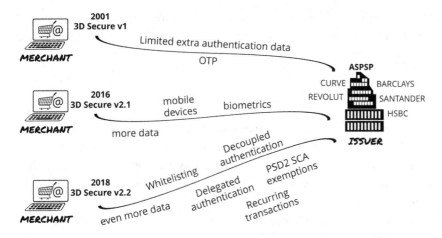

Figure 1.18   3D Secure then and now.
Source: drawing by the author.

Please assume that all the parties participating in the authorisation process as depicted in Figures 1.6–1.7 and 1.9–1.10 are still present and performing their functions. Figure 1.18 is just a simplified representation of the data flows.

To take advantage of 3D Secure functionality, **infrastructure must be deployed**:

- **By the issuer**: this is called an **Access Control Server (ACS)**. Most issuers outsource this to an **Independent Software Vendor (ISV)**, such as CardinalCommerce, Enfuce, Entersekt, or ACI Worldwide.
- **By the merchant**: this is called the **3D Secure Server (3DSS)** and used to be known as the **Merchant Plug-In (MPI)**. This technology is usually provided by the merchant's PSP, usually a payment gateway provider such as Adyen or checkout.com (some ACS providers also supply the 3DSS technology). This functionality provides the bridge between the cardholder (e.g. a pop-up window) and the acquirer during the authorisation process (see Figures 1.6–1.7 and 1.9–10).

Because there is an infrastructure deployment cost on both the issuer and merchant sides, 3D Secure version 1 is still widely deployed. Migration to newer versions will take time, although card schemes are pushing for migration through economic "incentives" (see Chapter 2, *Liability shift*), and

PSD2 in Europe has been a catalyst for 3D Secure migration to version 2.1 (see Chapter 5). At the time of writing, deployments of 3D Secure version 2.2 are still rare.

Decoupled and delegated authentication

Historically, 3D Secure functionality has been associated with e-commerce, and this is the case for versions 1 and 2.1. But this is set to change with version 2.2 and later versions, as they allow for **Decoupled Authentication**. This could allow telephone payments – the orphan channel of the card world (see Chapter 2, *Card payments channels*) with relation to fraud prevention – to take advantage of 3D Secure functionality (and therefore help telephone merchants with chargebacks). At the time of writing, I am not aware of this functionality being deployed for telephone payments interactions anywhere, but I believe this will change over time.

BOX 1.11 DELEGATED VS DECOUPLED AUTHENTICATION

Decoupled authentication is different from the standard authentication process shown in Figures 1.6–1.7 and 1.9–10. Here, cardholder authentication happens outside of their payment interaction with the merchant, at a different time, even if the cardholder is offline. Merchants can set a time limit (e.g. one minute, a week) for the cardholder to complete the authentication process, and this can take place on a device different to that used by the cardholder during the transaction. As the name suggests, with **Delegated Authentication**, issuers can delegate the authentication process to a third party (e.g. merchant, acquirer, digital wallet provider). For example, if a merchant can perform the cardholder authentication through a card-scheme-approved method, information can be passed on to the issuer to confirm the cardholder's identity, and there will be no need for the issuer to authenticate. This means a lot less friction for cardholders (e.g. one-click-payments).

Cardholder authentication has evolved over the last two decades, and it will continue to do so as technology advances and fraudsters innovate. 3D Secure is an overlay service that sits on top of the existing card infrastructures provided by the card schemes. Depending on their risk appetite and fraud profile, merchants may elect to deploy further fraud prevention measures provided by ISVs and other ecosystem actors. Initiatives are coming to market to prevent fraud and enhance customer experience, such as biometrics payment cards,[69] behavioural biometrics, [70] and many more. And these are needed more than ever, as evidenced in Table 1.15: CNP fraud and card ID theft are the two top fraud concerns in the card world.

One thing is certain: more and more data is flowing back and forth in an increasingly complex ecosystem, and that data must be protected from criminals.

Payment Card Industry Data Security Standard – PCI DSS (safe from harm)

What is the PCI DSS?

The **Payment Card Industry Data Security Standard (PCI DSS)** has been around since 2006. The PCI DSS aims to **protect cardholder information**.

The PCI DSS is a data security standard developed and maintained by an industry body similar to EMVCo, the **PCI Standards Security Council (PCI SSC)** of which American Express, Discover, JCB International, Mastercard, and Visa are founding members, and UnionPay a strategic member. The PCI SSC encourages industry participation through various programmes, including "Participating Organisations", "Affiliate Members", and "Special Interest Groups".

> The PCI DSS applies to all organisations who store, process, or transmit cardholder information, either electronically or manually. With version 4 of the standard, this scope was extended to include entities with environments that can impact the security of the **Cardholder Data Environment (CDE)**.

In other terms, the PCI DSS can apply to just about any card payment ecosystem actor.

The PCI SSC offers guidance to many stakeholders involved in the card payment ecosystem:

• **Software developers and payment application providers**: through the Software Security Framework, which includes the Secure Software

Lifecycle (Secure SLC) Standard and the Secure Software Standard. The framework promotes the secure design, development, and maintenance of card payment software.

- **Device manufacturers**: through other standards such as PIN Transaction Security (PTS), Point-to-Point Encryption (P2PE), and various mobile standards for payments using commercial off-the-shelf devices such as smart phones or tablets (e.g. contactless payments, software-based PIN entry, or mobile payment-acceptance solutions).
- **Other stakeholders**: including physical and logical card production and provisioning, token service providers, and 3D Secure providers.

Who enforces the PCI DSS?

The PCI SSC is not involved with enforcement or compliance. The PCI DSS is not law in most geographies (and therefore, it is not illegal not to comply), but some elements of the standard have become law in Nevada, Minnesota, and Washington[71] (at the time of writing).

 Practitioners should remember a few things:

- **Card schemes include compliance with PCI standards as part of their operating regulations.** From time to time, card schemes **enforce compliance through mandates** issued to their members (e.g. acquirers, issuers). This is to respond quickly to new crimes and new fraud without waiting for the next update of the operating regulations.
- **Acquirers are responsible for ensuring the PCI compliance of their merchant portfolios.**
- **Card schemes manage the compliance of service providers directly,** although this is difficult as they have to rely on members' reporting of their service providers (and the supply chain is vast).
- **Card schemes may levy penalties** on members and stakeholders for breaches of either operating regulations or mandates.

What are the requirements for PCI DSS compliance?

The PCI DSS has 12 requirements classified into six goals, which cover all aspects of card data security: people, process, and technology. This is shown in Table 1.17.

Table 1.17 PCI DSS v4 goals and requirements.

PCI DSS goal	PCI DSS requirements
Build and maintain a secure network and systems	1. Install and maintain network security controls 2. Apply secure configurations to all system components
Protect account data	3. Protect stored account data 4. Protect cardholder data with strong cryptography during transmission over open, public networks
Maintain a vulnerability management programme	5. Protect all systems and networks from malicious software 6. Develop and maintain secure systems and software
Implement strong access control measures	7. Restrict access to system components and cardholder data by business need-to-know 8. Identify users and authenticate access to system components 9. Restrict physical access to cardholder data
Regularly monitor and test networks	10. Log and monitor all access to system components and cardholder data 11. Test security of systems and networks regularly
Maintain an information security policy	12. Support information security with organisational policies and programmes

In my opinion, the PCI DSS is an excellent data security standard. Don't be put off by the fact that it is a card industry standard: if you take the standard document and do a bulk "find and replace all" for the terms "cardholder data" or "card data" or "authentication data" with "data I care about", you get best practice information security principles. This helps with other data protection compliance obligations.

This section will offer some practical advice.

How do you validate compliance with the PCI DSS?

Stakeholders in scope of the PCI DSS must comply with all PCI DSS requirements, but not all stakeholders are required to validate compliance. When compliance validation is required, stakeholders have options.

PCI DSS compliance validation

QSAS AND ISAS

Compliance validation may be done either through self-assessment, or by engaging with an accredited third party (the **Qualified Security Assessor,** or **QSA**) to perform the assessment. The PCI SSC maintains a list of QSAs and other qualified assessors.[72] An alternative to the QSA is the **Internal Security Assessor** (**ISA**), and this option is generally used by larger businesses. An ISA must go through a number of steps before they qualify, and these can be found on the PCI SSC website.[73]

SAQ, ASV, AND ROC

When compliance validation is performed through self-assessment, a **Self-Assessment Questionnaire** (**SAQ**) must be completed, and there are several options, depending on the type and size of the merchant. SAQs can be found in the PCI SSC document library.[74] An additional validation requirement applies to e-commerce merchants where they must also complete (where applicable) a quarterly network vulnerability scan performed by an **Accredited Scanning Vendor** (**ASV**). The PCI SSC maintains a list of ASVs and other qualified parties.

When compliance validation is performed by a QSA or ISA, a **Report on Compliance** (**ROC**) is produced. ROC templates can be found in the PCI SSC document library.

For merchants and service providers, choosing between a ROC and an SAQ will depend on their size, situation, and card scheme / acquirer requirements at the time of reporting (see *Merchant and service provider levels*). Merchants report compliance to their acquirer, which will in turn report to the card schemes for their merchant portfolios. Service providers report directly to the card schemes.

Merchant and service provider levels

In order to determine the validation type required for a business, merchants and service providers are classified into levels determined by the transaction volumes processed for any given card scheme. Luckily, both Visa and Mastercard agree on the volume bands. This is shown in Table 1.18 for merchants and Table 1.19 for service providers.

Table 1.18 Merchant Levels and PCI DSS compliance validation requirements. Source: Visa, Mastercard, 2023.

Merchant level	VISA Criteria Annual Visa transactions, all channels	Mastercard criteria Annual Mastercard and Maestro transactions	Validation requirement
Level 1	transactions > 6 million and Global merchants identified as Level 1 by any Visa region	Transactions > 6 million and Any merchant meeting the Level 1 criteria of Visa Any merchant that Mastercard, in its sole discretion, determines should meet the Level 1 merchant requirements to minimize risk to the system	Annual ROC by QSA Quarterly network scan by Approved Scan Vendor (ASV) Attestation of Compliance Form
Level 2	1 million < transactions < 6 million and Any merchant that has suffered a hack that resulted in an account data compromise may be escalated to a higher validation level	1 million < transactions < 6 million and Any merchant meeting the Level 2 criteria of Visa	Annual SAQ Quarterly network scan by ASV Attestation of Compliance Form
E-commerce transactions only			
Level 3	20,000 < transactions < 1 million and Any merchant that has suffered a hack that resulted in an account data compromise may be escalated to a higher validation level	20,000 < transactions < 1 million and Any merchant meeting the Level 3 criteria of Visa	Annual SAQ Quarterly network scan by ASV Attestation of Compliance Form
Level 4	E-commerce transactions < 20,000 and all other merchants processing up to 1 million Visa transactions annually Any merchant that has suffered a hack that resulted in an account data compromise may be escalated to a higher validation level	All other merchants.	Annual SAQ recommended Quarterly network scan by ASV, if applicable Compliance validation requirements set by acquirer

Table 1.19 Service provider levels and PCI DSS compliance validation requirements.

Service provider level	VISA criteria: annual Visa transactions, all channels	Mastercard criteria: annual Mastercard and Maestro transactions	Validation requirements
Level 1	VisaNet processors or any service provider that stores, processes, and/or transmits more than **300,000 transactions**	All Data Storage Entities (DSEs) and Payment Facilitators (Payfacs) with over **300,000 transactions** and All Third Party Processors (TPPs) All Staged Digital Wallet Operators (SDWOs) All Digital Activity Service Providers (DASPs) All Token Service Providers (TSPs) All 3D Secure Service Providers (3DSSPs) All AML/Sanctions Service Providers All Instalment Service Providers (ISPs) All Merchant Payment Gateways (MPGs)	Annual ROC by QSA. Quarterly network scan by Approved Scan Vendor (ASV) Attestation of Compliance (AoC) form Visa includes these providers on their list of PCI DSS Compliant Service Providers, and Mastercard doesn't specify
Level 2	Any service provider that stores, processes, and/or transmits fewer than **300,000 transactions**	All DSEs and PFs with less than **300,000 transactions** and All Terminal Servicers (TSs)3	Annual SAQ Quarterly network scan by ASV Attestation of Compliance Form Visa doesn't include these providers on their list of PCI DSS Compliant Service Providers, and Mastercard doesn't specify

Sources: Visa, Mastercard, 2023.

MERCHANT LEVELS

Table 1.18 is a summary of merchant levels and validation requirements, but there will be exceptional cases with variations, and these can
be found on the Visa and Mastercard website (and for any other card
scheme).

SERVICE PROVIDER LEVELS

For service providers, the requirements are slightly different between Mastercard and Visa, but the volume levels are similar, as shown in Table 1.19.

Table 1.19 is a summary of service provider levels and validation requirements, but there will be exceptional cases with variations, which can
be found on the respective Visa and Mastercard websites (and for any other
card scheme).

Protecting cardholder data

This section is not intended to cover the PCI DSS requirements in great
detail – the PCI SSC does an excellent job of that, supported by the third
parties they accredit (e.g. QSAs) – but it will give practitioners the opportunity to understand its fundamental principles, one of which is the protection of card data. As I said before, if you want to regulate something, you
have to define it.

PCI DSS data classification

The card data elements were shown in Table 1.13, and the PCI DSS classifies
these data elements into two categories: **Cardholder Data** and **Sensitive
Authentication Data**.

Table 1.20 adds this categorisation to our original classification.

The PCI DSS places stringent requirements on the storage security requirements of card account data, and this is shown in Table 1.21, which
must be looked at in conjunction with Table 1.20.

Table 1.20 Card data with PCI DSS classification.

Data element		Track 1	Track 2	Chip	Printed on card	PCI DSS classification
PAN		✓	✓	✓	✓	Cardholder data
Name		✓	✗	✗	✓	
Expiry date		✓	✓	✓	✓	
Service code		✓	✓	✓	✗	
CVV2		✗	✗	✗	✓	Sensitive authentication data
Discretionary data	CVV1	✓	✓	✗	✗	
	CVV3 (iCVV)	✗	✗	✓	✗	
	PIN / PIN block	✓	✓	✓	✗	
	Other data elements	✓	✓	✓	✗	

Source: ISO/ISE standards and PCI SSC.

Table 1.21 Elements of account data and storage requirements.

Account data	Data elements	Storage restrictions	Required to render stored data unreadable
Cardholder data	Primary Account Number (PAN)	Storage is kept to a minimum as defined in Requirement 3.2	Yes, as defined in Requirement 3.5
	Cardholder name	Storage is kept to a minimum as defined in Requirement 3.2	No
	Service code		
	Expiration date		
Sensitive authentication data	Full track data	Cannot be stored after authorization as defined in Requirement 3.3.13	Yes, data stored until authorization is complete; must be protected with strong cryptography as defined in Requirement 3.3.2
	Card Verification Code (CVV)		
	PIN / PIN block		

Source: PCI SSC, PCI DSS v4.0 Quick Reference Guide, p. 26, August 2022. Provided courtesy of PCI Security Standards Council, LLC and/or its Licensors. © 2009–2022 PCI Security Standards Council, LLC. All Rights Reserved.

"Required to Render Stored Data Unreadable".

Yes, I know, what does that mean? Essentially, data must be protected, and a number of methods are available: encryption, truncation, tokenisation, etc. The standard aims to remain technology-agnostic. The above definitions relate to version 4 of the PCI DSS, which introduced clarifications over the previous version. We can also see alignment between this standard and other data retention principles (as seen in the EU General Data Protection Regulation, or GDPR): the "Storage restrictions" column follows the principle of "don't keep data longer than needed for the original purpose". However, the data protection requirements are still somehow misaligned: for example, a cardholder name doesn't need any extra storage protection (e.g. encryption) according to the PCI DSS, but it is considered "personal data" by the GDPR so it is therefore subject to safeguards where applicable.

BOX 1.12 CONJUNCTION OF DATA ELEMENTS

You will notice that Table 1.21 classifies "full track data" as "sensitive authentication data". You know that the magnetic stripe contains the PAN, cardholder name (Track 1), expiry date, and service code. Why are these specific data elements classified as "cardholder data" and not "sensitive authentication data"? This is because on their own (i.e. the PAN only), they are of limited use to criminals, but **in conjunction** with other data elements, they are far more interesting. And the magnetic stripe contains all of them. This is a data protection principle similar to that used by the GDPR: an individual's name may not always be classified as "personal data" (e.g. John Smith), but the name in conjunction with a postcode and place of work may very well be.

Most important things to remember:

Operationally, one of the most important things to remember about the PCI DSS is this: **sensitive authentication data (which includes the card verification values) must not be stored post-authorisation**.

When it comes to the CVV2, we have seen far too many data breaches at e-commerce merchants where criminals were able to get hold of this piece of data, which is intended for the eyes of the cardholder only.

We have also seen far too many data breaches at brick-and-mortar merchants in non-EMV markets where magstripe cloning (thus obtaining the CVV1) is a problem.

You also know that the CVV3 (iCVV on the chip) is not an issue, because it is dynamic.

But data breaches still happen, although the PCI DSS has been a catalyst in raising awareness about information security best practices in merchant environments.

There is, however, one notable exception to sensitive authentication data storage rules: one ecosystem actor is allowed to store sensitive authentication data post-authorisation, and that is the issuer. It is logical, after all, because they are the ASPSP and responsible for managing the card account. As such, they need all of the card account data, but they are subject to additional PCI DSS requirements.

Another thing to remember is that for an organisation to comply with the PCI DSS, not only does the business need to meet the requirements, they also must ensure that any third parties in scope are also compliant with the standard. In our world of over-extended supply chains, partners and suppliers may expose businesses to unnecessary risks. Make use of all available lists of compliant providers from the PCI SSC and the card schemes.

Finally, the PCI DSS requirement details given in this section relate to version 4 of the standard. Version 3.2.1 of the standard (current at the time of writing) is less stringent but is expected to be retired in January 2024. During the transition period – between Q2 2022 and January 2024 – both versions can be used, and it's a clever idea to prepare for version 4 as soon as possible.

Card payments mechanics – conclusion (where do we go from here?)

In this whistle-stop of card payments mechanics, we covered:

- Ecosystem actors and models;
- Card payment processes: authorisation, clearing, and settlement;
- Exception processing and disputes;
- Transaction and card data;

- Card payment authentication; and
- The Payment Card Industry Data Security Standard (PCI DSS).

I have tried to explain the jargon and debunk a few myths. I have given you my opinion on some aspects of the ecosystem, but feel free to disagree. I always welcome a good debate!

If you read this book a few years from now, more innovation will have happened, new crimes will have emerged, innovative technologies will have been used, and behaviours will have evolved. Some businesses will grow, others won't; some will even disappear. In the future, more overlay services will be developed on card infrastructures, and card infrastructures will establish more links with other ecosystems. Cardholders will benefit from these advancements.

But as exciting as this all sounds, we must remember that the card payments ecosystem is centralised. It will, for the foreseeable future, continue to require centralised processes (e.g. authorisation, clearing settlement), infrastructure (card scheme networks), and operating regulations.

All the terms introduced in this chapter can be found in the glossary (Chapter 7). To complete our understanding of card payments, we must examine the economics of this fascinating value chain. Let's go on the second leg of our trip.

Notes

1 "Directive (EU) 2015/2366 of The European Parliament and of The Council", Official Journal of the European Union, 2015. Available at: https://eur-lex.europa.eu/legal-content/EN/TXT/?uri=celex%3A32015L2366 (Accessed 3 June 2023).

2 "RBS to sell 80% stake in WorldPay to Advent and Bain", Finextra, 6 August 2010. Available at: https://www.finextra.com/newsarticle/21679/rbs-to-sell-80-stake-in-worldpay-to-advent-and-bain (Accessed 5 June 2023).

3 "Why did Bank of America really terminate First Data JV?" Payment Cards & Mobile, 6 August 2019. Available at: https://www.paymentscardsand-mobile.com/why-did-bank-of-america-terminate-first-data-jv/ (Accessed 19 July 2023).

4 Marco Fava (2020) "Consolidation in payments – upsides, downsides, challenges", The Paypers, 9 December. Available at: https://thepaypers.

com/expert-opinion/consolidation-in-payments-upsides-downsides-challenges--1246145 (Accessed 4 June 2023).

5 Valerie Nowak (2023) "Blog from Valerie Nowak: Why this Maestro is retiring after 30 years", Mastercard, 19 October 2021. Available at: https://www.mastercard.com/news/europe/en/perspectives/en/2021/blog-from-valerie-nowak-why-this-maestro-is-retiring-after-30-years/ (Accessed 4 June 2023).

6 Alexandra Samet (2022) "Payment processing explained: payment methods and top payments industry companies in 2022", Insider Intelligence, 12 January. Available at: https://www.insiderintelligence.com/insights/payment-processing/ (Accessed 3 June 2023).

7 David Maurer (2009) "An examination of the economics of payment card systems", Swiss National Bank, July. Available at: https://www.snb.ch/en/mmr/reference/Zahlungskarten/source/Zahlungskarten.en.pdf (Accessed 4 June 2023).

8 "Closed loop network", American Express, Date unspecified. Available at: https://www.americanexpress.com/content/dam/amex/nz/staticassets/merchant/pdf/why-american-express/insights-and-trends/Closed-Loop-Network.pdf (Accessed 4 June 2023).

9 Nilson Report (2023), Nilson Report homepage. Available at: https://nilsonreport.com/ (Accessed 5 June 2023).

10 "Europe's largest acquirers, transactions (bil.) in 2013", Nilson Report, Featured Chart, Issue 1042, July 2014. Available at: https://nilson-report.com/publication_chart_of_the_month.php?1=1&issue=1042 (Accessed 4 June 2023).

11 "Europe's largest acquirers, purchase transactions (bil.) in 2021", Nilson Report, Issue 1219, May 2022. Available at: https://nilson-report.com/publication_newsletter_archive_issue.php?issue=1219 (Accessed 4 June 2023).

12 "Nexi acquires 30% stake in Computop", Finextra, 1 August 2023. Available at: https://www.finextra.com/newsarticle/42720/nexi-acquires-30-stake-in-computop (Accessed 1 August 2023).

13 Eric Auchard (2017) "Dutch payments processor takes pan-European license to bypass banks", Reuters, 23 June. Available at: https://www.reuters.com/article/us-banking-payments-adyen-idUSKBN19E1Y2 (Accessed 4 June 2023).

14 EMVCo (2023) EMVCo homepage. Available at: https://www.emvco.com/ (Accessed 5 June 2023).

15 EMVCo (2023) "Worldwide EMV® deployment statistics". Available at: https://www.emvco.com/about-us/worldwide-emv-deployment-statistics/ (Accessed 5 June 2023).

16 "Analysis of Oyster pay as you go journeys", Transport for London website. Available at: https://tfl.gov.uk/corporate/publications-and-reports/oyster-card (Accessed 1 August 2023).

17 "Analysis of contactless pay as you go journeys", Transport for London website. Available at: https://tfl.gov.uk/corporate/publications-and-reports/contactless-payment (Accessed 1 August 2023).

18 Dan Balaban (2021) "OMNY hits new usage milestone as open-loop payments rollout continues", Mobility Payments, 17 March. Available at: https://www.mobility-payments.com/2021/03/17/omny-hits-new-usage-milestone-as-open-loop-payments-rollout-continues/ (Accessed 5 June 2023).

19 Tom Philips (2022) "Central Bank rolls out national contactless transit ticketing system in Costa Rica", NFCW, 23 June. Available at: https://www.nfcw.com/2022/06/23/377608/central-bank-rolls-out-national-contactless-transit-ticketing-system-in-costa-rica/ (Accessed on 6 June 2023).

20 "Public transport in Malaysia to feature open-loop fare payments", Southeast Asia Infrastructure, 22 March 2022. Available at: https://southeastasiainfra.com/public-transport-in-malaysia-to-feature-open-loop-fare-payments/ (Accessed 6 June 2023).

21 "The Netherlands gets nationwide contactless public transport payments system", Finextra, 8 June 2023. Available at: https://www.finextra.com/newsarticle/42442/the-netherlands-gets-nationwide-contactless-public-transport-payments-system (Accessed 8 June 2023).

22 Mike Clark (2015) "St Petersburg Metro to go contactless" NFCW, 3 February. Available at: https://www.nfcw.com/2015/02/03/333869/st-petersburg-metro-go-contactless/ (Accessed 5 June 2023).

23 Tom Phillips (2021) "Moscow to complete contactless ticketing rollout by end 2021", NFCW, 22 January. Available at: https://www.nfcw.com/2021/01/22/370260/moscow-to-complete-contactless-ticketing-rollout-by-end-2021/ (Accessed 5 June 2023).

24 Mastercard (2020) "Contactless continent", Mastercard, 28 May. Available at: https://www.mastercard.com/news/europe/en-uk/newsroom/press-releases/en-gb/2020/may/contactless-continent/ (Accessed 5 June 2023).

25 UK Finance (2021) "Contactless limit to increase to £100 from 15 October", UK Finance, 27 August. Available at https://www.ukfinance.org.uk/press/press-releases/contactless-limit-increase-100–15-october (Accessed 5 June 2023).

26 WorldPay, Inc. (2018) "Vantiv and Worldpay complete combination to form Worldpay, Inc.", Cision PR Newswire, 16 January. Available at:

https://www.prnewswire.com/news-releases/vantiv-and-worldpay-complete-combination-to-form-worldpay-inc-300583008.html (Accessed 5 June 2023).

27 "WorldPay payments firm in $43bn sale to US rival", BBC, 18 March 2019. Available at: https://www.bbc.co.uk/news/business-47609536 (Accessed 3 June 2023).

28 FIS (2023) "FIS announces plans to spin off merchant business", FIS, 13 February. Available at: https://www.investor.fisglobal.com/news-releases/news-release-details/fis-announces-plans-spin-merchant-business (Accessed 6 June 2023).

29 "Buyout firm GTCR picks up majority stake valuing FIS unit Worldpay at $18.5 billion", Reuters, 6 July 2023. Available at: https://www.reuters.com/markets/deals/fis-sell-stake-merchant-business-gtcr-185-bln-deal-2023–07-06/ (Accessed 28 July 2023).

30 "Press release: Discover Financial Services completes Diners Club acquisition", Discover, 1 July 2008. Available at: https://investorrelations.discover.com/newsroom/press-releases/press-release-details/2008/Discover-Financial-Services-Completes-Diners-Club-Acquisition/default.aspx (Accessed 7 June 2023).

31 "Banks are becoming 'museums of technology' says ex-Barclays boss", Finextra, 12 June 2023. Available at: https://www.finextra.com/news-article/42458/banks-are-becoming-museums-of-technology-says-ex-barclays-boss (Accessed 27 June 2023).

32 Yltaevae, L. (2023) "Social commerce – statistics and facts", Statista, 27 February. Available at: https://www.statista.com/topics/8757/social-commerce/#topicOverview (Accessed 5 June 2023).

33 "Smarter STIP", Visa Inc., October 2020. Available at: https://usa.visa.com/dam/VCOM/regional/na/us/about-visa/research/documents/smarter-stip.pdf (Accessed 17 June 2023).

34 "Card-based payment instrument issuers – CBPIIs", UK Open Banking website. Available at: https://standards.openbanking.org.uk/customer-experience-guidelines/card-based-payment-instrument-issuers-cbpiis/latest/ (Accessed 28 June 2023).

35 "Visa core rules and Visa product and services rules", Visa, 17 April 2023. Available at: https://usa.visa.com/content/dam/VCOM/download/about-visa/visa-rules-public.pdf (Accessed 6 June 2023).

36 "Mastercard rules", Mastercard, 13 December 2022. Available at: https://www.mastercard.us/content/dam/public/mastercardcom/na/global-site/documents/mastercard-rules.pdf (Accessed 6 June 2023).

37 "Nigerian payments system – risk and information security management framework", Central Bank of Nigeria, 2020. Available at: https://www.cbn.gov.ng/out/2020/psmd/nigerian%20payments%20system%20risk%20and%20information%20security%20management%20framework.pdf (Accessed 19 August 2023).

38 "Payments and settlements", Bank of England, May 2023. Available at: https://www.bankofengland.co.uk/payment-and-settlement (Accessed 7 June 2023).

39 "Consumer credit agreements – an overview", Lexis Nexis, 2023. Available at: https://www.lexisnexis.com/uk/lexispsl/financialservices/document/393813/5N3C-M331-F18F-M265-00000-00/Consumer_credit_agreements_overview (Accessed 7 June 2023).

40 European Central Bank, Eurosystem (2019), "Glossary of terms related to payment, clearing and settlement systems", ECB, December. Available at: https://www.ecb.europa.eu/pub/pdf/other/glossaryrelatedtopaymentclearingandsettlementsystemsen.pdf (Accessed 7 June 2023).

41 https://logo.ethoca.com/ (Accessed 7 June 2023).

42 "Order insight", Visa, 2023. Available at: https://developer.visa.com/capabilities/vmpi (Accessed 7 June 2023).

43 "Mastercom", Mastercard, 2023. Available at: https://developer.mastercard.com/product/mastercom/ (Accessed 7 June 2023).

44 "Global Fraud Trends, Fraud & Payments Survey 2023", Ravelin, 2023. Available at: https://pages.ravelin.com/fraud-and-payments-survey-2023 (Accessed 7 June 2023).

45 "Consumer Credit Act 1974". Available at: https://www.legislation.gov.uk/ukpga/1974/39/section/75.

46 "Dispute Management Guidelines for Visa Merchants", Visa, 2018. Available at: https://usa.visa.com/content/dam/VCOM/download/merchants/chargeback-management-guidelines-for-visa-merchants.pdf (Accessed 7 June 2023).

47 "Chargeback Guide Merchant Edition", Mastercard, 25 October 2022. Available at: https://www.mastercard.us/content/dam/public/mastercardcom/na/global-site/documents/chargeback-guide.pdf (Accessed 7 June 2023).

48 "How to Manage and Help Prevent Disputes", Global Merchant Network Services 2019, American Express, 2019. Available at: https://www.americanexpress.com/content/dam/amex/us/merchant/pdf/US-Disputes-Reference-Guide-Updated.pdf (Accessed 7 June 2023).

49 "The year in chargebacks 2022", Midigator, 2022. Available at: https://midigator.com/chargeback-report-statistics/#chargeback-to-transaction-ratio-decreased (Accesses 8 June 2023).

50 Ronen Shnidman (2022) "Friendly fire: chargeback fraud has become a consumer weapon", Finextra, 24 July. Available at: https://www.finextra.com/blogposting/22640/friendly-fire-chargeback-fraud-has-become-a-consumer-weapon (Accessed 8 June 2023).

51 Patrick Wheeler (2022) "Collyer Bristow," 10 February. Available at: https://collyerbristow.com/shorter-reads/dsars-weaponised/ (Accessed 8 June 2023).

52 "CBA pilots police referral service for serial abusers", Finextra, 8 August 2023. Available at: https://www.finextra.com/newsarticle/42744/cba-pilots-police-referral-service-for-serial-abusers (Accessed 9 August 2023).

53 Ronen Shnidman (2022) "Customer attitudes towards chargebacks in 2022: a summary", Justt, 20 July. Available at: https://justt.ai/blog/customer-attitudes-towards-chargebacks-2022/ (Accessed 8 June 2023).

54 "American Express to acquire B2B payments automation company Nipendo", American Express, 12 January 2023. Available at: https://about.americanexpress.com/newsroom/press-releases/news-details/2023/American-Express-to-Acquire-B2B-Payments-Automation-Company-Nipendo/default.aspx (Accessed 8 June 2023).

55 "Report: 80% of B2B transactions expected to be digital by 2025", Pymnts.com, 23 September 2021. Available at: https://www.pymnts.com/news/b2b-payments/2021/report-80-pct-b2b-transactions-expected-to-be-digital-by-2025/ (Accessed 8 June 2023).

56 Mastercard (2021) "8-Digit BIN expansion and PCI standards", Mastercard, 20 October. Available at: https://www.mastercard.com/content/dam/public/mastercardcom/globalrisk/pdf/8-Digit%20BIN%20Expansion%20and%20PCI%20Standards%20-%20FINAL%20(10–20–2021).pdf (Accessed 9 June 2023).

57 Neira Jones (2015) "Target breach timeline January 2015". Available at: https://www.youtube.com/watch?v=5JvlwhnKE6o (Accessed 9 June 2023).

58 EMVCo (2023) "EMV Chip". Available at: https://www.emvco.com/knowledge-hub/emv-chip/ (Accessed 9 June 2023).

59 EMVCo (2023) "Worldwide EMV® Deployment Statistics – EMV Card-Present Transaction Percentage". Available at: https://www.emvco.com/about-us/worldwide-emv-deployment-statistics/ (Accessed 9 June 2023).

60 Gary Yamamura (2015) "Why are US credit card companies introducing 'Chip and Signature' cards instead of 'Chip and PIN'?" Quora, 14 February. Available at: https://www.quora.com/Why-is-the-USA-adopting-chip-signature-and-not-chip-pin/answers/9824261 (Accessed 10 June 2023).

61 "In India's mobile-payments boom, even beggars get QR codes", *Wall Street Journal*, 27 May 2022. Available at: https://www.wsj.com/articles/in-indias-mobile-payments-boom-even-beggars-get-qr-codes-11653653383 (Accessed 23 June 2023).

62 "EMV QR codes" EMVCo, January 2021. Available at: https://www.emvco.com/emv-technologies/qr-codes/ (Accessed 23 June 2023).

63 "QR code payments", Deloitte, 13 June 2023. Available at: https://www2.deloitte.com/content/dam/Deloitte/us/Documents/financial-services/us-deloitte-qr-code-payments-pov.pdf (Accessed 23 June 2023).

64 "Swiping left on magnetic stripes", Mastercard, August 2021. Available at: https://www.mastercard.com/news/perspectives/2021/magnetic-stripe/ (Accessed 2 August 2023).

65 "Signing off: Mastercard moves beyond signatures worldwide" Mastercard, 18 October 2018. Available at: https://www.mastercard.com/nn ews/press/2018/signing-off-mastercard-moves-beyond-signatures-worldwide/ (Accessed 2 August 2023).

66 "Cybercriminals can now block contactless payments", Finextra, 31 January 2023. Available at: https://www.finextra.com/newsarticle/41701/cybercriminals-can-now-block-contactless-payments (Accessed 10 June 2023).

67 Allan Glen (2023) "Police failed to solve a single burglary in HALF of English and Welsh neighourhoods over the last three years, data reveal amid warnings of 'no consequences' for committing crime", *Daily Mail*, 6 June. Available at: https://www.dailymail.co.uk/news/article-12164829/Police-failed-solve-single-burglary-HALF-English-Welsh-neighbourhoods.html (Accessed 11 June 2023).

68 "Mass deployment of biometric payment cards is coming globally", Payments Cards & Mobile, 15 June 2023. Available at: https://www.paymentscardsandmobile.com/mass-deployment-of-biometric-payment-cards-is-coming-globally/ (Accessed 19 June 2023).

69 "Mastercard biometric card: driving cardholder security and convenience", Mastercard, 2023. Available at: https://www.mastercard.us/en-us/business/overview/safety-and-security/authentication-services/biometrics/biometrics-card.html (Accessed 12 June 2023).

70 "Entersekt partners with Capitec Bank to boost security and reduce friction for e-commerce transactions", Business Wire, 10 May 2022. Available at: https://www.businesswire.com/news/home/20220510005083/en/Entersekt-partners-with-Capitec-Bank-to-Boost-Security-and-Reduce-Friction-for-E-Commerce-Transactions (Accessed 12 June 2023).

71 Medha Mehta (2020) "Infosec insights by SectigoStore," 21 April. Available at: https://sectigostore.com/blog/what-is-pci-dss-a-quick-guide-to-the-12-pci-dss-requirements/ (Accessed 13 June 2023).

72 "PCI qualified professionals", PCI Security Standards Council, 2023. Available at: https://www.pcisecuritystandards.org/program-listings-overview/ (Accessed 13 June 2023).

73 "How to become a PCI Internal Security Assessor (ISA)", PCI Security Standards Council, 2023. Available at: https://training.pcisecuritystandards.org/how-to-become-an-isa (Accessed 13 June 2023).

74 "PCI SSC document library", PCI Security Standards Council 2023. Available at: https://www.pcisecuritystandards.org/document_library/ (Accessed 13 June 2023).

2

CARD PAYMENTS ECONOMICS

Costs and value chain
(what do you do for money, honey?)

Any ecosystem requires investment, and the cost of developing and maintaining an ecosystem can be split into two main categories: infrastructure costs and operational costs. Ecosystem actors will provide technology infrastructure and resources, ensure ecosystem integrity, and generally ensure that the money flows. The global scale of payments is astounding. As an example, Visa's total gross revenue for fiscal year ended 2022 was $39.6 billion (net $29.3 billion),[1] most of it consisting of the fees it charges its members. In that same year, Visa processed 192.5 billion transactions worth $11.6 trillion. And that's just for Visa. You do the maths with relation to fees charged vs transaction value processed. No wonder startups and technology companies all want a piece of the payments pie.

DOI: 10.4324/9781032631394-3

Infrastructure costs

The total number of card transactions is estimated to reach 8.46 tril-lion in 2023 for Visa, Mastercard, and American Express alone.[2] That's more than 23 billion transactions per day across these three schemes. As examined in Chapter 1, the infrastructure runs all the time, and we take it for granted. But the technology must be able to process thousands of transactions per second every day and everywhere. And it must be dependable.

Card payment ecosystem actors will all incur infrastructure costs in dif-ferent ways, as shown in Figure 2.1.

- **The acquirer maintains the payment-acquiring infrastructure** and ensures its security, integrity, and availability.
- **The card scheme maintains the card network** (e.g. VisaNet for Visa), and ensures its integrity, security, and availability.
- **The issuer maintains the card-issuing infrastructure** and the bank-ing systems if they are also a bank. They ensure its integrity, security, and availability.

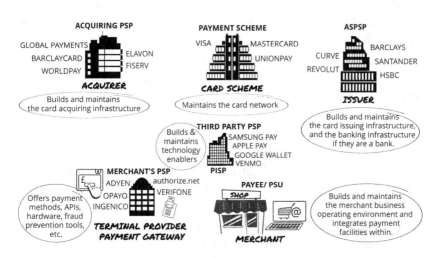

Figure 2.1 Infrastructure costs for card payments ecosystem stakeholders.

Source: drawing by the author.

- **The merchant's PSPs (e.g. payment gateways, card terminal suppliers) provide the payment facilities** (e.g. e-commerce payment page, card terminal), as well as the relevant connectivity (e.g. APIs) and fraud prevention tools (e.g. 3D Secure and others). They ensure that these facilities comply with rules and standards. Merchants will incorporate these facilities into their environment.
- **Merchants build their technical environment and integrate payment facilities** supplied by their PSP. They also have to ensure that their environment complies with rules and standards.
- **Third Party Payment Services Providers (TPPs) build technology enablers** to enable cardholders to manage their card accounts conveniently (e.g. make payments, see transaction history) and may also offer services to merchants and other businesses. They also have to ensure that their products comply with rules and standards.

The card network sits in the middle of this infrastructure, and it is of systemic importance. In geographies where card schemes are dominant systems, they may be designated by the regulators alongside bank settlement infrastructures, such as in the UK.[3] We all know the consequences of VisaNet or Banknet going down, even if it's just for a few hours. If cardholders are unable to use their Visa card or Mastercard, media headlines appear fast.[4] And we don't often think of the trickle-down effect to other stakeholders when this happens, because they are all interconnected. Despite all the existing mechanisms that ensure fallback and redundancy (e.g. Chapter 1, Box 1.3, *What is stand-in processing?*), things can still go wrong. But most of the time, they don't.

We covered technologies deployed in merchant environments in Chapter 1, either through merchants' PSPs and/or ISVs. Card schemes, acquirers, and issuers make major investments in infrastructure, and whilst they may develop some functionality themselves, they will usually use ISVs for infrastructure development. You may have heard of long-established players in this space such as ACI Worldwide (Base24®), BPC (SmartVista®), FIS, RS2 (BankWORKS®), Tieto, and Worldline. As the types of transactions (card and alternative payments, financial and non-financial, ISO 20022, etc.) have grown, so has their related functionality, meaning that these platforms have applicability in the greater payments domain. As these boundaries have stretched, so too has the number of suppliers, including new entrants, and their offerings. I don't propose to list these here, as the independent report from PayX, "Payment Platform Vendor Comparison Report, 2024 Edition"[5] does an excellent job for those considering these technologies.

We covered the transactional processes for card payments in Chapter 1, and these processes will run on infrastructure. But in order for an ecosystem to function, you need more processes – and people to make them work.

Operational costs

Now that we have the technology and we know we can make payments using cards, we need to grow the ecosystem to make it sustainable. This involves a number of steps, and they have associated costs:

- Sales and marketing;
- Merchant and cardholder onboarding and servicing;
- Fraud prevention, risk management, and compliance;
- Processing; and
- Much more.

And we need this every day.

Table 2.1 Card payments ecosystem operational costs per stakeholder.

	Acquirer	Card scheme	Issuer	Merchant's PSP	TPP (PISP)
Rule setting	✗	✓	✗	✗	✗
Sales and marketing	✓	✓	✓	✓	✓
Onboarding and servicing	✓	✗	✓	✓	✓
Card acquiring	✓	✗	✗	✗	✗
Processing	✓	✓	✓	✓	✓
Switching	✗	✓	✗	✗	✗
Clearing	✓	✓	✓	✗	✗
Settlement	✓	✓	✓	✗	✗
Write-off	✓	✗	✓	✗	✗
Card issuing	✗	✗	✓	✗	✗
Providing consumer credit	✗	✗	✓	✗	✗
Financing of cardholder interest-free period	✗	✗	✓	✗	✗

Table 2.1 provides an overview of the operational costs incurred by the card payment ecosystem actors providing services to merchants and cardholders.

This is not an exhaustive list of costs. For example, the merchant's PSP, acquirer, card scheme, and issuer all participate in the authorisation process (not included in Table 2.1, but shown in Chapter 1, Figures 1.6 through 1.10). Table 2.1 should be considered illustrative.

 Professionals should remember:

- **Operational costs are directly related to the functions performed** by the various actors, as introduced in Chapter 1. For example, only acquirers, card schemes, and issuers participate in the clearing and settlement processes (see Chapter 1, Figures 1.11, 1.12, and 1.13), and therefore are the only ones to incur operational costs for these functions.
- **The issuer, on the cardholder side in the two-sided market, has unique responsibilities** (i.e. card issuing, providing credit, bad debt write-offs) which have associated costs. It also has responsibilities to the other side of the market.
- **The acquirer, on the merchant side of the two-sided market, also has unique responsibilities** with associated costs (e.g. card acquiring, write-offs when a merchant goes bust and has liabilities towards the rest of the ecosystem). But unlike the issuer, the acquirer only has responsibilities on one side of the market.
- Within the confines of applicable national regulations, **the card scheme is the only entity that decides the rules for its ecosystem**. It seems unilateral, compared to other payments ecosystems, but it makes decision making much easier. However, some of the largest issuers and retailers sit on the Boards of Visa[6] and Mastercard,[7] and since both issuers and retailers can decide to leave a card network, they have influence.
- **The card scheme is not in direct contact with either merchants or cardholders**, and as such will not "onboard" or "service" either, unlike the other stakeholders (i.e. issuer with cardholder, acquirer with merchant, TPP with cardholder). They may, however, develop products and services for the market.
- Bear Table 2.1 in mind when you read the *Value chain* section.

Value chain

- The common definition of a **Value Chain** is a business model describing the steps involving bringing a product or service to market, from design to distribution, and everything in between.
- For successful value chains, efficiency is key so that maximum value can be derived for the least possible cost. It's about roles, risks, and rewards. The value chain is shown in Figure 2.2.

> The **Card Payments Value Chain** is the set of activities performed by its stakeholders to deliver valuable products and services to the card payments market.

In the following sections, we will examine the characteristics of each step of the value chain.

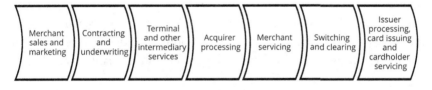

THE CARD PAYMENTS VALUE CHAIN

Figure 2.2 The card payments value chain.

Source: drawing by the author.

Merchant sales and marketing

What is it? Marketing and selling payment facilities to physical and virtual merchants.

Who is involved? The acquirer and the merchant's PSP (for physical or virtual payment facilities) will perform this function. Two card payments ecosystem actors not previously introduced can also market and sell to merchants: the **Independent Sales Organisation (ISO)** and the **Payment Facilitator (Payfac)**. Acquirers may have a direct sales force. They may also have telephone sales, generally targeting small- to medium-sized businesses, and they may also partner with ISOs or Payfacs, which are often referred to as **Merchant Services Providers** (**MSPs**). ISOs are popular in their chosen markets, as they typically offer a more tailored, one-stop-shop service. Visa publishes a list of ISOs[8] (as well as other service providers). In Chapter 1, we examined how a single ecosystem actor can play multiple roles (see Tables 1.1 and 1.2), and this will be the case in this step of the value chain: for example, an acquirer may sell their own merchant PSP services (e.g. payment gateway, such as Barclaycard's Smartpay), in which case they are competing against other merchant PSPs (e.g. Adyen, Opayo). For small to medium-sized merchants, acquirers may outsource the sales and marketing process to ISOs and give them buy and sell rates (see *Charges and fees*) so they can sell on to merchants at competitive prices. ISOs may have several acquiring partners. Similarly, acquirers may decide to partner with other merchant PSPs and Payfacs (who will also benefit from buy and sell rates from their own acquirers) who bring merchant volumes. In addition to payment-processing services provided by acquirers, ISOs, and Payfacs, terminal and payment gateway providers can also market and sell to merchants directly, and the technologies provided will have to integrate into the offerings of the merchant services providers (e.g. a merchant wants to use Adyen as the payment gateway and Worldpay as the acquirer). For the remainder of this section, we will concentrate on merchant services.

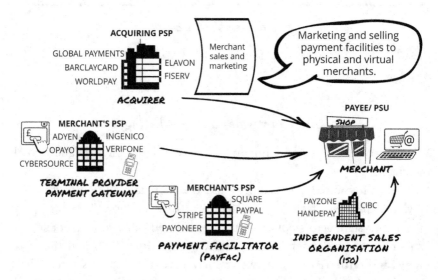

Figure 2.3 Card payments value chain: merchant sales and marketing.

Source: drawing by the author.

An **Independent Sales Organisation (ISO)** is a merchant PSP which isn't a card scheme member (either principal or affiliate) but has developed partnerships with card scheme acquiring members to provide merchant accounts. Acquiring partners will typically be responsible for merchant underwriting, although some ISOs (e.g. wholesale) may take on some of the process. ISOs will also have partnerships with other PSPs (e.g. POS, payment gateway, fraud prevention), as well as ISVs (e.g. CRM, accounting) to offer full-stack merchant services and support.

A **Payment Facilitator (Payfac)** is a merchant PSP that typically isn't a card scheme member (either a principal or affiliate). It provides their customers with the infrastructure necessary to accept card payments and receive the funds from those payments. Payfacs underwrite and onboard their "sub-merchants" directly and may be liable for associated merchant risk and provide a link between the merchant's environment and one or more acquirers.

What are the critical success factors? In this competitive and ever-evolving market, it is crucial that the following elements are present in any sales and marketing endeavour:

- Market sector knowledge (e.g. the hospitality sector will be different from the retail sector);
- Payments knowledge;
- Card scheme rules knowledge;
- Knowledge of applicable regulations (federal- and country-level);
- Competitive offerings;
- Pricing knowledge (it can be complicated, see *Charges and fees*);
- Value-added services; and
- Motivated sales force (if you're selling pretty much what everyone else has, you need to believe!).

Contracting and underwriting

What is it? Assessing merchant risk and contracting with the merchant. This step is about ascertaining whether the merchant's potential commercial value is worth the risk, and therefore the cost. This stage is also known as **Merchant Onboarding**. The stakeholders are the same as for Figure 2.3. The acquirer onboarding stage is quite stringent, as the acquirer has to perform **Customer Due Diligence (CDD)**, **Know Your Customer (KYC)**, and, where required, **Enhanced Due Diligence (EDD)** checks (see Chapter 5, *Anti-Money Laundering*), which may involve asking a merchant for official documentation and further information about their business (e.g. location, company structure, tax information, industry, annual sales volume). The ISO risk assessment is typically not quite as stringent for merchants (depending on where liabilities rest), and depending on the geography, they may (US) or may not (Europe) onboard the merchant. Where ISOs are responsible for the quality of the underwriting, they tend to be more stringent in their risk assessments. Where ISOs act as a referrer of "leads/opportunities", they tend to let the acquirer preform the in-depth risk assessment. The PSP onboarding stage is even less stringent (see *Merchant models and contract types*). At this stage, the merchant will be codified and assigned recognisable codes, which will be a merchant ID for merchants brought in by acquirers or ISOs, or a sub-merchant code for PSP-onboarded merchants. Figure 2.4 displays the contracting and underwriting process.

Who is involved? The acquirer, the ISO, and the merchant's PSP (e.g. a payment gateway or a Payfac) may perform this function.

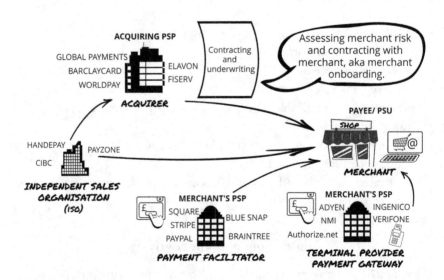

Figure 2.4 Card payments value chain: contracting and underwriting.

Source: drawing by the author.

MERCHANT CATEGORY CODE (MCC)

The MCC is used to classify a business by the types of goods or services they provide. And there's good news! In an attempt to provide consistency across the card payments ecosystem, an international standard (ISO 18245)[9] is used for this four-digit identifier, but there will be variations across card schemes. Large merchants may have their own specific MCC: 3005 for British Airways, 3359 for Hertz Rent-a-Car, and 3504 for Hilton Hotels, and many more. A merchant may have multiple MCCs, for example when a merchant operates a restaurant (MCC 5812) as well as a night club (MCC 5813), each having their own payment facilities.

Because onboarding is a risk assessment stage, there will be merchants that are recognised as "High Risk" by the card schemes. These merchants will usually belong to industries that generate the highest levels of cardholder disputes (see Chapter 1, *Exceptions and disputes*) and that represent higher levels of financial risk, or create additional brand risk for the card schemes (e.g. online pharmaceuticals, online gambling/gaming, online dating). In addition, card schemes may impose additional requirements for certain Card Not Present (CNP) merchants with MCCs not necessarily classified as high risk (e.g. online tobacco sales vs retail tobacco sales). A **High Risk MCC** is subject to additional requirements from the card schemes.

BOX 2.1 HIGH-RISK MERCHANTS

Merchants with a high-risk MCC may find it difficult to source acquiring services from mainstream acquirers. However, there are acquirers and payment facilitators specialising in high-risk sectors, typically offering to accept higher chargeback thresholds than mainstream acquirers, and additional resources tailored to managing high-risk businesses. They will typically charge higher fees for assuming higher risk.

Finally, MCCs evolve in line with card payments, as new risks emerge. For example, MCC 6051 and 6012 were amended by Visa in April 2023 to include "Liquid and Crypto Currency Assets" as well as the purchase of **Non-Fungible Tokens (NFTs)** and **Buy-Now-Pay Later (BNPL)** transactions.

MCCs are not easily classified into a small number of categories (at least, I couldn't do it); for more information, card schemes, such as Visa[10] and Mastercard,[11] have comprehensive lists.

MERCHANT ID (MID)

When onboarded by acquirers or ISOs, the merchant will also be given a customer identifier.

> The **Merchant ID (MID)** is given to a business when they are onboarded directly by an acquirer or by an ISO. This is, in effect, their customer number and is a unique code linked with the merchant's bank account. The MID identifies a merchant to their acquirer or payment facilitator, and also serves regulatory obligations with regard to business identification.

When a merchant is directly recruited by an acquirer, Payfac, or ISO, they are allocated an MCC that is appropriate for their business model or the goods and services that they sell. Typically, when an ISO onboards a merchant, they may have a lighter underwriting regime, but this will depend on where the liability rests (see *Merchant models and contract types*).

What are the critical success factors? Contracting and underwriting, the onboarding stage, is all about risk, and the following factors are crucial:

- **Risk management**: the higher the liability for a given ecosystem actor (e.g. acquirer, ISO), the greater the accountability and therefore the greater the stringency of the underwriting.
- **Correctly classifying a merchant**: doing it right the first time saves a lot of problems with card schemes in the long run. In my experience, smaller organisations may fail in that obligation, perhaps through lack of knowledge or lack of initial due diligence at the recruitment stage. Giving a merchant an incorrect MCC is a breach of card scheme rules.
- **Risk-based pricing**: MCCs will drive a lot of the real and perceived risks associated with a merchant.
- **Easy set-up and onboarding**: merchants don't want to wait too long before they can accept card payments.
- **Value-added services**: in this competitive market, merchant onboarding is an opportunity to upsell and cross-sell to merchants.
- **Card scheme compliance**: this is a permanent factor from the onboarding stage onwards in the card payments value chain. One must abide by the rules.

Terminal and other intermediary services

What is it? Providing payment facilities to enable merchants to take card payments either physically or virtually.

Who is involved? The same stakeholders who onboarded the merchant: acquirer, merchant's PSP, or ISO. In addition, typically, these stakeholders may have partnerships with other stakeholders to supply specific products and services, such as an acquirer partnering with a terminal manufacturer, or an ISO offering a one-stop-shop for all products and services.

There are differences depending on the payment facilities supplied to the merchant (physical or virtual). Figure 2.5 shows how terminal and other intermediary services operate.

In order to ensure that all payment transactions can be linked back to a specific merchant and a specific location for the merchant and, in some cases, a specific device at the specific location, the acquirer or ISO will issue a **Terminal ID (TID)** to the merchant, usually one per physical or virtual device. The TID combined with the MID ensure that the payment can be traced back to its source.

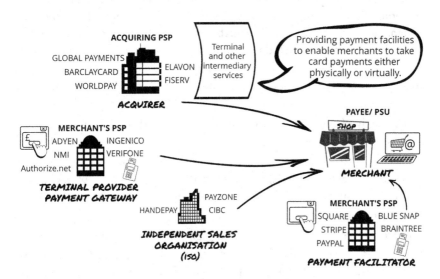

Figure 2.5 Card payments value chain: terminal and other intermediary services.

Source: drawing by the author.

PHYSICAL TERMINAL SERVICES

The **supply of physical terminal services** generally involves the following:

- **Supplying hardware** (e.g. card terminal, PIN pad) **and hardware support services**. The hardware may be owned or rented by merchants. There may also be other more specific hardware depending on the sector, such as top-up kiosks, vending machines, unattended payment terminals, and **Electronic Point of Sale** devices (EPOS) (see Box 2.2 and Figure 2.6).
- **Providing terminal software**, software management, training, etc.
- **Providing network connectivity.**
- **Providing sector-specific functionality and other value-added services** such as tipping, bill splitting, group payments, and BNPL services.

BOX 2.2 WHAT IS AN EPOS SYSTEM?

An **Electronic Point of Sale (EPOS)** system is a modern till system consisting of hardware and software that help merchants run their business. Their functionality may include features such as sales management, accounting, data collection, product, management, and stock management, as well as the capability to accept payments. Modern EPOS systems may include technologies such as touchscreens and apps.

The supply of card payment terminals has evolved over the years. For example, standard hardware terminals can enable new payment methods, such as Ingenico with Alipay[12] (barcode). New entrants – such as Zettle (formerly iZettle before PayPal's acquisition) and Square (Block) – have gained popularity with small businesses. These devices, which can be either attached to a standard mobile phone (e.g. a dongle) or used on their own, are referred to as **Mobile Point of Sale (mPOS)** systems and enable merchant mobility (e.g. market traders, window cleaners, and other peripatetic businesses) at a relatively low cost. mPOS solutions have evolved in recent years and may take many forms: tablet-based systems, mobile-phone-based systems, terminal-based systems, etc. The more recent iteration of mobile terminals is the **SoftPOS** which doesn't rely on additional hardware and allows merchants to accept card payments directly on a standard consumer smart phone or tablet (i.e. Android or iOS). mPOS is not to be confused with mobile money (see Chapter 4, *Open banking and alternative payments*). SoftPOS solutions are becoming popular, and in March 2023 Ingenico acquired Phos.[13] Even Zettle ditched the dongle[14] in May 2022, effectively providing a SoftPOS system.

In summary, **card payment terminals can be classified** into two categories:

- **Proprietary devices**: these are specific to a manufacturer (e.g. Ingenico, Verifone, Zettle). Chronologically, they are imprinting machines (aka zip-zap machines), traditional card terminals, EPOS, mPOS, SmartPOS (see Chapter 1, *What's in a card transaction?*).
- **Enabled consumer devices**: SoftPOS (software capability that runs on Android or iOS consumer devices). Essentially, a SoftPOS payment facility converts a consumer device into a secure payment terminal and enables acceptance of EMV contactless cards. The software facility supplied to the merchant, generally referred to as a **Software Development Kit (SDK)**, is **API**-based and complies with applicable standards (e.g. EMV).

Figure 2.6 gives a historical snapshot of card payment terminals.

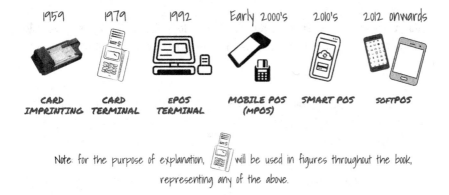

Figure 2.6 The evolution of card payments terminals.

Source: drawing by the author.

VIRTUAL TERMINAL SERVICES

The supply of virtual terminal services generally involves the following:

- **Enabling e-commerce and other virtual transactions through virtual terminals**. The cardholder-facing part of a virtual terminal is referred to as a **Payment Page** and would be integrated within a merchant's online shop. This is where a cardholder would type their card details at checkout. For telephone sales, a virtual terminal can be used by the merchant, and this is where they would enter the cardholder's details as supplied by the cardholder over the phone.
- **Supporting multiple shopping carts** such as Adobe Commerce (formerly Magento), Ecwid, and Square Online (formerly Weebly).
- **Supporting diverse payment methods,** as consumer demand dictates in any given market (e.g. PayPal, iDEAL, SOFORT, etc.) (see Chapter 4, *Fintech and alternative payments*).
- **Providing plug-ins and other tools** enabling merchants to accept virtual payment transactions and manage their business.
- **Providing the 3D Secure Server** (see Chapter 1, *3D Secure*) and other authentication solutions.
- **Providing fraud prevention solutions**.

What are the critical success factors? Providers of technology that enables merchants to accept card payments must ensure that their solutions exhibit the following:

- **Reliability and speed**: customers don't want to wait too long for their payment to be taken;
- **Simple integration**: merchants don't want to wait weeks or months to be able to accept card payments;
- **Relevant payment methods**, as dictated by the market and consumer preferences;
- Provision of **sector specific functions**; and
- **Card scheme compliance**.

Acquirer processing

What is it? Connecting merchants with card schemes to enable them to accept card payments for those schemes.

Who is involved? The acquirer. Some payment facilitators (hybrid) and merchants have direct connections to the card schemes, but they still need an acquirer contract to process transactions, as shown in Figure 2.7.

What are the critical success factors? For acquirers to be successful in their market, they must demonstrate the following:

- **Reliability, accuracy, and speed**;
- **Efficient authorisation routing** to the issuer via the card scheme (see Chapter 1, *Authorisation*);
- **Assessing applicable transaction fees** and other **value-added services** charges (see *Charges and fees*);
- **Efficient clearing and interbank settlement** (see Chapter 1, *Clearing and Settlement*);
- **Large volume capability**, in order for the acquirer to achieve economies of scale;
- **Risk management**; and
- **Card scheme compliance**.

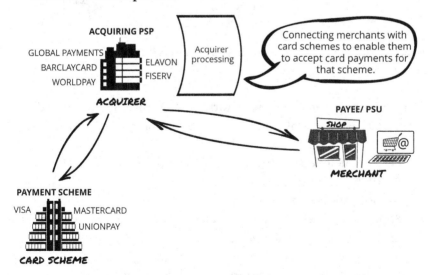

Figure 2.7 Card payments value chain: acquirer processing.

Source: drawing by the author.

Merchant servicing

CORE ACTIVITIES

What is it? Supporting the merchant for the duration of their contract (see *Merchant models and contract types*).

Who is involved? The **acquirer**, the **ISO**, and the **merchant's PSP**, including **Payfacs**, will perform this function for physical or virtual payment facilities, as shown in Figure 2.8.

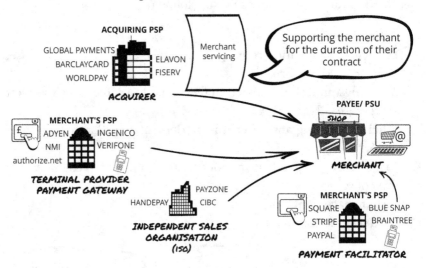

Figure 2.8 Card payments value chain: merchant servicing.
Source: drawing by the author.

What are the critical success factors? At this stage, efficiency and customer service are crucial, and the following factors are key to success:

- **Efficient helpdesk, support, and merchant self-provisioning**;
- **Resilient infrastructure**;
- **Authorisation approval rates**;
- **Supporting merchants with chargebacks and exceptions** (see Chapter 1, *Exceptions and disputes*);
- **Efficient merchant settlement and accounting**;
- Providing **management information**, both online and offline;
- **Fraud/credit monitoring and compliance**: the acquirer is responsible for merchant compliance and reporting to the card schemes, and they

have merchant-monitoring programmes to achieve this (see Chapter 1, *Chargeback* and *PCI DSS*). The ISO is responsible for merchant account-ing and reporting to the acquirer, which in turn reports to the card schemes. The compliance and monitoring models are simpler for ISOs and PSPs (see *Merchant models and contract types*);

- **Ability to upsell and cross-sell**: for example, the provision of new payment facilities or value-added services; and
- **Card scheme rules and regulatory compliance**.

VALUE-ADDED SERVICES

The acquiring market is very competitive, and it is crucial for acquir-ers, ISOs, and PSPs to be able to upsell and cross-sell. This is why many independent software vendors (ISVs) and other technology pro-viders offer solutions that may benefit merchants, and these include the following.

Dynamic Currency Conversion (**DCC**): as cardholders, you've all done it, even though you may not realise you have. This is where you travel abroad and use a card issued in your home country for payments. You may want to withdraw money from an ATM, or you may pay for goods at a physical retailer, and you would get a message of this type: "Would you like to see this transaction in your home currency, or in the local cur-rency?". Convenience suggests that you may want to see the transaction in your home currency, because it's familiar. For a cardholder, DCC conveni-ence may not be a friend if the stakeholders involved are not transparent. For example, if an issuer doesn't charge a fee for international transactions, DCC is not good for the cardholder. What enables this message to be dis-played is the DCC value-added service, as provided by organisations such as Fexco, Global Blue, and Corefy. At a high level, this service relies on a pricing structure involving exchange rates, conversion fees, transaction fees, etc. The pricing structure benefits the merchant, the acquirer, and the issuer, but not the cardholder. Therefore, it is worth selling, but, perhaps, in my opinion, this facility borders on the unethical for some players.[15] Unsurprisingly, Mastercard issued guidelines for DCC,[16] although they don't provide DCC services themselves. A breach of the rules would of course lead to compliance assessments, such as when applying DCC to contactless transactions within the cardholder verification method (CVM) limit (see

Chapter 1, *The acquiring market*), which goes against their desire to push for contactless adoption.

Merchant Financing: this value-added service, whilst a well-established one, has seen a resurgence in popularity with merchants due to the global cost-of-living crisis. There are two forms of merchant financing. A merchant **Cash Advance** is a form of debt financing that involves a merchant borrowing money based on their projected sales. Providers of such services include YouLend,[17] 365 Business Finance,[18] Nucleus Commercial Finance,[19] and Liberis Ltd.[20] **Factoring** (aka **Invoice Factoring**) is another form of merchant financing, which involves the sale of unpaid invoices to a third party at a discount. Providers include Team Factors,[21] Market Invoice,[22] and Bibby Financial Services.[23] Both cash advance and factoring providers may partner with acquirers or other stakeholders (e.g. Worldpay has a partnership with Liberis at the time of writing) and are often referred to as **Alternative Finance** or **Embedded Finance** solutions providers.

Merchant loyalty programmes: everyone loves perks, benefits, and rewards. The merchant loyalty solutions industry is vast, and I don't propose to cover it in any detail here, as others have done it very well already.[24] Popular loyalty programmes exist, and they can be free (e.g. Starbucks Rewards),[25] on the basis of a paid membership (e.g. Barnes & Noble,[26] which offers both a free and a premium membership), or on the basis of charitable undertakings (e.g. The Body Shop "Love Your Body™" programme offers members the ability to spend points for themselves or donate to charity), and new ideas are launched all the time. This industry has evolved to become digital, and long gone are the days where all programmes were based on a little card that the retailer had to stamp. Now you have apps, and the payments industry has been a driver for this. Acquirers may partner with loyalty ISVs, such as Elavon with LoyalZoo,[27] a venture targeting small businesses.

Other value-added services include tokenisation, payment card data storage (e.g. for recurring transactions), BNPL, mobile top-ups, and prepaid gift cards. Innovation will continue.

Switching and clearing

What is it? Providing and operating the network infrastructure, processes, and rules for card payments. The process is shown in Figure 2.9.

Who is involved? The card scheme(s).

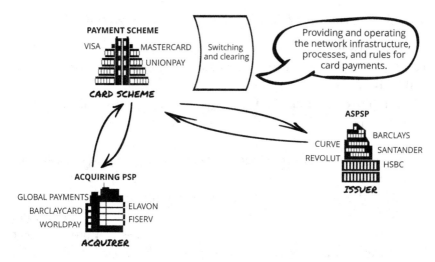

Figure 2.9 Card payments value chain: switching and clearing.
Source: drawing by the author.

What are the critical success factors? The card scheme is the central entity around which everything runs. As such, they have a lot of responsibility, and the critical success factors include:

- Network **scale, security**, and **availability**;
- Efficient **routing** between acquirers and issuers;
- Efficient **clearing** and **interbank settlement**;
- Providing **stand-in** processing (e.g. Chapter 1, Box 1.3);
- Managing scheme **memberships** (see *Scheme membership*);
- A **strong brand**: card schemes perform extensive brand marketing and also give incentives to their members for particular initiatives. This can take the form of partnerships with acquirers or merchants, sponsorship of major events (e.g. the Olympics, concert venues, etc.), TV adverts (to keep the card scheme brand front of mind for cardholders), etc.;
- Interoperable **standards, rules** and **certifications**: the card scheme creates and/or manages the interbank frameworks, as well as the technical standards and certifications to ensure interoperability across their network;
- Efficient **arbitration** in the event of disputes;
- **Product development**: increasingly, card schemes develop new products for the benefit of the market (e.g. tokenisation, fraud prevention); and
- **Marketing and product incentives to members**.

Issuer processing and cardholder servicing

What is it? Issuing cards and managing cardholder accounts on behalf of the card schemes. The issuers connects cardholders with the card schemes.

Who is involved? The issuer.

What are the critical success factors? For the issuer, this is all about card usage: they need volume. The following factors are the keys to success:

- **Driving consumer card usage**: marketing cards to consumers is impor-tant to issuers. This is why you still receive much junk mail offering you this card or that card, enticing you with even more features and bene-fits. Partnering with third parties is another way of driving volume, and smaller issuers may rely on third party companies that provide issuer services, and because the latter are generally larger organisations with scalable infrastructures which serve many issuers, they can operate at much lower costs that a small issuer would be able to do on their own.
- **Providing a trusted and convenient card payments environment**: issuers need cardholders to trust them and therefore customer service is important. Efficient cardholder support is key including help desk (physical or virtual), statements, collections, enquiries, disputes, etc.

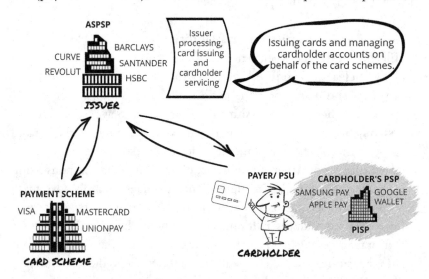

Figure 2.10 Card payments value chain: issuer processing, card issuing and cardholder servicing.

Source: drawing by the author.

- **Efficient clearing and interbank settlement.**
- **Efficient risk management**: issuers have extensive fraud prevention and risk monitoring systems as they are responsible for authorising cardholder transaction (see Chapter 1, *Authorisation*). They will also manage chargebacks and disputes. When they provide credit cards, they will also have the responsibility of assessing cardholder risk before contracting, and for the duration of the cardholder relationship, as well as managing bad debts and write-offs, and financing any interest free period.

BOX 2.3 WHAT IS A PROGRAMME MANAGER?

In the context of card issuing, a **Programme Manager** is an entity that acts as an aggregator between the different parties in the card payment value chain through a BIN Sponsorship agreement with an issuer (see Chapter 1, Box 1.8). Programme managers enable quick time to market[28] for their clients and are associated with the prepaid card industry. A programme manager is different from an issuer processor (see Chapter 1, *The issuing market*), as they build the card programme functionality and technology that will exist on the issuer processor platform. Some examples are EML,[29] Edenred Payment Solutions,[30] and Enfuce.[31] Some programme managers are also issuer processors.

For completeness purposes, cardholder servicing may also be performed by the cardholder's TPP (cardholder's PSP, PISP), as they will provide cardholders with convenient means to pay with cards (e.g. Apple Pay, Samsung Pay, Google Wallet, Venmo), but doesn't extend to card issuing (unless they perform that role as well, such as Apple with the Apple Card, although they do this in partnership with an issuer, Goldman Sachs). This is an overlay service on top of the infrastructure and economic models. Their critical success factors are different, as they only initiate payments and are concerned about adoption and usage.

Card payments value chain: recap

That's it. We've now added more colour as to the roles and responsibilities of the various stakeholders, and Figure 2.11 provides a summary.

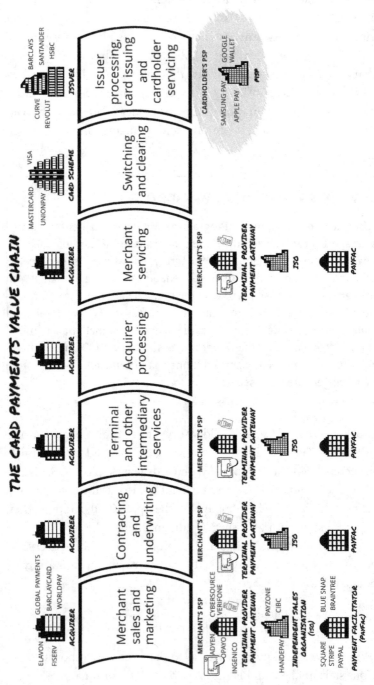

Figure 2.11 Card payments value chain: recap with stakeholders.

Source: drawing by the author.

Now that we understand the functions performed by the various stake-holders, we can start examining the economic implications of this ecosystem.

Merchant models and contract types (it's not what you do, it's the way that you do it)

Selling card payment facilities to merchants is hard. This is because you're trying to sell products and services in a market that is heavily commoditised. Success means one of three things:

- **Rely on the good old-fashioned human touch**: this is why mainstream acquirers have salespeople that specialise in corporate businesses, government, or other important sectors, primarily for large merchants; or,
- **Have something that no one else has**, which is difficult, but not impossible; or,
- **Have a near-frictionless digital merchant onboarding experience**, which is more suited to small and medium-sized business with straightforward requirements.

 Of course, you can have a combination of all three, but the most important thing to remember is: **one size doesn't fit all**.

Understanding the merchant's profile and needs is key to determining what payment service or product is best, and this will include, but won't be limited to:

- Transaction volume;
- Merchant type;
- Industry sector;
- Merchant risk profile;
- Merchant trading channel(s);
- Preferred payment methods; and
- Merchant competitive landscape.

As covered in the *Value chain* section, we now understand that merchants can be recruited either:

- **Directly by an acquirer**: the merchant will have a direct contract with the acquirer. The merchant will be known as a **Master Merchant**.

- **By an ISO** which may have one or more acquirer relationships: the merchant may have a contract with the ISO but will always have a contract with the acquirer. The merchant will be known as a **Master Merchant**.
- **By a merchant PSP**: the merchant will have a contract with the PSP only and will be known as a **Sub-Merchant**. Sometimes, depending on merchant volumes, the schemes will require that there is a tripartite agreement in place for large-volume merchants that receive services from a PSP (e.g. a payment facilitator).

But what does this mean in practical terms? Simply put: the onboarding party will determine whether the merchant's potential value is worth the cost.

Merchant onboarded directly by an acquirer

This is the simplest model. Figure 2.12 shows how it works.

When acquirers onboard merchants directly, underwriting is a crucial stage, because acquirers will only onboard merchants if their value is worth the cost. Acquirers will perform **Due Diligence**, **KYC**, and **Anti-Money Laundering** (**AML**) (see Chapter 5, *Anti-Money Laundering*) checks and further risk assessments – according to their risk appetite – and aim to meet their critical success factors (see *Contracting and underwriting*).

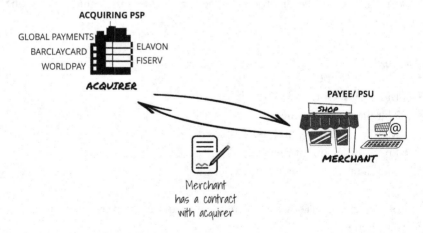

Figure 2.12 Merchant onboarded directly by an acquirer.
Source: drawing by the author.

Value vs cost: acquirer-onboarded merchant

In addition to previously mentioned risk factors, an acquirer will take the following into consideration:

- **Large volume** merchants attract **low fees** but enable acquirers to achieve **economies of scale**.
- Conversely, **too many large merchants could be detrimental** to acquirers, as this could adversely affect their margin. This is generally why mainstream acquirers have caps on the number of large merchants they are prepared to onboard.
- **Chargeback risk** is a contingent liability which is an important underwriting risk factor for acquirers, who need to assess merchants accordingly. This is particularly relevant for acquirers in the Four Party Model where the acquirer bets on the merchant remaining solvent. If a merchant goes bust, the acquirer will be left with the liability to resolve all chargebacks and refunds, and this has been a particular issue during the pandemic with industries such as airlines, furniture retail, and hospitality.
- **Small to medium businesses** (SMBs) presenting a **low to medium risk** profile can also bring volumes to acquirers. The proportion of SMBs vs large merchants in an acquirer portfolio is typically anywhere from 70/30 to 80/20, depending on the market.

Therefore, depending on the acquirer's risk appetite, higher-risk merchants or lower-volume businesses may not be attractive for acquirers to onboard directly. Acquirers may have a direct sales force as well as telephone sales for smaller merchants, and they may decide to partner with ISOs which would bring merchant volumes that acquirers may not necessarily be able to (or want to) recruit themselves.

Merchant recruited by an ISO

This contractual model is slightly more complicated in structure than direct acquiring, but once onboarded the merchant will only interact with the ISO throughout their lifecycle, as shown in Figure 2.13.

Whilst a merchant has a contract with an acquirer, the ISO will always remain their main contact throughout their lifecycle. In this construct, the

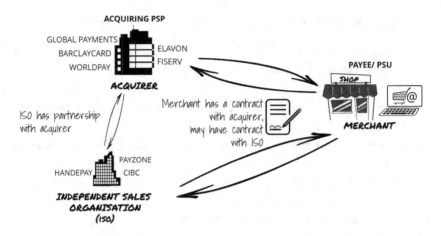

ACQUIRING PSP

GLOBAL PAYMENTS
BARCLAYCARD
WORLDPAY

ELAVON
FISERV

PAYEE/ PSU

ACQUIRER

ISO has partnership
with acquirer

Merchant has a contract
with acquirer,
may have contract
with ISO

MERCHANT

PAYZONE
HANDEPAY   CIBC

INDEPENDENT SALES
ORGANISATION
(ISO)

Figure 2.13 Merchant recruited by an ISO.

Source: drawing by the author.

ISO and the acquirer have different responsibilities. There will be geographical differences in the way this model works in practice, and these will be highlighted where applicable.

ISO responsibilities

The ISO acts as a one-stop-shop for the merchant and has the following responsibilities:

- **Sales and marketing**: ISOs may have a direct sales force, telephone sales, or extensive online marketing, or they may use independent salespeople on commission. Acquirers benefit from this arrangement, as they are essentially gaining an extra sales force.
- **Contracting and risk assessment**: in Europe and the UK, the ISO will perform an initial risk assessment to determine the suitability of the merchant for the available payment services. This merchant risk assessment stage is typically lighter than what would be performed directly by an acquirer. Essentially, the ISO adds an extra layer between the merchant and the acquirer, and therefore takes on additional risk. An ISO will charge a merchant for that risk, but this will be offset by the buy and sell rates they obtain from their partner acquirer(s). Therefore, ISOs will only sell products and services to a merchant

if their value is worth the cost, and this will also be determined by the decision of their partner acquirer to give the prospective customer a merchant account. In the US, ISOs may onboard merchants directly and may operate an aggregator model similar to a payment facilitator.

- As an ISO acts as a one-stop-shop; they have **multiple partnerships** (e.g. POS, payment gateway, fraud prevention), and offer valued-added services such as Customer Relationship Management (CRM) solutions. ISOs generally know their market very well (e.g. geographical region, industry sector) and are able to offer merchants ongoing **personalised support** with tools that are generally more sophisticated than those offered by acquirers (e.g. management information).
- In Europe, the ISO will perform **billing** for their merchants for any additional services they provide outside of their acquiring partner contract with the merchant. In the US, an ISO may be more similar to a Payfac and perform merchant settlement, which includes transactions.
- **ISOs support their merchants with chargebacks and exception processing.**
- The ISO may also be responsible for merchant **ongoing risk monitoring and compliance if they also provide gateway services**. They will then **report back to the acquirer(s)**, according to their contract with their acquirer(s).

Acquirer responsibilities

- In this model, the acquirer will have the following responsibilities:
- **Underwriting and contracting with the ISO** (i.e. full risk assessment and, in some instances, registration with the card schemes).
- **Underwriting and contracting with the merchant**: in Europe, the acquirer will onboard the merchant, and if their risk assessment is favourable, they will give the merchant a merchant ID (MID). In the US, this may be outsourced to the ISO.
- **Transaction routing**: the merchant has a MID and is therefore known to the acquirer which processes the merchant transactions as in the direct model. In the US, the ISO may aggregate transactions for their merchants.

- **Merchant settlement**: since the merchant has a MID, the acquirer will process and settle the transaction in the usual way to the merchant account (Europe) or the ISO account (US).

This construct can be considered a sales and servicing outsourcing arrangement in Europe, and **a form of merchant aggregation** in the US. In both cases, the construct relies on the relationship between the ISO and their partner acquirer(s). To this effect, acquirers will select ISO partnerships according to their risk appetite. This is why, generally, newly established merchants, with little or no credit history, are unlikely to interest ISOs. For these merchants, a PSP may be more suitable.

Merchant onboarded by a PSP (aggregation)

This contractual model, shown in Figure 2.14, is relatively fuss-free for small to micro-merchants, although larger merchants may also take advantage of it.

Why would a merchant choose this model? Because it makes life easier. Going through all the steps in the acquirer (or even ISO) onboarding process, fulfilling all the CDD, KYC, and EDD checks (see Chapter 5, *Anti-money laundering*), and dealing with some financial constraints might be difficult to achieve for small merchants.

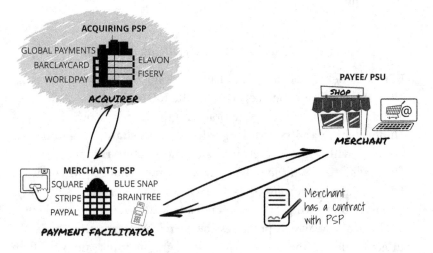

Figure 2.14 Merchant onboarded by a PSP.

Source: drawing by the author.

The **Payment Facilitator** (**Payfac**) model introduced earlier has three variations:

- **Where the merchant uses a Payfac and is a sub-merchant of the Payfac**: this would be the case where the merchant uses Stripe or WePay, whereby the Payfac will aggregate multiple sub-merchants under a single master merchant account, simplifying the process for smaller merchants. In this model, the Payfac is the merchant and has an acquirer or set of acquirers. The cardholder purchasing goods or services will see the merchant's name on their card statement. This is a type of merchant aggregation.

- **Where the merchant uses a Payfac for payment processing and the Payfac is responsible for payments and associated liabilities, such as collecting sales tax, processing refunds and chargebacks, and ensuring compliance with standards and regulations**: this is the case for merchants that want to operate cross-border without having to set up operations in each geography, and is especially advantageous for small- to medium-sized merchants which sell digital goods, such as SaaS businesses. This construct enables merchants to access other markets quickly without the burden of building relationships with local acquirers, complying with local laws, etc. The Payfac buys the goods/services from the merchant and sells them to the cardholder, who will see the Payfac's name on their card statement. Essentially, the Payfac acts as a reseller of the goods or services, and the merchant's only client is the Payfac. In this construct, the Payfac is called a **Merchant of Record** (**MOR**). For example, PayPal is a MOR for many of its customers.

- **Where the merchant uses a Payfac to sell goods or services to cardholders but the merchant is responsible for payments and associated liabilities, such as collecting sales tax, processing refunds and chargebacks, ensuring PCI DSS compliance, etc.**: this is the case when a merchant offers PayPal as a payment method – this model is used by larger merchants as well as smaller ones. Here, the cardholder paying for goods or services offered by the merchant will see the name of the merchant on their card statement. For example, when a cardholder pays for an airline ticket at British Airways using PayPal, they will see British Airways on their card statement, not PayPal. In this instance, the Payfac operates just like a payment gateway, and the merchant has the relationship with the acquirer (or ISO), which means that the Payfac is not involved in underwriting.

And it gets a bit more complicated, as this model is a cascading one. For example, I provide an e-learning website through a Software-as-a-Service (SaaS) company called Thinkific. They have payment integrations with Stripe, PayPal, and their own "Thinkific Payments" platform. I selected the Stripe option, and I have a separate Stripe account. On my site (hosted by Thinkific), learners can pay by card. I am a sub-merchant of Stripe, who is my Payfac, but the cardholder will see Thinkific on their statement (although it will be clear they purchased one of my courses). If I used "Thinkific Payments", payments would no longer be processed through my Stripe account, and Thinkific would be my Merchant of Record.

A business may decide to become a Merchant of Record (MOR) without becoming a Payfac, and this is another form of merchant aggregation. This is particularly useful for small and micro-enterprises wanting to take card payments and get traction in their target market: as cardholders prefer to deal with recognisable brand names, it is beneficial for those merchants to operate under that brand name (e.g. when you pay for an Uber, you will see "Uber" on your card statement, whereas the actual merchant is the driver). This is also the case when you purchase goods on marketplaces.

 ### What should professionals remember?

- To recap, the Payfac and MOR are both merchant aggregation models. Not all Payfacs are MORs and vice-versa, and both require the necessary permissions from the card schemes to operate their business.
- MORs may use Payfacs and other PSPs to provide their services.
- A business may decide to become a MOR for other merchants without becoming a Payfac. Famous examples of MORs are Uber, Airbnb, and Deliveroo. In the Uber example, Uber is the Merchant of Record, not the Uber driver.
- As per the ISO model, the responsibilities will be split between the PSP and the acquirer. The **acquirer's responsibilities are the same as in the ISO model with one exception: the MOR/Payfac will not perform transaction routing for each merchant transaction**; instead, they will route aggregated transactions.
- **Typically, MORs and Payfacs have lighter underwriting responsibilities**, and compliance monitoring and assessment will also be less stringent on merchants, unless the Payfac operates as a payment gateway,

in which case the acquirer will perform merchant underwriting in the usual way. These PSPs isolate the acquirer from underlying merchant risk, as they can aggregate many small businesses. As risk means cost, proactive risk management and monitoring of "sub-merchants" is crucial. So is having sufficient and sufficiently skilled back-office resources to ensure that exceptions and disputes are kept under control.

- **PSPs will not provide "personalised" support**, as they offer a one-size-fits-all solution. But they will have slick processes. To keep costs down, **digital automation and merchant self-provisioning** are critical.
- The aggregating PSP will also have one additional responsibility, and that is to **aggregate merchant transactions** for onwards submission to the acquirer.

With this "cookie-cutter" approach, pricing and fees are generally higher than with other options, which may make them unappealing for larger merchants. They are, however, very attractive to low-volume merchants, as they are relatively hassle-free.

In the future, if you come across the terms "merchant aggregator", "master merchant", "merchant of record", or "Payfac", you'll know what they are.

BOX 2.4 WHAT IS THE DIFFERENCE BETWEEN A PAYFAC AND A MARKETPLACE?

A **Marketplace**, such as eBay, Amazon, Uber, or Etsy, connects buyers with multiple sellers and maintains complete control over the payment transactions, their fulfilment, and the end-to-end customer experience, and are therefore MORs. With a marketplace, a cardholder intends to buy a product or service, and the marketplace will offer these products or services from multiple sellers. A Payfac, such as Stripe or PayPal, connects one buyer with one seller. The cardholder intends to buy from the seller and may not even know that a Payfac is involved, as they only facilitate the payment. With a Payfac, the seller is responsible for the fulfilment and end-to-end customer experience.

As you know, the payments industry evolves fast, especially in the digital space, as increasing numbers of merchants come online, and this trend was driven even further by the 2020–2021 pandemic. You may have heard of the term "e-commerce platform"; examples include Shopify, Magento, WooCommerce, and Squarespace. These platforms enable businesses to build e-commerce websites and include functionality such as inventory management, customisation, shipping options, dashboards, and merchant training. The payments functionality is usually provided by a Payfac or PSP, and indeed, in June 2023, Shopify announced its partnership with Adyen.[32] In addition, marketplaces don't have to be MORs, in which case they are platforms: eBay started as a platform (with buyers and sellers transacting directly), and then evolved into a MOR marketplace. Choosing a particular model depends on the stage of evolution of the business and their strategy.[33]

In our modern times, the waters get a bit muddied. Companies such as Uber, Airbnb, and others are often referred to as **Peer-to-Peer (P2P)** or sharing-economy platforms. But at least, you now understand the mechanics.

Value vs cost

Risk is perhaps the most important factor in determining merchant value. Merchants can adopt various models to accept card payments, depending on their size, structure, and the stage they have reached in their

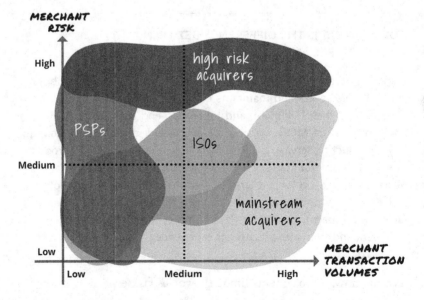

Figure 2.15 Another way of looking at merchant value.
Source: drawing by the author.

evolution. Consequently, merchants can move from one model to the other over time as their business evolves. The value of a merchant to a card payments ecosystem actor will depend on the model used and the merchant profile. Figure 2.15 will help you understand the market position of the ecosystem actors introduced in this section.

The next section will cover how cardholders interact with merchants to make payments, and how this has evolved over the years.

Card payment channels (I did it my way)

A card payment channel (Figure 2.16) is how customers interact when using their cards, either directly or through a PISP. **Interactions vary depending on customer preferences.**

For merchants, card payment acceptance can be:

- **Physical**: this is referred to as **Card Present** or **Customer Present** (**CP**). This is the type of transaction where a cardholder pays with a card at a physical shop or by using a elf-service payment terminal (e.g. vending machine, public transport terminal, toll booth terminal).
- **Virtual**: this is referred to as **Card Not Present** or **Customer Not Present** (**CNP**). Visa has tried to introduce the term **Card Absent** for these transactions, and as far as I can tell, this is not catching on.

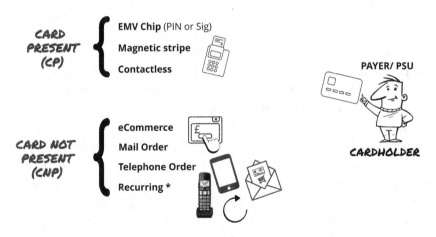

Figure 2.16 Card payment channels.
Source: drawing by the author.

Whilst the "recurring transaction" is not strictly speaking a "channel" (more a type of CNP e-commerce "transaction"), it is significant enough to warrant a special mention given the popularity of subscription services.

Card Present

We covered which products and services are supplied by which ecosystem actors in the *Value chain* section. Figure 2.17 gives a pictorial representation of the Card Present channel.

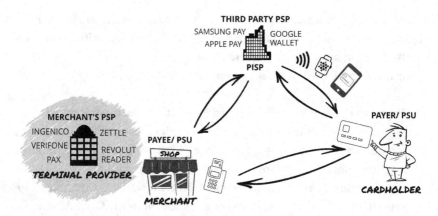

Figure 2.17 Card payment channels: Card Present.
Source: drawing by the author.

As seemingly old-fashioned as the physical card terminal industry may be perceived to be, this too has changed with the times, driven by consumer preferences and behaviours. As streamlined customer experiences are no longer a nice-to-have but a must-have, innovation abounds. We covered open loop card payments in public transport in Chapter 1 (*Contactless payments*) and how they are a driver for digital payments usage. We must also include self-service vending systems as a usage driver, as these are particularly popular in some geographies (e.g. Japan). In the UK, Monzo's BNPL product comes with a virtual card that lets cardholders make contactless payments in-store through Apple Pay or Google Wallet.[34] In Japan, 7-Eleven stores enable contactless payments for their customers through holographic terminals, removing the need to touch any hard surfaces.[35] In 2020, Amazon launched Amazon One, its palm-scanning contactless solution, and as of March 2023 it has been deployed in 200 locations within and out-side Amazon.[36] Of course Amazon is no stranger to innovation, having launched Amazon Go stores featuring their "Just Walk Out" technology in 2017 in Seattle. There are now more than 25 Amazon Go stores in the US and 19 in London[37] (where they are called "Amazon Fresh") at the time of writing, with more openings planned.

This is pointing more and more towards seamless authentication and digital identity through the use of technologies such as machine learning and biometrics. Apple paved the way when they launched their biometric authentication Touch ID in 2013. Biometric technology is now widely ac-cepted as a valid means of authentication for payments. As EMV standards support biometric authentication, there is no need for merchants to up-grade payment terminals (see Chapter 1, *Card payments authentication*). Both Visa[38] and Mastercard[39] are pushing for the adoption of biometric cards. And biometrics are not confined to fingerprint recognition: more and more solutions are coming to market that make use of facial recognition and other biometrics for payment authentication,[40] and in July 2023 Amazon rolled out palm recognition in 500+ Whole Food Market stores across the US.[41] Biometrics can also be used for digital identity verification, as dem-onstrated by Aldi Shop & Go in the UK, [42] featuring built-in age estimation facial recognition technology used for checkout-free sales of age-restricted products (such as alcohol). Watch this space.

Card Not Present – e-commerce

Nowadays in payments, this is where it's at: everything digital. E-commerce is part of our lives, and we see the effects everywhere. High Street shops, the leisure and hospitality sector, and many others are struggling. Those who saw the writing on the wall during the pandemic tried to do some-thing about it, and in an attempt to remain competitive, if not just afloat, these businesses implemented many new (or new to them) digital features to cater for changing habits and the global cost-of-living crisis. "Click-and-Collect", "Buy-Now-Pay-Later", "Social Commerce", "Pay-as-You-Go", and "One-Click", to name but a few, are now embedded in our lives. Technol-ogy innovations designed to make our digital lives even more convenient are the root of this trend: ever faster connectivity, mobile phones, tablets, wearable devices. Ask yourself this question: how often do you go to a physical shop? How do you choose a restaurant or a hotel, and how do you

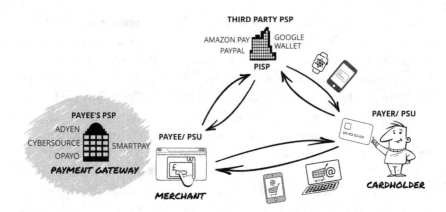

Figure 2.18 Card payment channels: Card Not Present, e-commerce.
Source: drawing by the author.

pay for your booking? Before buying something new, where do you check first? I can go on and on.

However, as pervasive and innovative as e-commerce can be, it still operates on the infrastructure within the rules introduced thus far and involves the same stakeholders. Typically, this will involve the customer entering their card details on a payment page, including the PAN, expiry date, cardholder name, CVV2, and billing and shipping addresses. Merchants may elect to use an AVS (see Chapter 1, *Authentication*) as a fraud prevention measure. If the merchant has deployed 3D Secure, and depending on the version used, the cardholder may see an additional pop-up window for a second step of authentication. The overall authentication step is important for merchants, because it will determine where the fraud liability resides (see *Liability shift*) in case they face a dispute later on (see Chapter 1, *Exceptions and disputes*). Because of the increased risk faced by issuers, e-commerce transactions are more expensive for merchants to process than CP transactions.

Figure 2.18 gives a pictorial representation of the CNP e-commerce channel.

Card Not Present – telephone order

If you don't do it online, you may very well order a pizza or a curry over the telephone, and you should be familiar with the process. The person on the other end of the line (the merchant), after having recorded your order and given you the price to pay, will ask you how you want to pay. You may very well decide to go and pick up your order from the outlet and pay there, in which case this is not a telephone sale, and we're back to a CP payment. If, however, you decide to pay by card over the telephone, regardless of how you choose to pick up your order, this is a telephone sale. You will be asked for all the details that were covered in Chapter 1, *Authentication*, including the PAN, expiry date, cardholder name, CVV2, and most probably your postcode (AVS). At this point, the merchant has three options:

- **Entering the cardholder's name in the virtual terminal and passing control over to the cardholder to enter the card details from their telephone keypad.** This gives control to the cardholder, as the merchant will (generally) not be aware of the card details, which will be masked as the cardholder enters them. In Figure 2.19, you may notice some merchant PSPs not introduced previously (e.g. Eckoh, PCI Pal, Semafone). These are PSPs which focus on telephone payments by offering specific features to enable merchant PCI DSS compliance (e.g. **DTMF Masking**), as well as other functions specific to the call centre industry.
- **Entering the card details on a virtual terminal themselves.** The merchant at this stage is in full possession of everything they need to make an e-commerce transaction (or several). What is stopping them from using them fraudulently at a later stage? This could of course result in disputes. This is why, generally, call centre operations that accept payments will have "clean room" policies (e.g. no paper, no pens, no personal devices, etc.) to minimise temptation.
- **Entering the card details on a physical terminal.** These are called **PAN Key Entry** transactions and are not authenticated (because there is nothing much to authenticate them with other than a PAN, expiry date, and cardholder's name), making it impossible for issuers to assess risk.

It is therefore unsurprising that these transactions are expensive to process for merchants, which will also bear the fraud risk (see *Liability shift*), regardless of the option deployed.

The need to reduce transaction costs saw the introduction of **Pay-By-Link**, effectively shifting the telephone interaction to an online one for the

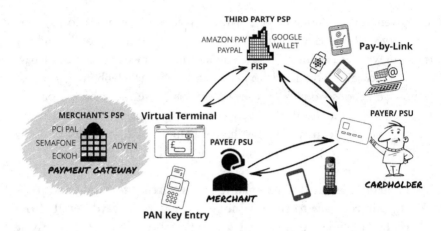

Figure 2.19 Card payment channels: Card Not Present, telephone channel.
Source: drawing by the author.

card payment (effectively making it an e-commerce transaction, which is less expensive to process than a telephone card payment).

Figure 2.19 gives a pictorial representation of the Card Not Present telephone channel.

The 2019–2022 pandemic led to a resurgence of telephone payments, as vulnerable segments were unable, or unwilling, to use digital payments or travel to shops. Retailers established telephone sales capabilities, such as Morrisons[43] in the UK which, at the time of writing, have kept this facility going.[44] In the UK, many local councils accept card payments over the telephone.[45] Utility suppliers[46,47] as well as telecommunications firms also accept card payments to pay bills over the telephone.[48,49] Some car dealers accept payments over the telephone (e.g. for a deposit), and, of course, so do businesses in the leisure and hospitality sector, although increasingly they are aiming to shift this to online channels.

Conclusion: there is a market.

Card Not Present – mail order

Long gone are the days where catalogue sales were extremely popular (well, in the UK, at least), where everyone waited to receive or collect the new season edition from their favourite retailer, cradling it back home in anticipation of the delights within, to be savoured over a cup of tea. Now, these very same retailers have put their catalogues online (and we're back

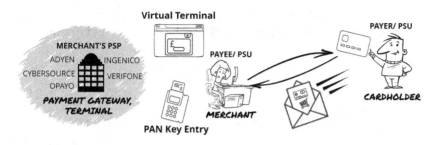

Figure 2.20 Card payment channels: Card Not Present, mail order channel.
Source: drawing by the author.

to e-commerce). They may still send you smaller edited versions of the catalogues by post, but, in the UK at least, these no longer contain order forms. But mail order still exists. Newspapers still feature businesses marketing and selling goods (e.g. plants, slippers, elasticated trousers, and even furniture), and the order forms are still there, reminiscent of a bygone era ... But this too has changed, and this is mostly due to risk and fraud. Prior to 2017, when completing a mail order form, a cardholder would have to specify their card number, expiry date, full address (for shipping), and the CVV2! (see Chapter 1, *What's in a card?*) When the merchant received the completed order form (assuming the form wasn't intercepted in transit to the merchant after the cardholder posted it), they would process the transaction using a virtual or physical terminal as shown in Figure 2.20.

At this point (prior to 2017), the merchant would be in full possession of card details, including the authentication details for e-commerce transactions: what is stopping them from going on an online shopping rampage? You can imagine the ensuing chargebacks and many unhappy issuers. In addition, PAN Key Entry transactions, which are merchant-initiated and not authenticated, make it impossible for issuers to assess risk. It is therefore unsurprising that these transactions are expensive to process for merchants, which also will bear the fraud risk (see *Liability shift*). Fortunately, the card scheme operating regulations changed after 2017, where the merchant is no longer allowed to collect the CVV2 on mail order forms (good for issuers and good for merchants, as this helps with chargebacks). To manage risk, merchants are left with just the AVS and potentially other fraud prevention features that may be provided by their PSP and other ISVs. These transactions are still expensive to process, and the merchant still bears the fraud risk. No wonder this is slowly getting abandoned!

MOTO is the collective term referring to Mail Order and Telephone Order transactions.

Card Not Present – recurring transactions

The popularity of subscription services, such as Netflix, Amazon Prime, and Spotify, established recurring transactions as an important addition to the card payment world. A recurring transaction is where a cardholder gives their card details to a merchant and authorises them to take subsequent regular payments. There are some variations and exemptions that may apply (such as in Europe with PSD2), but typically, with these transactions, if nothing changes (i.e. the amount remains the same and the frequency remains the same), then only the first transaction will be authenticated in the usual way … *ad infinitum* … or until the cardholder changes their mind and tries to cancel it, which is not impossible but somewhat difficult. Some may advise cardholders to ask their issuer to cancel the transaction, as they have no right to ask you to contact the merchant to do this (UK Citizens Advice Bureau),[50] but the process shows that this is not necessarily straightforward. Some issuers want the cardholder to contact the merchant first (Barclays,[51] Nationwide Building Society),[52] but advise that they could do it under certain conditions. Some sit in the middle (MoneySavingExpert).[53] Conclusion: the process is not straightforward, and suppliers of these services will compete for customers on convenience, ease of use, and fairness.

Recurring transactions are also known as **Continuous Payment Authority (CPA)** transactions. This is because the merchant is allowed to store the card details, excluding the CVV2 after the first transaction has been authorised (see Chapter 1, PCI DSS), and subsequently to take payments without the cardholder's involvement. This is one type of **Card on File** transaction, for which a pictorial representation is given in Figure 2.21. Another application of this arrangement is where a cardholder agrees for their card details to be stored in the merchant environment in a secure manner through a merchant PSP which would replace the card details by a "token" which can subsequently be used for payment transactions even if the amount and frequency of payments are not set in advance.

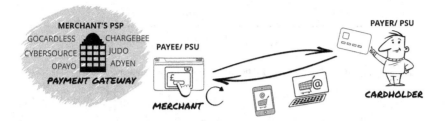

Figure 2.21 Card payment channels: Card Not Present, recurring transactions.
Source: drawing by the author.

BOX 2.5 WHAT IS A CARD ON FILE TRANSACTION?

A card on file transaction is where a cardholder consents to a merchant storing their card details for future use. There are several applications for card on file transactions, an early example of which is in the hospitality sector: this is when a hotel takes the cardholder's details at check-in time and enables them to use a fast check-out service, where any incidentals will be charged to the card by the hotel without the cardholder's intervention. Another famous example is Apple Pay. Modern businesses such as food delivery apps and ride-hailing and bike-sharing schemes also make use of card on file transactions, which renders checkout more streamlined. BNPL providers also make use of this facility to enable them to take split payments at regular intervals. More recently, modern retail outlets such as cashierless stores (e.g. Amazon Go) and those retailers that enable cross-channel interactions (e.g. buy online, refund in store, and vice versa) are also benefitting from this process. After the first authorised transaction initiated by the cardholder, the merchant's taking of a subsequent payment without the cardholder's intervention is known as a **Merchant-Initiated Transaction (MIT)**.

Risk and cost: CP vs CNP

The Card Present channel is considered less risky than the Card Not Present channel, and so it is therefore less expensive to process for merchants. This is because with CP transactions the customer is physically present in front of the merchant, simplifying authentication, especially with EMV chip and PIN. For the CNP channel, MOTO transactions are considered riskier than e-commerce ones, and therefore more expensive, as shown in Figure 2.22.

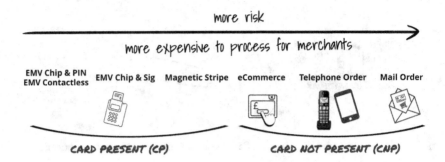

Figure 2.22 Card payment channels: risk and cost – CP vs CNP.

Source: drawing by the author.

Therefore, charges and liabilities will vary, depending on a number of factors, including the authentication used, whether the transaction is domestic or international (aka cross-border), the type of card (e.g. debit, credit, consumer, commercial), etc. Unsurprisingly, the card schemes "encourage" stakeholders to behave in the right way to preserve the integrity of the ecosystem. One such incentive is the liability shift.

Liability shift

The **Liability Shift** is a method by which the fraud liability of card transactions shifts from the merchant to the issuer, under certain conditions, in the event of disputes. Figure 2.23 illustrates this concept.

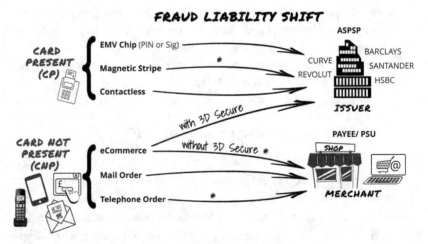

Figure 2.23 Card payment channels: liability shift.

Source: drawing by the author.

For the fraud liability to shift from the merchant to the issuer, specific conditions must be satisfied, and these are summarised below:

- **All EMV chip transactions are covered by the liability shift.** This means that in the event of a dispute the fraud liability rests with the issuer and the merchant doesn't incur any costs. This is a way of encouraging merchants to migrate from magnetic stripe to EMV-capable terminals.
- **Magnetic stripe transactions are typically covered by the liability shift. BUT.** This will depend on the geography. For example, in the US card schemes "encourage" merchants to migrate to EMV (see Chapter 1, *What's in a card?*), and in April 2021 they removed the liability shift for magnetic stripe transactions, leaving merchants to bear the fraud cost in the event of disputes. In other markets, this may not be possible, but ultimately the card schemes decide.
- **Contactless transactions are covered by the liability shift.**
- **E-commerce transactions that have been authenticated using an approved version of 3D Secure are covered by the liability shift.** As new versions of 3D Secure are released, card schemes may act to "encourage" merchants to migrate to new versions.
- **E-commerce transactions that have either (1) not been authenticated with 3D Secure, or (2) authenticated with a 3D Secure version that is no longer card-scheme-approved are not covered by the liability shift.** For example, on 1 January 2021, Mastercard doubled the authentication fees for 3D Secure (see Chapter 1, *3D Secure*) version 1, and on 15 October 2022 Visa discontinued support for 3D Secure version 1.0.2. This leaves merchants with the cost of fraud and the burden of disputes, even if they are compliant with applicable regulations, such as the Strong Customer Authentication (SCA) requirements of PSD2 in Europe – noting that 3D Secure version 1 is compliant with this regulation. Beware: compliance with applicable regulations doesn't necessarily imply compliance with card-scheme operating rules!
- **Mail order transactions are not covered by the liability shift.**
- **Telephone order transactions are typically not covered by the liability shift. BUT.** As explained in *Card Not Present – Telephone order*, modern telephone operations may shift the payment part of the transaction process to a pay-by-link step, effectively making it an e-commerce

transaction. In addition, as covered in Chapter 1, *Decoupled and delegated authentication*, 3D Secure version 2.2 may render telephone transactions suitable for a liability shift, but it is still early days, and at the time of writing, I haven't seen any deployment of this version for this purpose.

In summary, if all merchants behaved in the safe and secure way that card schemes expect, issuers would lose a lot of money. Of course, this is never the case, and I don't weep for issuers.

Fraud prevention and digital identity

As our world continues to become more digital and as online and mobile activity increases, so too does fraud. As a result, regulations are becoming more complex. As stakeholders in the card payments ecosystem endeavour to preserve its integrity, distinguishing legitimate customers from fraudsters and striking the right balance between fraud prevention and customer experience becomes harder. Juniper Research estimates that merchants will lose $38 billion to fraud globally in 2023[54] with an increase to $91 billion in 2028, making an estimated total of $362 billion in merchant losses between 2023 and 2028.

 Professionals should remember:

- To prevent fraud, the card payments ecosystem offers security and fraud prevention features as standard, such as EMV chip, 3D Secure, etc.
- These features on their own, whilst key elements of fraud prevention, are not sufficient to fight fraud.
- The key to success is to adopt a layered approach to fraud prevention as technology advances and criminals become more and more innovative (and knowledgeable).

Figure 2.24 explains this approach.

Digital Identity is fundamental to payments, especially when it comes to fighting fraud. We are starting to see a shift towards payment integration with digital identity services.

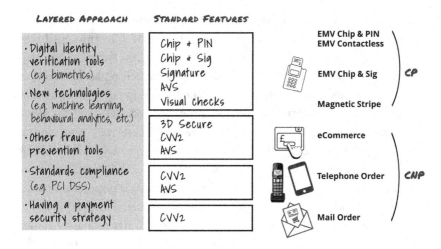

Figure 2.24 Card payment channels: a layered approach to fraud prevention.
Source: drawing by the author.

In **India**, the government already mandates the linking of **Aadhaar** to the PAN to pay their taxes, and taxpayers were subject to a fine of ₹500 for not doing so from April 2022 to June 2022, and this increased to ₹1,000 thereafter.

BOX 2.6 WHAT IS AADHAAR?

Aadhaar is a digital identity framework developed by the Unique Identification Authority of India (UIDAI) on behalf of the Government of India.[55] It consists of a 12-digit individual identification number and a set of rules governing the framework. The Aadhaar number serves as proof of identity and residence for any Indian resident, irrespective of age, and is valid for life. Through the Aadhaar deployment, the Indian government intends to promote financial inclusion for a largely rural and underbanked population by facilitating access to banking, mobile phone connections, and other government and non-government services. In March 2023, Aadhaar authentication transactions climbed to 2.31 billion,[56] and UIDAI claims that its digital KYC (eKYC) deployment has significantly reduced customer acquisition costs for financial services institutions, telcos, and others.

The **Nordic countries** have successful deployments of nation-wide digital identity systems, but unlike India's, which was government-driven, these were largely bank-driven. We have Sweden's BankID, Norway's BankID (a different one), and Denmark's MitID (which replaced NemID in June 2023). In Finland,[57] we have TUPAS (a partnership between all Finnish banks), the National Citizen ID (a government-issued eID), and the newer Mobiilivarmenne (a partnership between telcos). There are 8.4 million users of BankID in Sweden (81% of the population), most of which choose to use the mobile version. In 2022, it was used 6.7 billion times across 6,150 businesses and authorities.[58] In Norway, BankID is popular for several identity verification use cases such as online payments and signing official documents. The Norwegian BankID has successfully reduced payment fraud from 1% to 0.00042% of transactions.[59] You get the gist: the Nordics have got it sussed,[60] and digital identity is an essential tool for fighting fraud (amongst many other things).

In the US in April 2022, Early Warning, the consortium of seven of the largest banks behind Zelle, launched **Authentify**®,[61] an identity verification service for consumers and businesses that leverages trusted bank data. This enables merchants to reduce cart abandonment and fraud ratios whilst streamlining the identity verification process for consumers. It also gives financial services institutions the ability to provide value-added services to their customers outside of the banking experience. Consumers remain in control of their data, as they are able to share identity verification attributes with requestors without having to share their data. At the time of writing, I can't find any usage statistics, but Gartner lists some good reviews for this service.[62]

In June 2021, Stripe partnered with OpenAI (the founders of ChatGPT) to launch **Stripe Identity**,[63] which can validate official document authenticity (over 100 countries supported) and match user selfies with the image on the identity document. Stripe Identity can also validate user data input, such as name, date of birth, government identification number, and address. In October 2022, the mobile SDK was released, making the facility available on Android and iOS. At the time of writing, I can't find any usage statistics, but in my opinion, this product could be a great success.

In China, some university students have been trialling a digital yuan hard wallet device since May 2022.[64] The **Super SIM Hard Wallet** is a proprietary device developed by the Industrial and Commercial Bank of China in partnership with China Mobile because local regulations ban the use of conventional smart phones by students on school premises. The device enables them to make payments to "select high-quality merchants" on and off school premises using China's central bank digital currency (CBDC) as well as verify their identity using NFC. This is another example of digital identity and payments integration, although I think the intent may be different than for the earlier examples.

In the US in May 2022, Google launched a multipurpose digital wallet[65] (see Chapter 4, *Digital wallets*) capable of supporting identity cards, tickets for transit or events, payment cards, hotel room keys, driving licences, office badges, health passes, etc. **Google Wallet** was rolled out to a further 39 countries a couple of months later.[66]

In the meantime, the private sector is not standing still: in March 2023, Lloyds Bank invested £10 million in Yoti's digital identity solution,[67] and Mastercard became a certified digital identity provider in the UK.[68] Mastercard have been scaling their digital identity solution worldwide since 2019.

From a **policy-making** perspective, European Parliament members backed plans in February 2023 for a Digital Identity Framework[69] in an attempt to create an EU-wide scheme giving EU citizens digital access to key public services across EU borders without resorting to commercial providers. The scheme would also be interoperable with existing public national identity frameworks (e.g. myID.be in Belgium) and private ones (e.g. itsme app in Belgium). The technical specifications for the digital identity wallet were expected to be published in July 2023.[70] The EU aims to "become the first global region with a governance framework for trusted digital identities" (too late, the Nordics and India have pipped them to that post). Given the benefits that digital identity can bring to the payments industry, I find it extremely puzzling that the European Credit Sector Associations (ECSAs, a collective name for the European Banking Federation, the European Association of Co-operative Banks, and the European Savings and Retail Banking Group) called for the exclusion of payments (especially card payments) from the proposed Digital Identity Framework in April 2023![71] From Chapter 1, *Authentication*, we understand that robust processes and regulations are already in place. BUT, I think calling for "removal of payments" from the framework is counter-productive, although I believe provisions should be made to cater for card payments specifics, which could be achieved through consultation.

For completeness, I should mention the UK. Yes, the UK has a Digital Identity Strategy,[72] and it made some deployment attempts. Ill-conceived

Gov.UK Verify shut down in June 2023 after seven years,[73] and a new service, One Login, is expected to replace it for access to all government services. Deployment of One Login is not expected to be completed until 2025, and doesn't include the private sector, and therefore consumer payments (you should see my face as I write this). Separately, the pandemic led to the deployment of the NHS App for UK citizens' health and vaccination records, and as of December 2022 there were 30 million users.[74] That is 30 million authenticated and verified users (linked to their National Insurance Number), or about 45% of the UK population. Missed opportunity? In the meantime, there is a lot of talk: eight countries, including the UK, proposed 11 "high-level principles" for the mutual recognition and interoperability of digital ID schemes,[75] and Tony Blair and William Hague wrote a joint report in support of digital identity to foster economic growth.[76] Tony Blair said: "We risk doing what actually happened in the 19th century, which is when the industrial revolution happened, politics took decades to catch up with it." The UK is already behind.

Charges and fees (show me the money!)

In this section, we will explore how charges and fees are applied throughout the card payment ecosystem. Whilst the fundamentals will remain the same (or similar) across geographies, some real-life illustrative examples will be given, and the UK will be chosen as the sample market. Where fundamental differences exist, these will be pointed out.

An introduction to transaction fees

Let's start by busting one myth. When I deliver courses on payments, I always ask: "Which card payments ecosystem actors make the most money on transaction fees and charges?" (see Chapter 1, Figure 1.1), and I give three options: the acquirer, the card scheme, or the issuer. I rarely get the right answer, as it is a common misconception that the card scheme makes the most money in a card transaction. After all, card scheme fees are contentious worldwide. The correct answer is the issuer, as shown in Figure 2.25 for a typical UK example, taking an **Average Transaction Value (ATV)** of £65 for credit and £45 for debit, giving an overall ATV of £44 assuming a 70/30 split between debit and credit, respectively, in the

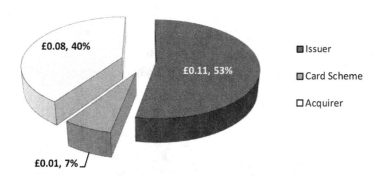

Figure 2.25 UK illustration of typical transaction fees and charges split between acquirer, issuer, and card scheme.

Source: chart by the author.

merchant portfolio. Given that merchant portfolios differ across players (see Figure 2.15), Figure 2.25 should not be taken as an absolute but as a comparative illustration.

The issuer makes the most money in card transactions, because they bear most of the risk (see *Costs and value chain*), although in Europe this is not as pronounced as before the **Interchange Fee Regulation (IFR)** introduced caps on interchange for consumer debit and credit card transactions.

In addition, debit and credit card transactions have different fee profiles, as shown in Figure 2.26.

Essentially, debit transactions are cheaper to process for merchants. But the differences in fees are more complex than just between debit and credit. Figure 2.27 gives a handy comparison and should be read in conjunction with Figure 2.22, as the UK is an EMV market.

Obviously, Figure 2.27 is a simplification of charges and fees, as other factors need to be considered, including whether the transaction is domestic or cross-border, the type of acquirer, the issuer, the card scheme, and the applicable regulations (e.g. interchange fee caps).

And of course, **acquirers, ISOs, and aggregators have other revenues** than just those applicable to transactions (see *Value chain*), including minimum monthly fees, terminal rentals, PCI administration fees, and value-added services. **Issuers also have other revenues**, such as cardholder fees, interest income, ATM fees, and foreign exchange fees.

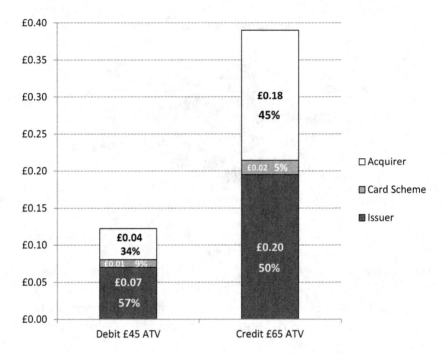

Figure 2.26 UK illustration of typical transaction fees and charges for debit and credit card transactions.

Source: drawing by the author.

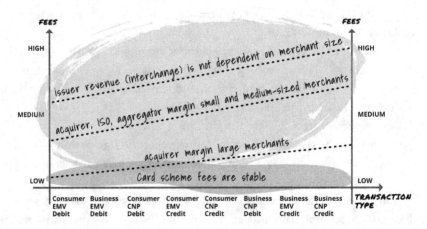

Figure 2.27 Transaction fees and charges, differences by merchant size and transaction type.

Source: chart by the author.

The Merchant Service Charge (MSC)

The **Merchant Service Charge** (**MSC**) represents the charges taken on every credit and debit card transaction that a merchant accepts. The MSC follows a simple formula:

MSC = interchange + card scheme fees + acquirer margin

The **Acquirer Margin** will depend on the factors highlighted in Figures 2.25, 2.26, and 2.27, as well as on the contractual arrangement (see *Merchant models and contract types*).

Interchange

Interchange is a funding mechanism specific to the card payment ecosystem used to compensate issuers for their costs, and it enables the ecosystem to function (see *Costs and value chain*). The interchange rules are determined by the card schemes, but these don't supersede applicable regulations (e.g. interchange fee caps). Interchange is collected by the acquirer from the merchant and flows from the acquirer to the issuer, for whom it is a fee income. Depending on the card programme, product type, etc., interchange may be the largest income line item for an issuer. Interchange rates are published by the card schemes[77] and are heavily regulated in Europe (see *Interchange fee regulations*) and other countries such as Canada and Australia. Interchange is a contentious concept, and you either love it or hate it, depending on which side of the fence you sit, and it is the cause of much litigation around the world.

Interchange is usually assessed by the acquirer and can vary at the individual transaction level (see Chapter 1, *Service code*). The calculation is relatively simple, and is set as one rate per card type, with variants if the card is not issued where the transaction takes place or is accepted without EMV chip and PIN, etc.

Card scheme fees

Card scheme fees, unlike interchange, are unregulated, although, according to the UK Payment Systems Regulator (PSR), this may change.[78] A card scheme fee is any fee that that is paid to a card scheme for their contribution to the ecosystem, and some of these fees are in the public domain.[79, 80] There are several types of card scheme fees, including membership fees for acquirers and issuers, and processing fees (e.g. authorisation, refund, chargeback, cross-border, and assessment). It's therefore difficult to give a definite answer, but in all my illustrations I use an average value of 0.03% of transaction value, which seems to be about right (I realise this rate may be much higher, but in any instance it will be lower than 0.10%, so please take this percentage as an example for illustrative purposes only). Card scheme processing fees are collected by the acquirer from the merchant, and they constitute revenue for the card scheme.

How to read a merchant statement

Depending on the contractual model (see *Merchant models and contract types*), a merchant statement can be very simple or it can be rather obscure. Figure 2.28 shows the elements you might find on a merchant statement, but the picture I give is much clearer than what a merchant would get in real life. Merchant statements are not known for their transparency and clarity unless regulations force acquirers to act differently (such as in the UK, with the PSR mandating summary boxes since July 2023).[81]

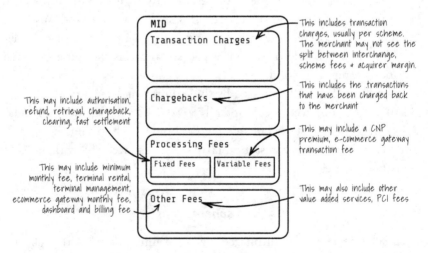

Figure 2.28 Transaction fees and charges, a utopian merchant statement.

Source: drawing by the author.

We have now pieced together all the financial elements introduced so far in Chapters 1 and 2. Fortunately, there is a trend in the payments world to move towards more transparency.

Pricing models – acquiring sales jargon

You would be forgiven for thinking that acquiring salespeople talk in a foreign language, which can be bamboozling for those who are not in the industry and for many that are … But selling acquiring (directly or indirectly) to merchants is in fact quite simple.

 Professionals should remember:

There are three broad pricing models for selling acquiring to merchants:

- **Interchange++**: this pricing model means that a merchant will be able to see the MSC split between interchange, card scheme fees, and acquirer margin. This **is the most transparent pricing model**. This model is typically used by acquirers for larger merchants, although regulations in some geographies may force acquirers (and others) to use this pricing model for all merchants.
- **Interchange+**: this pricing model will enable a merchant to see the interchange, but both card scheme fees and acquirer margin will be amalgamated into a fixed percentage on top of the interchange fee. This model offers **less transparency than Interchange++**, but the merchant still sees the interchange. This model is also typically used for larger merchants.
- **Blended or Tiered**: in this pricing model, the transactional fees are represented by **just one rate** which has no contractual link to interchange. This is **the least transparent model** and will be typically used for small to medium-sized merchants. ISOs and PSPs may favour this model, although acquirers will generally try to use it for smaller merchants if applicable regulations don't prevent them from doing so.

Figure 2.29 positions the different pricing models.

Figure 2.29 should be looked at in conjunction with Figures 2.22 and 2.27 for transaction risk and type.

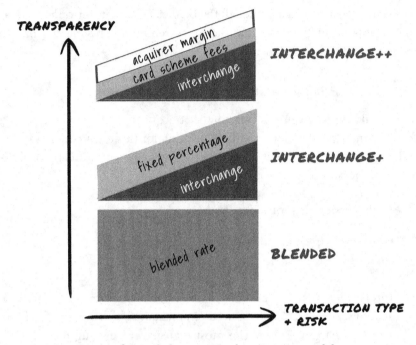

Figure 2.29 Transaction fees and charges: merchant pricing models.
Source: drawing by the author.

Interchange fee regulations

Europe: Interchange Fee Regulation (IFR)

The **Interchange Fee Regulation (IFR)**[82] has been in force since December 2015 for all EU member states. The IFR aims to benefit consumers, merchants, cardholders, acquirers, and issuers by promoting fairness, innovation, and competition across the block with no distinction between national and cross-border payments. This section will not cover the IFR in detail but will introduce the most important of its measures.

Interchange fee caps

• consumer debit transactions capped at 0.2% of transaction value; and
• consumer credit transactions capped at 0.3% of transaction value.

The caps are weighted annual averages across a merchant's total transactions.

Commercial transactions are out of scope for the IFR, although the interchange fee caps apply to individually settled business credit cards because the funds used to settle the card balance come from the individual cardholder and not the business. Also, Three Party Model cards are not in scope for the IFR, except when they are co-branded, and neither are international cards, but issuers are urged to act on a "best endeavour" basis.

TRANSPARENT PRICING

Practices such as the "blending" of fees (see Figure 2.29) are prohibited, and acquirers must clearly show their merchants the individual elements of merchant service charges, interchange fees, and card scheme fees for each category and brand of card. For merchants, surcharging cardholders is not allowed for the cards in scope, but they have a choice in the types of card products they accept. This means that a merchant accepting debit cards can't be forced to accept credit cards, and those accepting credit cards can't be forced to accept commercial cards (unless these cards are subject to the same regulated interchange fee).

REMOVING TERRITORIAL RESTRICTIONS

This effectively gives choice to merchants and cardholders in terms of issuing and acquiring across the EU block.

IFR IMPACT

In the years following the IFR coming into force, we can safely say that merchants didn't benefit much, and neither did cardholders, as the ecosystem has a way of economically balancing itself. This is also due to the fact that regulators were slow to enforce the regulation (although the caps were applied in each geography), especially regarding the transparency element. Some deadlines in the regulation were set at 2020 to allow ecosystem players a reasonably long runway for reporting requirements (for example, the caps are based on weighted averages calculated yearly), although enforcement actions started making the news in 2022.[83] At the time the IFR came into force, the UK was part of the EU block, and therefore subject to the regulation.

The IFR mandates transparent pricing for merchants, and there is confusion as to which pricing model should be applied. The European Commission issued a clarification on 9 June 2016,[84] stipulating that acquiring banks must specify individually the different fees they will charge (merchant service charges, interchange fees, scheme fees) for each category and brand of payment card. Therefore, the only applicable pricing model in the EU is Interchange++ (see Figure 2.29). This fact is either little known, or altogether ignored.

The UK and Brexit

Brexit happened in 2020, and prior to this the UK card payment ecosystem benefitted from the IFR's provisions. More specifically, UK merchants benefitted from the IFR cap on consumer credit and debit card fees for all UK–EU transactions. This changed after Brexit, but domestic transactions remained capped, as did Card Present cross-border transactions. However, the pandemic led to an increase in Card Not Present transactions, including cross-border, just as the UK became a "third country". This led to public outcry, and, notably, in November 2021 Amazon announced that they would stop accepting Visa credit cards on 19 January 2022 due to the high fees[85] (see Figure 2.27 for the differences between the fees for each type of card). The cynic in me says that Amazon had no intention of doing this, and I think all they wanted to do was negotiate a better deal with Visa and gain some kudos (they can, they have enough influence). In the meantime, some ecosystem players took advantage of this announcement to make pretty shrewd marketing moves: Curve in the UK announced an "Amazon Ban Hack"[86] two days before the deadline. Curve weren't doing anything other than what they usually do, which is issue a prepaid Mastercard for which a Visa card can be the funding mechanism. Neat. But as expected, on the same day as the Curve announcement Amazon made a media U-turn and scrapped its ban on Visa credit cards[87] in the UK and even reached a global agreement with Visa.[88] Funny that. Curve should have made their move in November 2021.

A few months later, the UK PSR instigated two market reviews of Visa's and Mastercard's fees,[89] and at the time of writing these reviews are in the consultation stage, and the PSR hasn't issued any timeline for completion.

In addition, the PSR published its final remedies on the card acquiring market,[90] which were aimed at benefitting small- to medium-sized businesses. The final remedies, which came into force in January 2023, include limiting POS terminal contract lock-in (contract duration cannot exceed 18 months and notice after renewal cannot come later than one month after the lock-in). The remedies also aim to address transparency by mandating clear summary boxes, online quotation tools, and trigger messages for directed entities; they came into effect in July 2023. The PSR didn't mandate the development of comparison tools, as it is hoping the industry will do that for itself, as happened with the insurance sector.

Interchange remains contentious, and in November 2022 the UK Competition Appeals Tribunal dismissed an appeal from Mastercard in a long-standing class action against them,[91] and a new class action against Visa and Mastercard was launched in February 2023.[92] Many more are on the horizon.[93]

Rest of the world

This section doesn't give a comprehensive overview of the interchange fee regulations worldwide (or lack thereof) but highlights the main differences for some markets. For those interested in more details, please refer to CM-SPI's "Global Review of Interchange Fee Regulations".[94]

US: the US has a weaker interchange regulation than the EU. In 2010, the US Congress passed the **Durbin Amendment** to the Dodd-Frank Act, instructing the Federal Reserve to establish a cap on interchange fees for debit cards only and exempting issuers with less than $10 billion in assets. In 2011, the Fed set the cap at $0.21 + 0.05% of transaction value.[95] As this regulation only applies to debit cards, and because high reward/premium cards are popular in the US, the effect has been an overall rise in interchange. In addition, Visa and Mastercard had planned an increase in interchange in 2019, which was delayed by the pandemic; they finally implemented this increase in April 2022 to public outcry.[96] In October 2023, The US Federal Reserve proposed lowering the caps on debit interchange fees.[97]

Brazil: Brazil is similar to the US, in as much as it doesn't cap interchange on credit cards, and the cap on debit transactions is set at 0.5% (weighted average) with a maximum of 0.8% for individual transactions.

Australia: the Reserve Bank of Australia set the cap at 0.5% on credit cards (with a maximum of 0.8% on individual transactions) and 0.08%

on debit cards (with a maximum of 0.2% on individual transactions). Co-branded cards are in scope.

China: legislation was passed in 2016 capping consumer debit and pre-paid cards at 0.35% and consumer credit at 0.45%, and this also includes commercial cards. In addition, China introduced a cap on card scheme fees of 0.065% and an exemption on "public welfare" (e.g. non-profit, schools, and medical institutions), where the interchange should be null.

Russia: interchange caps were not introduced and therefore will vary between 1.10% and 2.10% for consumer cards, depending on the card type, processing, and card scheme. For commercial cards, this is even worse, with rates somewhere between 1.45% and 2.15%.

Malaysia: the interchange cap on credit cards ranges from 1.0% to 1.1%, and debit interchange is set at a minimum of 0.21% and RM0.7 (£0.12) + 0.01% for global card brands. For domestic schemes (see Chapter 1, *Domestic card schemes*), the minimum on debit interchange is set at 0.15% and RM0.5 (£0.084) +0.01%.

Switzerland: the caps are similar to those introduced by the EU, with an interchange cap of 0.44% on credit cards and 0.31% on debit cards.

Europe side note: interchange is so controversial, that European initiatives were launched to build alternative cross-border payment schemes to rival those of Visa and Mastercard: P27 for the Nordics and the European Payment Initiative (EPI) across the EU block. Whilst P27 collapsed in April 2023, the EPI still has life in it (see Chapter 3, *Payment schemes in Europe*).

How do TPPs make money?

One more thing on interchange: there are major ecosystem players on the card rails that haven't been mentioned in this section, such as the Payment Initiation Service Providers (PISPs). These were introduced in Chapter 1 (*Overview and jargon buster*, see especially Figure 1.1). One may justifiably wonder how they make money; after all, there is no mention of them in the clearing and settlement processes (Chapter 1, *Authorisation, clearing, and settlement*) or acquiring contract types. When delivering my courses, I'm happy to say that attendees often give the right answer, in as much as it is understood that the existing clearing and settlement processes will not change to accommodate new entrants. Yet, those new entrants make money, albeit more in some markets than others. Businesses like Apple and Samsung have large customer bases, most of which are likely users of their payment facilities (i.e. Apple

Pay and Samsung Pay). To issuers, they can bring volumes and demographics to which they won't necessarily have access. Therefore, PISPs of this type are able to negotiate directly with issuers, and this is a win-win situation:

- **PISPs bring card volume** to issuers and get paid by the issuers for the volume they bring.
- **Issuers need card volume**, and depending on the geography and applicable interchange rule, they are able to fund what they give to PISPs through the interchange they collect.

You now understand how PISPs make money, however, what they get is totally dependent on the issuer and geography. It is also dependent on the size of the PISP, as smaller entities may not have the kind of influence that larger players have.

Decoupled debit

A concept emerged more than a decade ago by which non-bank issuers could issue debit cards that are not tied to a specific bank account: **Decoupled Debit**. Decoupled debit cards are usually associated with retailers (e.g. Target's REDcard™ Debit) and can only be used at that retailer (closed loop). Why is this interesting? Simply put, retailers (and other organisations) could issue debit cards with associated incentives, such as **Cashback**, which are not tied to a specific bank (i.e. the cardholder chooses the bank(s) to associate with the card). If the retailer manages to encourage their customers to use those cards for payment (e.g. loyalty, rewards), not only can they increase loyalty and spend, but they can also avoid interchange fees, because these cards use the bank rails (see Chapter 1, *Interbank settlement*), not the card rails. This could mean substantial savings for the merchant. As a fundamental principle, the ASPSP (on any payment rail) is the only entity that authorises transactions, because they manage the account and hold the funds (see Chapter 1, *Authorisation, clearing, and settlement*). Therefore, with decoupled debit, the underlying bank will still be the entity that authorises the transaction, but that would be done on the bank rails (see Figure 2.30 and Chapter 3, Figure 3.4).

From figure 2.30, we can see that acquirer and card scheme are not involved and that the merchant is also the issuer of the card. If you look at the Target REDcard™ Debit, you will see that it hasn't got a card scheme logo

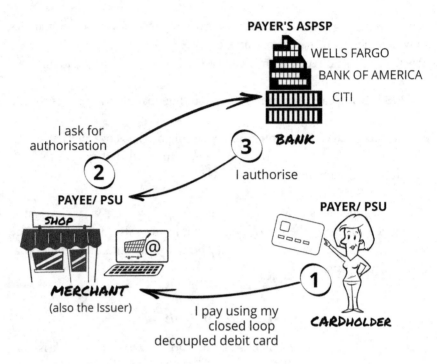

Figure 2.30 Closed loop decoupled debit.

Source: drawing by the author.

on it. The back-end processes take place on the bank rails, thus avoiding interchange, and the merchant relies on their own banking relationships to settle payments. This is an early form of **Account-to-Account (A2A) Payment**, where the exchange of value is from the cardholder's bank account to the merchant's bank account (see Chapter 3, *Account-to-Account payments*).

The newer form of decoupled debit that runs on the card rails is the open loop **CBPII**, as introduced in Chapter 1, and these cards run on card scheme networks (unlike closed loop decoupled debit cards) and will therefore attract debit interchange for merchants.

Fintech and interchange

Another mystery we can elucidate is the reason behind the popularity of **airline cards** in the US and the lack thereof in Europe (see Chapter 1, *Ecosystem actors and models*). The benefits (i.e. air miles) offered to cardholders for these cards are funded by the issuers through the interchange they collect.

Therefore, the higher the interchange, the more the issuer is able to fund benefits to entice cardholders. As interchange is so much lower in Europe, and the benefits so much lower, it's no wonder that either issuers are shying away from issuing these products or that cardholders are not interested in them.

The same principle applies to credit cards that offer cardholders a percentage cashback on spend: the cashback is also largely funded by interchange. In the US, the cashback rate typically ranges from 1.5% to 6.0% (!) on allowed spending categories (some issuers even offer welcome bonuses). In the UK, this drops down to between 0.25% and 1.25% (although some issuers may offer a higher rate for a limited introductory period). Of course, established issuers understand the economics of interchange and are adept at making it work for them (e.g. membership fees can be flexed, cashback caps can be applied, etc.).

Card issuing is a part of the market that is also evolving with the times, and many new issuers have made a few mistakes by not understanding the dynamics of interchange. An example was the Crypto.com debit card, which, on launch, offered very high rewards, making their crypto cards (Visa co-branded) very popular. They were forced by economics to drastically lower cardholder benefits in June 2022 to community outcry,[98] and at the time of writing, they have significantly dropped in the popularity stakes. Some crypto debit cards offer significant rewards in their own tokens, but they are not immune to the mechanics of interchange (see *Merchant Category Code*). All of this is, of course, subject to abuse, and to add insult to injury think of the scenario when a cardholder makes a BNPL purchase (e.g. payment split into three monthly transactions) using a crypto reward card. Is the cashback reward applied on the first instalment? On the last instalment? What if the cardholder cancels their purchase and has already spent their reward on crypto? If, as an issuer, you're not clear on the transaction and cashback processes and the interchange dynamics, you could be in a lot of trouble.[99]

Scheme membership (the "in" crowd)

Wanna play on the card rails? You need permissions from the operators and rule-setters: the cards schemes, who allow any eligible financial institution to become a member.

Table 2.2 Card scheme memberships.

Membership type	Issuing	Acquiring	Disburse cash	Settlement	Sponsor others	Direct BIN licencing	Ongoing fees payment	Reporting	Rules compliance
Principal	✓	✓	✓	✓	✓	✓	✓	✓	✓
Affiliate	✓	✓	✓	✗	✗	✓	✗	✗	✓

There are two types of **Scheme Membership**:

- **Principal members**: these members are allowed to settle with the scheme (see Chapter 1, *Interbank settlement*).
- **Affiliate members**: these members are sponsored and supervised by principal members, who are in turn responsible for the settlement and other activities of their sponsored affiliates.

For principal members, this is similar to operating an agency business, where the affiliate is essentially an "agent" of the principal. This is summarised in Table 2.2.

The most obvious thing in Table 2.2 is that all members have to comply with the rules. Visa[100] and Mastercard[101] publish their membership application processes at a high level.

As card-scheme operating rules never supersede applicable regulations, card schemes require that principal members have the appropriate regulatory credentials, which should be obtained from the competent authorities prior to applying for membership. In the EU and the UK, this would be an authorised **Payment Institution (PI)** licence, or an authorised **eMoney Institution (EMI)** licence (see Chapter 5, *Licences to operate a payment business*).

Principal members will be responsible for settlement and reporting to the card schemes, including reporting on behalf of their affiliates. Of course, affiliate members still have to pay their fees and have reporting obligations, but they are accountable to their principal and they have their own regulatory obligations and must comply with the card scheme rules.

Card payment economics – conclusion (what's next?)

In this whistle-stop of Card Payment economics we covered:

- Costs and value chain;
- Merchant models and contract types;
- Card payment channels;
- Charges and fees; and
- Scheme membership.

I have tried to explain the jargon and debunk a few myths, and you'll find the key terms in the glossary (Chapter 7) for future reference. I have given you my opinion on some aspects of the economics of the card payment ecosystem, but feel free to disagree: I always welcome a good debate!

If you read this book a few years from now, new business models will have emerged, and regulatory pressure will likely have increased. More overlay services will have been developed on card infrastructures, and card infrastructures will have established more links with other ecosystems, making the relevant economic principles even more confusing. Ecosystem actors may benefit from some advancements, and not from others. Cardholders might turn to methods of payment other than cards, although this might remain transparent to them. Card schemes, acquirers, and issuers will try to get their fingers in other pies. This has already happened, such as with the Vocalink acquisition by Mastercard and the Tink acquisition by Visa (after their failed bid for Plaid). One thing is certain: the future won't be boring.

To complete our understanding of payments, we must examine the options we have beyond card payments.

Notes

1 "Year-end financial highlights", Annual Report, Visa website. Available at: https://annualreport.visa.com/financials/default.aspx (Accessed 22 August 2023).

2 "Number of purchase transactions on payment cards worldwide in 2023, by brand", Statista, 11 August 2023. Available at: https://www.statista.com/statistics/1080669/credit-card-transactions-worldwide-by-brand-forecast/ (Accessed 22 August 2023).

3 "Who we regulate", Payment Systems Regulator website. Available at: https://www.psr.org.uk/payment-systems/who-we-regulate/ (Accessed 26 August 2023).

4 "Millions warned of issues with Mastercard payments", The Telegraph, 12 June 2023. Available at: https://www.telegraph.co.uk/business/2023/06/12/ftse-100-markets-news-ubs-credit-suisse-takeover/ (Accessed 15 June 2023).

5 "Payment Platform Vendor Comparison Report, 2024 Edition", PayX, 2024. Available at: https://payxintl.com/shop (Accessed 26 August 2023).

6 "Board of Directors", Visa website. Available at: https://investor.visa.com/corporate-governance/board-of-directors/default.aspx (Accessed 22 August 2023).

7   "Board of Directors", Mastercard website. Available at: https://investor.
    mastercard.com/corporate-governance/board-of-directors/default.
    aspx (Accessed 22 August 2023).

8   "Search Service Providers", Visa Inc., 2023. Available at: https://www.
    visa.com/splisting/searchGrsp.do (Accessed 16 June 2023).

9   "ISO 18245:2023. Retail financial services – Merchant category codes",
    ISO, 2023. Available at: https://www.iso.org/standard/79450.html
    (Accessed 17 June 2023).

10 "Merchant Data Standards Manual", Visa Inc. April 2023. Available
    at: https://usa.visa.com/content/dam/VCOM/download/merchants/
    visa-merchant-data-standards-manual.pdf (Accessed 17 June 2023).

11 "Quick Reference Booklet – Merchant Edition", Mastercard, 15 November
    2018. Available at: https://www.mastercard.us/content/dam/mccom/
    en-us/documents/rules/quick-reference-booklet-merchant-edition.pdf
    (Accessed 17 June 2023).

12 "Ingenico to enable the rollout of Alipay+ to millions of merchants and
    thousands of banks and acquirers with PPaaS, its cloud-based Payments
    Platform as a Service", Cision PR Newswire, 18 May 2022. Available at:
    https://www.prnewswire.com/in/news-releases/ingenico-to-enable-
    the-rollout-of-alipay-to-millions-of-merchants-and-thousands-of-banks-
    and-acquirers-with-ppaas-its-cloud-based-payments-platform-as-a-
    service-817882662.html (Accessed 17 June 2023).

13 "Ingenico acquires Phos, extending its offer for Merchant Payment Accep-
    tance via Smartphone", Ingenico, 28 March 2023. Available at: https://
    ingenico.com/en/newsroom/press-releases/ingenico-acquires-phos-
    extending-its-offer-merchant-payment-acceptance (Accessed 17 June
    2023).

14 "Zettle ditches the dongle", Finextra, 13 May 2022. Available at: https://
    www.finextra.com/newsarticle/40241/zettle-by-paypal-ditches-the-
    dongle (Accessed 17 June 2023).

15 "Dynamic Currency Conversion: Always choose local currency", One
    Mile at a Time, 3 May 2023. Available at: https://onemileatatime.com/
    guides/dynamic-currency-conversion/ (Accessed 22 June 2023).

16 "Dynamic Currency Conversion – Compliance Guide", Mastercard Inc.,
    2016. Available at: https://www.mastercard.com/elearning/dcc/docs/
    DCC%20Guide%2020.02.17%20EN.pdf (Accessed 22 June 2023).

17 YouLend website. Available at: https://youlend.com/ (Accessed 22 June
    2023).

18 365 Business Finance website. Available at: https://www.365business-
    finance.co.uk/ (Accessed 22 June 2023).

19   Nucleus Commercial Finance website. Available at: https://nucleuscommercialfinance.com/ (Accessed 22 June 2023).

20   Liberis website. Available at: https://www.liberis.com/ (Accessed 22 June 2023).

21   Team Factors website. Available at: https://www.teamfactors.co.uk/ (Accessed 23 June 2023).

22   Market Invoice website. Available at: https://invoice-funding.co.uk/marketinvoice/ (Accessed 23 June 2023).

23   Bibby Financial Services website. Available at: https://www.bibby-financialservices.com/ (Accessed 23 June 2023).

24   Philip Shelper *Loyalty Programs: The Complete Guide*, Loyalty & Reward Co Pty Ltd, Sydney, 2021.

25   Starbucks Rewards website. Available at: https://www.starbucks.co.uk/rewards (Accessed 23 June 2023).

26   Barnes & Noble B&N Rewards website. Available at: https://www.barnesandnoble.com/membership/ (Accessed 23 June 2023).

27   "LoyalZoo partners with Elavon to deliver loyalty systems to SMB retailers using Poynt Smart POS", LoyalZoo, 1 August 2020. Available at: https://www.loyalzoo.com/elavon-poynt/ (Accessed 23 June 2023).

28   Gloria Methri "Visa and Enfuce launch prepaid cards for Ukrainian refugees in France", IBS Intelligence, 5 January 2023. Available at: https://ibsintelligence.com/ibsi-news/visa-and-enfuce-launch-prepaid-cards-for-ukrainian-refugees-in-france/ (Accessed 18 June 2023).

29   EML website. Available at: https://www.emlpayments.com/payment-solutions/ (Accessed 18 June 2023).

30   Edenred Payment Solutions website. Available at: https://eps.edenred.com/ (Accessed 18 June 2023).

31   Enfuce website. Available at: https://enfuce.com/ (Accessed 18 June 2023).

32   "Adyen and Shopify partner to power new payment capabilities for enterprise merchants", Adyen, 21 June 2023. Available at: https://www.adyen.com/press-and-media/adyen-and-shopify-partner-to-power-new-payment-capabilities-for-enterprise-merchants (Accessed 21 June 2023).

33   "Are you a platform or a marketplace?" Fin, Published by Plaid, 28 February 2019. Available at: https://fin.plaid.com/articles/are-you-a-platform-or-a-marketplace/ (Accessed 25 June 2013).

34   "Monzo add virtual card for contactless payments to Flex BNPL product", Finextra, 26 November 2021. Available at: https://www.finextra.com/newsarticle/39295/monzo-adds-virtual-card-for-contactless-payments-to-flex-bnpl-product (Accessed 19 June 2023).

35 "7-Eleven stores in Japan trial holographic payment terminal", Finextra, 16 March 2022. Available at: https://www.finextra.com/ newsarticle/39870/7-eleven-stores-in-japan-trial-holographic-payment-terminal (Accessed 19 June 2023).

36 "Amazon has rolled out contactless tech to 200 locations including Panera cafes", Reuters, 22 March 2023. Available at: https://www. reuters.com/technology/amazon-has-rolled-out-contactless-tech-200-locations-including-panera-cafes-2023-03-22/ (Accessed 19 June 2023).

37 "Amazon Go and Amazon Fresh: How the 'Just walk out' tech works" Pocket-Lint, 16 May 2023. Available at: https://www.pocket-lint.com/ what-is-amazon-go-where-is-it-and-how-does-it-work/ (Accessed 19 June 2023).

38 "Fingerprint authentication moves from phones to payment cards", Visa, 7 May 2023. Available at: https://usa.visa.com/visa-everywhere/ security/biometric-payment-card.html (Accessed 19 June 2023).

39 "Mastercard biometric card, Driving cardholder security and convenience", Mastercard Inc. 2023. Available at: https://www.mastercard.us/ en-us/business/overview/safety-and-security/authentication-services/ biometrics/biometrics-card.html (Accessed 19 June 2023).

40 "Dubai welcomes biometric face verification for payments into 'hypermarkets'", Fintech Times, 13 February 2023. Available at: https:// thefintechtimes.com/dubai-welcomes-biometric-face-verification-platform-into-hypermarkets/ (Accessed 19 June 2023).

41 "Amazon rolls out palm payment tech to 500+ Whole Food Market stores", Finextra, 24 July 2023. Available at: https://www. finextra.com/newsarticle/42674/amazon-rolls-out-palm-payment-tech-to-500-whole-food-market-stores (Accessed 24 July 2023).

42 "Aldi Shop & Go Privacy Policy", Aldi Shop & Go, 2023. Available at: https://www.aldi.co.uk/shopandgo-privacy (Accessed 19 June 2023).

43 "Morrisons introduces new measures aimed at helping vulnerable and elderly during crisis", Morrisons, 14 April 2020. Available at: https://www.morrisons-corporate.com/media-centre/corporate-news/ morrisons-introduces-new-measures-aimed-at-helping-vulnerable-and-elderly-during-crisis/ (Accessed 20 June 2023)

44 "Morrisons doorstep delivery-telephone ordering", NHS Live Well Cheshire & West, 11 May 2023. Available at: https://www.livewell. cheshirewestandchester.gov.uk/Services/4040/Morrisons-Doorstep-D (Accessed 20 June 2023).

45 "Paying bills and invoices", Milton Keynes City Council, 2023. Available at: https://www.milton-keynes.gov.uk/pay-report-and-apply/payments-council (Accessed 20 June 2023).

46   "How to pay your energy bill", SSE Energy Services website. Available at: https://sse.co.uk/help/bills-and-paying/how-to-pay-your-energy-bill (Accessed 20 June 2023).

47   "Ways to pay my bill", Welsh Water website, 2023. Available at: https://www.dwrcymru.com/en/my-account/paying-your-bill (Accessed 20 June 2023).

48   "Ways to pay your mobile phone bill", EE website, 2023. Available at: https://ee.co.uk/help/help-new/billing-usage-and-top-up/paying-my-bill/how-do-i-pay-my-phone-bill (Accessed 20 June 2023).

49   "How can I pay my BT bill?", BT Broadband website, 2023. Available at: https://www.bt.com/help/account-and-billing/payments—bills-and-charges/how-do-i-pay-my-bill-/how-can-i-pay-my-bt-bill- (Accessed 20 June 2023).

50   "Stopping a future payment on your debit or credit card", Citizens Advice, 20 February 2020. Available at: https://www.citizensadvice.org.uk/debt-and-money/banking/stopping-a-future-payment-on-your-debit-or-credit-card/ (Accessed 21 June 2023).

51   "How can I cancel a recurring card payment?", Barclays website. Available at: https://www.barclays.co.uk/help/payments/payment-information/recurring-card-payments/cancel/ (Accessed 21 June 2023).

52   "How to cancel a recurring card payment", Nationwide Building Society website. Available at: https://www.nationwide.co.uk/help/payments/regular-payments/recurring-card-payment-cancel/ (Accessed 21 June 2023).

53   "Recurring card payments. How to cancel & reclaim cash", MoneySavingExpert, 21 March 2023. Available at: https://www.moneysavingexpert.com/banking/recurring-payments/ (Accessed 21 June 2023).

54   "Online Payment Fraud: Market Forecasts, Emerging Threats & Segment Analysis 2023–2028", Juniper Research, 26 June 2023. Available at: https://www.juniperresearch.com/researchstore/fintech-payments/online-payment-fraud-research-report (Accessed 23 June 2023).

55   "Unique Identification", Authority of India website. Available at: https://www.uidai.gov.in/en/16-english-uk/aapka-aadhaar/14-what-is-aadhaar.html (Accessed 23 June 2023).

56   "Aadhaar authentication rose to 2.31 billion in March 2023: IT Ministry data", The Statesman, 27 April 2023. Available at: https://www.thestatesman.com/technology/aadhaar-authentication-rose-to-2-31-billion-in-march-2023-it-ministry-data-1503176008.html (Accessed 23 June 2023).

57 "Finnish Mobile ID – A Lesson in Interoperability", GSMA, February 2013. Available at: https://www.gsma.com/identity/wp-content/uploads/2013/03/GSMA_Mobile-Identity_Finnish_Case_Study.pdf (Accessed 24 June 2023).

58 "Sweden's BankID launching new digital ID card", Biometric Update.com, 24 April 2023. Available at: https://www.biometricupdate.com/202304/swedens-bankid-launching-new-digital-id-card (Accessed 24 June 2023).

59 "APP fraud costing banks and their customers dearly", Retail Banker International, 29 March 2022. Available at: https://www.retailbankerinternational.com/comment/app-fraud-expert-comment-martin-wilson/ (Accessed 24 June 2023).

60 "Electronic ID in the Nordics – A model for other countries?" Computer Weekly, 14 May 2019. Available at: https://www.computerweekly.com/news/252463291/Electronic-ID-in-the-Nordics-a-model-for-other-countries (Accessed 24 June 2023).

61 "Early Warning announces Authentify®, a new identity verification service", Cision PR Newswire, 4 April 2022. Available at: https://www.prnewswire.com/news-releases/early-warning-announces-authentify-a-new-identity-verification-service-301517075.html (Accessed 23 June 2023).

62 "Authentify reviews", Gartner Peer Insights, 2023. Available at: https://www.gartner.com/reviews/market/user-authentication/vendor/early-warning/product/authentify (Accessed 23 June 2023).

63 "Stripe launches Stripe Identity, an identity verification tool to increase trust online", Stripe, 14 July 2021. Available at: https://stripe.com/gb/newsroom/news/stripe-launches-identity (Accessed 23 June 2023).

64 "China pilots NFC devices that combine digital currency payments with student IDs", NFC World, 30 May 2022. Available at: https://www.nfcw.com/2022/05/30/377308/china-pilots-nfc-devices-that-combine-digital-currency-payments-with-student-ids/ (Accessed 23 June 2023).

65 "Google launches multipurpose digital wallet with support for digital IDs, tickets and payment cards", NFC World, 12 May 2022. Available at: https://www.nfcw.com/2022/05/12/377096/google-launches-multipurpose-digital-wallet-with-support-for-digital-ids-tickets-and-payment-cards/ (Accessed 23 June 2023).

66 "Google begins rolling out its new multifunction mobile wallet to 39 countries", NFC World, 20 July 2022. Available at: https://www.nfcw.com/2022/07/20/378135/google-rolling-out-new-multifunction-mobile-wallet-to-39-countries/ (Accessed 23 June 2023).

67 "Lloyds invests GBP 10 mln in Yoti's digital ID solution", The Paypers, 13 March 2023. Available at: https://thepaypers.com/digital-identity-security-online-fraud/lloyds-invests-gbp-10-mln-in-yotis-digital-id-solution--1261754 (Accessed 23 June 2023).

68 "Mastercard certified as digital ID provider in the UK", Finextra, 16 March 2023. Available at: https://www.finextra.com/newsarticle/41981/mastercard-certified-as-digital-id-provider-in-the-uk (Accessed 23 June 2023).

69 "MEPs back plans for an EU-wide digital wallet", European Parliament, 9 February 2022. Available at: https://www.europarl.europa.eu/news/en/press-room/20230206IPR72110/meps-back-plans-for-an-eu-wide-digital-wallet (Accessed 23 June 2023).

70 "Technical guidelines for EU digital ID wallet expected in 2 weeks", Identity Week, 19 June 2023. Available at: https://identityweek.net/technical-guidelines-for-eu-digital-id-wallet-expected-in-2-weeks/ (Accessed 23 June 2023).

71 "European Credit Sector Associations call for removing payments from the scope of the Digital Identity Regulation", European Banking Federation, 11 April 2023. Available at: https://www.ebf.eu/ebf-media-centre/european-credit-sector-associations-call-for-removing-payments-from-the-scope-of-the-digital-identity-regulation/ (Accessed 24 June 2023).

72 "Enabling the use of digital identities in the UK", Gov.UK, 22 March 2023. Available at: https://www.gov.uk/guidance/digital-identity (Accessed 24 June 2023).

73 "UK government officially shuts down beleaguered Verify ID service", Global Government Forum, 8 May 2023. Available at: https://www.globalgovernmentforum.com/uk-government-officially-shuts-down-beleaguered-verify-id-service/ (Accessed 24 June 2023).

74 "NHS App hits over 30 million sign-ups", Gov.UK, 31 December 2022. Available at: https://www.gov.uk/government/news/nhs-app-hits-over-30-million-sign-ups (Accessed 24 June 2023).

75 "Eight countries jointly propose principles for mutual recognition of digital IDs", ZDNet, 17 February 2022. Available at: https://www.zdnet.com/article/eight-countries-jointly-propose-digital-id-principles-for-mutual-recognition-and-interoperability/ (Accessed 24 June 2023).

76 "Tony Blair and William Hague call for digital identity cards", Finextra, 24 February 2023. Available at: https://www.finextra.com/newsarticle/41858/tony-blair-and-william-hague-call-for-digital-identity-cards (Accessed 24 June 2023).

77 "Understanding interchange (Europe)", Mastercard website. Available at: https://www.mastercard.com/europe/en/regulatory/european-interchange.html (Accessed 24 June 2023).

78 "Market review into card scheme and processing fees", UK Payment Systems Regulator website, 23 February 2023. Available at: https://www.psr.org.uk/our-work/market-reviews/market-review-into-card-scheme-and-processing-fees/ (Accessed 24 June 2023).

79 "Visa Canada Standard Acquiring Network Assessment Fees", Visa Canada, February 2017. Available at: https://www.visa.ca/content/dam/VCOM/regional/na/canada/Support/Documents/visa-canada-standard-acquiring-network-assessment-fees-feb2017.pdf (Accessed 22 August 2023).

80 "Mastercard interchange rates and fees", Mastercard Canada website. Available at: https://www.mastercard.ca/en-ca/business/overview/interchange/merchant-interchange-rates.html (Accessed 22 August 2023).

81 "Implementation advice for summary boxes, online quotation tools and trigger messages Version 1", Payment Systems Regulator, October 2022. Available at: https://www.psr.org.uk/media/5xvboekx/implementation-advice-summary-box-oqt-trigger-oct-2022-v3-final.pdf (Accessed 1 August 2023).

82 "Regulation (EU) 2015/751 of the European Parliament and of the Council of 29 April 2015 on interchange fees for card-based payment transactions", Official Journal of the European Union, 19 May 2015. Available at: https://eur-lex.europa.eu/legal-content/EN/TXT/HTML/?uri=CELEX%3A32015R0751 (Accessed 25 June 2023).

83 "Barclays slapped with £8.4 million interchange fee fine", Finextra, 2 December 2022. Available at: https://www.finextra.com/newsarticle/41418/barclays-slapped-with-84-million-interchange-fee-fine (Accessed 25 June 2023).

84 "Antitrust: Regulation on interchange fees", European Commission, 9 June 2026. Available at: https://ec.europa.eu/commission/presscorner/detail/fr/MEMO_16_2162 (Accessed 25 June 2023).

85 "Amazon to stop accepting Visa credit cards in UK", BBC News, 21 November 2021. Available at: https://www.bbc.co.uk/news/business-59306200 (Accessed 25 June 2023).

86 "Curve promises Amazon Visa ban hack", Finextra, 17 January 2022. Available at: https://www.finextra.com/newsarticle/39522/curve-promises-amazon-visa-ban-hack (Accessed 25 June 2023).

87 "Amazon U-turn as it scraps ban on Visa credit card just two days before new rules were due to kick in", The Sun, 17 January 2022. Available at:

https://www.thesun.co.uk/money/17346650/amazon-shoppers-scraps-visa-credit-card-ban/ (Accessed 25 June 2023).

88 "Amazon reaches deal to continue accepting Visa payments world-wide", TechCrunch, 17 February 2022. Available at: https://techcrunch.com/2022/02/17/amazon-reaches-deal-to-continue-accepting-visa-payments-worldwide/ (Accessed 25 June 2023).

89 "Market review into card scheme and processing fees", UK Payment Systems Regulator, 21 June 2022, updated 23 February 2023. Available at: https://www.psr.org.uk/our-work/market-reviews/market-review-into-card-scheme-and-processing-fees/ (Accessed 25 June 2023).

90 "PS22/2: Card-acquiring market remedies: Final decision", Payment Systems Regulator, October 2022. Available at: https://www.psr.org.uk/publications/policy-statements/ps22-2-card-acquiring-market-remedies-final-decision/ (Accessed 25 June 2023).

91 "Court dismisses Mastercard appeal against £14 billion class action lawsuit", Finextra, 29 November 2022. Available at: https://www.finextra.com/newsarticle/41406/court-dismisses-mastercard-appeal-against-14-billion-class-action-lawsuit (Accessed 25 June 2023).

92 "Mastercard and Visa to face another card interchange class action suit", Finextra, 22 February 2023. Available at: https://www.finextra.com/newsarticle/41840/mastercard-and-visa-to-face-another-card-interchange-class-action-suit (Accessed 25 June 2023).

93 "Visa, MasterCard fight off new UK mass actions over fees for now", Reuters, 9 June 2023. Available at: https://www.reuters.com/technology/visa-mastercard-fight-off-new-uk-mass-actions-over-fees-now-2023-06-08/ (Accessed 25 June 2023).

94 "Global Review of Interchange Fee Regulations", CMSPI, November 2020. Available at: https://cmspi.com/nam/en/resources/content/cmspi-global-interchange-report-available-now/ (Accessed 1 August 2023).

95 "Federal Reserve issues a final rule establishing standards for debit card interchange fees and prohibiting network exclusivity arrangements and routing restrictions", Federal Reserve, 29 June 2011. Available at: https://www.federalreserve.gov/newsevents/pressreleases/bcreg20110629a.htm (Accessed 25 June 2023).

96 "Retailers call out Visa and Mastercard for fee hikes that could make inflation worse", CNN Business, 18 May 2022. Available at: https://edition.cnn.com/2022/05/18/economy/credit-card-swipe-fees-inflation/index.html (Accessed 25 June 2023).

97 "Fed proposes rule to slash interchange fee cap", American Banker, 25 October 2023. Available at: https://www.americanbanker.com/news/ fed-proposes-rule-to-slash-interchange-fee-cap (Accessed 16 November 2023).

98 "Crypto.com is significantly lowering the rewards of its popular debit cards", ZDNet, 4 May 2022. Available at: https://www.zdnet.com/ finance/credit-cards/crypto-com-is-significantly-lowering-the-rewards-of-its-popular-debit-cards/ (Accessed 26 June 2023).

99 "Adding crypto to payment cards is playing with fire", New Money Review, 9 January 2023. Available at: https://newmoneyreview.com/ index.php/2023/01/09/adding-crypto-to-payment-cards-is-playing-with-fire/ (Accessed 26 June 2023).

100 "Licensing Program", Visa website. Available at: https://partner.visa. com/site/programs/licensing-program.html (Accessed 25 June 2023).

101 "Who can receive an issuing and/or acquiring license from Mastercard?", Mastercard website. Available at: https://www.mastercard. com/fintechexpressEU/en/fintech-express/access.html (Accessed 25 June 2023).

3

BANK PAYMENTS SYSTEMS

Bank payments – overview and jargon buster (all the way to the bank)

Good news! We've busted most of the jargon in Chapter 1, *Overview and jargon buster*, and we'll therefore continue to use the same terminology here and follow the same structure.

What are bank payments?

At a high level, bank payments are similar to card payments, in as much as they enable users to pay and get paid, BUT …

- they use **different technology infrastructures**;
- they have **different rules and regulations**;

DOI: 10.4324/9781032631394-4

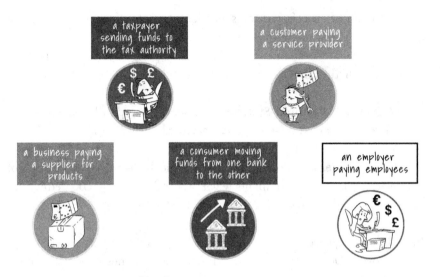

Figure 3.1 Common uses of bank payments.

Source: drawing by the author.

- they operate **different processes** (e.g. authorisation, clearing, and settlement); and
- they are **subject to different oversight**.

Common uses of bank payments are shown in Figure 3.1.

Bank payment systems

Similarly to the way card networks operate, bank payment systems will provide the clearing and settlement infrastructure for bank payments.

> Payment ecosystems are often referred to as "rails", hence the bank payment ecosystems are also known as **Bank Rails**.

Today, there are many payment schemes for bank payments: RTP and FedNow (US), SIBS (Portugal), BEPS (China), BECS (Australia), BACS and Faster Payments System (UK), STET (EU), SIC (Switzerland), Pix (Brazil), etc. These are often referred to as "settlement infrastructures" and are of national (or federal) systemic importance.

Generally, bank settlement infrastructures (rails) can be classified according to whether they operate in real time or not:

- **Large-Value Payment Systems** (**LVPS**): these typically handle large-value payments and time-critical payments (e.g. CHAPS in the UK or Fedwire in the US).
- **Retail Payment Systems** (**RPS**): these typically handle high volumes of relatively low-value payments (e.g. BACS and FPS in the UK, FedACH in the US, Pix in Brazil).

In addition, payment systems which only operate in one geography are referred to as **Domestic** or **Local**, whilst other schemes may allow international payments.

Bank ecosystem actors

Main bank ecosystem actors

As far as the bank payment ecosystem actors are concerned, they follow a similar classification to the card rails:

- The actor which provides the centralised payments infrastructure and operating rules is the **Payment Scheme**. This entity operates according to a set of rules that ecosystem participants must follow and manages the required technical infrastructure, which may be provided by a third party. Payment schemes can be domestic (i.e. used within a geography) or cross-border (i.e. allow international payments). In addition, some payment schemes will be used for high-value payments whilst others will concentrate on retail payments.
- The actor which uses payment services: on the bank rails, the **Payment Service User** (**PSU**) is **a bank account holder**, and therefore it can be a person, a business, or another organisation holding a bank account and making (**Payer**) or receiving (**Payee**) payments.
- The actor which manages the payer's and payee's bank account: here, the **Account Servicing PSP** (**ASPSP**) is a bank. Similarly to the card rails, the ASPSP's role is to manage the payer's account (i.e. the bank account) throughout its lifecycle, but unlike the card rails, this is not a

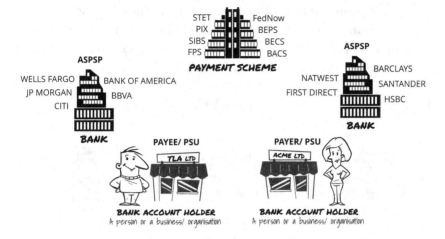

Figure 3.2 Bank payment ecosystem actors.

Source: drawing by the author.

two-sided model and a bank (not necessarily the same bank) will also manage the payee's account. The ASPSP (bank) is the **Payer's PSP** (for the sending account) or the **Payee's PSP** (for the receiving account).

Already, we can see that the structure is simpler than for card payments, and the main stakeholders are shown in Figure 3.2.

New bank ecosystem actors

Payment ecosystems evolve fast, and similarly to the card world, well-established bank infrastructures have also seen their fair share of new entrants. Just as we introduced TPPs in Chapter 1 for the card rails, so too we will introduce different entities who **provide payment services to payers and payees** (i.e. bank account holders) for bank payments.

PISP AND AISP

- A **Payment Initiation Service Provider** (**PISP**). For bank payments, this could be a technology provider that supplies bank account holders (payers) with the means to make a payment through their bank account (e.g. Cash App, Venmo when funded by a bank account, Zelle, iDEAL, SOFORT).
- An **Account Information Service Provider** (**AISP**). For bank payments, these providers would enable bank account holders to use their

bank account data for several purposes (e.g. check balance, last payment, transaction history, prepare their tax return, or calculate a credit score). Players in this space include Xero, QuickBooks, and Credit Kudos (acquired by Apple in May 2023).

Let's complete our visual summary, which Figure 3.3 provides.

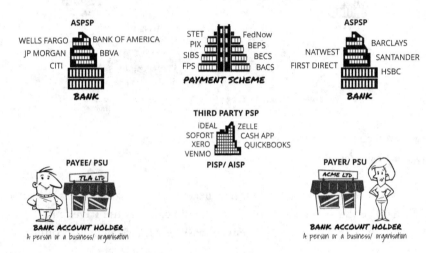

Figure 3.3 Bank payment ecosystem actors including TPPs.
Source: drawing by the author.

BOX 3.1 WHAT ARE PEER-TO-PEER (P2P) PAYMENTS?

Digital apps such as Venmo and Zelle are popular with younger demographics but became even more popular with broader demographics during the pandemic. Because they enable convenient payments between payers and payees, they are often referred to as **Peer-to-Peer Payment (P2P)** services. This is because to the users it looks like you're making a payment directly to your friend (or supplier, etc.) without intermediaries. This is not the case. Regardless of the rails used (i.e. card or bank), these payments still need to go through the existing mechanisms covered in Chapters 1 and 2 (i.e. authorisation, clearing, and settlement), and therefore through intermediaries which provide the settlement infrastructure. From a payer's point of view, it looks like "peer-to-peer", but underneath the ducks still paddle ... For true "peer-to-peer", you must look at decentralised rails, which will be covered here in Chapter 4 (*A crash course on DLT and blockchain*) and more extensively in my second book, *Beyond Payments*.

CLOSED LOOP CBPII

We introduced the Open Loop Card-Based Payment Instrument Issuer (CB-PII) in Chapter 1 (Figure 1.8), which runs on the card rails and would therefore attract debit interchange, and we also looked at closed loop retailer-issued cards, which enable retailers to avoid interchange altogether. Finally, we looked at decoupled debit in Chapter 2 (*Decoupled debit* and Figure 2.30). The **Closed Loop CBPII** is another variation where the only difference is that the merchant is not the issuer (the CBPII is) and the authorisation process is the same as for closed loop retailer cards (doesn't involve card schemes), thus avoiding interchange. Some may argue that the closed loop CBPII shouldn't appear in this chapter on bank payments, but where else would you put it, as there's no card scheme involved? You could also argue that the closed loop decoupled debit card (retailer card) shouldn't appear in Chapter 1, which is all about card rails, but how would you explain the differences related to interchange? You see my dilemma. In any instance, you should now understand the mechanics and decide for yourself.

Figure 3.4 shows how closed loop CBPII works.

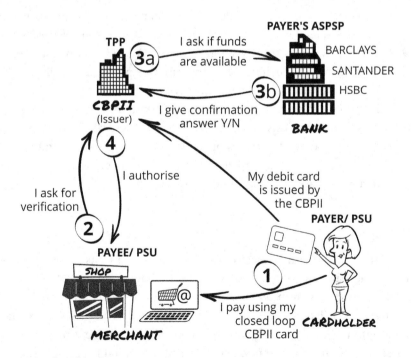

Figure 3.4 Closed loop CBPII.

Source: drawing by the author.

In this instance, Suzie's debit card can be linked to several of her bank accounts, and she can choose which bank account to use for the payment transaction.

Payment messaging

Payment systems will exchange data between the various stakeholders; as with any ecosystem, conventions must be applied so all ecosystem actors talk the same "language".

ISO 8583

ISO 8583 is a messaging standard that was originally developed for card payments. The official name of this standard is "Financial Transaction Card-Originated Messages – Interchange Message Specifications", and you already understand the mechanics for card ecosystems. In Chapter 1, *What's in a card?*, we explained that the message contains either 63 (Track 2 and chip) or 127 characters (Track 1). ISO 8583 is an old standard and uses a bitmap format where each data element is assigned a specific position and is processed sequentially (i.e. as it is being read). It has been used since 1987 and is now on its third version (2003). ISO 8583 is now considered a legacy standard, although card schemes use this protocol and there is no evidence that they are planning to move away from it.

Although ISO 8583 was developed for card systems, most mature bank payment schemes use this standard as well (e.g. UK FPS). But unlike card schemes, bank payment schemes globally either have plans to migrate to the newer ISO 20022 standard (e.g. UK New Payments Architecture) or have already migrated (see Figures 3.18 through to 3.21).

ISO 20022

ISO 20022 is a modern messaging standard, and prior to its release in 2004 large-value payment systems used SWIFT messaging and retail payments used ISO 8583. Unlike ISO 8583, data is machine-readable (not sequential) and uses XML (Extensible Markup Language) and ASN.1 (Abstract Syntax Notation). It can significantly streamline payment messaging by providing richer data, more transparency, and better interoperability (e.g. standardising non-Latin alphabets) and by adapting to changing needs and business models. ISO 20022 involves the processing of much larger data volumes, and payments ecosystem actors need to update their infrastructures to manage the additional information, which means substantial investment. ISO 20022 is particularly fundamental to modern real-time payments infrastructures.

Bank payment scheme participation

Traditionally, access to bank clearing and settlement infrastructures was only open to banks (hence the term "clearing bank"), and this is still largely the case. In modern times, increasingly, these infrastructures are opening up to non-banks and fintechs. The UK was at the forefront of this phenomenon[1] with TransferWise (now Wise) becoming the first fintech to open an RTGS account at the Bank of England in April 2018.[2] By contrast, the new US FedNow real-time bank payment scheme which launched in July 2023 is only directly accessible to banks and credit unions.[3] However, non-banks have other options to access these infrastructures. Bank payment scheme participation is similar in concept to card scheme membership (see Chapter 2, *Scheme membership*).

Participation models

There are three participation models for bank payment schemes:

- **Directly connected settling**: these participants are directly connected to the scheme and settle directly through the settlement agent, with whom they have an RTGS account.
- **Directly connected non-settling**: these participants are directly connected to the scheme but can't settle directly with the settlement agent (i.e. they don't have an RTGS account), although they can use the services of settling participants.
- **Indirectly connected**: these participants are neither connected directly to the scheme nor able to settle directly through the settlement agent. But they can still access the payment scheme through participants which are able to do so.

Bank payment scheme participation models are described in Figure 3.5.

The suitability of each participation model for a given organisation will depend on the type of institution (e.g. credit institution) and the cost

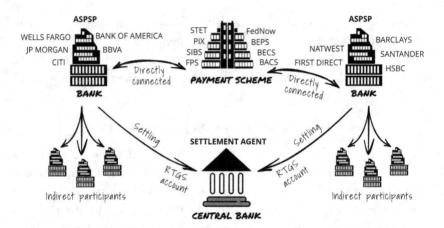

Figure 3.5 Bank payment scheme participation models.

Source: drawing by the author.

involved (e.g. technology, liquidity, connectivity, scheme fees, settlement account cost, security, etc.). To understand this a bit more, you need to look at specific payment schemes.

Participation costs

The suitability of each access model for a given organisation will depend on its type (e.g. a credit institution) and the costs involved. Costs to scheme participants will vary depending on the payment scheme and the participation model selected, so it is difficult to give a quantitative scale. However,

Table 3.1 Bank payment scheme – scale of participation costs.

Scale of cost	Description
High	• Technology build • Assurance costs • Operational costs
Medium	• Connectivity costs • Security costs: e.g. Public Key Infrastructure (PKI), Hardware Security Module (HSM) • Transaction costs
Low	• Liquidity • Scheme membership • Settlement account costs

Table 3.1 gives a comparative scale of the costs that may be incurred by scheme participants.

Those businesses wanting to access a bank payment scheme will incur costs depending on the scheme, the access model chosen, and the jurisdiction.

Bank payments types (one way or another)

Bank payments, from an account holder's point of view, are easy. For the most part, we're not really aware we're using them (e.g. when we pay a utility bill by Direct Debit), and in some geographies they are even more popular than card payments (e.g. in Germany with SOFORT, or iDEAL in the Netherlands). Depending on the payment scheme, several payment types exist:

Common bank payments types

See Figure 3.1 for common uses of bank payments.

Direct Debit (DD)

A Direct Debit (DD) is a payment instruction from the account holder to their bank authorising a biller (e.g. a utility company) to collect payments from their account at regular intervals (e.g. monthly). Usually, the amount remains the same for a long time, but it may vary from time to time, as happened with the cost-of-living crisis and as is continuously happening with energy companies increasing their prices on a regular basis. When the biller must increase the payment amount, they must give advance notice (i.e. new amount and date of collection) to the bank account holder. This is a type of **recurring transaction** (see Chapter 2, Card Not Present – recurring transactions), but unlike card recurring transactions, Direct Debits can easily be cancelled by the account holder, as it's only a couple of clicks on their online banking facility. This type of payment is not supported by all payment schemes.

Credit transfer

A credit transfer is a payment instruction from the bank account holder to their bank to transfer funds to a payee. The payee can be the same person as the instructing bank account holder (e.g. a bank account holder moving funds between their own accounts), and this includes single ad hoc payments, or a different person (e.g. a bank account holder moving funds to another person's account). For retail payments, these generally have lower-value thresholds than credit transfers on Large-Value Payment Schemes (LVPS) and are mostly associated with consumer transactions. Credit transfers can also be submitted in batch by the account holder's bank to the payment scheme (e.g. salaries, pension contributions, etc.), but in this case, each fund transfer in the batch counts as a single transaction. This type of payment usually has high-value minimum thresholds (not necessarily by the scheme rules, but mostly due to economics) and is not supported by all payment schemes.

Standing order

A standing order is a payment instruction from the bank account holder to their bank to transfer funds to a payee for a **fixed amount at a fixed frequency**. The payee can be the same person as the instructing bank account holder (e.g. a bank account holder moving funds between their own accounts). This is another type of **recurring transaction**, albeit one that is completely controlled by the payer, unlike Direct Debit. Examples would be when a bank account holder transfers a fixed sum from their bank account to their savings account at the end of every month, or when they transfer money to their children every month. This type of payment is not supported by all payment schemes.

As another testimony to the fast pace of change in payments, new payment types have emerged as overlay services on top of bank payment infrastructures.

Emerging payment types

Request-to-pay

RtP is similar in intent to sending an invoice. RtP involves a payee (e.g. a supplier of goods or services) issuing a digital payment request to a payer, without having to send an invoice. This is a type of overlay service that sits on top of existing bank payment infrastructures, and it caters to modern behaviours. For example, the payer can receive the request through their mobile device, or their banking app, or via a TPP. But RtP is not just about digital invoicing: it gives more flexibility to payers. For each payment request, a payer may choose to pay in full, pay in installments, or decline to pay altogether. Payers can also communicate with the payee through this service. Because of this flexibility, and the hoped-for outcome that it will help people avoid falling into debt, it could save money at a national level. In the UK, where this service has been deployed over the FPS real-time retail payment scheme, the savings estimates are between £2 billion and £3 billion annually.[4]

Not all payment schemes can support RtP, and of course banks and other PSPs need to deploy it for it to be available to bank account holders (see *Real-time payments drivers and challenges*).

Variable Recurring Payments (VRPs)

A VRP is a payment instruction issued by a bank account holder to their bank authorising a biller (e.g. a subscription service) to collect payments from their account at regular intervals (e.g. weekly, monthly, yearly), within agreed limits, without the bank account holder's intervention after the first instruction. It is a bank payment overlay service and is a type of recurring transaction, but it offers more flexibility and transparency than alternatives such as Direct Debit and card recurring transactions, as the bank account holder remains in **control** of the payment limits, and the payment instruction's end date is agreed up front. At any point up to clearing and settlement, the bank account holder can change any of the agreed parameters, enabling them to respond to changes in circumstances as they happen. In addition, bank account holders can see a list of all their VRP instructions, bringing more **transparency** to the transaction.

Not all payment schemes can support VRP, and of course banks and other PSPs need to deploy it for the service to be available to bank account holders (see *Real-time payments drivers and challenges*).

There are two main use cases for VRPs:

- **Sweeping**: for example, covering a short-term deficit in a bank account with funds from another account with a positive balance, or moving surplus funds from one account to another offering higher savings interest.
- **Non-sweeping**: this may cover a range of scenarios, such as offering an alternative to DD, managing subscription services, or managing tax and other duties at the point of invoice collection by setting funds aside in an account until such tax and other duties are due.

Table 3.2 Differences between card recurring transactions, Direct Debits, standing orders, and VRPs.

		Card recurring transactions	Direct Debit	Standing orders	Variable Recurring Payments
Transparency	See payment instruction mandate	✗	✓	✓	✓
	See last transaction amount	✓	✓	✓	✓
	See transaction history	✗	✓ (Not through the bank, but usually available on the biller's website)	✓	✓
	See frequency	✗	✓	✓	✓
Control	Set payment instruction end date	✗	✗	✓	✓
	Set payment instruction amount limit	✗	✗	✓	✓
	Control each amount	✗ (Dynamic, but only the biller controls the amount)	✗ (Dynamic, but only the biller controls the amount)	✓ (Although a standing order is for a fixed amount, this amount can be changed by the account holder, but it has to be done each time)	✓ (Dynamic within the set limits, controlled by the account holder)
	Cancel payment instruction	Difficult to cancel (see Chapter 2, Card payment channels – recurring transactions)	Through the bank or biller, generally, notice must be given	Can be cancelled or amended online up to the point the transaction becomes irrevocable	Can be cancelled or amended online up to the point the transaction becomes irrevocable
	Chargeback	✓	✓ or ✗ (Depending on the geography's payment scheme and regulations)	✓ or ✗ (Depending on the geography's payment scheme and regulations)	✓ or ✗ (Depending on the geography's payment scheme and regulations)

Table 3.2 shows the differences between the four types of recurring payments and the control and transparency features available to account holders.

SEPA payments types

Most Euro credit transfers and DDs rely on the **European Payments Council (EPC) Payments Schemes**. The EPC payment schemes are used by thousands of PSPs across Europe to facilitate some 43 billion transactions each year. There are a number of EPC SEPA payment schemes[5]:

- **SEPA Credit Transfer (SCT)**;
- **SEPA Instant Credit Transfer (SCT Inst)**;
- **SEPA Direct Debit (SDD Core)**;
- **SEPA Direct Debit B2B (SDD B2B)**; and
- **SEPA One Leg Out Instant Credit Transfer** (between SEPA and non-SEPA countries).

Please note a difference in terminology: what the EPC calls a "payment scheme" is not how we have used the term in this book up till now. To the EPC, a payment scheme represents a payment type and the set of rules which PSPs have agreed upon to execute transactions through a specific instrument (e.g. credit transfer). What we have called a "payment scheme" so far (i.e. card scheme, bank payment scheme) refers to the set of governing rules as well as the technical infrastructure that processes transactions (the EPC refers to these as "payment systems").

The EPC provides the following:

- A **rulebook**: technical standards, steps, transaction duration, etc.;
- **Implementation Guidelines (IGs)**: technical translations of the rulebook into ISO 20022 payment messages enabling SEPA transactions;
- **Management rules**: principles governing the administration and evolution of the scheme; and
- **Clarification papers**: published on a case-by-case basis covering specific topics related to the scheme's implementation.

PSPs wanting to use EPC schemes must follow the rules but are free to use any compliant payment scheme for clearing and settlement.[6]

In addition to payment schemes, the EPC provides other schemes to cater for evolving consumer behaviours, and these are **overlay services** (not payment schemes):

- **SEPA Proxy Lookup (SPL)**[7]: this provides a data lookup function to be used before initiating a payment and covers mobile payments where the mobile number or associated email address is used as a proxy to an **IBAN**. This scheme may evolve over time to include additional proxy types and identifiers. This may lead to the development of a Confirmation of Payee service.
- **SEPA Request-to-Pay – (SRTP)**[8]: see *Emerging payment types*.
- **SEPA Payment Account Access (SPAA)**[9]: this service provides ASPSPs the ability to offer value-added services to TPPs by capitalising on the account data they hold (**Proxy Lookup Scheme**). This could potentially lead to a new surge of **Open Finance** services based on data-sharing (see Chapter 5, *What's next for PSD2?*).

This will continue to evolve, and who knows, we might soon see a SEPA EPC scheme for Variable Recurring Payments (VRPs), or perhaps more identity-proofing services on the basis of the Proxy Lookup scheme.

Account-to-Account payments (from me to you)
Definition

The term **Account-to-Account Payments** has been used, abused, and confused with other terms. Some use **A2A Payments** and **Open Banking Payments** interchangeably, but they are not the same thing.

> **Account-to-Account (A2A) Payments** allow a payer to move money from their bank account to a payee's bank account.

That's it. All payments listed under *Common bank payment types* are A2A payments, and all payment types listed under *Emerging payment types* are A2A payments and also open banking payments. Card payments are not A2A payments. If you Google the terms, you will find many descriptions, each showing varying degrees of accuracy, some even describing A2A payments as involving the movement of funds between accounts without the need for intermediaries. If you're reading this page, I assume you've read the previous sections and chapters, and therefore are fully aware of the fact that centralised payments ecosystems always involve intermediaries whose function it is to preserve the integrity of the ecosystem (e.g. authorisation, clearing, and settlement).

To a payer, however, A2A payments may look simple and convenient, and they may look like peer-to-peer payments (i.e. not needing intermediaries), such as when making a payment using Venmo. Underneath, the ducks still paddle. If you want a glimpse of true peer-to-peer payments (I'm a purist, granted), see Chapter 4, *Centralised vs decentralised ledgers*, or for a fuller dive, check out my second book, *Beyond Payments*.

I just thought I'd clarify that.

A2A payments in practice

Global A2A payment transaction value exceeded $525 billion in 2022, and this is expected to grow at a 13% four-year CAGR to 2026, driven by further open banking developments and process improvements. In 2022, there were 64 live payment schemes providing the real-time payment rails enabling new A2A payment use cases (see Figures 3.18 through 3.21).

Figures 3.6 and 3.7 aim to give an overview of A2A payments in various geographies.

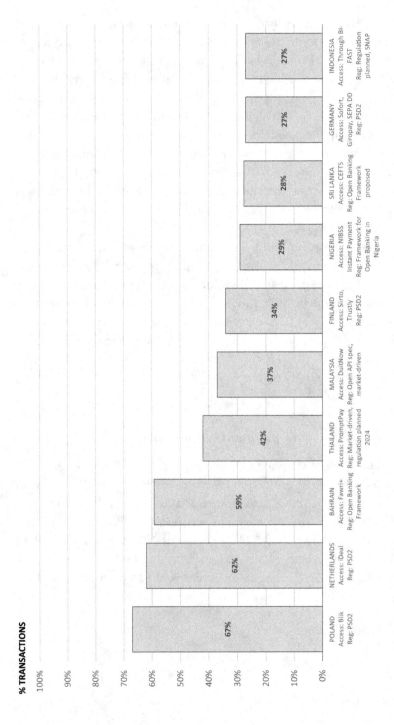

Figure 3.6 Top ten countries by A2A payments' share of e-commerce transactions in 2022.

Source: Worldpay Global Payments Report 2023.

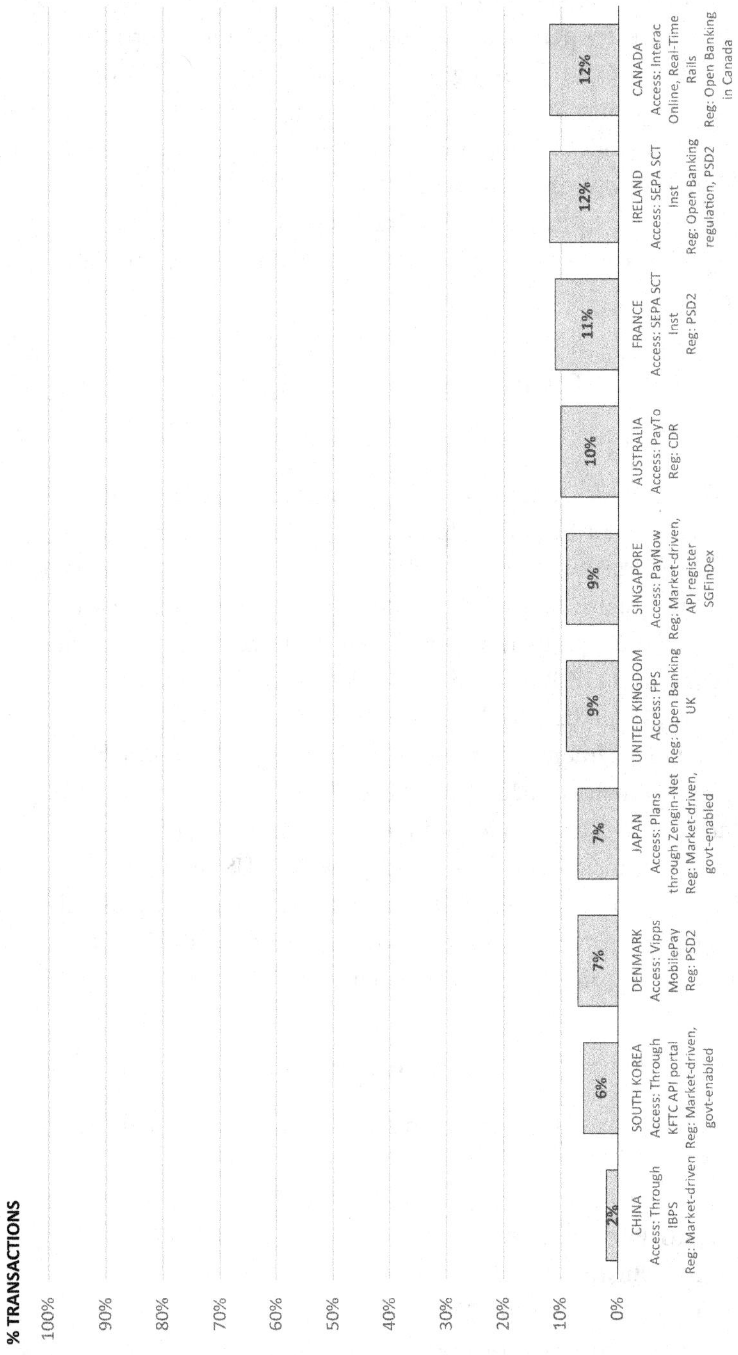

% TRANSACTIONS

CHINA	SOUTH KOREA	DENMARK	JAPAN	UNITED KINGDOM	SINGAPORE	AUSTRALIA	FRANCE	IRELAND	CANADA
2%	6%	7%	7%	9%	9%	10%	11%	12%	12%

CHINA
Access: Through IBPS
Reg: Market-driven, govt-enabled

SOUTH KOREA
Access: Through KFTC API portal
Reg: Market-driven, govt-enabled

DENMARK
Access: Vipps MobilePay
Reg: PSD2

JAPAN
Access: Plans through Zengin-Net
Reg: Market-driven, govt-enabled

UNITED KINGDOM
Access: FPS
Reg: Open Banking UK

SINGAPORE
Access: PayNow
Reg: Market-driven, API register SGFinDex

AUSTRALIA
Access: PayTo
Reg: CDR

FRANCE
Access: SEPA SCT Inst
Reg: PSD2

IRELAND
Access: SEPA SCT Inst
Reg: Open Banking regulation, PSD2

CANADA
Access: Interac Online, Real-Time Rails
Reg: Open Banking in Canada

Figure 3.7 Bottom 10 countries by A2A payments share of e-commerce transactions in 2022.

Source: Worldpay Global Payments Report 2023.

For each country, the share of A2A transactions is shown, and the labels will also show the open banking status (see Chapter 4, *Open banking and alternative payments*). Open banking payments are a subset of A2A payments, and the share, whilst it can't be easily determined, will be lower than that. Figures 3.6 and 3.7 should be looked at in conjunction with Figures 3.17–3.20 to position real-time payments in the mix. This will be a moving feast: for example, in July 2023 Pix (ranking 11, hence not in the top 10 in Figure 3.6) was used for more transactions than credit and debit cards combined.[10]

Terminology (say it right)

Real-time vs batch

Now, I must introduce you to the term **Automated Clearing House** (**ACH**). I know, this may not be very helpful, but in centralised payments ecosystems we are obsessed with the term "clearing", and you will find that many bank payment systems around the world will feature the term "clearing" in their name. ACH is a globally accepted term for legacy bank payment infrastructures (such as UK BACS and US FedACH) that have longer settlement cycles than real-time bank rails such as UK FPS and US FedNow.

Newer retail payment schemes, such as Brazil's Pix (launched 2020), US FedNow (launched 2023), and the UK's FPS (launched in 2008), are referred to as **Real-Time Payment Systems**. To complicate matters further, large-value payment systems such as UK CHAPS or US Fedwire also operate in real time, and, in practice, whilst these are technically and usually real-time payment systems, they are commonly referred to as **Wire Transfer** to distinguish them from "retail" real-time payment systems.

Payments interactions

Depending on the payment scheme, a number of payment interactions may be available:

- **Person-to-Person (P2P)**;
- **Person-to-Business (P2B)**;
- **Person-to-Government (P2G)**;
- **Government-to-Person (G2P)**;

- **Business-to-Business (B2B)**; and
- **Business-to-Person (B2P)** (here, I use the Bank of International Settlements description; in practice, the term "business-to-consumer", or "B2C", is mostly used).

Settlement cycles

In order to understand whether a bank payment system operates in "real time", you have to understand the **Settlement Cycle** (method), which is dependent on the payment scheme and which could be performed:

- **In batch at the end of the day (Deferred Net Settlement)**: this is where banks batch their transactions at the end of the day and submit them in one go according to the scheme rules. This settlement method is used by older ACH Schemes and involves a multi-day settlement cycle, such as with UK BACS and US FedACH.
- **In near real time (e.g. Deferred Net Settlement several times a day)**: this is where banks batch their transactions at several points during the day and submit the batch each time. This is used by some real-time retail payment schemes. To a payer, a payment looks like it has settled instantly.
- **In real time (Real-Time Gross Settlement)**: RTGS is a real-time settlement method, and each payment instruction is cleared and settled as it is presented, and the payments are irrevocable. Each payment is presented and settled immediately, and this has traditionally been applicable to LVPS used for money market transactions, for time-critical payments such as the settlement of commercial payments and financial market transactions, and for the funding of other systemically important financial market infrastructures. This method requires increased liquidity to manage risk, as high-value payments present the largest potential systemic risk when compared to retail payments, and payment schemes using it are usually managed by central banks.

RTGS is a relatively new process (in the history of banking), and as I mentioned before it was originally confined to large-value payments. For example, RTGS was only introduced to UK CHAPS in 1996. Before that, the process was largely manual and paper-based, and involved messengers going on "walks" to the central bank to present their large cheques for processing before the banking hall closed for that day. How times have changed! Nowadays, the concept of payment systems becoming more automated, as well as implementing more mechanisms to manage risk, is referred to as **Straight Through Processing (STP)**.

Bank payment mechanics (follow the money)

As examined in earlier sections, there are many payment schemes around the world, and each scheme will have its own operating rules, but we will cover the fundamental principles that apply anywhere. In addition, this is a book about payments, so we will not cover mechanisms and economic factors that apply to money markets (e.g. liquidity risk, etc.) and confine ourselves to the mechanics of retail payments. (If you're interested in more details on bank settlement mechanisms, the Bank of England explains this very well on their website, [11] but you can find information from any central monetary authority.)

Similarly to the card rails, it's about moving money from a payer to a payee. The main difference is that it involves bank accounts directly in the transactional payment process, but the fundamental processes are the same:

- **Authorisation**;
- **Clearing**; and
- **Settlement**.

However, in my opinion, these processes are much simpler than on the card rails. There are several reasons for this: in Europe, until SEPA, bank settlement infrastructures were largely domestic; in the US, some schemes (see *Deferred net settlement ACH retail payment schemes*) may lack a strong authorisation process when compared to Europe. In the following sections, I'll use Europe to illustrate authorisation.

Bank payments transaction authorisation

For the remainder of this chapter, we will assume that the closed loop CBPII process is understood (Figure 3.4) and is merely adding steps to the standard authorisation process; therefore, I will omit closed loop CBPIIs from the graphics and explanations.

Bank account numbers

The way bank accounts are constructed is different from the way card numbers are constructed, in as much as a PAN follows ISO/IEC 7812 (see Chapter 1) and whilst there is an international standard (ISO 13616) for an **International Bank Account Number** (**IBAN**), each country may implement its particular national IBAN format. The ISO 13616 standard specifies the structure of an ISO-compliant national IBAN format. ISO has designated SWIFT to act as the registration authority for national IBAN formats.

In the UK, a bank account is identified by a combination of **Sort Code** and Bank Account Number. In the US, a bank account is identified by a combination of **ABA Routing Number** and Bank Account Number.

Direct payment instruction

Figure 3.8 shows the bank payment transaction authorisation for a bank account holder directly issuing a payment instruction to their bank (e.g. they make a payment through online or mobile banking).

This is a simple process.

Step 1: the **payment instruction** is initiated by the bank account holder, and they will supply the amount to pay, and the name, bank sort code/ routing number, and account number of the receiver.

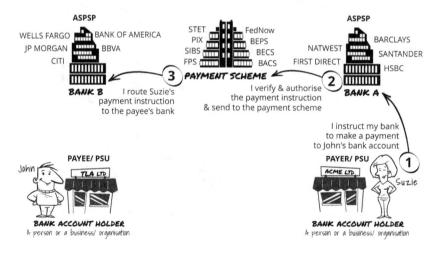

Figure 3.8 Bank transaction authorisation.

Source: drawing by the author.

Step 2: the bank (ASPSP) will **verify the transaction and authorise it** according to applicable regulations/payment scheme rules. In Europe, authorisation must be completed according to PSD2 with Strong Customer Authentication (or applicable exemptions), which means the use of multi-factor authentication for bank-account-holder verification.

Step 3: the payment scheme **routes the payment instruction to the payee's bank**. Just like a card scheme, the payment scheme operates as a switch between the sender's and the receiver's banks.

Payment instruction through a PISP

PISPs can also be involved in this process, but the principles remain the same, and this is shown in Figure 3.9.

Depending on the geography (and therefore applicable laws/rules), the PISP may be subject to additional authentication requirements (see Chapter 5, *Secure communications*). For example, in Europe, PSD2 mandates that a PISP (or an AISP, although they don't initiate payments) be authenticated separately from the account holder. This means that a PISP would have their own credentials to initiate a payment so that the sending bank could identity that the payment instruction was initiated by a PISP authorised by the account holder (who has their own separate credentials), and not directly by the bank account holder.

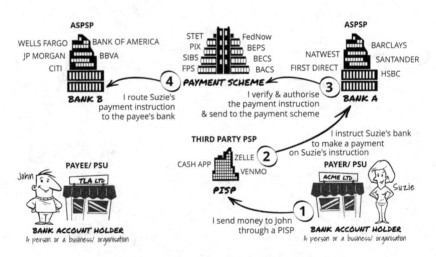

Figure 3.9 Bank transaction authorisation using a PISP.

Source: drawing by the author.

Confirmation of Payee (CoP)

Confirmation of Payee (CoP) is an overlay service that sits on top of bank payment infrastructures and happens at the authorisation stage. Where deployed (such as in the UK),[12] this service will enable a bank account holder (payer) to check the name of the receiving account (payee) before submitting a payment instruction to their bank (ASPSP), which must enrol in the service. The bank may return four possible answers to the account holder:

- **full match**: name supplied and name on the account match;
- **partial match**: name supplied and name on the account are a close match;
- **no match**: name supplied and name on the account are different; or
- **unavailable**: the ASPSP is unable to check for reasons such as timeout or invalid account.

This service is aimed at reducing the impact of mistakes and scams on bank account holders. Not all bank payment schemes can support CoP, and, of course, banks and other PSPs must support it for the service to be available to bank account holders.

Similarly to the card rails, settlement on the bank rails will have two phases: interbank settlement and retail settlement.

An introduction to bank clearing and settlement

Similarly to the card rails, when the authorisation stage is complete, transfer of funds between payer and payee has yet to happen. Clearing and settlement will be the next step, and this is where banking transactions are reconciled between banks and funds move from payer to payee. The process is facilitated by the payment scheme and is different from the card rails, as there is no concept of acquiring and issuing on the bank rails. In addition, there are many schemes around the world, each with their own rules and governance frameworks, and the way payment transactions are processed will also depend on the settlement method (real-time gross settlement or deferred net settlement). However, we can abstract the mechanics at a fundamental level.

Clearing

The clearing process is quite simple. Each bank will, at the frequency defined by the scheme rules, present their payment instructions. The way payment instructions are presented to the scheme depends on the settlement method:

- **For RGTS**, each transaction is cleared (processed) by the payment scheme as it is presented, and settlement follows straight through.
- **For Deferred Net Settlement**, the process will be similar to clearing on the card rails, in as much as participants will batch their transactions in clearing files presented to the payment scheme according to the rules for the payment scheme. This can happen several times a day as for some real-time payment schemes (e.g. UK FPS), or at the end of the day in one go for older ACH Schemes (e.g. UK BACS or US FedACH).

Please note that "having an RTGS account" and "using a RGTS payment scheme" are two different things. You need to have an RTGS account to settle directly on a bank payment scheme, regardless of the settlement method used.

The clearing process is explained at a high level in Figure 3.10.

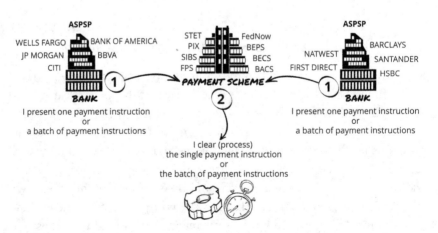

Figure 3.10 Bank transaction clearing.

Source: drawing by the author.

Interbank settlement

This is a centralised function coordinated by the payment scheme, supported by a settlement agent, with participation from both sending and receiving banks. Its purpose is to exchange value between banks, and this is shown at a high level in Figure 3.11.

Because not all accounts are held at the same bank, when a bank account holder makes a payment to a business or a person, the payer's bank (Bank A) owes the payee's bank (Bank B) the value of the payment. This creates a level of risk, and a payment scheme must use an intermediary (the settlement agent) for the final settlement of funds between banks. The settlement agent will hold accounts for banks, which are used to settle funds moved between them. On the bank rails, **the settlement agent is usually a central bank** (i.e. not a commercial bank). For example, in the UK the settlement agent for all UK payment schemes is the Bank of England. An account held by a bank at the settlement agent (aka central bank or monetary authority) for settlement purposes is called a **Real-Time Gross Settlement (RTGS) Account**.

On the bank rails, clearing and settlement can be continuous in real time on an individual-payment-instruction basis (gross settlement), or periodically in batch between the settlement members of the scheme (net settlement).

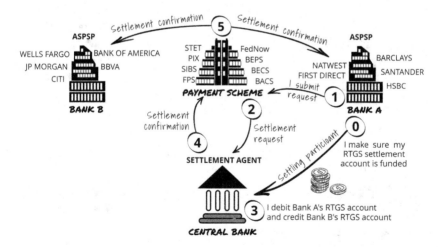

Figure 3.11 Interbank settlement.

Source: drawing by the author.

You can compare Figure 3.11 with Chapter 1, Figure 1.12 (inter-bank settlement on the card rails) for the main differences, but in the same way as merchant settlement happens after interbank settlement, retail settlement on the bank rails also happens after interbank settlement.

Retail settlement

To complete the settlement process, the funds will need to move from Suzie's bank account to John's, and this is shown in Figure 3.12.

How long does it take for a payee to receive their funds? Unlike on the card rails, where merchant settlement is dependent on the contract a merchant has with an acquirer (or ISO, or PSP), a payee on the bank rails will receive their money according to the rules governing the payment scheme, and **settlement times apply to everyone according to the scheme governance rules**, because there is only one set of rules per bank payment scheme, and this is not commercially negotiable. Whilst a bank account holder has a commercial contract with their bank (just like cardholders with issuers), all banks are bound by the payment scheme rules and applicable regulations, especially towards consumers.

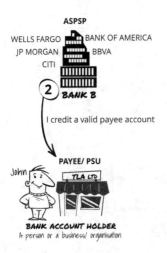
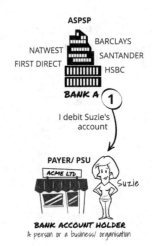

Figure 3.12 Bank retail settlement.

Source: drawing by the author.

Banks have some leeway (e.g. limits), but payment scheme settlement times apply to **Direct Payment Instructions**. Settlement times may increase for the end users if:

- overlay services are used (as these may be **Indirect Payment Instructions** to the bank), such as with **Digital Wallets**. Depending on the underlying settlement infrastructure and the payer's and payee's bank participation models, times may vary for payment service users according to the terms agreed with the overlay service; or
- the participant banks (Bank A and Bank B) are indirect participants, as they have to rely on the services of direct participants.

You will notice that at Step 2 of Figure 3.12 ("I credit a valid payee account [...]"), I didn't say "I credit John's account". This is one of the unfortunate characteristics of established (read "older") payment systems around the world. Whilst a payer will specify a payee's name, bank sort code/routing number, and bank account number, the payment messaging on older systems (e.g. ISO 8583) is such that only the bank sort code and bank account number are validated, not the payee's name. This means that John might not necessarily receive his money:

- If Suzie mistypes the bank sort code or account number, but the mistyped account is still a valid one (although not John's); or
- If Suzie has been misled by a fraudster into sending the money to their account (different sort code and account number altogether) but giving John's name as the account holder (which is not checked if an overlay service such as Confirmation of Payee (CoP) is not used).

This is bad news for bank account holders, because there is little equivalent – except in the UK and the EU going forward (see Chapter 5, *Authorised fraud*) – to the card rails chargeback process (see Chapter 2, *Exceptions and disputes*) for some types of bank payments (e.g. direct payment instruction), whilst some others offer recourse to payers (e.g. Direct Debits [DDs]; see Table 3.2). Bank account holders who make mistakes on direct payment instructions, or those who are scammed, have a hard job recovering their money. This led to the development of the CoP service (see *Bank payment transaction authorisation*).

The next sections will give real-life examples of the different types of payment schemes worldwide.

Bank payments schemes worldwide (all around the world)

Wire transfer payment schemes

International payments and correspondent banking

Whilst wire transfer payment schemes can be used for domestic transactions, they also allow for international (cross-border) transactions. When making cross-border payments, ecosystem actors need a communication mechanism by which payment schemes can facilitate funds transfer across national (and linguistic) boundaries so that a payer in one geography (one payment scheme) can make a payment from their bank account to a payee's bank account in another geography (another payment scheme).

Correspondent banking

Of course, for all this to work settling participants in a cross-border payment scheme (e.g. UK CHAPS) will need to hold funds with settling participants in cross-border payment schemes in other geographies so that the funds can eventually reach the payee's bank account. This is called **Correspondent Banking** and is explained in Figure 3.13.

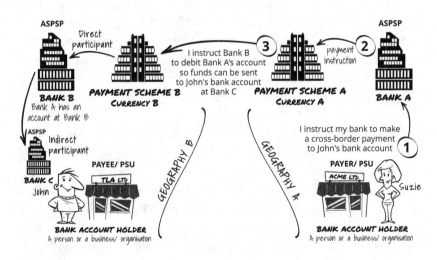

Figure 3.13 Correspondent banking.

Source: drawing by the author.

At a high level, **Correspondent Banking** is defined as an arrangement under which one bank holds funds owned by other banks and provides payment and other services to those respondent banks.

In Figure 3.13, Bank B is the correspondent bank for Bank C (the respondent bank). Evidently, the more banking "hops" you have in a cross-border payment, the more charges and fees accrue, which is why these funds transfers are relatively expensive for payers.

In each geography, the payment scheme mechanics are understood. But how does the instruction from Payment Scheme A get to Payment Scheme B? Well, prior to 1973 banks used TELEX, a wire system similar to telegraph, to transmit text messages with their payment instructions. This is why, to this day, some still refer to these payments as "wire transfers". But TELEX was slow and prone to human error and security breaches.

You may have heard of the terms **Nostro** and **Vostro** accounts. These are Latin words describing a bank account held by a bank at another bank. The two terms describe the same account, but from the point of view of either the bank that holds the account for another bank, or the bank that is the account holder. Nostro means "our money held at your bank", and Vostro means "your money held at our bank".

SWIFT

In 1973, **SWIFT**[13] (**Society for Worldwide Interbank Financial Telecommunications**) was founded to address this issue. SWIFT is a **messaging system** used between banks for same-day electronic funds transfer, and there is no upper limit (as the limits are with the payment schemes using this facility). This is little understood: SWIFT doesn't actually move funds; the payment schemes do that. SWIFT specifies a set of standard messages and formats that the industry agrees on, thus minimising translation and counterparty verification costs, as well as improving security. If you hear the term "MT message", you know you're talking about SWIFT messaging. There are several categories of MT messages, but for payments MT 1xx, MT

Table 3.3 Examples of SWIFT MT messages.

MT message	Description
MT 103	Single Customer Credit Transfer
MT 101	Request for Transfer
MT 104	Direct Debit and Request for Debit Transfer Message (STP)
MT 190	Advice of Charges, Interest, and Other Adjustments
MT 191	Request for Payment of Charges, Interest, and Other Expenses
MT 195	Queries
MT 196	Answers
MT 200	Financial Institution Transfer for Its Own Account
MT 205	Financial Institution Transfer Execution
MT 207	Request for Financial Institution Transfer
MT 900	Confirmation of Debit
MT 910	Confirmation of Credit

2xx, and MT 9xx messages are the most relevant, and some examples are given in Table 3.3.

The SWIFT messaging format uses the ISO 150022 standard. SWIFT counts more than 11,000 members in more than 200 countries. Because of recent geopolitical tensions[14] and the resulting sanctions banning many Russian top banks from SWIFT (also enabling the freezing of Russian assets abroad), Russia has developed an alternative network to SWIFT, the System for Transfer of Financial Messages (SPFS), which gained support from other countries.[15] China has also developed its own system, CIPS.[16]

Of course, because SWIFT is only a messaging system (albeit a systemically important one), there is no technical impediment to building an alternative (but there is no guarantee that it will be used),[17] and of course states can revert back to other means (which would be either less secure or more costly).

SWIFT migration to ISO 20022

In addition, SWIFT is replacing, between November 2022 and November 2025, three of its current message categories (MTs 1, 2, and 9) with ISO 20022 messages for cross-border payments,[18] although large-value payment systems (e.g. UK CHAPS, US Fedwire) have already migrated (interbank settlement). US CHIPS, however, has postponed its migration to 2024.[19] This is commonly referred to as the "MT to MX migration".

Example wire transfer schemes

CHAPS

The UK **Clearing House Automated Payment System**[20] (**CHAPS**), a wire transfer payment scheme, was launched in 1984. It can be used in several ways, as described in Figure 3.14.

CHAPS is one of the largest large-value wire transfer payment systems in the world, and as it uses real-time gross settlement (requiring more liquidity), it is more suited to high-value payments. As such, there are few CHAPS payments (0.5% of the total number payments in the UK), but they represent 92% of the total value of UK payments with an average value of £1.8 million. Traditional UK banks have access to the CHAPS scheme, but increasingly challenger banks and non-bank PSPs have been allowed access. The all-time record (at the time of writing) was set on 3 October 2022 when £642.7 billion was settled in CHAPS. Table 3.4 shows its main characteristics.

Figure 3.14 Common uses of CHAPS payments.

Source: drawing by the author.

Table 3.4 CHAPS payment scheme characteristics.

CHAPS	Description
Payment types	• **Same-day high-value wholesale credit transfers** • **Time-critical high-value retail credit transfers**
Payment limits[21]	No upper limit
Settlement cycle	**Real-Time Gross Settlement**
Settlement time	For a payer/payee, this is **immediate on instruction.** Payments are irrevocable.
Participation models	• Directly connected settling • Indirectly connected
Scope	UK domestic and cross-border, £ (currency conversion applies to cross-border)
Operator	Bank of England
Rules	Bank of England
Infrastructure	Bank of England

CHAPS offers two participation models: directly connected settling and indirectly connected (see Figure 3.5). Directly connected participants include traditional banks and a number of international and custody banks, but the Bank of England allows indirect access to other financial institutions which can settle via direct participants. In addition, the Pay.UK Confirmation of Payee overlay service is available for the CHAPS scheme. CHAPS uses SWIFT messaging.

FEDWIRE

Fedwire is a Large-Value Payment Scheme (LVPS) similar to UK CHAPS and is operated by the Federal Reserve. In the US, LVPS can be operated by both public (Fedwire) and private sector (CHIPS) organisations. Its scheme characteristics are presented in Table 3.5.

There are 12 federal reserve banks across the US, so not every state has one, but each state is assigned a federal reserve, which amounts to the same thing, meaning that Fedwire operates across all US states and therefore payments can be made seamlessly across US national boundaries. International cross-border transfers will use SWIFT messaging. In that sense, Fedwire is an alternative to SWIFT for messaging (see *Correspondent banking*), and it also moves the funds across states (unlike SWIFT), but only within the US.

Table 3.5 Fedwire payment scheme characteristics.

Fedwire	Description
Payment types	• **Same-day high-value wholesale credit transfers** • **Time-critical high-value retail credit transfers**
Payment limits[22]	No upper limit
Settlement cycle	**Real-Time Gross Settlement**
Settlement time	For a payer/payee, this is **immediate on instruction**. Payments are irrevocable.
Participation models	• Directly connected settling • Indirectly connected
Scope	US domestic and cross-border, $ (currency conversion applies to cross-border)
Operator	Federal Reserve
Governance	Federal Reserve

CHIPS

The **Clearing House Interbank Payments System** (**CHIPS**) is privately operated by The Clearing House and operates across its member banks in a similar fashion to Fedwire, although it has less coverage and is slower (deferred net settlement). It is, however, cheaper for its members. Its payment scheme characteristics are presented in Table 3.6.

Table 3.6 CHIPS payment scheme characteristics.

CHIPS	Description
Payment types	• **Same-day high-value wholesale credit transfers**
Payment limits[23]	No upper limit (average transaction $3 million)
Settlement cycle	**Deferred Net Settlement**, once a day
Settlement time	Slower than Fedwire, but cheaper
Participation models	• Directly connected settling • Indirectly connected Usually large US banks or US branches of international banks
Scope	US domestic and cross-border, $ (currency conversion applies to cross-border)
Operator	The Clearing House (TCH)
Governance	The Clearing House (TCH)

CHIPS will use SWIFT messaging for international cross-border transfers. Because member banks are in several US states, CHIPS is an alternative to SWIFT for messaging (see *Correspondent banking*), and also moves the funds across states (unlike SWIFT), but only within the US.

Deferred net settlement ACH retail payment schemes

These payment schemes are the oldest and are generally referred to as **ACH Schemes**. But they are still used today, and I'll give some examples here for the UK and the US.

BACS – Bankers Automated Clearing Services[24]

The first retail ACH System in the world was BACS,[25] and it was launched in the UK in 1968, and its common uses are shown in Figure 3.15. It is so old that it doesn't even use ISO 8583 for messaging but another specification called "Standard 18" (the price of being first!), although mapping between Standard 18 and ISO 20022 is available.[26]

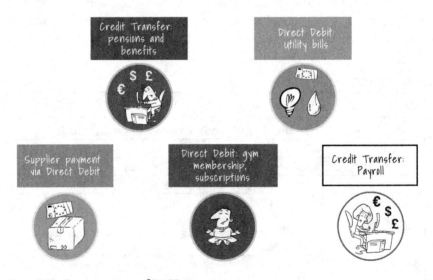

Figure 3.15 Common uses of BACS payments.

Source: drawing by the author.

Table 3.7 BACS payment scheme characteristics.

BACS Payment Scheme	Description
Payment types	• **Batch credit transfers** (aka "Direct Credits"). • **Direct Debits**: a type of **recurring transaction**. BACS DDs offer payers a money-back guarantee
Payment limits[27]	£20 million for customer grade, £999 million for government and bank grade
Settlement cycle	**Deferred Net Settlement**, once a day
Settlement time	For a payer/payee, this is a **three-day cycle**.
Participation models	• Directly connected settling • Directly connected non-settling • Indirectly connected
Scope	UK domestic, £
Operator	Pay.UK
Rules	Pay.UK
Infrastructure	Vocalink

Table 3.7 shows the main payment scheme characteristics of BACS.

BACS facilitated 6.7 billion payments totalling £5.3 trillion in 2022, including 4.7 billion Direct Debits[28] (nearly 90% of British adults have at least one Direct Debit commitment, and 73% of household bills are paid this way). The all-time record (at the time of writing) was set in November 2019 when 124 million transactions were settled in BACS. More than 150,000 organisations in the UK use BACS Direct Credit, and nearly 90% of the UK's workforce is paid this way. BACS is also used for a variety of bills (e.g. mobile phone, broadband packages, energy, council), subscriptions, insurance, dividends, refunds, and even holidays. At the time of writing, there were 31 BACS direct participants.

FedACH

The first ACH System in the US, FedACH, was launched in 1972 and is operated by the Federal Reserve. There is one governance body for US retail payment ACH Schemes, the **National Automated Clearing House Association**[29] (**NACHA**), which is also an accreditation body. These schemes

Table 3.8 FedACH payment scheme characteristics.

FedACH	Description
Payment types	• **Batch credit transfers** (aka "Direct Credits") • **Direct Debits**: recurring and single • **FORWARD-dated payments**
Payment limits	Up to $1 million
Settlement cycle	Deferred net settlement
Settlement time	For a payer/payee, this is a **three-day cycle**, although FedACH offers same-day ACH processing for eligible payments,[31] but this hasn't experienced growth due to cost and the fact that faster processing doesn't mean faster settlement.
Participation models	• Directly connected settling • Directly connected non-settling • Indirectly connected
Scope	US domestic, $
Operator	Federal Reserve
Governance	NACHA

typically handle high volumes of relatively low-value payments and can be operated by both public (FedACH) and private sector (EPN) organisations. In the US, ACH Schemes have long been established, and I don't propose to cover these in detail in this book, as it's already been done.[30] Table 3.8 shows the main FedACH payment scheme characteristics.

EPN (Electronic Payments Network)

EPN is privately operated by The Clearing House but is still governed by the NACHA rules. Its payment scheme characteristics are laid out in Table 3.9.

FedACH[33] operates across all US states, and EPN[34] operates across its member banks, essentially performing cross-border payments across states, similarly to SWIFT's messaging operating across international borders. In that sense, FedACH and EPN are alternatives to SWIFT (see *Correspondent banking*) for messaging but also move the funds across states (unlike SWIFT), but only within the US.

Table 3.9 EPN payment scheme characteristics.

EPN	Description
Payment types	• **Credit transfers** (aka "Direct Credits"), including batch • **Direct Debits**, including recurring
Payment limits[32]	Up to $1 million
Settlement cycle	Deferred net settlement
Settlement time	For a payer/payee, this is a **three-day cycle**, but same-day processing is available for a fee.
Participation models	• Directly connected settling • Directly connected non-settling • Indirectly connected • EPN only handles transactions from the private sector, whereas FedACH handles government transactions.
Scope	US domestic, $
Operator	The Clearing House (TCH)
Governance	NACHA

Globally, there is a trend to move towards real-time retail settlement infrastructures.

Deferred net settlement real-time retail payment schemes

Worldwide overview

Table 3.10 lists real-time payment schemes using deferred net settlement around the world, listing their payment capabilities.

It is important to note that most of these schemes will allow Business-to-Person (B2P) payments; however, the BIS paper is inconsistent. For example, the UK FPS allows for B2P payments in instances such as insurance claim settlements or remittances from savings accounts at one bank to current accounts at another, but the BIS paper doesn't list FPS as offering B2P (which is clearly wrong). I have therefore omitted the B2P element in Table 3.10, as you can have a look at the individual schemes to see which scheme does what. The same comment applies to Table 3.12.

Table 3.10 Deferred net settlement real-time retail payment schemes around the world.

Country	Payment scheme	Operator	Year introduced	P2P	P2B	P2G	G2P	B2B
South Africa	RTC	BankServAfrica	2006	✓	✓	✗	✗	✓
South Korea	CD/ATM	KFTC	2007	✓	✓	✓	✓	✓
United Kingdom	FPS	Pay.UK	2008	✓	✓	✓	✓	✓
China	IBPS	China NCC	2010	✓	✓	✓	✓	✓
India	IMPS	NPCI	2010	✓	✓	✓	✓	✓
Argentina	IT	Redlink SA & Prisma SA	2011	✓	✓	✓	✗	✓
Singapore	FAST	BCS	2014	✓	✓	✓	✓	✓
India	UPI	NPCI	2016	✓	✓	✓	✓	✓
Spain	SNCE	Iberpay	2016	✓	✓	✓	✓	✓
Switzerland	Twint	Twint Ltd	2017	✓	✓	✗	✗	✗
Japan	More Time System	Zengin-Net	2018	✓	✓	✗	✓	✓
Saudi Arabia	sarie	SAMA	2021	✓	✓	✓	✓	✓

Source: Bank of International Settlements (BIS), "Developments in retail fast payments and implications for RTGS systems", December 2021.[35]

The UK's Faster Payments System (FPS)[36]

FPS is a real-time retail payment scheme which launched in 2008 and allows account holders to make payments almost instantaneously, seven days a week, 24 hours a day. In 2022, FPS processed 3.4 billion transactions with a value of £2.6 trillion. Its many uses are shown in Figure 3.16.

Its characteristics are shown in Table 3.11.

The VRP and RtP **overlay services** developed by Pay.UK are **only available on FPS**.

Prior to February 2022, FPS was described as a scheme for low-value retail payments, and the maximum limit was £250,000, but after that the limit increased to £1 million, giving businesses a choice

Table 3.11 UK Faster Payments System (FPS) characteristics.

Faster Payments System	Description

Payment types	• **Credit transfers** (aka "Direct Credits"), including:
	  • single immediate payments
	  • forward-dated payments
	  • direct corporate access: for business customers, enables bulk files (batched transactions) to be submitted to the scheme
	• Standing order: a type of recurring transaction where a fixed amount is sent to the same payee on a regular date

Payment limits[37]	£1 million. Individual participants are free to set their own limits within this threshold, and there can be different limits depending on the type of customer (e.g. personal, business) and the channel used (e.g. branch, phone, online).
Settlement cycle	**Deferred Net Settlement, three times a day.**
Settlement time	For a payer/payee, this is a **quasi-immediate payment**; however, the scheme rules allow for up to two hours.
Participation models	• Directly connected settling • Directly connected non-settling • Indirectly connected
Scope	UK domestic, £
Operator	Pay.UK
Rules	Pay.UK
Infrastructure	Vocalink

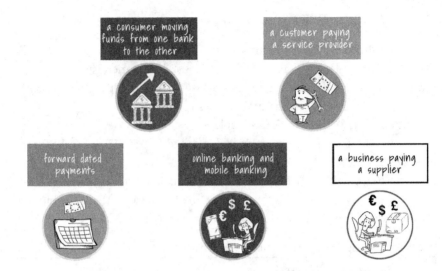

Figure 3.16 Common uses of the UK Faster Payments System (FPS).
Source: drawing by the author.

between BACS batch credit transfers and FPS direct corporate access for payments up to £1 million. Indeed, in 2021 payments using FPS overtook BACS Direct Credit as the preferred payment method for businesses.[38]

In addition, the UK has been progressive in allowing access to FPS to non-bank PSPs, thus promoting innovation. At the time of writing, there were 40 FPS direct participants, from traditional banks to fintech firms (e.g. Banking Circle, Mettle, Modulr, Revolut, Square, and Wise), and thousands of indirect participants.[39]

Real-time gross settlement (RTGS) retail payment schemes
Worldwide overview

Increasingly, this settlement method is being used for retail payment systems.

Table 3.12 lists real-time payment schemes using RTGS around the world.

Table 3.12 Real-time gross settlement (RTGS) retail payment schemes around the world.

Country	Payment scheme	Operator	Year introduced	P2P	P2B	P2G	G2P	B2B
Japan	CTS	BOJ-Net	1973	✓	✓	✗	✓	✓
Sweden	BiR	Bankgirot	2012	✓	✓	✓	✗	✗
Mexico	SPEI	Banxico	2015	✓	✓	✓	✓	✓
South Korea	EBS	KFTC	2016	✓	✓	✓	✓	✓
Europe	RT1	EBA Clearing	2017	✓	✓	✓	✓	✓
United States	RTP	The Clearing House	2017	✓	✓	✗	✗	✓
Australia	NPP	NPPA	2018	✓	✓	✓	✓	✓
Europe	TIPS	Eurosystem	2018	✓	✓	✓	✓	✓
France	SEPA EU	STET	2018	✓	✓	✗	✗	✓
Hong Kong	FPS	HKICL	2018	✓	✓	✓	✓	✓
Belgium	CEC.IP	CEC	2019	✓	✓	✓	✓	✓
Netherlands	eW IP CSM	eW	2019	✓	✓	✓	✓	✓
Russia	FPS	CBR	2019	✓	✓	✗	✗	✗
Brazil	Pix/SPI	BCB	2020	✓	✓	✓	✓	✓
Indonesia	BI-FAST	BI	2021	✓	✓	✓	✓	✓
Turkey	FAST	CBRT	2021	✓	✓	✗	✗	✗
Canada	RTR	Payments Canada	2022	✓	✓	✓	✓	✓
Sweden	RIX-INST	Riksbank	2022	✓	✓	✓	✓	✓
Switzerland	SIC-IP (provisional name)	SIX	2023	✓	✓	✓	✓	✓
United States	FedNow	Federal Reserve	2023	✓	✓	✗	✗	✓

Source: Bank of International Settlements, "Developments in retail fast payments and implications for RTGS systems", December 2021.

FedNow

The US is a relatively new player in the real-time payments game, and the **FedNow** service, operated and governed by the Federal Reserve, was originally due to launch in 2024, but this was brought forward by a full year in 2021[40] with an official launch on 20 July 2023.[41] Full roll out is expected in 2025, and there's even a 3D theatre to visit![42]

RTP

The **RTP** real-time retail payment scheme is privately operated by The Clearing House (TCH) and launched in 2017. RTP was the only operational real-time payment system in the US up to the point when FedNow launched in July 2023. TCH also controls the rules (not NACHA). RTP volumes have increased substantially since launch, and the scheme now has in excess of 280 bank and credit union participants, a number which increases weekly. Its popularity largely stems from digital wallet usage, such as PayPal, Venmo (owned by PayPal), and Zelle (owned by Early Warning Services), and the newer POS service Pay by Bank (owned by Sionic) also launched in February 2023. Surprisingly, Cash App (owned by Block) doesn't use RTP, and whilst the payment may seem instantaneous to the user (i.e. Cash App balance), the settlement happens later using FedACH or EPN (i.e. withdraw to bank account), although users may elect to pay a fee for faster settlement.

Europe – SEPA

What is SEPA?

The **Single Euro Payment Area** (**SEPA**) is an initiative that aims to enable payers anywhere in the EU (as well as in a number of other countries) to make fast, safe, and efficient cashless Euro **Credit Transfers** (introduced in 2008) and **Direct Debits** (introduced in 2009) to anywhere within the area, just like national payments. SEPA gave Europe three building blocks:

- A **common set of payment instruments** (see SEPA *payments types*);
- **Common standards**:
  - The IBAN (International Bank Account Number);
  - ISO 20022 XML migration;

- Payment card migration from magnetic stripe to EMV chip (see Chapter 1, *Acquiring in Europe*); and
- Standards for payment cards and terminals (**SEPA card frameworks**); and
- A **legal framework**:
  - Regulation 260/2012 for Euro Credit Transfers and Direct Debits;
  - Regulation 924/2009 for Euro-denominated cross-border transfers and Direct Debits; and
  - Regulation 2025/2366, The Payment Services Directive (PSD2 and IFR [Interchange Fee Regulation], and PSD1 before that).

Payment schemes in Europe

I won't cover in detail all payment schemes in Europe, as you now understand the mechanics, and you can use tables similar to Tables 3.8 or 3.10 to understand the specifics of each scheme. I will just say that for consumer payments SEPA introduced the **TARGET Instant Payment Settlement** (**TIPS**) system for messaging across the EU, essentially the EU equivalent to SWIFT (for EURO-denominated payments). SEPA encouraged EU countries to migrate their national payment schemes to TIPS messaging, and this was completed in 2022.[43] The payment schemes that migrated to TIPS are shown in Table 3.13.

It is important to note that the German central bank (*Bundesbank*) operates its own Retail Payments System (RPS), which was extended to incorporate SEPA Credit Transfers (SCTs) in 2008 and Direct Debits (SDDs) in 2009, using the services of other payment schemes (e.g. EBA Clearing).[44] In addition, Table 3.13 shows the payment schemes that have migrated to TIPS, but individual countries may also have domestic payment schemes, such as FLIK in Slovenia.[45]

In addition, the **P27** cross-border real-time A2A payment system aimed to combine eight bank payment schemes across the Nordics into one integrated real-time A2A payment scheme, but it collapsed in April 2023[46] due to a lack of political alignment, not achieving critical mass, and conflicts of interest.

In February 2021, 31 major European banks created a joint venture with acquirers Worldline and Nets (now owned by Nexi) aiming to build a pan-European network rival to Visa and Mastercard: the **European Payments**

Table 3.13 EU payment schemes migrated to TIPS.

Payment scheme	Country
BANKART (BIPS)	Slovenia
CEC	Belgium
CENTRO	Lithuania
DIAS	Greece
EBA Clearing (STEP2 & RT1)	SEPA countries
EKS	Latvia
EquensWorldline	The Netherlands
Iberpay	Spain
Nexi (formerly Sia)	Italy
SIBS	Portugal
STET	France

Initiative (EPI).[47] In March 2022, we thought that was the end of it, as the EPI seemingly disbanded.[48] But in April 2023, at the time P27 collapsed, in a surprising move the EPI acquired Dutch payment facility iDEAL and Belgian mobile payments app Payconiq,[49] progress which was welcomed by the European Central Bank. Watch this space, as we may soon see a European equivalent to the American Zelle.

Bank payments economics (where does all the money go?)
Generic principles

We examined the costs of participating in a bank payment scheme in *Bank payment scheme participation*, and we now need to have a look at the costs of bank payments to both business users and consumers (payment service users, or PSUs). Because costs will vary depending on the geography, I will give UK examples, but it's easy to find out costs and fees in other geographies.

 Professionals should remember the following:

- **Not all bank payment schemes are available to everyone as a user (PSU).** For example, some schemes are only available to businesses, not consumers, such as BACS in the UK.

- **Not all bank payment schemes are accessible to all business partici-pants** (banks and non-banks), as this will depend on the jurisdiction and the participation models available for the scheme.
- **Bank payment schemes that allow cross-border transfers** (e.g. CHAPS in the UK, FedWire in the US) will generally **charge higher fees** to users. In the UK example, consumers can expect to pay between £25 and £35 for a CHAPS transfer, but charges for business users will be lower than this.
- **Transactional fees to business users are largely negotiable**, as they will depend on the tariff businesses being able to negotiate with their bank. Unlike on the card rails (see Chapter 2, *Charges and fees*), transactional fees are **based on volume**, not value. This means that fees can amount to just a few pence per transaction.
- There is **no concept of interchange on the bank rails**. (Yet. But more on that later.)
- **The way a monetary system evolves** for consumer transactions **depends on consumer behaviours** and the willingness of the government and central banks to move with the times.

Costs to users

Business users

Business users of bank payments incur costs as part of their banking tariff, and this is therefore negotiable and largely volume-based (unlike for the card rails, where transactional costs are largely value-based). Nevertheless, for business users bank payments are cheaper than card payments. For very low monthly volumes (e.g. less than 200 transactions), it may be £0.50 (this is a UK BACS example, but this depends on the bank). For volumes exceeding 5,000 transactions, it may be as low as £0.05 plus the bank set-up fee and transaction fees. Approved entities (e.g. bureaus or PSPs) can also offer these services, which means that businesses don't necessarily have to go through a bank to use a scheme.

Consumers

Consumers may incur costs depending on the jurisdiction and the payment scheme. For example, the UK population at large is used to the illusion of "free banking", and this has been discussed in the media for many years.[50,51] We've seen the closure of bank branches, the rise of digital-only banks, the controversy on overdraft rates which led to the intervention of the Financial Conduct Authority (FCA),[52] and much more. Nowadays, more and more UK bank accounts are in fact not free (if they ever really were), and more and more people are happy to pay the fees in exchange for the perks (e.g. cash back for each Direct Debit set up on the account). In the UK, using **online or mobile banking to make payments** (conducted on the FPS scheme) **is free to consumers**, and it would be a difficult job for the industry to change that (especially as consumers don't incur transactional fees to make card payments, so why should they if they make bank payments?). In other geographies, consumers may very well be used to paying for banking services and are probably wondering why the Brits are getting so hot under the collar about it. UK consumers may use the CHAPS payment scheme for high-value transactions, and, depending on the bank they use, this may cost them between £20 and £30 per transaction.

Bank vs card payments

It's all about context. I could quote global market statistics in terms of the dominance of various payment methods globally, or in Europe, or in Asia, or in the US, but, whilst interesting, they won't be of much use to you. Global figures only give you an appreciation of global trends. If you want to do something in a particular market (i.e. sell something, regulate something, stop something, encourage something, disrupt something), you need to understand that market.

This is what I'm getting at: you may want to say that for merchants bank payments are cheaper than card payments, and in theory they are, so why aren't merchants flocking to them? In practice, for merchants to deploy bank payments, the economics of such an action is not the only deciding factor. Consumer preference is one driver, and this is why bank payments are more popular in some geographies than others (e.g. iDEAL). The availability of services and their ease of integration into the merchant environment is another driver (e.g. again iDEAL). Government drivers also play a role, as measures can be implemented to influence behaviours (e.g. India with demonetisation). Undeniably, interchange is a pain for merchants, and some will seek to minimise it, but these will primarily be larger businesses, as smaller ones may not have the knowledge, or indeed the choice. And who's to say that, as A2A payments (and open banking) develop, the payments services that will come to market won't, in time, attract fees and charges that we haven't anticipated? The industry has a way of balancing itself.

Real-time payments drivers and challenges (life in the fast lane)

UK perspective

There are several potential drivers for the development of real-time payments infrastructures, ranging from boosting the economy, through fostering innovation, to financial inclusion. The UK FPS launched in 2008 and is therefore a mature system. The launch of FPS was not to foster innovation, but to boost the economy and to benefit UK businesses. Indeed, the 2007–2008 financial crisis, dubbed by some the biggest crisis since the Great Depression, was the catalyst for the launch. This is why innovation didn't happen during the first seven years of FPS and, in fact, why only one new business type emerged: payday lenders. As an example, Wonga launched in July 2008, their business model enabled by real-time payments, and many others followed. But this is a cautionary tale, as payday lenders paid the price for irresponsible lending and extortionate rates, although it took a decade to see regulations in the space. Wonga faced troubles in other jurisdictions (e.g. Canada), until they eventually collapsed into administration in 2018. Nowadays, payday lenders have all but disappeared (in the UK at least), leaving space for the popular BNPL products. And the UK is preparing for its New Payments Architecture (NPA).

Global perspective

Fast forward to 2023, and the UK expectations for their NPA[53] are in line with global ones:

- **Technology**, especially smart phones, has been the main driver behind the creation of real-time payment systems.
- **Consumer expectations** have changed, and modern real-time payments systems are fulfilling a customer need driven by technology.

- New business opportunities and enabling competition **will foster innovation**.
- **Financial inclusion** will be heavily promoted.

At the time of writing, we are experiencing an even bigger economic crisis, which is changing the landscape yet again. Globally, drivers for real-time payments will come from open banking, digital identity, and regulations. The challenges are shown in Table 3.14.

Approaches to real-time payments differ across the globe, but success depends on conducive regulations, messaging standardisation, and adequate infrastructure (e.g. 5G).

To take the UK as an example, the New Payments Architecture (NPA) originally aimed to unify CHAPS, BACS, FPS, and the cheque clearing infrastructure. Its scope has since been narrowed to just BACS and FPS, essentially concentrating on retail payments.[54] The NPA is expected to go live at the end of 2024, with a full migration at the end of 2025. In the meantime, at the time of writing, Canada is experiencing delays in the delivery of its Real Time Rail (RTR) infrastructure.[55]

The following sections show the top and bottom ten countries by real-time transaction volumes specifying the payment scheme, messaging, 5G deployment, and open banking status.

Table 3.14 Real-time payments drivers and challenges.

Drivers	Challenges
Open banking	<ul><li>Access through APIs brings API security into focus</li><li>Fraud prevention models</li><li>Customer care models</li></ul>
Digital identity	<ul><li>Disparate digital identity framework</li><li>Lack of digital identity framework</li><li>Portability and integration issues</li><li>Interoperability issues</li></ul>
Regulations	<ul><li>Increased complexity</li><li>Increased disparity</li><li>Increased stringency (especially with AML)</li><li>Balancing regulatory obligations, security,fraudprevention,privacy,andcustomerexperience</li></ul>

Top ten countries

As a testimony to the dynamism of the payments industry, Brazil stole second position from China since the last report, and if you read this book years from its publication, the picture will be different again. In any instance, it is apparent that real-time payments still have massive growth opportunities in most countries as their proportion of electronic payments is still low. Will there be similar opportunities in India, Thailand, Nigeria, Oman, and Mexico? Maybe, if they manage to massively reduce the use of cash.

Figure 3.17 doesn't give the complete picture, as you also have to look at growth opportunity projections, and Figure 3.18 offers this.

Of note is Croatia, which exhibits a healthy 210.9% five-year CAGR.

Bottom ten countries

Finally, Figures 3.19 and 3.20 chart the bottom ten countries.

Surprised to see markets such as Canada and the UK in this chart? Well, what you have to remember is that those markets are heavily card-penetrated, so it will take a lot of effort from policy makers, and a lot of communication, to convince consumers to switch from cards, which are convenient and ubiquitous ... History will tell.

Bank payments risks (danger zone)

There are a number of risks associated with bank payments, be they related to demographics and consumer preferences, governance, and processes, or to the fact that payments are so much faster.

Unauthorised fraud

Unauthorised Fraud is a type of fraud where the account holder hasn't provided authorisation for the payment and the transaction is carried out by a criminal (e.g. the victim's card details are used without their knowledge or consent), or when the account holder acts fraudulently (e.g. a mule account).

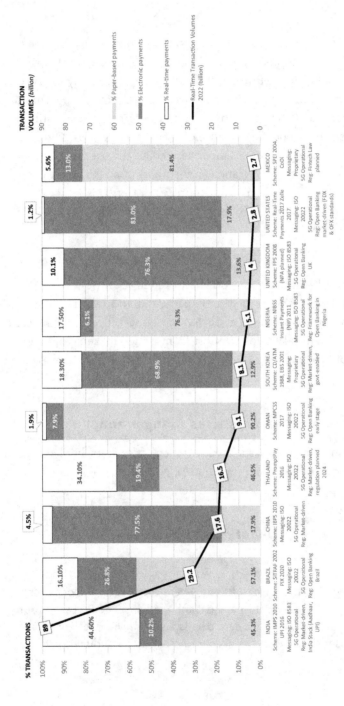

Figure 3.17 Top ten countries by real-time transaction volume, including messaging, 5G deployments, and open banking status, 2022. Chart by the author.

Sources: ACI Worldwide, "It's Prime Time for Real Time 2023"[6], Global Mobile Suppliers Association, "5G Market Snapshot May 2023"[7], and individual country reports.

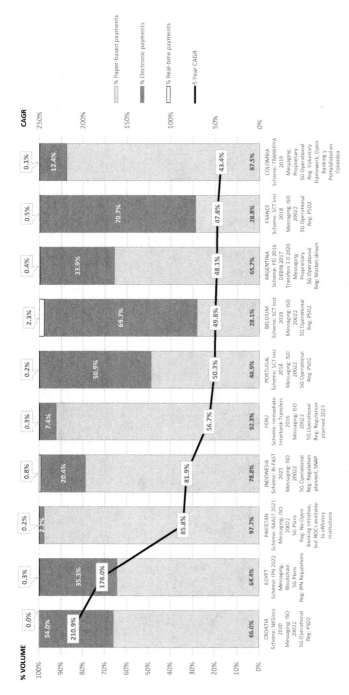

Figure 3.18 Top ten countries by real-time five-year CAGR, including messaging, 5G deployments, and open banking status, 2022–2047. Chart by the author.

Sources: ACI Worldwide, "It's Prime Time for RealTime 2023"; Global Mobile Suppliers Association; "5G Market Snapshot May 2023"; and individual country reports.

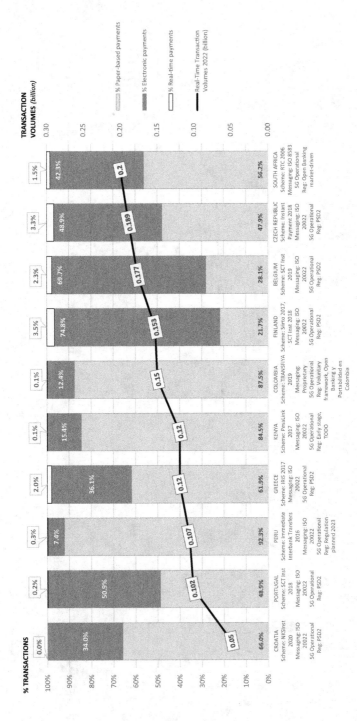

Figure 3.19 Bottom ten countries by real-time transaction volumes, including messaging, 5G deployments, and open banking status, 2022. Chart by the author.

Source: ACI Worldwide, "It's Prime Time for Real Time 2023"; Global Mobile Suppliers Association, "5G Market Snapshot May 2023"; and individual country reports.

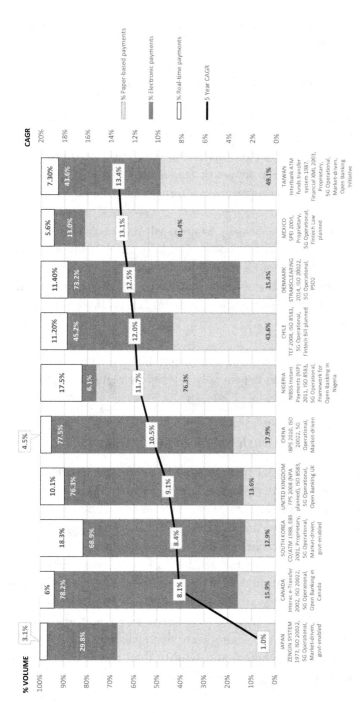

Figure 3.20 Bottom 10 countries by real-time five-year CAGR, including messaging, 5G deployments, and open banking status, 2022–2047. Chart by the author.

Sources: ACI Worldwide, "It's Prime Time for Real Time 2023"; Global Mobile Suppliers Association, "5G Market Snapshot May 2023"; and individual country reports.

Unauthorised fraud can take many forms, and you probably have heard of the following examples:

- **Account Takeover Fraud (ATO)**: this usually happens when a fraudster compromises a genuine payment account and conducts transactions fraudulently with that account. This is generally linked to identity theft crimes and is a particular issue in financial services in general (but also other industries). As data breaches continue to plague our lives, large volumes of stolen credentials are continuously being dumped on underground forums and offered for sale to criminals.
- **New Account Fraud**: this usually happens when a fraudster or money mule has been successfully onboarded by a financial institution after applying using their own identity (first party fraud), a stolen identity (third party fraud), or a synthetic identity (i.e. identity created from real and fake identity information over time). This is also referred to as **Application Fraud**.

There are more examples of unauthorised fraud, but I won't dwell on this subject, as this type of fraud is generally covered by regulations globally and has been for a long time.

Authorised Push Payment (APP) fraud

This type of fraud is a global phenomenon. As real-time payments infrastructures suggest a move from multi-day settlement cycles to almost immediate settlement for retail transactions, the impact on consumers is significant. This is due to the fact that governance arrangements are different from those applicable to Large-Value Payment Schemes (LVPS) (e.g. CHAPS, FedWire), where the sending and receiving parties are heavily regulated, authenticated, and generally know what they're doing. Consumers are showing an increasing preference for faster digital retail payments, and digital fraud is on the rise as a result. Indeed, in the UK in 2022, 98% of APP scams were conducted through the FPS real-time retail payment scheme, and, within that, the most common channel was mobile banking followed by Internet banking. But what is APP fraud?

> **Authorised Push Payment (APP) Fraud** happens when a bank account holder is tricked into sending a payment to a fraudster posing as a genuine payee.

This is different from unauthorised fraud, where a fraudster takes over a genuine bank account without the account holder's knowledge (account takeover), and subsequently makes payments or applies for products. Across geographies, consumers are largely covered against unauthorised fraud if they can prove that they weren't party to the fraud. The picture is very different with APP fraud, and consumers may be left with the liability depending on the jurisdiction. APP fraud is generally linked to real-time payments, as there may be little time for action from the point of a payment instruction to when the funds irrevocably leave the account.

Business Email Compromise (BEC)

One scenario for APP fraud is called "Business Email Compromise (BEC)" and is described in Figure 3.21.

BEC happens when a cybercriminal compromises the email of a trusted party (e.g. a solicitor), which is generally the case if the trusted party's

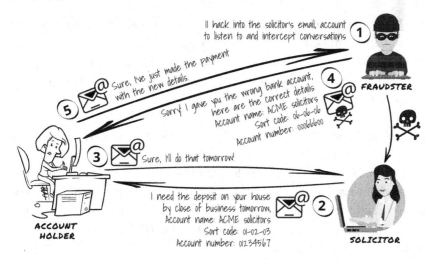

Figure 3.21 A Business Email Compromise (BEC) scenario.

Source: drawing by the author.

device or environment is insecure. Once the fraudster has access to the trusted party's email environment, they sit and watch email conversations between the trusted party and their client.

At the point when a payment transaction is about to happen (e.g. the deposit on a house purchase is about to be paid), the fraudsters would send an email from the trusted party's email address notifying the client that the payment should be made to a different bank account, giving the fraudster's sort code and bank account number, but the trusted party's name. If the client doesn't verify the validity of this request through another channel (e.g. over the phone or in person), they would authorise the payment through their banking facility with the new payee's details.

This is considered an authorised payment by the bank, and current payment schemes would route the payment on the basis of the sort code/routing number and bank account number. The name would not be checked, unless the bank has deployed additional services to cater for this scenario (see *Confirmation of Payee*).

Types of APP scams

In their Annual Fraud Report 2023, UK Finance offers a helpful classification of APP fraud into two categories and eight types:

- **Malicious payee**: this includes purchase scams, investment scams, romance scams, and advance fee scams.
- **Malicious redirection**: this includes invoice and mandate scams, CEO fraud, law enforcement or bank staff impersonation, and other impersonation.

Figures 3.22 and 3.23 show the proportion of APP scam types in the UK in 2022.

In 2022, £485.2 million was lost through APP scams in the UK, with social engineering of victims as the main driver and investment scams and impersonation of police, bank, or telco staff as the top categories by volume. This has pushed the Payment Systems Operator (PSR) to develop a world-first regulation to force the ecosystem to act for the benefit of victims (see Chapter 5, *Authorised fraud*). In the US, victims of APP scams are largely not covered, as banks argue that they already cover unauthorised fraud, which has pushed the US Congress to question bank bosses.[58] APP scams in the US

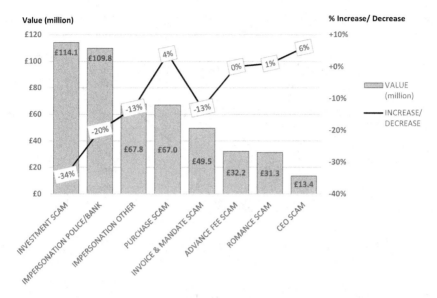

Figure 3.22 APP scam types by value in the UK in 2022. Chart by the author.
Source: UK Finance Annual Fraud Report 2023.

happen on Zelle, as you would expect, and the media at large and members of the US Congress are pointing the finger at Zelle for being insecure, which I think is unfair since over 99.9% of Zelle transactions are clean transactions, according to Early Warning Services, the Zelle operator, and I believe the US banking and regulatory system as a whole is not (yet) conducive to combatting authorised fraud (some may disagree). In addition, Zelle is not the only medium through which this type of scam happens. In any instance, this would probably mean an amendment to Regulation E (Electronic Fund Transfers, 12 CFR 205.11), [59] so as to mandate reimbursement of authorised payment scams, an idea which is starting to draw more media attention. Perhaps lessons can be learnt from the UK regulation on reimbursement of APP scams (see Chapter 5, *Authorised fraud*), but bearing in mind that it took about six years for UK regulators to do anything about it, the US has a long way to go yet.[60] In October 2023, the US banks members of Zelle started reimbursing APP fraud victims following pressure from Washington.[61]

There are many opportunities for PSPs and technology providers to deliver products and services. For example, Mastercard launched their AI tool, Consumer Fraud Risk, in July 2023 to help banks prevent real-time payment scams.[62]

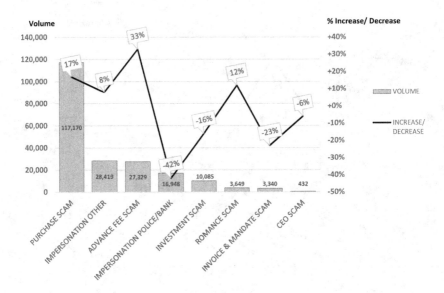

Figure 3.23 APP scam types by volume in the UK in 2022. Chart by the author.

Source: UK Finance Annual Fraud Report 2023.

Other risks

Real-time payments have many benefits for businesses (e.g. cash flow) and users (convenience) alike, but by their very nature they leave **little margin for error because of the fast settlement times**. Once a fraudster gets hold of the money, it disappears very quickly. Users can also make mistakes: if a mistyped sort code and bank account number (ABA Routing Number and account number in the US) corresponds to a valid account, the effect would be the same as for an APP scam (unless other safeguards are in place).

Distinguishing fraudsters from genuine account holders is a concern, and a well-designed digital identity framework would address this concern (see Chapter 2, *Fraud prevention and digital identity*), but deployments vary around the globe. In the meantime, we just apply plasters (i.e. technology and half-hearted regulations) to solve a systemic issue.

Aside from fraud, there are also concerns amongst businesses and consumers alike over the **lack of refund and reimbursement processes**, as we're all used to these processes on the card rails (see Chapter 1, *Exceptions and* *disputes*). I admit that there could be more thought put into the arbitration of exceptions (a role which should be performed by a payment scheme or their governing entity) and that processes should be clear, but, when it comes to consumer retail payments, is this really an issue? When something is wrong with a retail purchase, I go directly to the retailer. If they have a good "refunds and returns" policy, I will be happy. That's called customer service. Why would I need to bother with the intricacies of my rights under any payments regulation?

It would be remiss of me to ignore the elephant in the room: **Big Tech**. Social media platforms and search engines act as a launch pad for criminals, but they are largely left out of the accountability loop. If an advert for a fake investment site is placed on a social media platform or ranks on a search engine, it can reach multitudes. Figure 3.22 shows that investment scams are the biggest fraud by value in the UK, and crypto scams contribute to this.

Finally, real-time payments are relatively new, and infrastructures and processes must be developed with security in mind because **cybercrime will not abate**. This is not specific to real-time payments but applies to the financial services industry in general. Building secure and resilient infrastructures is key, and in recent years global financial services regulations have increasingly included stringent provisions for cybersecurity and resilience.

Of course, all of this may have **unintended consequences** because any change or improvement to an ecosystem means that investment will have to be made somewhere. Financial infrastructures, especially for banking, have been funded by the banks. On the card rails, card schemes have made that investment, but they unilaterally make their own rules to make their model economically viable (within applicable regulations of course), which is why, for example, we have interchange. On the bank rails, we have very complex, and stringent, regulatory frameworks, and any change to the monetary system, especially when related to liability, has economic implications which the banking industry might resist. Indeed, in the UK as far back as 2018, UK Finance, a banking trade association, proposed an additional tax on banking transactions to fund any potential fraud reimbursement to victims[63] (isn't this a bit like interchange?). Watch this space.

Fraud prevention best practice

Payment ecosystems have been around for a long time, and lessons can be learnt (although we don't ever seem to do a lot of that). In any instance, best practice can be classified into three categories: detection, prevention, and response. These three fundamental elements should follow the well-known organisational principles of process, people, and technology.

Detection

Success in detecting fraud will depend on:

- **The processes in place**: the mechanics of payments are understood, and processes must ensure that they cater for all fraud origination scenarios, new and upcoming, and these must be reviewed regularly to cater for new crimes. It is not sufficient to comply with applicable regulations: organisations have a duty to protect themselves and the end users. This protection consists of the underwriting stage when opening an account and the monitoring processes in place once an account is opened.
- **The technologies used**: transactional data monitoring and customer analytics (including behavioural) are crucial, especially in real-time environments. Because processes are so much faster, automation plays a crucial role. Long gone are the days where we could rely on fraud prevention technologies solely based on static rules. These systems look at the past, and whilst historical data is good for modelling, the world and technology have moved on to become more forward-thinking: predictive analytics, machine learning, and AI in general are here to help. In addition, sharing threat intelligence is fundamental to fighting fraud, and there are many sources, both from industry and the public sector. This is also where digital identity, KYC, and a multitude of identity-proofing mechanisms come into their own.
- **The people performing the processes and using the technologies**: educating staff and partners is key, and this means giving them the ability to identify fraudulent account openings and payments that are at risk of fraud, as well as the processes to do something about it, including improving the processes themselves.

Prevention

The way fraud is prevented is not always visible to the end users. For example, as covered in Chapter 1, *Exceptions and disputes*, chargebacks and retrievals can be initiated by the issuer independently of the cardholder. This suggests that the issuer has fraud prevention mechanisms that allow them to do that. Firms should take reasonable steps to prevent fraud, according to their duty of care, and this will depend on:

- **The processes in place**: processes must be adequate to prevent known fraud origination scenarios, but they must also prevent new and upcoming ones. These processes must be reviewed regularly to keep up with criminals. At a basic level, payment accounts must only be opened in line with legal and regulatory requirements on Customer Due Diligence. In addition, once an account is opened, firms should use all available threat intelligence sources and industry fraud databases to screen accounts and identify abnormal usage patterns. At an end-user level, organisations should also provide end users with effective warnings, including the appropriate actions for customers to take to protect themselves against fraud. Where possible, firms should also deploy available mechanisms provided by the payment schemes and infrastructures (e.g. 3D Secure, CoP), and keep up to date with developments and upgrades.
- **The technologies used**: these will be essentially the same as those used for detection, and success in preventing fraud is largely dependent on the processes in place. Similarly to the previous step, automation is key, as no one has unlimited resources, and success will depend on the organisation's ability to minimise the volumes of manual interventions, leaving only the most complex cases for actual people.
- **The people performing the processes and using the technologies**: educating staff and partners is key, and this means giving them the ability to identify genuine accounts being used fraudulently or behaving strangely, new accounts opened fraudulently, and payments that are at risk of fraud. The processes in place, supported by technology and automation, should reflect this, which should include a process to improve the processes.

Response

Fraud will happen, and when it does, or when it is suspected, firms still have a chance to do something about it:

- **The processes in place**: processes must be able to flex to enable a delay in the actual payment before the payment becomes irrevocable, whilst the firm investigates the case and communicates with the payee's PSP. This is mostly a procedural step, and it relies heavily on effective communication mechanisms. This is perhaps one of the hardest things to achieve, as the financial services industry is not best known for its effective communications and transparency. However, provisions should be made for the freezing of funds whilst an investigation is performed, as well as the repatriation of funds to the end user as soon as practical (see Chapter 5, *Customer care*).

- **The technologies used**: these will be essentially the same as those used for detection and prevention, but success in fraud response is largely dependent on best practice communication mechanisms between ecosystem actors, and effective communication technologies should be deployed for both end users and ecosystem partners. Neo-banks do this well, whilst it can be convoluted for incumbent players (Do I call? Do I go on the website? Is there a chat facility? Can I email? Where can I find instructions?).

- **The people performing the processes and using the technologies**: educating staff and partners is key, and this means giving them the ability to deal with the cases not only in line with applicable regulations, but with empathy too. This is a customer services matter, and effectiveness will be contingent to the processes in place and the technology used, as well as the law (which sometimes may not allow for good outcomes for end users).

 ## Lessons learnt

We can learn a lot from our rich history.

Educating end users is fundamental, and as everyone becomes increasingly more digital, this responsibility shouldn't fall solely on financial services institutions. Communicating the danger of mule accounts, identity theft, phishing, and cybercrime in general should be a top agenda item for everyone, public and private sector firms alike.

Industry cooperation is also crucial, and this manifests itself in the development of new services (e.g. CoP, digital identity services), intelligence sharing, and contribution to the evolution of existing regulations. The cooperation should also extend to non-financial services organisations that are systemically important to the payments ecosystem, such as Big Tech and other platform providers. In addition, industry cooperation shouldn't confine itself to the private sector, and public–private cooperation is also crucial.

Customer aftercare is often left to the industry, but regulators have a part in this. Defining fair contingent reimbursement models for fraud victims or erroneous payments is fundamental. The cards industry already does this well with the chargeback process. Bank payment rails are not so far advanced, except in the UK (see Chapter 5, *Authorised fraud*). This step also relies on effective communication mechanisms and a clear definition of "duty of care".

What next for bank payments?

Environmental changes will continue to affect the payments industry. The pandemic's impact will continue to affect businesses and people alike, as will the geopolitical environment. Economic implications will drive the adoption of payment methods to ease the burden for both consumers and businesses (e.g. BNPL, merchant financing, mobile money). This will also lead to further consolidation, with more acquisitions and divestments, and more partnerships between incumbent and new entrants. The industry will continue to strive for innovation, ranging from not-for-profit organisations, such as Innovate Finance[64] in the UK, to incumbent players, such as the Barclays Accelerator[65] programme.

Bank payment infrastructures will continue to evolve towards more real-time operations for the benefit of businesses and consumers. The role of central banks may evolve as a result.

Payment fraud and cybercrime will continue to increase. Financial crime will not abate, and criminals will find ever more innovative ways to try and compromise ecosystems. Industry and regulators will continue to implement measures to preserve ecosystem integrity. Payment fraud in general will continue to increase, especially real-time payment fraud (e.g. UK FPS, UK FedNow, EU instant payments). The worldwide increase in faster payments of all types, including A2A, will lead regulators to increase their focus on financial services institutions, particularly for authorised fraud where controls are lacking, (and this is already catered for on the card rails). This will also lead to more cooperation with, and even regulations for, technology firms (e.g. telcos, social media, platforms, etc.) to ensure good outcomes for consumers (e.g. communications, liability, and reimbursement).

Competition and convergence across centralised payment rails will continue, and these are not mutually exclusive. Rivals to Visa and Mastercard will continue to emerge, some will die, and some might even be successful (e.g. EPI). In July 2023, traditionally closed systems like Alipay and WeChat Pay started to let people link Visa, Mastercard, and JCB as funding mechanisms.[66] Open banking will hopefully drive further adoption of A2A payments, and traditional card rails will continue to embed themselves. Mastercard started early with the acquisition of Vocalink in 2017.

The drive for standardisation will continue, as exemplified by the wide adoption of the ISO 20022 standard, and this will contribute to increased interoperability between bank payment rails and other centralised rails. And of course, cash is not dead and will remain a part of the mix for as long as consumers want it to.

Customer experience and convenience will continue to be a major innovation driver. This is a familiar phenomenon in the consumer space, and B2C payment innovation will continue, but B2B payments will remain a growth area, as, increasingly, businesses demand the same seamless experiences that consumers already enjoy. In addition, in 2023 a number of fintech firms operating in both B2C and B2B sectors shuttered B2C operations to concentrate on their B2B portfolios. As an example, both open banking loyalty firm LoyalBe[67] and crypto firm Bakkt[68] shut down their consumer operations in 2023 to concentrate on the B2B sector. As a result, we will also see an increase in innovation and services for B2B payments, including those related to embedded finance: MarketsandMarkets predicts that the global B2B payments market will grow from $1,025.5 billion in 2022 to $1,682.4 billion by 2028 at a CAGR of 8.6% to 2028.[69] In our hyper-connected world, cross-border payments will also continue to grow.

Big Tech will continue to insert themselves further into payments ecosystems (and into financial services in general). Big Tech companies' proficiency at using data, combined with their size, customer base, and reach, has incumbent industry players and regulators worried.

The world of payments is evolving.

Bank payment systems – conclusion (where do we go from here?)

In this whistle-stop of bank payments, we covered:

- Bank payments, their mechanics, and economics;
- The different types of payment systems and their settlement infrastructures; and
- Real-time payments and their drivers, challenges, and risks.

I have tried to explain the jargon and debunk a few myths, and the main terms introduced in this chapter will be found in the glossary (Chapter 7). I shared some insights as to what the future might look like, supported by global market trends, graphs, and charts which I hope readers will find useful. The fundamental principles were covered, and I also gave you my opinion on some aspects of the industry. I know some may disagree with me, and I always welcome a good debate, but I hope I have equipped you to ask the right questions.

If you read this book a few years from now, new business models will have emerged, and regulatory pressure will have increased. Some businesses will have thrived, some will have pivoted, and others will have simply disappeared.

To complete our understanding of payments, we must examine open banking and alternative payments.

Notes

1 "Access to UK Payment Schemes for Non-Bank Payment Service Providers", Bank of England, 2019. Available at: https://www.bankofengland. co.uk/-/media/boe/files/markets/other-market-operations/accessfor nonbankpaymentserviceproviders.pdf (Accessed 28 June 2023).

2 "TransferWise becomes first non-bank to open settlement account with BofE RTGS", Finextra, 18 April 2018. Available at: https://www.finextra.com/newsarticle/31969/transferwise-becomes-first-non-bank-to-open-settlement-account-with-bofe-rtgs (Accessed 28 June 2023).

3 "FedNow Service – Frequently Asked Questions", US Federal Reserve website. Available at: https://www.federalreserve.gov/paymentsystems/fednow_faq.htm (Accessed 28 June 2023).

4 "Request to Pay", Pay.UK website. Available at: https://www.wearepay.uk/what-we-do/overlay-services/request-to-pay/ (Accessed 29 June 2023).

5 "EPC payment scheme management", European Payments Council website. Available at: https://www.europeanpaymentscouncil.eu/what-we-do/sepa-payment-scheme-management (Accessed 30 June 2023).

6 "Clearing and settlement mechanisms", European Payments Council website. Available at: https://www.europeanpaymentscouncil.eu/what-we-do/sepa-payment-scheme-management/clearing-and-settlement-mechanisms (Accessed 30 June 2023).

7 "SEPA proxy lookup", European Payments Council website. Available at: https://www.europeanpaymentscouncil.eu/what-we-do/other-schemes/sepa-proxy-lookup (Accessed 30 June 2023).

8 "SEPA Request-to-Pay" European Payments Council website. Available at: https://www.europeanpaymentscouncil.eu/what-we-do/other-schemes/sepa-request-pay (Accessed 30 June 2023).

9 "SEPA payment account access" European Payments Council website. Available at: https://www.europeanpaymentscouncil.eu/what-we-do/other-schemes/sepa-payment-account-access (Accessed 30 June 2023).

10 "Brazil's Pix used for more transactions than credit and debit cards combined", Finextra, 26 July 2023. Available at: https://www.finextra.com/newsarticle/42695/brazils-pix-used-for-more-transactions-than-credit-and-debit-cards-combined (Accessed 26 July 2023).

11 "Payment and settlement", Bank of England website. Available at: https://www.bankofengland.co.uk/payment-and-settlement (Accessed 28 June 2023).

12 "Confirmation of Payee", Pay.UK website. Available at: https://www.wearepay.uk/what-we-do/overlay-services/confirmation-of-payee/ (Accessed 28 June 2023).

13 SWIFT website. Available at: https://www.swift.com/ (Accessed 30 June 2023).

14 "Geopolitical fragmentation risks and international currencies", European Central Bank, June 2023. Available at: https://www.ecb.europa.eu/pub/ire/article/html/ecb.ireart202306_01~11d437be4d.en.html (Accessed 30 June 2023).

15 "60 Percent of Iran-Russia Trade Is Already De-Dollarized" teleSUR[HD], 2 June 2023. Available at: https://www.telesurenglish.net/news/60-Percent-of-Iran-Russia-Trade-Is-Already-De-Dollarized-20230602-0015. html (Accessed 30 June 2026).

16 "Expanding global use of CIPS, e-CNY the best way to resist US' sanctioning", Global Times, 14 May 2023. Available at: https://www.globaltimes. cn/page/202305/1290672.shtml (Accessed 30 June 2023).

17 "China's CIPS: A potential alternative in global financial order", The Diplomat, 25 April 2022. Available at: https://thediplomat.com/2022/04/chinas-cips-a-potential-alternative-in-global-financial-order/ (Accessed 30 June 2023).

18 "We are live: what are the next steps during coexistence?" SWIFT website. Available at: https://www.swift.com/standards/iso-20022/iso-20022-payments-financial-institutions (Accessed 15 July 2023).

19 "TCH reschedules CHIPS ISO 20022 implementation to April 2024", The Clearing House, 9 February 2023. Available at: https://www. theclearinghouse.org/payment-systems/Articles/2023/02/02-09-2023_ TCH_Reschedules_CHIPS_ISO_20022_ImplementationApril_2024 (Accessed 16 July 2023).

20 "A brief introduction to the Real-Time Gross Settlement system and CHAPS", Bank of England website. Available at: https://www.bank ofengland.co.uk/payment-and-settlement/a-brief-introduction-to-the-real-time-gross-settlement-system-and-chaps (Accessed 30 June 2023).

21 "An Introduction to the UK's Interbank Payment Schemes", Payment Systems Regulator, 2016. Available at: https://www.psr.org.uk/media/ wnahveui/for-information-only-an-introduction-to-the-uks-interbank-payment-schemes.pdf (Accessed 29 June 2023).

22 "An Introduction to the UK's Interbank Payment Schemes", Payment Systems Regulator, 2016. Available at: https://www.psr.org.uk/media/ wnahveui/for-information-only-an-introduction-to-the-uks-interbank-payment-schemes.pdf (Accessed 29 June 2023).

23 "An Introduction to the UK's Interbank Payment Schemes", Payment Systems Regulator, 2016. Available at: https://www.psr.org.uk/media/ wnahveui/for-information-only-an-introduction-to-the-uks-interbank-payment-schemes.pdf (Accessed 29 June 2023).

24 "BACS Service Principles", Pay.UK, February 2023. Available at: https:// www.wearepay.uk/wp-content/uploads/Pay.UK-Bacs-Service-Principles. pdf (Accessed 29 June 2023).

25 BACS website. Available at: https://www.bacs.co.uk/ (Accessed 28 June 2023).

26 BACS, "Translation Guide", Version 1.1. BACS website. Available at: https://www.bacs.co.uk/media/1cqbf21x/iso20022bacstranslationguide.pdf (Accessed 3 October 2023).

27 "An Introduction to the UK's Interbank Payment Schemes", Payment Systems Regulator, 2016. Available at: https://www.psr.org.uk/media/wnahveui/for-information-only-an-introduction-to-the-uks-interbank-payment-schemes.pdf (Accessed 29 June 2023).

28 Pay.UK website. Available at: https://www.wearepay.uk/what-we-do/payment-systems/bacs-payment-system/ (Accessed 30 June 2023).

29 NACHA website. Available at: https://www.nacha.org/ (Accessed 14 July 2023).

30 See Carol Coye Benson, Scott Loftesness, and Russ Jones, *Payments Systems in the U.S.: A Guide for the Payments Professional*, 3rd ed., Glenbrook Press, San Francisco, 2017.

31 "FedACH® Processing Schedule", The Federal Reserve, 12 September 2022. Available at: https://frbservices.org/resources/resource-centers/same-day-ach/fedach-processing-schedule.html (Accessed 12 July 2023).

32 "An Introduction to the UK's Interbank Payment Schemes", Payment Systems Regulator, 2016. Available at: https://www.psr.org.uk/media/wnahveui/for-information-only-an-introduction-to-the-uks-interbank-payment-schemes.pdf (Accessed 29 June 2023).

33 "FedACH® Services Resources", Federal Reserve website. Available at: https://www.frbservices.org/resources/financial-services/ach (Accessed 16 July 2023).

34 "About ACH", The Clearing House website. Available at: https://www.theclearinghouse.org/payment-systems/ach (Accessed 16 July 2023).

35 "Developments in Retail Fast Payments and Implications for RTGS Systems", CPMI, December 2021. Available at: https://www.bis.org/cpmi/publ/d201.pdf (Accessed 11 August 2023).

36 "Faster Payments System", Pay.UK website. Available at: https://www.wearepay.uk/what-we-do/payment-systems/faster-payment-system/ (Accessed 1 July 2023).

37 "Transaction limits", Pay.UK website. Available at: https://www.wearepay.uk/what-we-do/payment-systems/faster-payment-system/transaction-limits/ (Accessed 1 July 2023).

38 "UK Payment Markets Summary 2022", UK Finance, August 2022. Available at: https://www.ukfinance.org.uk/system/files/2022–08/UKF%20Payment%20Markets%20Summary%202022.pdf (Accessed 1 July 2023).

39 "Payment system participant list", Pay.UK website. Available at: https://www.wearepay.uk/participants-list/ (Accessed 1 July 2023).

40 "Fed moves up FedNow launch date", Consumer Finance Moni-
    tor, Ballard Spahr LLP, 18 February 2021. Available at: https://www.
    consumerfinancemonitor.com/2021/02/18/fed-moves-up-fednow-
    launch-date/ (Accessed 13 July 2023).

41 "Launching in Late July – Get on board!", FedNOW website. Available at:
    https://explore.fednow.org/ (Accessed 13 July 2023).

42 "Explore the City", FedNow website, July 2023. Available at: https://
    explore.fednow.org/explore-the-city (Accessed 21 July 2023).

43 "Successful completion of ACH migration to TIPS", European Central
    Bank, 28 March 2022. Available at: https://www.ecb.europa.eu/paym/
    intro/news/html/ecb.mipnews220328.en.html (Accessed 30 June 2023).

44 For SCTs, see https://www.bundesbank.de/en/tasks/payment-systems/
    services/sepa/content/sepa-credit-transfer-626664 (Accessed 3 October
    2023). For DDs, see https://www.bundesbank.de/en/tasks/payment-
    systems/services/sepa/content/sepa-direct-debit-626654 (Accessed 3
    October 2023).

45 "Instant payment environment in Slovenia", European Payments Coun-
    cil, 26 January 2021. Available at: https://www.europeanpaymentscouncil.
    eu/news-insights/insight/instant-payment-environment-slovenia
    (Accessed 30 June 2023).

46 "P27 has withdrawn its clearing license application", P27 website, 20
    April 2023. Available at: https://news.cision.com/p27-nordic-payments-
    platform/r/p27-has-withdrawn-its-clearing-license-application,c3750183
    (Accessed 12 July 2023).

47 "Changing the way Europe pays", EPI, 2021. Available at: https://www.
    epicompany.eu/ (Accessed 25 June 2023).

48 "EPI abandons plan for Visa and Mastercard rival as member banks
    quit", Finextra, 22 March 2022. Available at: https://www.finextra.com/
    newsarticle/39907/epi-abandons-plan-for-visa-and-mastercard-rival-as-
    member-banks-quit (Accessed 25 June 2023).

49 "EPI Company announces acquisitions, additional shareholders and
    the coming launch of its new instant payment solution", EPI website,
    25 April 2023. Available at: https://www.epicompany.eu/epi-company-
    announces-acquisitions-additional-shareholders-and-the-coming-
    launch-of-its-new-instant-payment-solution/ (Accessed 12 July 2023).

50 "Is free banking on the way out?" Choose, 10 February 2015. Available
    at: https://www.choose.co.uk/news/end-of-free-banking-say-pricewater-
    housecooper.html (Accessed 1 July 2023).

51 "Negative interest rates could put an end to free banking, experts warn",
    The Telegraph, 12 October 2020. Available at: https://www.telegraph.

co.uk/business/2020/10/12/bank-england-asks-banks-ready-negative-interest-rates/ (Accessed 1 July 2023).

52 "Millions of customers together save nearly £1 billion due to overdraft rule changes", Financial Conduct Authority website, 19 April 2023. Available at: https://www.fca.org.uk/news/press-releases/millions-customers-together-save-nearly-1billion-due-overdraft-rule-changes (Accessed 1 July 2023).

53 "The New Payments Architecture Programme: Delivering a New Payments System for the UK", Pay.UK, July 2023. Available at: https://www.wearepay.uk/wp-content/uploads/2023/07/Pay.UK_NPA_Prospectus.pdf (Accessed 17 July 2023).

54 "About the NPA", Pay.UK website. Available at: https://www.wearepay.uk/npa/about-the-npa/ (Accessed 13 July 2023).

55 "Payments Canada update on Real-Time Rail (RTR)", Payments Canada website, 13 June 2023. Available at: https://payments.ca/payments-canada-update-real-time-rail-rtr (Accessed 13 July 2023).

56 "It's Prime Time For Real-Time", ACI Worldwide, 2023. Available at: https://www.aciworldwide.com/real-time-payments-report (Accessed 9 July 2023).

57 "5G-market snapshot May 2023", Global Mobile Suppliers Association, May 2023. Available at: https://gsacom.com/paper/5g-market-snapshot-may-2023/ (Accessed 10 July 2023).

58 "Congress drills bank brass on Authorized Push Payments fraud", Pymnts.com, 22 September 2022. Available at: https://www.pymnts.com/bank-regulation/2022/congress-drills-bank-brass-on-authorized-push-payments-fraud/ (Accessed 14 July 2023).

59 "Electronic Fund Transfers, 12 CFR 205", Federal Reserve website. Available at: https://www.ecfr.gov/current/title-12/chapter-II/subchapter-A/part-205/section-205.11 (Accessed 14 July 2023).

60 "Will the US embrace the UK Contingent Reimbursement Model to fight online scam losses?", Thomson Reuters, 10 April 2023. Available at: https://www.thomsonreuters.com/en-us/posts/investigation-fraud-and-risk/us-embrace-contingent-reimbursement/ (Accessed 14 July 2023).

61 "Payments app Zelle begins refunds for imposter scams after Washington pressure", Reuters, 13 November 2023. Available at: https://www.reuters.com/technology/cybersecurity/payments-app-zelle-begins-refunds-imposter-scams-after-washington-pressure-2023-11-13/ (Accessed 16 November 2023).

62 "Mastercard AI tool helps UK banks take on real-time payment scams", Finextra, 6 July 2023. Available at: https://www.finextra.com/newsarticle/42602/mastercard-ai-tool-helps-uk-banks-take-on-real-time-payment-scams (Accessed 16 July 2023).

63 "UK Finance proposes payments tax to compensate fraud victims", Finextra, 10 October 2018. Available at: https://www.finextra.com/newsarticle/32762/uk-finance-proposes-payments-tax-to-compensate-fraud-victims (Accessed 14 July 2023).

64 Innovate Finance website. Available at: https://www.innovatefinance.com/ (Accessed 27 July 2023).

65 Barclays Accelerator website. Available at: https://home.barclays/who-we-are/innovation/barclays-accelerator/ (Accessed 27 July 2023).

66 "Chinese payment app giants start accepting Visa and Mastercard", Finextra, 26 July 2023. Available at: https://www.finextra.com/news-article/42689/chinese-payment-app-giants-start-accepting-visa-and-mastercard (Accessed 26 July 2023).

67 "Rewards app loyalBe shuts down consumer operations", Finextra, 17 July 2023. Available at: https://www.finextra.com/newsarticle/42651/rewards-app-loyalbe-shuts-down-consumer-operations (Accessed 18 July 2023).

68 "Bakkt kills off consumer app", Finextra, 16 February 2023. Available at: https://www.finextra.com/newsarticle/41792/bakkt-kills-off-consumer-app (Accessed 18 July 2023).

69 "B2B Payments Market: Global Industry Trends, Share, Size, Growth, Opportunity and Forecast 2023–2028", MarketsandMarkets, March 2023. Available at: https://www.researchandmarkets.com/reports/5769041/b2b-payments-market-global-industry-trends (Accessed 18 July 2023).

4

OPEN BANKING AND ALTERNATIVE PAYMENTS

Open banking (open your heart)

What do we mean by open banking?

Real-time payments are fundamental to **Open Banking**. I am not saying that you can't have open banking payments without real-time payments, this is technically perfectly feasible, but the services provided would be so slow that they would be unappealing to users, thus making them pointless. As previously mentioned, open banking payments are a type of A2A payment (see Chapter 3, *Account-to-Account payments*) that follow agreed standards of interoperability. The bank infrastructure overlay services I mentioned in the previous chapter (see Chapter 3, *Variable Recurring Payments* and *Request-to-pay*) are open banking services.

> **Open Banking** aims to promote innovation and competition through standardisation.

DOI: 10.4324/9781032631394-5

Open banking requires traditional financial institutions to open up customer and/or payment account data to TPPs, thus breaking up monopolies and enabling fairer competition and innovation in financial services. This is illustrated in Figure 4.1.

Consumers can benefit from innovative services, such as Budgeting, Comparison, etc.

Small businesses can link their accounting package to their bank account to streamline their money management and tax returns

With access to bank data, Open Banking enables fairer competition and innovation in financial services

Financial inclusion can be improved with lenders now able to assess credit risk through banking behaviour rather than traditional credit references

Consumers remain in control of their data, which is never shared without their consent, and consent can be withdrawn at any time

Figure 4.1 Open banking use cases.

Source: drawing by the author.

Access to Account data is provided through "open", standardised methods, such as public **Application Programming Interfaces (APIs)**.

An **Application Programming Interface (API)** is a software interface that allows parties to communicate with each other through an agreed set of definitions and protocols. The document or standard that describes how to build or use such an interface is called an "API specification."

Because access is "open", security is paramount, which is why open banking is traditionally linked to a trust framework involving the authentication of participants and users. Open banking is also intrinsically linked to modern real-time payments infrastructures. But data sharing is not new, and bank data was accessible to third parties long before open banking came along. Back then, TPPs like Intuit (QuickBooks) accessed bank data via a method called **Screen Scraping**. This matter was very controversial in Europe because PSD2 banned screen scraping, which was a method used by many PISPs, which claimed the ban would destroy their business. A few years on, PISPs are still doing very well in Europe, and the ecosystem is more secure.

BOX 4.1 WHAT IS SCREEN SCRAPING?

Screen Scraping is a method of accessing data by which an account holder shares their account login credentials with a Third Party Provider (TPP). The TPP then uses the account holder's credentials to access the account and to copy or "scrape" the data for use outside of the account holder's account facility (e.g. an online banking portal). This is, outside of Europe, still a popular method. Apart from the fact that bank account holders would most probably be in breach of their bank's terms and conditions (i.e. they would be sharing credentials with outside parties), this method is not very secure, especially in financial services.

Open vs private APIs

A **Private API** is a communication interface specific to one organisation, and its use can only be granted by that organisation, as shown in Figure 4.2.

Figure 4.2 shows that when a TPP develops a service that needs access to banks which only offer their own private APIs, they need to develop an

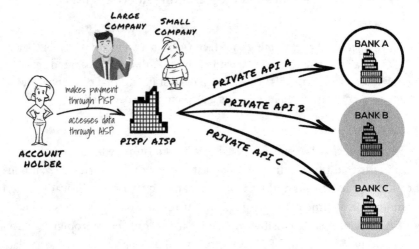

Figure 4.2 How private APIs work

Source: drawing by the author.

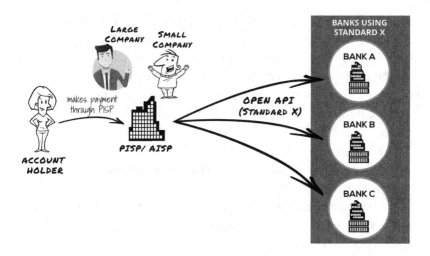

Figure 4.3 How open APIs work.

Source: drawing by the author.

interface specific to each bank. The more private APIs a TPP must interface with, the more development effort and resources are needed. And this is fine if the TPP is a large company like Apple, but it is not so fine if you're a young fintech with limited resources.

By contrast, an **Open API** is a communication interface that follows a public standard or a set of standards that is available for developers to use, as shown in Figure 4.3.

Figure 4.3 shows that when a TPP develops a service using an interface to an API that follows an open standard, they automatically have access to all the banks participating in the published standard, cutting the development effort to just one interface for the set. This establishes a level playing field for all players, big or small.

> **Data sharing** is fundamental to open banking, and open APIs enable fairer competition as well as business innovation.

The trust framework

Open banking relies on the sharing of data between different parties. Data is precious, and in modern economies, where data privacy is a well-understood concept, consumers are aware of their rights. This means that an effective trust framework must be implemented, where ecosystem players can be trusted and interactions are safe. You are already familiar with the concept of authentication, and the security measures (e.g. data, processes) that are implemented on both card and bank rails.

A trust framework for open banking combines all these elements and should cover:

- The **elements necessary to identify and secure connections** between ecosystem participants;
- The **elements necessary to deploy security best practices** (preferably to acknowledged standards) to ensure data exchanges are protected and secure (e.g. API security);
- The **elements necessary to mitigate the risks of financial crime** (e.g. payment limits, KYC, threat intelligence sharing, data collection, fraud prevention tools); and
- The **elements necessary to ensure that the framework is dynamic** so as to enable the detection of any change in participant status (e.g. conformance, coverage) to enable ecosystem players to act accordingly.

Deploying a trust framework for open banking is the responsibility of the open banking implementation entity in any country. You can look at how the UK is evolving their framework in a paper published by the Joint Regulatory Oversight Committee in April 2023.[1]

The portability challenge

Undeniably, open APIs are essential to levelling up the playing field, BUT ... there are various open API standards. In Europe, for example, there is one standard in the UK (Open Banking), a different one in Germany (Berlin Group), one in France (STET), and yet a different one in Poland (PolishAPI), and so on and so forth (although in Europe, all standards are based on the NextGenPSD2 standard originally proposed by the Berlin Group). Of course, the situation is much better than it was before, and standards allow for fairer competition, and if a TPP is only operating in one geography, they only have to interface with one standard. But if they want to expand across borders, they must use the applicable standard(s). As always in the payments industry, innovation flourishes, and this gap was rapidly filled by new entrants. Let's call them **API Aggregators**.

API aggregators

These TPPs enable businesses to operate across borders by taking the interfacing work unto themselves and offering their clients one set of APIs to operate across standards (and therefore geographies), as shown in Figure 4.4.

Figure 4.4 shows that an API aggregator is essentially a TPP which has obtained the necessary permissions (see Chapter 5, *Licences to operate a payment business*) to enable users to access different markets. But the model shown in Figure 4.4 is theoretical, at least at the time of writing. This is because API aggregators are currently B2B businesses, and in order for Suzie to take advantage of their services, they would need to offer a B2C payment facility (e.g. a digital wallet), which hasn't happened yet.

In practice, these TPPs enable innovation by offering their permissions and infrastructures to enable other businesses (e.g. retailers or other PSPs) to operate across geographies, as shown in Figure 4.5.

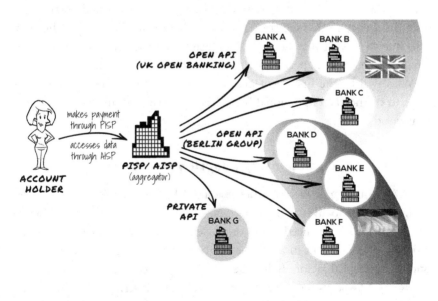

Figure 4.4 API aggregators.

Source: drawing by the author.

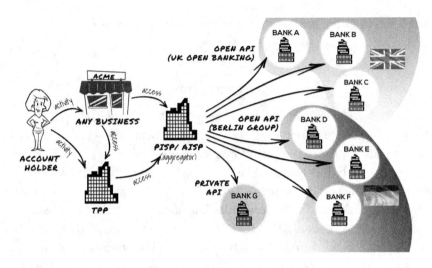

Figure 4.5 API aggregators enabling access across boundaries.
Source: drawing by the author.

Figure 4.5 shows that API aggregators (e.g. Plaid, Tink, Token, Truelayer, Salt Edge) can enable businesses of any type (e.g. retailers, PSPs) to access different markets, even for geographies that haven't developed open standards (in theory), provided this is commercially viable for them. They can also interface with private APIs. This fosters innovation and enables even smaller companies to participate in this modern ecosystem.

Who will be the first domestic digital wallet to make use of these services to operate across national boundaries for bank payments? Your guess is as good as mine.

Open banking adoption worldwide

PSD2 (see Chapter 5, *Payment services regulations*) has been instrumental in creating the open banking phenomenon. Other geographies have followed suit, some more advanced than others. Successful implementation of open banking is contingent to a number of behavioural (customer perception) and technological factors (what the infrastructure can do).

Figure 4.6 shows the status of open banking initiatives worldwide.

If you look at Figure 4.6 in conjunction with Figures 3.17 through 3.20, you will see a lot of opportunities.

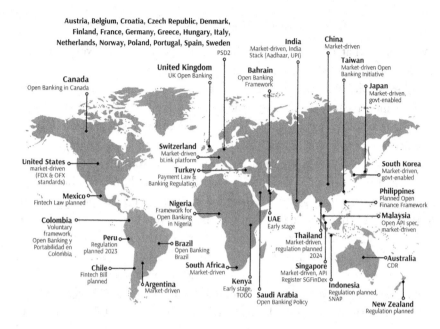

Austria, Belgium, Croatia, Czech Republic, Denmark,
Finland, France, Germany, Greece, Hungary, Italy,
Netherlands, Norway, Poland, Portugal, Spain, Sweden
PSD2

India
Market-driven, India
Stack (Aadhaar, UPI)

China
Market-driven

United Kingdom
UK Open Banking

Bahrain
Open Banking
Framework

Taiwan
Market-driven Open
Banking Initiative

Canada
Open Banking in Canada

Japan
Market-driven,
govt-enabled

Switzerland
Market-driven,
bLink platform

United States
market-driven
(FDX & OFX
standards)

South Korea
Market-driven,
govt-enabled

Turkey
Payment Law &
Banking Regulation

Mexico
Fintech Law planned

Philippines
Planned Open
Finance Framework

Nigeria
Framework for
Open Banking
in Nigeria

Colombia
Voluntary
framework,
Open Banking y
Portabilidad en
Colombia

UAE
Early stage

Malaysia
Open API spec,
market-driven

Peru
Regulation
planned 2023

Thailand
Market-driven,
regulation planned
2024

Brazil
Open Banking
Brazil

Australia
CDR

Chile
Fintech Bill
planned

South Africa
Market-driven

Singapore
Market-driven, API
Register SGFinDex

Argentina
Market-driven

Kenya
Early stage,
TODO

Indonesia
Regulation planned,
SNAP

Saudi Arabia
Open Banking Policy

New Zealand
Regulation planned

Figure 4.6 Open banking status worldwide.

Source: drawing by the author.

Why is open banking so hard?

In the US, open banking may become a reality in 2024, as the Consumer
Financial Protection Bureau (CFPB) plans to implement a rule that sets expectations for the market, expressing a wish for more standardisation but
favouring a market-driven approach.[2] Open banking is evolving, and many
states across the EU are pushing for more open banking services. New
regulatory frameworks will aim to clarify and simplify existing regulations
whilst preserving the integrity of the ecosystem.

In markets where card payments are predominant (see Figures 3.17
through 3.20), the adoption of open banking services has been relatively
slow (only seven million users of open banking services in the UK[3] at
the time of writing). Some argue that this might be due to the fact that
consumers are worried that the protections available to them for card payments (e.g. refunds, chargebacks) are not available (or largely not available or convoluted) with open banking services. This may very well be
true, BUT ...

The next evolution of closed loop retailer cards?

Who knew that closed loop retailer cards could become very success-ful for their issuers, as exemplified by the Target REDcard™ Debit (see Chapter 2, *Decoupled debit*)? Indeed, Target earned in excess of $100 billion in revenue in 2022, and these cards contributed to nearly 20% of it. This again comes down to consumer preferences, and it is safe to say consum-ers don't care about the card brand. They care about the benefits they get out of a particular payment instrument. For example, Target gives a 5% discount on all purchases, and when customers have a problem with a purchase, they can go to a Target for a refund, and the problem is all sorted out for them (indeed, Target seems to have a very good returns and refunds policy, giving extra incentives for purchases made with a RED-card).[4] The inconvenience of only being able to use this card at Target, and therefore having to hold many cards depending on the retailer, is offset by the benefits. Indeed, Andreessen Horowitz estimates that if Target were to convince customers to use the REDcard for all Target purchases, it could bring them an additional $2.2 billion in income.[5] And because the card is directly connected to a bank account, Target avoids the interchange fees and opens itself up to innovative partnerships with fintech firms, potentially bringing to market even more interesting services. Of course, 5% cash back may not be sustainable where potential interchange savings are not so high (e.g. in Europe), but if you consider customer acquisition costs, a one-time joining bonus offered by the retailer for switching cards might just do the trick.

Why am I telling you this? Because the closed loop CBPII introduced in Chapter 3 (Figure 3.4) could give open banking a boost if innovative part-nerships between large retailers and CBPIIs were to happen.

Does open banking have a branding problem?

Maybe. Whilst open banking is about making data access fairer for all play-ers in order to foster competition and innovation, the term itself is only useful to the industry. From a consumer's point of view, the term "open" associated with "banking" is a bit (if not a lot) worrying, especially a few years after major data protection and privacy regulations were introduced. Now, most people know about – or at least are vaguely aware of – their data rights, especially those around privacy.

We come along with our big boots to say that we're "opening up bank data". Yikes. No matter how much you explain that the consumer remains in control of what data they share, with whom, and for how long, the headline sticks. This, combined with consumer preferences (e.g. markets where card payments are dominant), and perhaps unjustified perceptions, is what is making progress slow.

As an industry, we don't learn from past experiences. In the UK, for example, when the Faster Payments System was launched in 2008, it took a few years to reach any kind of volume. And that's because people were worried about (1) banking online and (2) doing it fast, which raised the question: if payments can be so much faster, will fraud become equally fast as a result? FPS volume growth was slow in the early years.

A fraud increase in any area of payments is generally a good indicator of transaction volumes, because criminals have to make their efforts pay, and this is just plain economics. Therefore, the fact that Authorised Push Payment (APP) fraud only started to appear in the UK in 2014 (see Chapter 3, *Authorised fraud*), with the Owners Direct holiday rental affair,[6] suggests that it took about eight years for fraudsters to understand Faster Payments processes and exploit loopholes and for volumes to be viable. We had eight years to do something about it, including better communications to consumers at large, and to address the root of the problem. What's happening with open banking is merely history repeating itself.

In any instance, open banking should be transparent to consumers, as it should simply be another way to pay and manage financial affairs.

The industry might just do it for itself

Unlike for closed loop retailer cards, open banking standardisation means that services could be available anywhere, should the services be deployed where they need to be and a conducive regulatory framework be available. I'm just waiting for a large retailer or a high-volume subscription services provider to realise this. In any instance, global take-up of open banking services is expected to grow as:

- the range, quality, and reliability of APIs increase;
- people realise the benefits of value-added services; and
- businesses realise the financial benefits.

Table 4.1 Open banking APIs and platforms by region.

Region	Open banking APIs	Open banking platforms
Europe	2,537	1,160
Asia Pacific	1,638	203
Middle East & Africa	485	79
US and Canada	320	34
UK	300	51
Latin America	284	51

Source: Platformable, 21 July 2022, Open Banking / Open Finance Trends Q3 2022.[7]

But that on its own won't be sufficient, and the industry might just do it for itself whilst the regulators are playing catch-up (see Chapter 5, *Authentication at large*).

In the meantime, in Q2 2022, there were 1,578 open banking platforms, supported by 5,564 open banking API products worldwide at an annual growth rate of 8% when compared to Q1 2021. Table 4.1 shows the contribution of each region.

What are banks doing?

Good question. It's been a bit of a shock for banks, because in jurisdictions where open banking is law, banks have been forced to open up access to bank data (sometimes kicking and screaming) and may have adopted

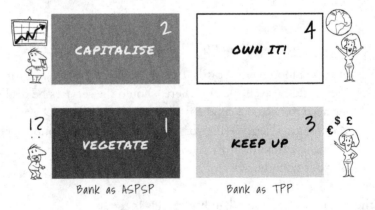

Figure 4.7 Open banking strategies for banks.
Source: drawing by the author.

one of four strategies. Where no relevant laws are in effect, it's a bit slow, as seen in the previous section. Possible bank strategies are described in Figure 4.7.

Strategies 1 and 2 are defensive ones for banks, as either regulations have been "done unto them" and they had to react, or no regulations are in force, in which case they don't have to do much.

Strategy 1: Vegetate

When regulations are in force, taking the example of PSD2 in Europe, banks (regulated entities) have to comply, and they will do so to the most minimal extent. They will develop basic infrastructure and provide bank account data access to TPPs as mandated by the regulators. Where no regulations are enforced and/or government incentives or consumer and business communications are lacking, well, see Figure 3.20. This is basically the "wait and see" game.

Strategy 2: Capitalise

At this stage, banks realise that they have developed new infrastructure, and they decide to make their investment pay. Of course, they still do all the Strategy 1 things, but they also develop and expose new services through APIs that go beyond basic account information and payment initiation services. This could potentially generate new revenue streams, such as, for example, leveraging bank account data to provide bank-driven digital identity services,[8] such as with Early Warning's Authentify® service.[9] In the meantime, Europe continues to develop its pan-European digital identity framework[10] (see Chapter 2, *Fraud prevention and digital identity*).

Strategies 1 and 2 are inward-looking and defensive, and the bank sees itself in the role of an ASPSP. As banks mature on the idea of digital transformation, they may start taking a more offensive stance and start looking at themselves as TPPs. This is evident in the increased popularity of **Banking-as-a-Platform** (**BaaP**) solutions on the market, as these enable banks to integrate innovative fintech services within their infrastructure to enable them, in turn, to offer innovative services to their customers, thus kick-starting digital transformation.

Strategy 3: Keep up

This is where banks start to compete. Of course, Strategies 1 and 2 are still going on, but banks now start offering payment initiation and account information services themselves, leveraging the open access to other ASPSPs. This is where a lot of banks modify their banking apps to offer their customers access to all their bank accounts under one roof. HSBC, for example, launched their separate Connected Money app in May 2018[11] (dip toe in water), only to withdraw it in June 2019 (OK, some stuff works),[12] claiming that they would integrate its best features (e.g. balance after bills) into their main banking app. As far as I can tell, the app is no longer "connected", meaning that it only works for HSBC accounts. In the meantime, Barclays launched a similar feature on their banking app in September 2018,[13] and customers can (still, at the time of writing) link their accounts at other participating banks.[14] This is of course hardly "keeping up", as neo-banks have been doing funky things with their mobile apps for a while. Some, like Monzo, will offer to connect accounts at other banks through a premium service and see this as additional revenue generation. Incumbents still have a way to go to become truly digital, but it's a start.

Strategy 4: Own it!

And this is where it's at. This strategy is about achieving true digital transformation. Of course, all the elements of the previous strategies still have to be there, but at this point banks will enable third parties to build applications and services around the bank. Banks then become true digital players, enabled by open APIs, competing for customer relevance and ownership. If successful, they would effectively create an ecosystem. Who knows, maybe a bank will become the next super app of the Western world! Somehow, I doubt it. Antony Jenkins, ex-Barclays boss, described banks as "museums of technology".[15] In the Eastern world, WeChat launched in 2011 and achieved super-app status in 2018, and users (some 1.3 billion of them) literally conduct their lives on the app (including payments, which are largely invisible). For digital innovation, look East.

What's next for banks?

It's not as bad as it sounds. Juniper Research have been producing their digital banking report for a few years, and they use a strategy classification similar to mine, although they label the strategies differently ("Establish", "Focus", "Mature", "Evolve") and their 2021 report[16] (no banks in "Establish") shows definite progress from their 2018 report[17] (no banks in "Evolve"). It's moving in the right direction, albeit slowly. And banks have generally moved on from being frightened by fintech firms to partnering with them,[18] which is a win-win situation. In the meantime, market consolidation will continue, and Big Tech players will continue to try and grab bigger pieces of the payments pie.

Towards open finance

I believe that the open banking model works, in theory at least. Consequently, many geographies are starting to look at the next iteration, **Open Finance**, which is a logical evolution. As ecosystem actors are getting used to sharing payment data through better standardisation, trust frameworks, and processes, direct beneficiaries (consumers, businesses small and large) should start seeing the effects, and this should eventually trickle down through society and economies at large.

To some extent, open finance started to happen as soon as open banking was launched. After all, what is an account information service? Arguably, you could assess bank account data to determine whether a bank account

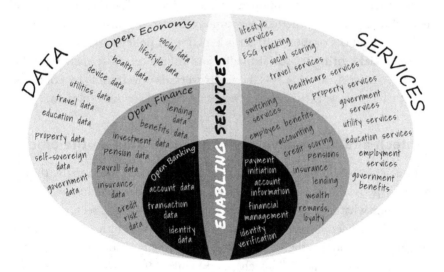

Figure 4.8 Open banking towards open finance, leading to open economy.

Source: drawing by the author.

is "well-behaved", potentially providing a new kind of (limited) credit scoring to foster financial inclusion (e.g. Credit Kudos), but the fact that a user allows QuickBooks (for example) to access bank data to produce a tax return is an accounting service, not a banking one. The evolution of open banking towards open finance, leading to open economy is shown in Figure 4.8.

> **Open Finance** is an evolution of **Open Banking** where data sharing extends beyond payment account data into wider financial services data.

This diagram in Figure 4.8 shows us how the scope of data provided affects the services that may be developed and how each layer will enhance services provided by the previous layer. Enabling services (e.g. API aggregation, overlay services, fraud prevention, infrastructure) will be provided by various ecosystem actors such as PSPs, TPPs, payment schemes, and other technology providers.

To follow from the earlier credit-scoring example, the basic open banking service is just the provision of account information, while open finance credit scoring can look at more data (e.g. lending), essentially enhancing traditional credit scores (e.g. Experian offers open banking services).[19] And if the latter is extended to an open economy, it could lead to social scoring (e.g. China,[20] Italy[21]). Whether government-driven social scoring is beneficial to individuals or more sinister is a matter for policy makers, but we all accept social scoring on social media, and influencers base their business on it ... Aside from this specific controversial aspect, and the concerns about data privacy, the diagram gives us an idea of service evolution.

Fintech and alternative payments (new kids on the block)

"Fintech" is a term that is used and abused, and it can mean many things to many people. In this section, you will see a number of industry classifications for what is generally considered "fintech". Many fintech types will already have been covered in this book, as these will either use the card or bank rails and are therefore related to payments. There is no formally adopted classification for "fintech", and Figure 4.9 attempts to do this (as many have done).

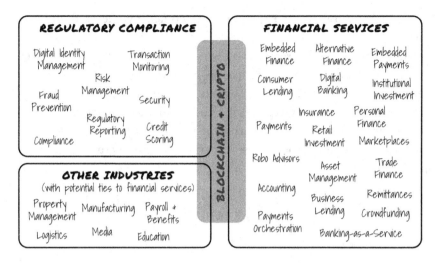

Figure 4.9 What is fintech?
Source: drawing by the author.

Figure 4.9 shows that the term "Fintech" is not very helpful with regards to payments. The term "Paytech" started to appear, but so far, it's only used on in specialist communities. In addition, there are subdivisions of fintech (e.g. InsureTech, WealthTech, etc.), and similar terms are used for other sectors (e.g. EdTech, PropTech, GovTech), and you can see how all these subsets fit together. "Fintech" suggests the use of technology in financial services, and below is a definition. The diagram also gives an appreciation of how various PSPs and technology providers (e.g. TPPs) fit into the model (i.e. Enabling Services).

BOX 4.2 A FINTECH DEFINITION

The term **Fintech** refers to any business that **uses technology** to improve, digitise, automate, or provide enablers to **financial services** aimed at businesses or consumers.

Undeniably, payments constitute a large part of fintech, and in Figure 4.9 I have also overlayed the space where decentralised infrastructures (i.e. blockchain, crypto) can fit (this is where you would get **DeFi** services, which are covered in *Beyond Payments*).

The term **Alternative Payments** was coined by the cards industry and is meant to represent anything that is not a traditional card payment. Therefore in this section you won't be surprised to find very well-established payment methods: bank transfers, digital wallets, money remittance, other card-based payments, and delayed payments, as well as the relatively more recent digital and virtual assets. We covered the mechanics for both card and bank rails in Chapters 1 and 3, respectively, and here you will find how these underlying infrastructures are used by payers.

Bank transfers

Bank transfers come in two types.

Real-time bank transfers

These payment methods allow users to make online payments in real time using the bank rails. Examples include SOFORT, a Klarna company (Germany and German-speaking markets), iDEAL (the Netherlands), eNETS (Singapore), Giropay (Germany and German-speaking markets), and SafetyPay, a Paysafe company (Latin America). A user would typically see the payment method displayed at the checkout of an online shopping site (e.g. "Pay with SOFORT").

Offline bank transfers

These payment methods break the payment process into two stages. First, the user would complete a transaction on the platform used and will be given the destination bank account details and other information, including a transaction identifier. Second, the user will make a payment through their bank to the platform with the details provided. They could also pay cash later at an affiliated outlet or store. Once the second stage is completed, the transaction would be considered complete on the platform. This is a form of delayed payment. Many PSPs offer this payment method to merchants (e.g. SafetyPay offers both online and offline bank transfers), and it is popular in some geographies.

Other card-based payments

Prepaid

This term generally refers to open loop prepaid cards (see Chapter 1, *Eco-system actors and models*) and will run on card scheme networks such as Visa or Mastercard. To a cardholder, they are used in the same way as debit or credit cards, the only difference being that they have to be pre-loaded with funds (i.e. stored value cards). Issuers of such cards are usually eMoney institutions (EMIs) and continue to gain popularity as they enable unbanked or under-served demographics to gain access to financial services. The COVID-19 pandemic accelerated prepaid card usage, as people sought alternatives to cash and governments wanted means to deliver benefits quicker. Moreover, as many people turned to gig work, prepaid cards also enabled timely payments.

Prepay

A prepay card is just like a gift card (e.g. for a fixed amount), but it can be used for payments just like any other card, in person or virtually. These can be referred to as "stored value cards" and will be denominated in the currency in use for the specified amount (e.g. €10). The load amounts will be low, as regulators (in Europe, for example) are increasingly restricting or banning the use of anonymous prepaid instruments. When issuers (or resellers) market these cards, they highlight their anonymity-preserving nature, their immediacy (you can obtain a virtual card number and code is seconds), and the fact that an account is not needed to make a payment using the card (within the limits of applicable regulations). Prepay cards are favoured by users of online services such as sports betting, gaming, dating, and gambling. Increasingly, these are delivered online only, such as with Neosurf and paysafecard.

An early version of this concept was the paper gift certificates that were issued by department stores and other merchants (only to be spent at these institutions) before prepaid cards and virtual currencies came into being. This is, however, a cautionary tale, as exemplified by the 2008 demise of US appliance and computer retail leader Circuit City. When Circuit City closed its doors, it left thousands of people holding worthless gift certificates[22] that were worth millions of dollars prior to that day. This is one of the concerns that led the US Congress to pass laws—specifically for gift certificates and, later, for prepaid gift cards and prepaid debit cards—that provided some level of consumer protection.

Digital wallets

Digital wallets come in three types.

e-Wallet

This is a web application used to make payments, and it can be accessed from any connected user device, usually with several funding mechanisms, such as a card or a bank account. It is probably the oldest and most popular digital payment method. Popular e-wallets include Alipay, PayPal, Amazon Pay, and YooMoney (formerly Yandex.Money).

Mobile wallet

This is a payment facility generally tied to a mobile device, and funding is usually provided by cards. Nowadays, these as very popular given the extensive usage of mobile phones and have been given massive impetus by social media platforms, especially with Asia's super apps, such as WeChat. Popular examples include Apple Pay, WeChat Pay, PayTM, Android Pay, and Samsung Pay.

Crypto wallet

This is a different beast altogether and is included here for the sake of completeness. As you may imagine, crypto wallets are associated with cryptocurrencies, but they don't store cryptocurrencies (as cryptocurrencies are stored on a blockchain). They store the user's proof of ownership of cryptocurrencies or other crypto assets, which takes the form of public and private key combinations. Examples of crypto wallets include Electrum, Mycelium, Trezor, Ledger Wallet, and MetaMask, and some exchanges also offer online wallets, such as Coinbase. Crypto wallets can enable users to send, receive, and spend cryptocurrencies. Please see my second book, *Beyond Payments*, for comprehensive coverage.

Money remittance

Money Remittance is a payment service by which funds are sent by a payer to a payee where no payment account needs to be opened in the name of either the payer or payee.

Money Transfer Operators (MTOs)

PSPs offering these services are financial firms (usually not banks) called **Money Transfer Operators** (**MTOs**) and they facilitate **Money Remittance** including the cross-border transfers of funds. They use either their internal infrastructure or access to banking networks. You've seen how bank payments work in Chapter 3. The existence of multiple currencies and banking systems means that sending money from one country to another is different from sending money domestically (see Chapter 3, *Correspondent banking* and Figure 3.13). An MTO will therefore use existing infrastructures to provide their services, as shown in Figure 4.10.

Many banking parties can be involved in the traditional MTO process, and you can see where each one would take a fee to provide their services. The MTO will use their own banking relationships and each country's bank settlement infrastructure where they can. They will also

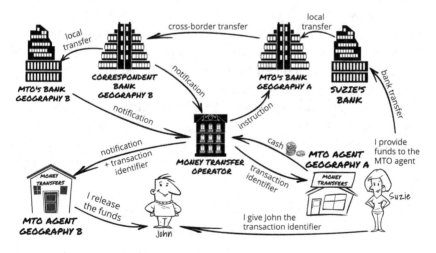

Figure 4.10 A Money Transfer Operator (MTO).

Source: drawing by the author.

define their own currency conversion rates and, combined with the cost of cross-border transactions, this can make transactions expensive. However, these services are becoming popular as the global workforce becomes more and more mobile. Indeed, according to the World Bank, money remittances are expected to grow to $626 billion in 2023,[23] although they are now experiencing a slow down due to the cost-of-living crisis.

Peer-to-peer (P2P) money exchanges

As expected, the payments industry evolved here too, and some fintech firms challenged the model for both MTOs and bank wire transfers (see Chapter 3, *Correspondent banking*). These firms use a different model (although they are still based on existing infrastructures and processes) and are referred to as **Peer-to-Peer (P2P) Money Exchanges**. Instead of correspondent banking and cross-border transactions, they "crowd-source" transfer matches in each of the geographies involved in a transfer. This means that they only have to perform domestic bank transactions at each end, making them much cheaper for the users. Well-known players in this space are Wise (formerly TransferWise), Remittly, and WorldRemit.

Of course, crowd-sourcing transfer matches is not without risks, and in an ideal world you would have 100% transfer matches in all covered geographies. But we live in the real world, and that never happens, and to bridge the funding gap in matches you need to have a pretty good treasury department and faithful investors. How did these fintech firms make money? Good management and operations have a lot to do with it, as well as relevant partnerships in the banking industry. Indeed, it took Wise (then TransferWise) six years from launch to become profitable, and it's doing very well at the time of writing.[24] Not everybody is that lucky: Azimo, a challenger in that space, closed its operations in 2022 after ten years.

Delayed payments

We covered one type of delayed payment earlier (offline bank transfer), but there are other types.

Buy-Now-Pay-Later (BNPL)

Driven by the pandemic and the cost-of-living crisis, this payment method is experiencing a boom, and market consolidation has led to a few acquisitions. **Buy-Now-Pay-Later (BNPL)**, sometimes referred to as "e-invoice", is a method by which consumers can pay for goods by instalments (usually over a few weeks or a few months) after delivery, interest free. It is a popular form of credit that is attracting regulatory scrutiny in a number of geographies, as it may make it easier for users to fall into unaffordable debt.[25] Some established players offer this service, including PayPal with its Pay in 4 (which allows card and bank accounts as funding options), Apple with its Apple Pay Later (which only allows debit cards as a funding option), and PaySafe with its Pay Later (sold to heidelpay in 2020, now trading as Unzer). Fintech firms in this space include Klarna, Affirm, Sezzle, AfterPay (acquired by Block, the owners of Square, in 2022), Zip (now struggling after a failed merger with AfterPay),[26] Flex, and Splitit.

Post pay

This is a payment method by which consumers order goods online and pay for them later at affiliated outlets or shops. The delay between the order and the payment makes this method unsuitable for perishable goods or time-sensitive purchases. It is, however, a popular method in some geographies, as evidenced by Boleto Bancário in Brazil and Konbini in Japan.

Cash on delivery (CoD)

For the sake of completeness, we can't ignore cash as a payment method (it's not dead yet) … Cash on delivery is a method by which the consumer pays for the goods with cash at the time of delivery, and therefore will be specific to countries and suppliers. It is a popular payment method in Central Europe. It is sometimes referred to as "collect on delivery (CoD)", since delivery may allow for cash, cheques, or electronic payments to be used.

Mobile money

Definition

The term **Mobile Payments** can be confusing, and it encompasses payment methods covered in earlier sections, such as mobile wallets and mobile banking. It merely refers to conducting banking activities, including bank payments, through an app on a mobile device. With increased digitisation in our post-pandemic world, mobile banking is set to overtake internet banking in most geographies due to changes in consumer behaviours[27] and increasing digital demographics.[28] Mobile payments also include payment acceptance through mobile devices (see Chapter 2, *Physical terminal services*).

We can classify mobile payments into two broad categories: those that necessitate a formal payment instrument as the underlying funding mechanism (e.g. card or bank account), and those that don't (e.g. use of cash). The former will rely on the formal infrastructures already covered in this book (e.g. e-wallet, mobile wallet, mobile acceptance), but the latter won't and is referred to as **Mobile Money**. Mobile money relies on infrastructures and services provided by telecommunications operators, and these services don't rely on existing financial services infrastructures. As mobile money is a cash substitute, telcos offering this service are eMoney issuers (see *eMoney*) and must have the necessary regulatory permissions to operate. Mobile money primarily targets the underbanked, underserved, or financially excluded, and is a path to the formal economy.

Direct Carrier Billing (DCB)

Direct Carrier Billing (**DCB**) is an online payment method by which users can make purchases by charging the payment to their mobile phone bill for a single payment or recurring payments. DCB is simply a type of overlay service that introduces a new ecosystem actor: the **Mobile Network Operator** (**MNO**), or mobile carrier. In the Western world, the carrier account would typically be on a monthly personal contract of good standing, but two options are technically feasible: **postpaid** (purchase amount added to the mobile carrier's monthly bill) and **prepaid** (purchase amount deducted from the current load balance).

DCB is usually confined to digital goods, and spending limits may apply, but this will depend on the geography, mobile carrier, and applicable regulations. The types of organisations offering this payment method include gaming platforms (e.g. Riot Games), marketplaces (e.g. Facebook Games Marketplace, Microsoft Marketplace), charity donations, ePublishing, online gambling, eSports, media, and entertainment (e.g. Spotify, YouTube

TV). Companies offering DCB services include Bango, Boku, Centili, De-gica, Digital Virgo, DIMOCO, Fonix, and Fortumo. Juniper Research pre-dicts that this market will grow by 74% between 2023 and 2027,[29] as DCB expands to physical goods and digital ticketing.

The mechanics of DCB are quite simple, and for a payer rather con-venient, as they don't need to have a card or a bank account as a funding mechanism to create an account because their "payment" account is their mobile account, identified by their mobile number. Of course, depending on the jurisdiction and the types of goods purchased, extra checks may be required by either the carrier or the merchant, but all in all it's quite sim-ple, and the payer is not even aware that they are using a DCB provider, just that they can "pay-by-phone" or "text-to-pay" at the merchant.

DCB gives merchants another channel to reach consumers, the mo-bile carrier customer base. For mobile carriers (aka **Mobile Network Operators, MNOs**), it is another revenue source. This is explained in Figure 4.11.

We can see the similarity with other processes on centralised rails: here the telco effectively acts as the ASPSP, as they "authorise" the payer through their mobile phone number at Step 3; the only difference is that there is no link to a bank account or card account.

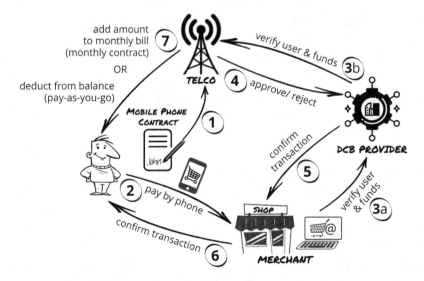

Figure 4.11 Direct Carrier Billing (DCB) process.

Source: drawing by the author.

The funding mechanism for the "mobile payment account" will be through cash-in outlets provided by the telcos, and this is what enables financial inclusion in cash-dominated markets. In the background, the telcos will use their own banking relationships for "real money" movements.

Mobile money deployment

Looking back at Figures 3.17 through 3.20, DCB is generally more popular in cash-dominated markets (e.g. Japan), and this is fuelled by the availability and adoption of low-cost mobile devices, expanding connectivity (e.g. internet, smart-phone penetration, 5G), and cloud services. Other indicators of success are the number of cash-in cash-out agents in a given geography and the number of merchants and public sector services that accept this payment method, as it is a means of access to financial services.

In addition, DCB is experiencing growth in card-dominated markets (e.g. South Korea, the US, and the UK), as it is fuelled by the increased popularity of subscription services and its adoption by younger demographics, although in Europe PSD2 (and regulations in general) may act as a limiting factor.

Mobile money was a boon for underserved populations during the pandemic, as it enabled quicker delivery of benefits. The Global System for Mobile Communications Association (GSMA) produces valuable statistics and reports, including the State of the Industry Report on Mobile Money 2023,[30] which gives an excellent account of the industry.

Some DCB providers have also partnered with mobile wallets, giving users even more payment options, and an additional emerging use case is the purchase of cryptocurrency through crypto exchanges (although this might store some problems for the future, certainly if decentralised crypto exchanges offer the service, but more on that in *Beyond Payments*). Numerous analyst reports are available, and global CAGR forecasts will vary, so I'll let you make your own mind up, but undoubtedly this is a growth market.

Finally, you are probably aware of a very successful mobile money service: M-Pesa, a joint venture launched in 2007 between Vodafone and Safaricom in Kenya, where it had a major impact on the economy, including helping increase the country's financial inclusion from only 26% in 2006 to 84% in 2021,[31] lifting a portion of the population out of poverty. M-Pesa has since expanded to other African geographies and has over 50 million monthly active customers. There are other popular mobile money services, such as Airtel Money, MTN, and Afrimoney. But professionals should re-member that being successful in one geography doesn't automatically mean success in another. Indeed, M-Pesa, whilst successful in Kenya and other African countries, had to withdraw from India, Romania, and Albania be-cause of low market uptake. Possible causes may have been the availability of an established payments/banking infrastructure, unconducive regula-tions, customer preferences, or the existence of a dominant player. I'll let you decide. Another interesting story is Myanmar, where the destabilising military coup of February 2021 resulted in the traditional banking infra-structure largely being shut down,[32] leaving people unable to withdraw or exchange money and making today's payments landscape rather interest-ing: you'll find bank-led systems (KBZ Pay, CB Pay, Ongo), telco-led initia-tives (MPT Pay, M-Pitesan, Mytel-Pay), and independent e-wallets (Wave Money, Easy Pay, TrueMoney, OK$, Oway Pay, Mandalay Smart Pay, Shal Pay, City Sky Pay, Trusty). Ongo, founded in 2015 in partnership with MOB Bank, has become one of the largest B2B digital payment platforms in My-anmar, providing essential services to over one hundred businesses with its payment platform through a network of over 10,000 agents. On the consumer side, people in major cities will use bank-led applications, as they have access to banks, whereas the majority of people in rural areas use telco-led applications or independent e-wallets (as bank access is dif-ficult and interoperability is lacking). At the time of writing, the dominant players in Myanmar are Wave Money and KBZPay, and as the military junta imposed identification of mobile money users in order to clamp down on funding to resistance groups, people are now going back to the old hundi system,[33] an informal and unregulated value transfer system, which is un-fortunately associated with money laundering and the financing of terror-ism (the hundi system is one of the reasons why Myanmar is on the FATF's black list; see Chapter 5, *Financial Action Task Force*).

Whilst these stories are very different, they show how pervasive pay-ments are and how they can bring change to even the most challenging environments.

About money

In order to understand what can and can't be used for the "exchange of value" in the various payments ecosystems, we need to understand what we mean by "money".[34] Payments rely on money, and it comes in different

BRITISH POUND   US DOLLAR   EURO

FIAT SINCE 1931   FIAT SINCE 1971   CREATED FIAT

Figure 4.12 Fiat money.
Source: drawing by the author.

forms. Money is a medium of exchange and is accepted by people for the payment of goods and services, as well as for the repayment of debt.

Fiat Money is government-issued currency that is not backed by a physical commodity, such as gold or silver, but rather by the government that issued it. It derives its value from supply and demand, and the stability of the issuing government. Fiat money gives central banks greater control over the economy, as they can control how much money is printed.

Fiat money has therefore no intrinsic value, and it is often referred to as **Paper Money**. Governments have to make it **Legal Tender** by setting it as the standard for debt repayment.

Most modern currencies are fiat money, which is explained in Figure 4.12.

We need to understand the concept of fiat money before we can understand virtual and digital assets.

Digital and virtual assets

Digital and virtual assets are difficult to categorise. This is because, depending on what we mean, the regulations might not be there to give us a reference framework, and so the terminology is therefore inconsistent. These gaps in the global regulatory framework have created significant loopholes for fraudsters and criminals to abuse.

To enable us to cover all types of virtual assets, regulated or unregulated, we will use the term "virtual asset" as a generic term and use the following definition.

The term **Virtual Asset** refers to any digital representation of value that can be digitally traded, transferred, or used for payment or investment purposes.

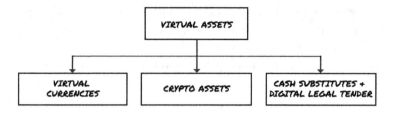

Figure 4.13 A proposed classification for virtual assets.
Source: drawing by the author.

Virtual assets may have many potential benefits. They could make pay-ments easier, faster, and cheaper. They could provide alternative methods of payment for those without access to regular financial products. There are many types of virtual assets, as shown in Figure 4.13.

Virtual currencies

At some point, you must have come across virtual currencies, especially if you play online games that enable you to buy assets in the game (e.g. lives, boosters, weapons, etc.). These games generally have private currencies that enable you to purchase those assets. Some examples of those virtual assets are V-Bucks in Fortnite, Robux in Roblox, or, one of the oldest, the Linden Dollar on Second Life. These currencies are issued, managed, and controlled by private issuers, developers, or the founding organisation (e.g. Epic Games, the owners of Fortnite, manages V-Bucks). A virtual currency is used in a specific community and relies on a system of trust defined by the private issuer. As such, they are a kind of closed loop medium of ex-change. For Web 2.0 games, such as those mentioned, these currencies are not interchangeable with other virtual currencies in other games (e.g. V-Bucks are not interchangeable with Robux). Virtual currencies are unregu-lated, so the integrity of each ecosystem using a virtual currency is ensured by the private issuer, which attracts its own risks.

Crypto assets

This is where it gets tricky. There is no formally accepted classification of crypto assets, and this is due to the lack of consistent regulations. Here, I attempt to give you a categorisation to help understand this space better.

In this book, the various types of crypto assets will not be covered in de-tail (you'll have to read *Beyond Payments* for this), but fundamental principles will be given. And the first thing I should mention is that classifying crypto assets is difficult, because their purpose may change over time from what they were originally intended for. The crypto asset classification model proposed here is based on the **primary purpose** of the crypto asset, as listed in the **white paper** defining that asset.

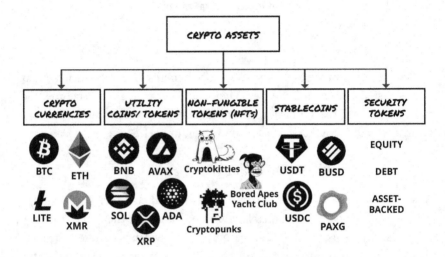

Figure 4.14 A proposed classification of crypto assets.
Source: drawing by the author.

BOX 4.3 WHAT IS A CRYPTO WHITE PAPER?

A crypto **white paper** is a document explaining the purpose, technology and current state of a crypto project, as well as any plans for it. It is meant as a high-level guide that enables investors to ascertain whether a project has future potential and to raise the interest of potential users. The original crypto white paper is the Bitcoin white paper, entitled "Bitcoin: A Peer-to-Peer Electronic Cash System", and it was written under the pseudonym of Satoshi Nakamoto in October 2008. Bitcoin was intended to give users an alternative payment system free of central control but otherwise operating just like any other currency. As such, the **primary purpose** of Bitcoin was to be a crypto currency.

Here, I will only expand on those crypto assets more pertinent to the payments space; the others are extensively covered in *Beyond Payments*. In Figure 4.14, the words "Coin" and "Token" are used, which may seem confusing. I will use either term in the following sections, as the difference is merely technical.

BOX 4.4 THE DIFFERENCE BETWEEN A COIN AND A TOKEN

A coin is a crypto asset native to its blockchain, such as Bitcoin (BTC) on the Bitcoin blockchain, or Ethereum (ETH) on the Ethereum blockchain. **Tokens are crypto assets foreign to the blockchain they live on**, such as Tether (USDT), Uniswap (UNI), or Chainlink (LINK). The Ethereum blockchain is the most popular for building tokens. Tokens can eventually become coins when the crypto project is successful and able to develop its own blockchain. An example of a successful migration from token to coin is the Binance coin (BNB), which previously existed on the Ethereum blockchain and is now native to the Binance Smart Chain (BSC).

A crypto asset is a type of virtual asset that lives on a blockchain, is secured by cryptography, and comes in five types: **Cryptocurrencies**, **NFTs**, **Utility Tokens**, **Stablecoins**, and **Security Tokens**.

In any instance, as you move from left to right looking at Figure 4.14, those assets will be more regulated (e.g. a stablecoin is more regulated than a cryptocurrency).

There is a rule which I call the **Regulations at the Edges Principle**. It goes like this:

BOX 4.5 THE REGULATIONS AT THE EDGES PRINCIPLE

When something unregulated starts touching something regulated, regulations will soon affect the unregulated thing, until, in time, what is unregulated becomes regulated.

Look at this principle as some sort of reverse contagion risk.

This rule applies to financial services in general, as well as to payments (remember how TPPs became regulated under PSD2 after a long stint of relative freedom) and crypto more specifically. Stablecoins, especially fiat-collateralised, "touch" fiat currencies, which are regulated. It is therefore unsurprising that regulators globally are getting edgy, and many have started regulating these instruments.[35]

CRYPTOCURRENCIES

Perhaps the most well-known of crypto assets, their intended purpose is to be a medium of exchange. This was the original purpose of Bitcoin BTC, but over the years it has morphed into a store of value used for speculative purposes. Some even refer to Bitcoin as "digital gold", which is a misnomer since gold is a stable asset and **cryptocurrencies are highly volatile and unregulated**. To this day, no cryptocurrency can claim to be a true medium of exchange, although some retailers accept crypto as payment, such as Ralph Lauren in Miami[36] and some stores in London.[37] Two notable exceptions are El Salvador[38] and the short-lived experiment in the Central African Republic[39] (the second-poorest country in the world), which made Bitcoin legal tender.

STABLECOINS

Stablecoins were created to address the volatility risks associated with cryptocurrencies and can be either pegged to a collateral (e.g. fiat currency, commodity, another cryptocurrency), or rely on a "mint and burn" stabilising mechanism to control the supply. The former is referred to as a **collateralised stablecoin** and the latter as a **non-collateralised or algorithmic stablecoin**. The primary purpose of a stablecoin is to facilitate trades on crypto exchanges. Instead of buying cryptocurrency with fiat currency, traders often exchange fiat for stablecoins and then execute trades between the stablecoin and another cryptocurrency, as this mitigates crypto-exchange fees. It's a bit like using poker chips (stablecoins) at a casino (the crypto exchange).

As a side note, I think that economically challenged states considering the adoption of cryptocurrencies as legal tender should perhaps consider fiat-collateralised stablecoins instead of volatile cryptocurrencies, but that is not without risk either (dollarisation anyone?). More specific to the payments industry, acquirers (WorldPay[40] and Checkout.com[41]) have started to offer round-the-clock merchant settlement (see Chapter 1, *Merchant settlement*) in USD Coin (USDC). In August 2023, PayPal started offering its own USD-pegged stablecoin, PayPal USD (PYUSD) in collaboration with Paxos, with plans to make it available on Venmo.[42]

As far as algorithmic stablecoins are concerned, you will undoubtedly remember the spectacular collapse of the TerraUSD (UST)/Luna stablecoin in 2022[43] and the effect it had on financial markets globally. Subsequently, the Fei Protocol discontinued their algorithmic stablecoin FEI in August 2022,[44] citing future regulatory risks, leaving only one significant player, MakerDAO's DAI. And this is a shame, because the concept of an algorithmic stablecoin is, in my opinion, interesting and in fact not dissimilar to that of a fiat currency. The major difference is of course governance and oversight. My prediction, following my Regulations at the Edges Principle, is that stablecoins will be regulated across the board (they are already in regulated some geographies).

UTILITY TOKENS

The primary purpose of a utility token is for crypto-project developers to raise interest in their project, to encourage developers to create applications, and generally to create more value in a blockchain ecosystem. These tokens can be used to redeem a special service or receive a special treatment, and they are often given out for free to promote the project (airdrop). An example of this is the Brave web browser Basic Attention Token (BAT), where users are rewarded in BAT tokens for viewing ads on the browser.

However, utility tokens are mostly issued in the context of Initial Coin Offerings (ICOs), which are a bit similar to Initial Public Offerings (IPOs) on the stock market. But unlike in traditional investments, the utility token value is not in any way linked to the valuation of the issuer, but more to the faith of the community.

There are sub-types of utility tokens: **exchange tokens**, which are only used in a specific exchange (e.g. Binance BNB, Crypto.com CRO), and **governance tokens**, which are an upgraded version of utility tokens and give more rights (e.g. voting) to their holders (e.g. Solana's SOL).

Utility tokens are unregulated. Here too, my Regulations at the Edges Principle applies. XRP, the utility token for Ripple, a permissioned blockchain (see *A crash course on DLT and blockchain*) is used in their xRapid service to offer banks and payment providers on-demand liquidity to service cross-border payments. More than one hundred financial institutions are members of the RippleNet community, suggesting that the governance processes around it should be pretty robust, as RippleNet positions itself at an alternative to SWIFT[45] (see Chapter 3, *Correspondent banking*).

But even regulators are not immune to confusion: Ripple is, at the time of writing, fighting a lawsuit from the US Securities and Exchange Commission (SEC) for breaching securities laws by selling XRP without first registering them,[46] although it secured a partial win against the SEC for retail trading.[47] But XRP's primary purpose is to be a utility token, not a security token, and therefore it shouldn't be considered a security. Or should it? The fact that XRP is in the top ten list of cryptocurrencies by market capitalisation doesn't help their cause, as XRP is also clearly used for investment purposes (and institutional trading should be regulated). Whilst the SEC continues to argue that all crypto assets are securities, the Belgian Financial Services and Markets Authority (FSMA) clarifies that crypto assets without issuers (e.g. BTC, ETH) are not to be considered securities,[48] unlike instruments that have a payment or exchange function (e.g. XRP), which may be subject to additional rules. And in the meantime, in August 2023, the Bank of England and Ripple explored synchronised interbank settlement using the Interledger Protocol.[49]

My conclusion is that use cases are numerous, confusion reigns still, and my Regulations at the Edges Principle applies here too.

NON-FUNGIBLE TOKENS (NFTS)

There is a lot of hype around **Non-Fungible-Tokens** (**NFTs**). In May 2014, digital artist Kevin McCoy minted the first-known NFT, "**Quantum**", on the Namecoin blockchain (the first fork of the Bitcoin blockchain). Sotheby's sold it for $1.47 million in 2021 as the first of its kind. The Bitcoin blockchain was, however, never designed for recording asset ownership, and Ethereum became the home of NFTs.

Non-fungible means "unique", and therefore refers to something that can't be replicated. NFTs are crypto assets that have been tokenised on a blockchain and assigned a unique identification. This is different from other crypto tokens or coins, or fiat currencies, which are interchangeable.

Even if 1,000 NFTs of the same item are minted, each token is unique and distinguishable from all the others. It's a bit like having limited edition prints of a painting, or tickets to an event or a film.

NFTs originally focussed on art and collectibles but have since expanded to other markets (e.g. virtual world assets, sports and trading cards, and domain names). Without going through the intricacies of the various types of NFTs (covered in *Beyond Payments*), it is fair to say that most are unregulated, unless they fall within the definition of a security, in which case regulations apply. However, because of their popularity, incumbent payments players dabble: Visa has launched an NFT programme to help creators grow their business,[50] Mastercard has partnered NFT marketplaces on card purchases,[51] and Amazon is laying the foundation to give its customers the ability to purchase NFTs tied to real-world goods (e.g. a pair of jeans) by launching an NFT marketplace.[52]

SECURITY TOKENS

These tokens are included here for the sake of completeness, but they don't have much relevance to the payments space. Security tokens are investment contracts and represent legal ownership of a digital, physical, or intangible asset. Security token investors aim to generate a profit (e.g. dividend payments, interest, profit share, residual rights).

Equity tokens, a type of security token (see Figure 4.14), are like stock, as token holders are entitled to the profits and losses of the business and also have the right to vote on company decisions. The main difference is that ownership is recorded on a blockchain (instead of on a centralised ledger for traditional investments).

Security tokens are obviously subject to applicable securities regulations and can only be traded through regulated platforms. Still, projects of this type can get into trouble, as regulatory uncertainty, disparity, and incompatibility across geographies is a technical and operational challenge which has caused many companies operating in this space to close down, such as Neufund.[53]

eMoney

eMoney is issued by a regulated entity called an **eMoney Institution (EMI)** (see Chapter 5, *Licences to operate a payment business*). and may be used for making payments to entities other than the issuer (unlike virtual currencies).

Types of eMoney include prepaid cards, electronic prepaid accounts, and virtual payment accounts for use online. It is an electronic store of monetary value that acts as a cash substitute, but unlike cash, which is a direct claim on the central bank, eMoney is a claim on the issuing organisation.

An example of an eMoney issuer familiar to everyone is PayPal.

CBDC

A **Central Bank Digital Currency** (**CBDC**) is a digital currency issued by a central bank and pegged to the value of that nation's fiat currency. It is regulated by the central bank or monetary authority and holds the status of legal tender. It is a direct claim on the central bank and therefore **the digital equivalent of notes and coins**.

There are two types of CBDCs, which are not mutually exclusive:

- **Retail CBDC**: for general purpose domestic use, including B2C, B2B, P2P, and G2C; and
- **Wholesale CBDC**: aimed at financial firms holding reserve deposits with a central bank and used to settle interbank payments and other financial market transactions.

In this book, we will concentrate on retail CBDCs. Globally, opinions vary regarding the deployment of CBDCs, but a lot of research and cooperation is taking place. A CBDC represents a change to the monetary system, and because the monetary system is a public good that underpins an economy and pervades people's lives, it must serve the public interest by:

- Providing economic benefits;
- Ensuring the quality of oversight and governance arrangements; and
- Preserving basic rights (e.g. data privacy).

There are many design and infrastructure choices for policy makers to choose from:

- The **roles** that the central bank and intermediaries will play;
- The **technology** used (e.g. centralised, decentralised, hybrid);

- How users **access** it (e.g. will it be privacy preserving?); and
- Its **interoperability** (e.g. domestic, cross-border, hybrid, available to non-residents).

China has been at the forefront of CBDC deployment with the eCNY, but other countries have deployed them such as Nigeria (eNaira) and the Bahamas (Sand Dollar).[54]

The various CBDC options will not be covered in this book (you will have to refer to *Beyond Payments*), but a comparison between cash, eMoney, and CBDC is given in the next section.

Virtual assets vs traditional payments

Cash vs eMoney vs CBDC

The differences between these payment instruments must be understood, as usage implications are different for ecosystem actors and users alike. This is explained in Figure 4.15.

As shown in Figure 4.15, a retail CBDC, just like cash, is a direct claim on the central bank, which means users are protected by law and their money is safe.

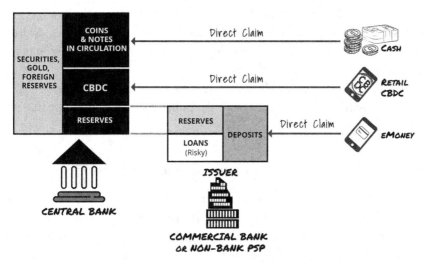

Figure 4.15 Cash vs eMoney vs CBDC.

Source: drawing by the author.

When users deposit their money with a bank, their money is safe up to a limit, as banks are usually covered by a compensation scheme (e.g. up to £85,00 with the Financial Services Compensation Scheme – FSCS – in the UK, and up to $250,000 with the Federal Deposit Insurance Corporation – FDIC – in the US).

When a bank is showing signs of stress, bank account holders may decide to take their money out completely, or enough to remain within the limits. If this has a cascading effect, and many bank account holders decide to do the same, you may have a **bank run**. In modern days, social media exacerbates this problem, as news travels ever faster.

Usually, in the Western world at least, failed banks will be rescued by the government, such as happened with Silicon Valley Bank in the US in March 2023 (described as the "first Twitter-fuelled bank run"), which was bought by First Citizen Bank from the FDIC.

The story is different for non-bank PSPs (see Chapter 5, *eMoney regulations*), as while the structure of the deposits and reserves is the same, there is no equivalent compensation scheme (unless bank partnerships exist), despite the existence of safeguarding requirements for customer deposits. We saw this in 2020[55] with the very public demise of Wirecard, the once darling of the EU fintech world. The scandal affected all ecosystem participants – even the German regulator, the Federal Financial Supervisory Authority (BaFin) – leading to the dismissal of a top official over wrongdoings.[56] In the aftermath, regulators worldwide tightened regulations, safeguarding requirements, and new proposed regulations are now including supplemental processes for wind-downs.

But I don't want to put a downer on EMIs: they bring innovation, and it must be fostered. This is a matter for the policy makers, and I hope that we have learnt valuable lessons.

Differences in functionality and settlement

Please note that we are only covering retail payments here. A roundup of the differences between different payment instruments is given in Table 4.2.

From Table 4.2, we can derive that CBDCs have a lot of potential to be equivalent to cash and promote financial inclusion, but much is contingent on the design choices made by central banks and policy makers. For further information, the Bank of International Settlements (BIS) produced papers in collaboration with a number of central banks in 2020[59] and again in 2023.[60] This topic is also covered extensively in *Beyond Payments*.

Table 4.2 Differences between payment instruments.

	Cash	Retail CBDC	Real-time bank payments	eMoney (incl. cards)	Stablecoin	Cryptocurrency
Safety as a settlement asset	Central bank liability	Central bank liability (Note 1)	Commercial bank liability	Issuer, or merchant or PSP liability	No (Note 2)	No
Finality of payment	Immediate on receipt	Immediate on confirmation	Immediate on confirmation	Immediate on authorisation	After validation	After validation
Finality of underlying payment	No interbank settlement required	Central bank settlement. Can be a blockchain but doesn't have to be	Deferred net settlement or RTGS	Interbank and merchant settlement	Blockchain settlement	Blockchain settlement
Speed of settlement	Fast	Fast	Depends on payment scheme	Depends on contract	Depends on blockchain	Depends on blockchain
Cost for users	No	No (Note 3)	Low, but depends on bank and payment scheme	Low, but depends on product	Depends on blockchain (Note 4)	Depends on blockchain (Note 4)
Cost for merchants/ businesses	Relatively low (cost of handling cash)	Low, but depends on design	Low, but depends on bank	Medium to high	Low	Low
User access identification	No (Note 5)	Depends on design (Note 6)	Yes	Yes	No	No
User anonymity/ confidentiality	Yes	Depends on design (Note 7)	No	No	Yes (Note 8)	Yes (Note 8)

(Continued)

Table 4.2 (Continued)

	Cash	Retail CBDC	Real-time bank payments	eMoney (incl. cards)	Stablecoin	Cryptocurrency
Offline payments	Yes	Depends on design	No	Yes	No	No
Cross-border use	Yes (physical transport)	Depends on design.	Yes	Yes	Yes	Yes
New digital functions (programmability)	No	Yes	Yes	Yes	Yes	Yes
Transaction speed	Fast	Fast, but depends on design choice	Fast	Fast	Can be slow (Note 9)	Can be slow (Note 9)

Note 1: for a retail CBDC, a central bank is ultimately liable, but there are CBDC models by which the CBDC is issued by a central bank and private issuers issue what is referred to as a **Synthetic CBDC (sCBDC)**, which is very similar to how eMoney works. The inner workings of liability (e.g. balance sheet) are of course a matter for policy makers (this is covered in *Beyond Payments*).

Note 2: stablecoins are in theory less volatile in nature than other cryptocurrencies, but limitations apply, as shown in earlier sections.

Note 3: *cost to users of a CBDC, as well as limits, are ultimately a matter for policy makers.*[57]

Note 4: this entirely depends on the blockchain and the facility used (e.g. crypto wallet, exchange). Transaction fees can be high, especially if a blockchain network is congested.

Note 5: some jurisdictions may require identification for high-value cash payments (I have this cinematic image of people carrying briefcases full of cash that are cuffed to their wrists).

Note 6: this is also a policy decision. For example, the Bank of England is developing a "privacy" layer for a potential CBDC.[58]

Note 7: *for example, the Chinese eCNY uses NFC for proximity payments.*

Note 8: as long as no linkage can be established between a wallet address and a real identity.

Note 9: for speed of transaction, blockchain scalability solutions exist (i.e. Layer 1, Layer 2), but please also refer to Figure 4.18 for comparative actual transaction speeds.

And this, my friends, concludes our tour of centralised payment ecosystems and alternative payments. Read on if you'd like to know what comes next!

Centralised vs decentralised ledgers (spread your wings)

You know by now that both card and bank rails use centralised mechanisms for processing payments. Each fundamental process in these value chains relies on trusted centralised entities to perform functions on behalf of the entire ecosystem (e.g. authorisation, clearing, settlement). For example, on the card rails settlement is performed by banks chosen by the card schemes or bilateral agreements. On the bank rails, settlement is performed by a central bank or monetary authority. Each of the trusted entities performing functions on behalf of the system will keep centralised ledgers for recording and reconciling, and the processes governing them aim to ensure integrity. These centralised ledger infrastructures have been developed over a long time and have mostly been provided by banks and financial services institutions.

The idea of eliminating the need for a "central authority", or "intermediary", to preserve the integrity of a network led to the development of **Distributed Ledger Technology (DLT)**. I don't intend to cover this topic in detail here, as this is covered extensively in *Beyond Payments*, but professionals should get enough in this section to understand the fundamental principles as they apply to payments.

A crash course on DLT and blockchain

This concept is not new, and it first appeared in 1991, when cryptographers Stuart Haber and W. Scott Stornetta wrote "How to time-stamp a digital document".[61] But it is not until 2008, when Satoshi Nakamoto wrote the Bitcoin whitepaper,[62] that Distributed Ledger Technology entered the world of payments. The idea of DLT, based on **Peer-to-Peer Networking**, was to eliminate the need for a central authority or intermediary, where peers communicate directly with each other and where data, trust, and control are distributed through the network – a self-governing democratic ecosystem if you will. Many confuse DLT and blockchain, using the terms interchangeably, but blockchain is but one type of DLT. There are others, such as Hashgraph, Directed Acrylic Graph (DAG), and Tempo (Radix), but blockchain is undeniably the most popular. The Bitcoin blockchain is the oldest one and was launched in 2009. See Figure 4.16 for a graphic representation of the blockchain.

A **blockchain** is essentially a form of DLT where time-stamped "blocks" of data are stringed together in a "chain". These blocks of data are intermittently validated (through consensus) by users of the network. Put simply, a DLT is a kind of distributed relational database.

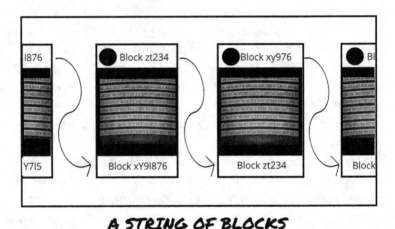

A STRING OF BLOCKS

Figure 4.16 A blockchain: blocks stringed to blocks.
Source: drawing by the author.

Data on a blockchain

The data in a block is equivalent to what you would refer to as a "batch of transactions" on centralised systems.

The **data recorded in a block is immutable** and therefore cannot be changed. If a change needs to happen, a block doesn't get "rewritten"; instead, a new block is created recording the change and added to the chain, recording that a change happened at a particular date and time, thus keeping a full historical ledger of all transactions that ever happened on the blockchain. Sound familiar? That's because this concept is based on that old book, the general ledger, where entries are recorded chronologically.

Conceptually, each entry comes after the previous one. On a blockchain, each new digital block (new entry on the ledger) contains information about the previous block.

The **data recorded on a blockchain is secure**: each block of transactions on a blockchain is secured by cryptography. A blockchain works like this by design, and participants don't have to do anything for this to happen. The equivalent on centralised networks (bank rails or card rails) is encrypting data in transit or at rest, but this means that ecosystem players must make a conscious decision to do this and add something to the infrastructure.

The **data recorded on a blockchain is transparent**: this means that each participant can see the data, as they all have a copy of the ledger, removing the need for a central authority to keep a single source of truth (the centralised ledger, as used for clearing and settlement processes by schemes and settlement agents) on behalf of the network.

The **data recorded on a blockchain is anonymous**: well, this can cause confusion, and the anonymity debate is still going on. What we can say, however, is that blockchain transactions can be anonymous if there is no way of linking a user's wallet address to their real identity (a better way of describing this is "pseudonymous": as long as you don't know the real person behind the "pseudonym", anonymity is achieved).

Blockchain mechanics

When comparing them to centralised networks (card rails or bank rails), blockchain networks have three main characteristics:

- **Decentralisation**: the way they track and store data is decentralised across multiple participants who can all see a copy of the ledger.
- **Distributed trust**: Blockchains minimise the amount of trust required from any single entity. The way data and transactions are validated is distributed across multiple participants in the ecosystem through a trust framework that incentivises ecosystem actors to cooperate with the rules defined by the blockchain. The main mechanism to achieve this is the blockchain **Consensus Protocol**, which is a kind of economic game. The two main consensus protocols are **Proof of Work (PoW)** and **Proof of Stake (PoS)**, but there are others. Regardless of which consensus protocol a blockchain

uses, the process is the same: validating nodes will listen to the network for incoming transactions and will each create blocks of valid transactions in a staging area (the **mempool**). The equivalent of this stage on centralised networks is a combination of **authorisation** and **clearing** (and as you know, no value changes hands at that stage). Then, validating nodes participate in the economic game (the consensus protocol), the winner of which gets to add their block to the chain, and everyone else deletes the losing blocks and gets a new copy of the ledger. This is the equivalent of the **settlement** process on centralised networks and what gives blockchains their immutability. Of course, not every participant on the blockchain will be a validating node, as you need resources to do this (and some users just want to trade crypto). Some blockchains require that a transaction be validated by at least 51% of validating nodes, but others may set a higher threshold for approval. This is why blockchains will reward validating nodes for their efforts through incentives (e.g. coins or tokens, transaction fees, etc.).

• **No intermediaries**: the network performs functions on a peer-to-peer basis. Participants in a blockchain network can be called "nodes" or "validators", and blockchains will have the equivalent of participation models on centralised systems (e.g. directly connected settling), but these models don't generally rely on centralised entities for "membership". The way they work will depend on the type of blockchain used.

Blockchain types

There are two types of blockchains: permissionless and permissioned, as shown in Figure 4.17.

PERMISSIONLESS BLOCKCHAINS

These allow any user to join the network, and there is no central authority. The most famous permissionless blockchain is the Bitcoin blockchain, being the oldest, but you also have the Ethereum, Litecoin, and Monero blockchains and many others. These are primarily associated with cryptocurrency trading and mining.

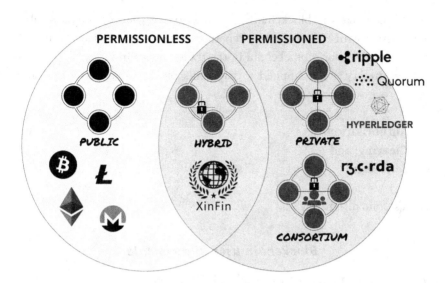

Figure 4.17 Permissionless and permissioned blockchains.
Source: drawing by the author.

PERMISSIONED BLOCKCHAINS

These are controlled by a central entity and restrict access to certain nodes. Rights can also be restricted. In the world of payments, there are some successful permissioned blockchains, such as Ripple, Quorum, and Hyperledger, and some banks have also created their own private blockchains, such as JP Morgan with Onyx.[63] These are generally associated with trade finance and interbank settlement. Figure 4.17 shows that permissioned blockchains introduce some degree of centralisation, as they are controlled by one entity or a set of entities, making control not as democratic as blockchain's original intent. In fact, a private blockchain is sometimes called a "managed blockchain", and the controlling entity not only determines who can be a node, it also decides which rights a node has to perform functions. A consortium blockchain is sometimes called a "federated blockchain".

HYBRID BLOCKCHAINS

These are a combination of both models. They are controlled by a central authority but will also have some permissionless elements. The controlling entity can make the blockchain accessible to everyone (through a public blockchain) whilst a private blockchain controls ledger updates. XinFin is an example of hybrid blockchain in the trade finance industry.[64]

In summary, when applied to payments blockchains follow the same basic processes as centralised ledgers:

- **Authorisation**;
- **Clearing**; and
- **Settlement**.

But it's done differently.

Blockchain uses in payments

In order to compete with centralised payments ecosystems, blockchain networks must be highly scalable (at least for consumer transactions). Just like legacy banks are plagued with a legacy problem,[65] blockchains face the **Blockchain Trilemma**,[66] which states that optimal levels of **decentralisation, security**, and **scalability** are hard to achieve, as one of the three elements must be sacrificed in favour of the other two. For example, the Bitcoin blockchain traded off scalability in favour of decentralisation

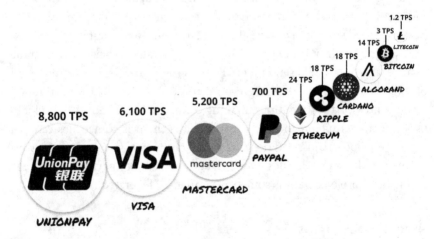

Figure 4.18 Centralised payment network's actual TPS vs blockchain's actual TPS.

Source: drawing by the author. Data source: Capital One Shopping, June 2023,[67] and annual reports showing transaction volumes for the various entities listed.

and security; this was also the case for the Ethereum blockchain prior to their consensus protocol migration (The Merge) from PoW to PoS in September 2022. Figure 4.18 gives a comparative illustration for transaction speeds.

Some may argue that Figure 4.18 doesn't relate to what you may Google for various transaction speeds, and they would be partly right. The Transaction per Second (TPS) figures given here relate to **actual TPS** rather than theoretical TPS. For example, VisaNet is capable of processing 65,000 TPS, and Algorand is theoretically able to handle 6,000 TPS. The reality is, of course, quite different.

Interlinkages between centralised and decentralised infrastructures

Interconnectivity is fundamental, as ecosystem actors fulfil different roles in the crypto ecosystem and most parts interact with and rely on each other. Some providers could be both competitors and clients. Traditional PSPs offering crypto trading could source liquidity from brokerages. Banks providing custody solutions can white-label services from custody providers. Crypto traders can use crypto wallets, or they can use more

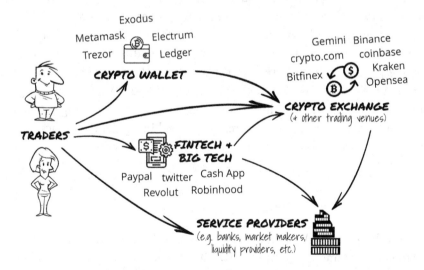

Figure 4.19 Transacting in a decentralised ecosystem.

Source: Drawing by the author.

familiar PSPs (e.g. Cash App, PayPal, Revolut). As an example, Twitter (now X) is offering cryptocurrency trading via eToro.[68] This is illustrated in Figure 4.19:

As shown in Figure 4.19, decentralised services will "touch" centralised ones, and as soon as that happens, my Regulations at the Edges Principle will apply.

In any instance, here's a fun exercise for you: have a look at the "PayPal Cryptocurrency Terms and Conditions ('Cryptocurrency Terms')"[69] (UK example given here), which specifies the terms for cryptocurrency trading on their platform, and try and determine which partnerships they may have.

For a more comprehensive treatment of this topic, see *Beyond Payments*.

Future outlook (I can see clearly now)

Consumer behaviours drive change, and technology advancements lead to new behaviours. In 2016, the worldwide population counted 7.4 billion people, and we had 6.4 billion connected things. In 2025, the world is predicted to have 8.2 billion people and 22.2 billion connected devices.[70] That's a lot of people, and even more devices! I won't bore or annoy you by quoting specific statistics on the constituents of workforce demographics, as opinions and forecasts vary. However, they all seem to agree that Gen Z and millennials will amount to more than 50% of the workforce in 2025 (my conservative take). The remote working trend has been exacerbated by the pandemic, and Gartner[71] estimates that 48% of knowledge workers around the world will work either remotely (9%) or in a hybrid arrangement (39%) – in the US, this estimate rises to 71% for working remotely and in a hybrid arrangement combined. Combining demographics, connectivity and workforce mobility serve to exacerbate technology usage and data gathering.

Our changing world

Technology has evolved and created new possibilities: big data, quantum computing, connectivity (IoT, RFID, Bluetooth, Zigbee, Zwave, 5G, etc.), social media (the third shopping channel),[72] AI, biometrics, etc. It has enabled new entrants to challenge incumbents, who are still hobbling through their digital transformation endeavours. New technology-driven business models have been created to fill that gap (e.g. Platform-as-a-Service, Banking-as-a-Service, API aggregation, etc.). As a result, consumers have more choice, and they take advantage of this fact by demanding more, or walking away if they are not satisfied.

Undeniably, **Big Tech** firms want more and more of the payments pie. Meta (Facebook, Instagram, WhatsApp), Apple, and TikTok make no bones about it. Apple is building its own payments infrastructure, acquired Credit Kudos (open-banking credit scoring), and is releasing a feature enabling merchants to accept contactless payments directly on an iPhone without the need for additional hardware.[73] Of course, this is not new in the Eastern world, where super apps such as WeChat have been dominating the payments space. No wonder that this systemically important and largely unregulated space is giving regulators the jitters!

Metaverse – Web 2.0 vs Web 3.0

And then we have the Metaverse, and the surrounding hype may lead some to not take this space seriously. Metaverse Fashion Week on Decentraland happened in March 2022, and any fashion brand worth its name had to be seen there. Estée Lauder was the exclusive launch partner for the event[74] and created an NFT wearable that allowed users' avatars to get a glowing and radiant aura inspired by their iconic night cream Advanced Night Repair™. In March 2022, nearly seven million people had visited the Nike Metaverse store, Nikeland.[75] Many retailers are experimenting with the Metaverse and trying to figure out how to monetise it, but is it not just a place to have fun with immersive experiences?[76]

Serious entities like Citi predict that the Metaverse economy could reach $13 trillion by 2030.[77] American Express filed Metaverse trademark applications for its name, logo, and slogans for a range of payment services.[78] HSBC purchased a plot of land on The Sandbox to engage with sports, e-sports, and gaming enthusiasts.[79] Worldline built a white-label shopping mall to make it easier for businesses to open stores in the Metaverse.[80] In June 2023, PKO Bank Polski ran a job fair in the Metaverse to attract new tech talent.[81] Is it worth exploring?

The concept of a metaverse is not new; in fact, we can trace its origin back to 1838![82]

> A **Metaverse** is defined as a virtual reality space in which users can inter-act with a computer-generated environment and other users.

Essentially, the Metaverse refers to virtual worlds where users interact, usually through digital avatars. There are well-known metaverses such as those created by the games Second Life, Fortnite, Roblox, and Minecraft. These metaverses operate on the current version of the internet, Web 2.0. Newer metaverse environments are associated with Web 3.0, the next it-eration of the World Wide Web. Web 3.0 is a decentralised infrastructure

Table 4.3 Differences between Web 2.0 and Web 3.0 infrastructures.

		Web 2.0	Web 3.0
Example virtual worlds		Second Life, Roblox, Fortnite, Minecraft, World of Warcraft	Decentraland, The Sandbox, Somnium Space, Voxels, Axie Infinity
Payments	**In-world medium of exchange**	Virtual currency (e.g. Robux, V-Bucks)	Cryptocurrency (e.g. ETH)
	In-world medium of exchange portability	Closed loop	Open loop
	Obtaining the medium of exchange	Traditional payments method (e.g. credit or debit card)	Crypt currency to cryptocurrency or fiat to crypto
	Payments infrastructure	Card rails or bank rails or mobile money	Blockchain, crypto exchanges
Digital assets	**Digital assets**	In-world digital assets	NFTs
	Digital asset ownership	Leased or purchased within world	Owned through NFT
	Digital asset portability	Locked within world	Portable across world
Identity	**In-world identity**	Avatar	Avatar
	Identity portability	Not portable across worlds	Interoperable across worlds
	Identity sovereignty	Linked to real-world identity (e.g. email, payment account)	Self-sovereign
	Anonymity	Not anonymous	Can be anonymous, but it depends on the mechanisms

built on blockchain technologies and applications. Web 3.0 is also referred to as the "Semantic Web" and is currently mostly associated with gaming environments.

But what's that got to do with payments, I hear you say. Well, whilst the environments are different, payments will still be conducted on Web 3.0. But these will use different infrastructures, different payment mechanisms, different digital asset structures, and different identity mechanisms, as shown in Table 4.3.

For payments professionals, Table 4.3 illustrates why Web 3.0 and the Metaverse can't be ignored, and Bloomberg predicts that the total Metaverse market size may triple that of gaming software, services, and advertising combined by 2024.[83] This is not without risks, however, and online gaming perhaps gives us lessons for the future of the Metaverse, from cybercrime and privacy[84,85] to money laundering.[86] Indeed, Valve, the creators of the Steam game platform, banned cryptocurrencies and NFTs from their platform due to "sketchy behaviour" and "out of control" fraud.[87]

For more comprehensive coverage of Metaverse business opportunities and associated risks, please see *Beyond Payments*.

What's next for payments?

Competition and convergence across centralised payment rails will continue, following in the footsteps of the Mastercard Vocalink acquisition, Visa acquired Tink in 2021 and American Express partnered with open-banking fintech firms Plaid and Yodlee in a data-sharing agreement enabling members to connect their accounts to thousands of apps and services across the digital-banking ecosystem. Amex also offers a debit card checking account with rewards not traditionally seen on debit card products. Venmo users can transfer cryptocurrency to friends and family and to PayPal accounts, external wallets, and exchanges, all without leaving the app. Interchange will continue to be contentious, and businesses may develop more closed loop products to try and get away from it. Standardisation will contribute to increased interoperability between bank payment rails and other centralised rails. And of course, cash is not dead and will remain a part of the mix for as long as consumers want it, although several jurisdictions are exploring CBDCs as an alternative. In our hyper-connected world, cross-border payments will continue to grow.

Convergence between centralised and decentralised payment rails will also continue. Ripple is already successful in the interbank settlement area, but traditional infrastructure providers are also positioning themselves to take advantage of the opportunity. ClearBank, a UK BaaS provider secured investment in 2022 to expand in the US and Europe and to move into newer areas such as cryptocurrency exchanges.[88] Crypto debit cards are gaining traction.[89] Worldpay offers US merchants direct settlement in stablecoin USDC.[90] Visa is building the Universal Payment Channel, an infrastructure to connect multiple blockchain networks to allow for the secure transfer of digital currencies.[91] Ralph Lauren accepts crypto payments at its Miami stores,[92] and Amazon dabbles in NFTs.[93]

Convergence between physical and digital domains will continue. There's even a term for it: "phygital" (physical + digital). Far be it from me to introduce more jargon, but this one is worth mentioning. The term was first coined by Australian marketing agency Momentum Worldwide in 2007[94] to describe the connection between physical and digital ecosystems. This is relevant to payments as stakeholders seek to accommodate diverse user preferences and offer seamless and immersive experiences for both B2B and B2C interactions. This has been happening for a while, as exemplified by using "click-and-collect", using a QR code to display a restaurant menu whilst at the restaurant, and trying clothes on through a video avatar, and converting physical loyalty cards to loyalty apps. Advancements in technology will encourage many more use cases to bridge the digital world with the physical world to provide unique and interactive user experiences.[95]

Payments are becoming more open. Consumers, regulators, and innovators have driven increased standardisation. Consumers are demanding more seamless and ubiquitous payment interactions. Innovators are demanding more open and standardised platforms to level the playing field. Regulators are increasingly promoting standardised platforms to foster innovation and financial inclusion. Indeed, in China internet companies are mandated to accommodate rival links and payment services on their platforms. In India, all licenced mobile wallets must connect with each other, and all merchants must accept payments from all wallets.

Digital identity will continue to be a focus area, not only for the provision of better streamlined services, but also to combat fraud and cybercrime. Deployments will vary across countries and jurisdictions, but ecosystem players will position themselves to take advantage of any opportunity. In March 2023, Mastercard was certified as a trusted digital identity provider in the UK.[96] In April 2023, Sweden's well-established bank-owned identity framework BankID launched a digital identity card supported by their app.[97] On 29 June 2023, the EU reached political agreement on the provision of a pan-European digital identity framework, amending the previous eIDAS framework.[98] In the meantime, Google has quietly added support for digital IDs through Google Wallet.[99]

Payments ecosystems' increased complexity and risks will drive new and more stringent regulations globally. This is turn will lead to more industry cooperation and automation. The regtech industry will grow as a result, and Exactitude Consultancy predicts that the global regtech market will grow from $6.5 billion in 2022 to $28.83 billion in 2029 at a CAGR of 17.55%.[100]

The world of payments is changing for the better.

Open banking and alternative payments – conclusion (where do we go from here?)

In this whistle-stop of open banking and alternative payments, we covered:

- Open banking, its mechanics, drivers, challenges, and the prospect of open finance;
- Fintech and alternative payments;
- Payment methods, their differences, and future prospects;
- Digital and virtual assets, from cash substitutes and digital legal tender to crypto assets;
- The differences between centralised and decentralised payment ecosystems;
- Blockchain and Distributed Ledger Technology and potential uses in payments; and
- What Web 3.0 and the Metaverse mean for payments.

I have tried to explain the jargon and debunk a few myths, and the main terms introduced in this chapter will be found in the glossary (Chapter 7). I shared some insights as to what the future might look like, which I supported by presenting global market trends, graphs, and charts which I hope readers will find useful. The fundamental principles were covered, and I also gave you my opinion on some aspects of the industry. I know some may disagree with me, and I always welcome a good debate, but I hope I have equipped you to ask the right questions.

If you read this book a few years from now, new business models will have emerged and regulatory pressure will have increased. Some businesses will be thriving, some will have pivoted, and others will have just disappeared.

To complete our understanding of payments, we must now examine the regulatory environment.

Notes

1 "Recommendations for the next phase of open banking in the UK", Joint Regulatory Oversight Committee, 17 April 2023. Available at: https://assets.publishing.service.gov.uk/government/uploads/system/uploads/attachment_data/file/1150988/JROC_report_recommendations_and_actions_paper_April_2023.pdf (Accessed 28 July 2023).

2 "Laying the foundation for open banking in the United States", Consumer Financial Protection Bureau, 12 June 2023. Available at: https://www.consumerfinance.gov/about-us/blog/laying-the-foundation-for-open-banking-in-the-united-states/ (Accessed 9 July 2023).

3 "UK reaches 7 million Open Banking users milestone", UK Open Banking, 20 February 2023. Available at: https://www.openbanking.org.uk/news/uk-reaches-7-million-open-banking-users-milestone/ (Accessed 10 July 2023).

4 "Returns and receipts", Target website. Available at: https://www.target.com/returns (Accessed 10 July 2023).

5 "Target competes with Visa and Mastercard", Leaders, 29 March 2023. Available at: https://leaders.com/news/business/target-competes-with-visa-and-mastercard/ (Accessed 10 July 2023).

6 "Holiday misery for the scam victims who believed they'd booked a villa through Owners Direct", The Guardian, 24 August 2014. Available at: https://www.theguardian.com/money/2014/aug/23/holiday-book-online-owners-direct-homeaway-scam (Accessed 11 July 2023).

7 "Open banking / open finance trends Q3 2022", Platformable, 21 July 2022. Available at: https://platformable.com/q3-2022-open-banking-open-finance-trends (Accessed 21 July 2023).

8   "The Rise of Digital Identity Wallets: Will banks be left behind?" Mobey
    Forum, 31 January 2023. Available at: https://mobeyforum.org/the-rise-
    of-digital-identity-wallets-will-banks-be-left-behind/ (Accessed 10 July
    2023).

9   "Early Warning Announces Authentify®, a New Identity Verification Ser-
    vice" Cision PR Newswire, 22 October 2022. Available at: https://www.
    prnewswire.com/news-releases/early-warning-announces-authentify-a-
    new-identity-verification-service-301517075.html (Accessed 10 July 2023).

10 "Council and Parliament strike a deal on a European digital identity
    (eID)" European Council, 29 June 2023. Available at: https://www.
    consilium.europa.eu/en/press/press-releases/2023/06/29/council-
    and-parliament-strike-a-deal-on-a-european-digital-identity-eid/
    (Accessed 10 July 2023).

11 "HSBC launches Connected Money app", Finextra, 9 May 2018. Avail-
    able at: https://www.finextra.com/newsarticle/32074/hsbc-launches-
    connected-money-app (Accessed 10 July 2023).

12 "HSBC drops Connected Money and integrates best features to main
    mobile banking app", Computer Weekly, 6 June 2019. Available at:
    https://www.computerweekly.com/blog/Fintech-makes-the-world-go-
    around/HSBC-drops-Connected-Money-and-integrates-best-features-
    to-main-mobile-banking-app (Accessed 10 July 2023).

13 "Barclays app lets customers see accounts from other providers",
    Finextra, 12 September 2018. Available at: https://www.finextra.com/
    newsarticle/32638/barclays-app-lets-customers-see-accounts-from-
    other-providers (Accessed 10 July 2023).

14 "Manage accounts with other banks in your Barclays app – Power is see-
    ing every penny", Barclays website. Available at: https://www.barclays.
    co.uk/ways-to-bank/account-aggregation/ (Accessed 10 July 2023).

15 "Banks are becoming 'museums of technology' says ex-Barclays
    boss", Finextra, 12 June 2023. Available at: https://www.finextra.com/
    newsarticle/42458/banks-are-becoming-museums-of-technology-says-
    ex-barclays-boss (Accessed 10 July 2023).

16 "Over half of global population to use digital banking in 2026; driven
    by banking digital transformation", Juniper Research 19 June 2021.
    Available at: https://www.juniperresearch.com/press/over-half-global-
    population-digital-banking (Accessed 10 July 2023).

17 "Digital banking users to reach 2 billion this year, representing nearly
    40% of global adult population", Juniper Research, 27 February 2018.
    Available at: https://www.juniperresearch.com/press/digital-banking-
    users-to-reach-2-billion (Accessed 10 July 2023).

18   "Why banks are chasing fintech partnerships", Raconteur, 2 June 2023. Available at: https://www.raconteur.net/growth-strategies/why-banks-are-chasing-fintech-partnerships/ (Accessed 10 July 2023).

19   "Experian approved to offer open banking services by the FCA", Experian website, June 2018. Available at: https://www.experian.co.uk/blogs/latest-thinking/automated-credit-decisions/experian-approved-to-offer-open-banking-services-by-the-fca/ (Accessed 12 July 2023).

20   "How China's social credit system actually works – it's probably not how you think", South China Morning Post, 7 January 2023. Available at: https://www.scmp.com/magazines/post-magazine/long-reads/article/3205829/how-chinas-social-credit-system-actually-works-its-probably-not-how-you-think (Accessed 12 July 2023).

21   "Bologna introduces social credit app to promote 'virtuous behavior'", The European Conservative, 27 April 2022. Available at: https://europeanconservative.com/articles/news/bologna-introduces-social-credit-app-to-promote-virtuous-behavior/ (Accessed 12 July 2023).

22   "Beware Circuit City cards, but don't pitch them", The Columbus Dispatch, 18 April 2009. Available at: https://eu.dispatch.com/story/business/2009/04/18/beware-circuit-city-cards-but/23832384007/ (Accessed 23 August 2023).

23   "Remittances remain resilient but likely to slow", World Bank, 13 June 2023. Available at: https://www.worldbank.org/en/news/press-release/2023/06/13/remittances-remain-resilient-likely-to-slow (Accessed 3 July 2023).

24   "TransferWise becomes profitable six years after being founded", BBC News, 17 May 2017. Available at: https://www.bbc.co.uk/news/business-39943651 (Accessed 3 July 2023).

25   Britain sets out legislation to regulate buy-now-pay-later credit", Reuters, 14 February 2023. Available at: https://www.reuters.com/business/finance/britain-sets-out-legislation-regulate-buy-now-pay-later-credit-2023-02-13/ (Accessed 3 July 2023).

26   "BNPL firm Zip exiting most markets and selling assets as stock plummets", Pymnts, 1 March 2023. Available at: https://www.pymnts.com/buy-now-pay-later/2023/bnpl-firm-zip-exiting-most-markets-and-selling-assets-as-stock-plummets/ (Accessed 3 July 2023).

27   "Digital banking experience trends for 2022", UK Finance, 2 November 2021. Available at: https://www.ukfinance.org.uk/news-and-insight/blogs/digital-banking-experience-trends-2022 (Accessed 16 July 2023).

28   "How Gen Z are reshaping the banking landscape", UK Finance, 13 June 2023. Available at: https://www.ukfinance.org.uk/news-and-insight/blog/how-gen-z-are-reshaping-banking-landscape (Accessed 16 July 2023).

29 "Carrier billing: Regional Analysis, Key Verticals & Market Forecasts 2023–2027", Juniper Research, 24 April 2023. Available at: https://www.juniperresearch.com/researchstore/operators-providers/carrier-billing-research-report (Accessed 16 July 2023).

30 "State of the Industry Report on Mobile Money 2023", GSMA, 2023. Available at: https://www.gsma.com/sotir/ (Accessed 17 July 2023).

31 "Driven by purpose: 15 years of M-Pesa's evolution", McKinsey, 29 June 2022. Available at: https://www.mckinsey.com/industries/financial-services/our-insights/driven-by-purpose-15-years-of-m-pesas-evolution (Accessed 23 August 2023).

32 "Myanmar's unfolding banking crisis", The Diplomat, 20 May 2021. Available at: https://thediplomat.com/2021/05/myanmars-unfolding-banking-crisis/ (Accessed 22 August 2023).

33 "Myanmar embraces mobile payments under military rule", Nikkei Asia, 19 January 2023. Available at: https://asia.nikkei.com/Spotlight/Myanmar-Crisis/Myanmar-embraces-mobile-payments-under-military-rule (Accessed 23 August 2023).

34 Naaman Helfield, "The meaning of money: its purposes and functions", Gold-Eagle, 27 February 2003. Available at: https://www.gold-eagle.com/article/meaning-money-its-purposes-and-functions (Accessed 6 October 2023).

35 "Global regulators back 'same risk, same regulation' for stablecoins", Reuters, 13 July 2022. Available at: https://www.reuters.com/technology/global-regulators-back-same-risk-same-regulation-stablecoins-2022-07-13/ (Accessed 6 July 2023).

36 "Ralph Lauren debuts crypto-friendly Miami store", Charge Retail Tech News, 5 April 2023. Available at: https://www.chargedretail.co.uk/2023/04/05/ralph-lauren-crypto/ (Accessed 6 July 2023).

37 "7 Places you can spend your bitcoin in London", London Post, 2 September 2022. Available at: https://london-post.co.uk/7-places-you-can-spend-your-bitcoin-in-london/ (Accessed 6 July 2023).

38 "El Salvador's bitcoin experiment: How is it working out?", Be In Crypto, 7 April 2023. Available at: https://beincrypto.com/el-salvadors-bitcoin-experiment-how-is-it-working-out/ (Accessed 6 July 2023).

39 "CAR bitcoin failure: Is Africa ready to legalize cryptocurrencies[?]", Further Africa, 6 June 2023. Available at: https://furtherafrica.com/2023/06/06/car-bitcoin-failure-is-africa-ready-to-legalize-cryptocurrencies/ (Accessed 6 July 2023).

40 "Worldpay to offer merchants direct settlement in USDC", Finextra, 7 April 2022. Available at: https://www.finextra.com/newsarticle/40022/worldpay-to-offer-merchants-direct-settlement-in-usdc (Accessed 6 July 2023).

41   "Checkout.com makes around the clock liquidity a reality with stable-coin settlement", Checkout.com website. Available at: https://www.checkout.com/blog/post/checkout-com-makes-around-the-clock-liquidity-a-reality-with-stablecoin-settlement (Accessed 6 July 2023).

42   "PayPal launches its own stablecoin", Finextra, 7 August 2023. Available at: https://www.finextra.com/newsarticle/42746/paypal-launches-its-own-stablecoin (Accessed 8 August 2023).

43   "What really happened to LUNA Crypto?", Forbes Digital Assets, 20 September 2022. Available at: https://www.forbes.com/sites/qai/2022/09/20/what-really-happened-to-luna-crypto/?sh=10727 3d14ff1 (Accessed 6 July 2023).

44   "Fei stablecoin project closed", Binance, 19 August 2022. Available at: https://www.binance.com/en/news/top/7181132 (Accessed 6 July 2023).

45   "AWS partner profile: Ripple", AWS website. https://aws.amazon.com/partners/success/ripple/ (Accessed 6 July 2023).

46   "Ripple CEO says more crypto firms may leave U.S. due to 'confusing' rules", CNBC, 18 May 2023. https://www.cnbc.com/2023/05/18/ripple-ceo-says-more-crypto-firms-may-leave-us-due-to-confusing-rules.html (Accessed 6 July 2023).

47   "Ripple scores partial win in SEC lawsuit", Finextra, 14 July 2023. Available at: https://www.finextra.com/newsarticle/42646/ripple-scores-partial-win-in-sec-lawsuit (Accessed 17 July 2023).

48   "Bitcoin, Ethereum, and Other Cryptos are not securities, says Belgian financial regulator", Be In Crypto, 25 November 2022. Available at: https://beincrypto.com/btc-eth-other-cryptos-not-securities-says-belgian-financial-regulator/ (Accessed 6 July 2023).

49   "BoE and Ripple explore synchronised settlement of payments using Interledger Protocol", Finextra, 4 August 2023. Available at: https://www.finextra.com/newsarticle/42728/bofe-and-ripple-explore-synchronised-settlement-of-payments-using-interledger-protocol (Accessed 4 August 2023).

50   "Visa Creator Program", Visa website. Available at: https://usa.visa.com/partner-with-us/info-for-partners/visa-creator-program.html (Accessed 6 July 2023).

51   "Mastercard partners NFT marketplaces on card purchases", Finextra, 10 June 2022. Available at: https://www.finextra.com/newsarticle/40426/mastercard-partners-nft-marketplaces-on-card-purchases (Accessed 6 July 2023).

52 "Amazon NFT marketplace: The future of digital collectibles", NFT News Today, 23 May 2023. Available at: https://nftnewstoday. com/2023/05/23/amazon-nft-marketplace-the-future-of-digital-collectibles/ (Accessed 6 July 2023).

53 "Why we're shutting down Neufund", Neufund website, 10 January 2022. Available at: https://blog.neufund.org/why-were-shutting-down-neufund-e553d990e8b1 (Accessed 6 July 2023).

54 "Central Bank Digital Currency Tracker", Atlantic Council website. Available at: https://www.atlanticcouncil.org/cbdctracker/ (Accessed 7 July 2023).

55 "How the biggest fraud in German history unravelled", The New Yorker, 23 February 2023. Available at: https://www.newyorker.com/ magazine/2023/03/06/how-the-biggest-fraud-in-german-history-unravelled (Accessed 7 July 2023).

56 "German regulator's top official dismissed over Wirecard wrongdoing", Pymnts, 29 January 2021. Available at: https://www.pymnts.com/news/ international/2021/german-regulators-top-official-dismissed-over-wirecard-wrongdoing/ (Accessed 7 July 2023).

57 "UK Finance baulks at proposed £20,000 upper limit for future Britcoin", Finextra, 7 July 2023. Available at: https://www.finextra.com/ newsarticle/42603/uk-finance-baulks-at-proposed-20000-upper-limit-for-future-britcoin (Accessed 7 July 2023).

58 "BofE taps Nuggets for digital pound privacy layer", Finextra, 7 July 2023. Available at: https://www.finextra.com/newsarticle/42606/bofe-taps-nuggets-for-digital-pound-privacy-layer (Accessed 7 July 2023).

59 "Central bank digital currencies: Foundational principles and core features", Bank of International Settlements, October 2020. Available at: https://www.bis.org/publ/othp33.pdf (Accessed 7 July 2023).

60 "Central bank digital currencies: Ongoing policy perspectives", Bank of International Settlements, May 2023. Available at: https://www.bis.org/ publ/othp65.pdf (Accessed 7 July 2023).

61 Stuart Haber and W. Scott Stornetta, "How to time-stamp a digital document", January 1991. Available at: https://link.springer.com/ article/10.1007/BF00196791 (Accessed 1 July 2023).

62 Satoshi Nakamoto, "Bitcoin: A Peer-to-Peer electronic cash system", Nakamoto Institute, 31 October 2008. Available at: https:// nakamotoinstitute.org/bitcoin/ (Accessed 1 July 2023).

63 "Onyx by JP Morgan", Onyx website. Available at: https://www. jpmorgan.com/onyx/index (Accessed 3 July2023).

64 "Enterprise ready hybrid blockchain for global trade and finance", XinFin website. Available at: https://www.xinfin.org/ (Accessed 3 July 2023).

65 "Banks are becoming 'museums of technology' says ex-Barclays boss", Finextra, 12 June 2023. Available at: https://www.finextra.com/newsarticle/42458/banks-are-becoming-museums-of-technology-says-ex-barclays-boss (Accessed 2 July 2023).

66 "What is the Blockchain Trilemma?", coinmarketcap website. Available at: https://coinmarketcap.com/alexandria/glossary/blockchain-trilemma (Accessed 30 July 2023).

67 "Number of credit card transactions per second, day & year", Capital One Shopping, 9 June 2023. Available at: https://capitaloneshopping.com/research/number-of-credit-card-transactions/ (Accessed 2 July 2023).

68 "Twitter to offer crypto trading via eToro", Finextra, 13 April 2023. Available at: https://www.finextra.com/newsarticle/42135/twitter-to-offer-crypto-trading-via-etoro (Accessed 18 July 2023).

69 "PayPal cryptocurrency terms and conditions ('cryptocurrency terms')", PayPal UK website. Available at: https://www.paypal.com/uk/webapps/mpp/ua/cryptocurrencies-tnc (Accessed 17 July 2023).

70 "State of IoT 2023: Number of connected IoT devices growing 16% to 16.7 billion globally", IOT Analytics, 24 May 2023. Available at: https://iot-analytics.com/number-connected-iot-devices/ (Accessed 17 July 2023).

71 "Gartner forecasts 39% of global knowledge workers will work hybrid by the end of 2023", Gartner, 1 March 2023. Available at: https://www.gartner.com/en/newsroom/press-releases/2023-03-01-gartner-forecasts-39-percent-of-global-knowledge-workers-will-work-hybrid-by-the-end-of-2023 (Accessed 17 July 2023).

72 "It's showtime! How live commerce is transforming the shopping experience", McKinsey, 21 July 2021. Available at: https://www.mckinsey.com/capabilities/mckinsey-digital/our-insights/its-showtime-how-live-commerce-is-transforming-the-shopping-experience (Accessed 17 July 2023).

73 "Apple reportedly looking to build its own payments and lending infrastructure", Fintech Futures, 5 April 2022. Available at: https://www.fintechfutures.com/2022/04/apple-reportedly-looking-to-build-its-own-payments-and-lending-infrastructure/ (Accessed 17 July 2023).

74 "Estée Lauder participates in Decentraland's Metaverse fashion week as exclusive beauty partner", Business Wire, 24 March 2022. Available at: https://www.businesswire.com/news/home/20220323005934/en/

Est%C3%A9e-Lauder-Participates-in-Decentraland%E2%80%99s-Metaverse-Fashion-Week-as-Exclusive-Beauty-Partner (Accessed 17 July 2023).

75 "Nearly 7 million people have visited Nike's Metaverse store", The Drum, 22 March 2022. Available at: https://www.thedrum.com/news/2022/03/22/nearly-7-million-people-have-visited-nike-s-metaverse-store (Accessed 17 July 2023).

76 "Shopping in the Metaverse could be more fun than you think", CNET, 23 March 2022. Available at: https://www.cnet.com/tech/computing/features/shopping-in-the-metaverse-could-be-more-fun-than-you-think/ (Accessed 17 July 2023).

77 "Metaverse economy could hit $13 trillion by 2030 – Citi", Finextra, 4 April 2022. Available at: https://www.finextra.com/newsarticle/39991/metaverse-economy-could-hit-13-trillion-by-2030---citi (Accessed 17 July 2023).

78 "Amex files metaverse-related trademark applications", Finextra, 16 March 2022. Available at: https://www.finextra.com/newsarticle/39878/amex-files-metaverse-related-trademark-applications (Accessed 17 July 2023).

79 "HSBC buys virtual plot of land in the Metaverse", Finextra, 16 March 2022. Available at: https://www.finextra.com/newsarticle/39883/hsbc-buys-virtual-plot-of-land-in-the-metaverse (Accessed 17 July 2023).

80 "Worldline makes it easier for companies to enter the Metaverse", Worldline, 9 March 2023. Available at: https://worldline.com/en/home/top-navigation/media-relations/press-release/worldline-makes-it-easier-for-companies-to-enter-the-metaverse.html (Accessed 17 July 2023).

81 "PKO Bank Polski to run jobs fair in the Metaverse", Finextra, 30 May 2023. Available at: https://www.finextra.com/newsarticle/42384/pko-bank-polski-to-run-jobs-fair-in-the-metaverse (Accessed 18 July 2023).

82 "A short history of the Metaverse", Forbes, 21 March 2022. Available at: https://www.forbes.com/sites/bernardmarr/2022/03/21/a-short-history-of-the-metaverse/?sh=d6d4d0a59688 (Accessed 18 July 2023).

83 "Metaverse may be $800 billion market, next tech platform", Bloomberg, 1 December 2021. Available at: https://www.bloomberg.com/professional/blog/metaverse-may-be-800-billion-market-next-tech-platform/ (Accessed 18 July 2023).

84 "Fortnite bug gave hackers access to millions of player accounts, researchers say", The Washington Post, 16 January 2019. Available at: https://www.washingtonpost.com/technology/2019/01/16/major-

bug-fortnite-gave-hackers-access-millions-player-accounts-researchers-say/ (Accessed 18 July 2013).

85 "NFT game Axie Infinity loses $600 million in security breach", The Gamer, 29 March 2022. Available at: https://www.thegamer.com/nft-axie-infinity-security-breach/ (Accessed 18 July 2023).

86 "Fortnite V-Bucks linked to large-scale money laundering scheme", GamesRadar+, 16 January 2019. Available at: https://www.gamesradar.com/fortnite-v-bucks-linked-to-large-scale-money-laundering-scheme/ (Accessed 18 July 2023).

87 "Gabe Newell banned NFTs from Steam due to 'sketchy behavior' and 'out of control' fraud", IGN, 25 February 2022. Available at: https://www.ign.com/articles/gabe-newell-nft-steam (Accessed 18 July 2023).

88 "ClearBank, a UK banking rails provider, raises $230M from Apax to expand into Europe and the US", TechCrunch, 18 March 2022. Available at: https://techcrunch.com/2022/03/18/clearbank-a-uk-banking-rails-provider-raises-230m-from-apax-to-expand-into-europe-and-the-u-s/ (Accessed 18 July 2023).

89 "The rise of crypto debit cards", Hydrogen, 19 October 2022. Available at: https://www.hydrogenplatform.com/blog/the-rise-of-crypto-debit-cards (Accessed 18 July 2023).

90 "Worldpay to offer merchants direct settlement in USDC", Finextra, 7 April 2022. Available at: https://www.finextra.com/newsarticle/40022/worldpay-to-offer-merchants-direct-settlement-in-usdc (Accessed 18 July 2023).

91 "Making digital currency interoperable", Visa website, 30 September 2021. Available at: https://usa.visa.com/visa-everywhere/blog/bdp/2021/09/29/making-digital-currency-1632954547520.html (Accessed 18 July 2023).

92 "Ralph Lauren now accepts crypto payments at Miami Design District Store", Finextra, 6 April 2023. Available at: https://www.finextra.com/pressarticle/96390/ralph-lauren-now-accepts-crypto-payments-at-miami-design-district-store (Accessed 18 July 2023).

93 "Amazon NFTs will be tied to real-world assets, token possible", Blockworks, 6 March 2023. Available at: https://blockworks.co/news/amazon-nfts-real-world-assets-token (Accessed 18 July 2023).

94 "What is 'phygital'? The blending of physical and digital", Yahoo! News, 7 September 2022. Available at: https://news.yahoo.com/phygital-blending-physical-digital-153000395.html (Accessed 24 August 2023).

95 "What is phygital commerce? Customers pay how they want. Your business grows sales like you want", Rapyd website, 17 June 2023. Available at: https://www.rapyd.net/blog/phygital-ecommerce/ (Accessed 24 August 2023).

96 "Mastercard certified as digital ID provider in the UK", Finextra, 16 March 2023. Available at: https://www.finextra.com/newsarticle/41981/mastercard-certified-as-digital-id-provider-in-the-uk (Accessed 18 July 2023).

97 "Sweden's BankID launches digital identity card", Finextra, 28 April 2023. Available at: https://www.finextra.com/newsarticle/42228/swedens-bankid-launches-digital-identity-card (Accessed 18 July 2023).

98 "Council and Parliament strike a deal on a European digital identity (eID)", European Council, 29 June 2023. Available at: https://www.consilium.europa.eu/en/press/press-releases/2023/06/29/council-and-parliament-strike-a-deal-on-a-european-digital-identity-eid/ (Accessed 18 July 2023).

99 "Google Wallet for Android now supports digital IDs", Ars Technica, 2 June 2023. Available at: https://arstechnica.com/google/2023/06/google-wallet-for-android-now-supports-digital-ids/ (Accessed 18 July 2023).

100 "Regtech market, global trends and forecast from 2022 to 2029", Exactitude Consultancy, April 2022. Available at: https://exactitudeconsultancy.com/reports/4330/regtech-market/#description (Accessed 18 July 2023).

5

PAYMENTS REGULATIONS AND LICENSES

Introduction

This chapter covers the most relevant regulations and licences for the payments industry. It is an overview of a complex matter, but readers will be able to understand the most salient points and access further readings. For more extensive reviews of global regulations, good books are already available, and regulations don't change that fast.

The payments world is incredibly dynamic, where new ecosystem risks, new business models, new products, and new infrastructures are challenging the existing order. Crypto's growth can threaten financial stability through contagion risk, as we have seen with the Terra/Luna and FTX collapses, calling for better oversight.[1]

Fraud continues to increase, and in the UK the Home Office estimated that one in five businesses across industries collectively suffered about 4.5 million fraud incidents between 2018 and 2023. With financial crime incidents remaining largely unreported,[2] the actual total could potentially be much higher.

DOI: 10.4324/9781032631394-6

New business models and new products create new ecosystem risks: for example, merchants operating across borders and currencies may face exposure to foreign exchange fluctuations or difficult-to-resolve defaults when they offer BNPL products[3] (risks which are well understood for traditional credit).

The geopolitical environment creates new challenges, and sanctions make it difficult for all ecosystem players to keep track of their compliance obligations, and this is even tougher for new entrants.

In their Global Risks Report 2023,[4] the World Economic Forum reports that, whilst environmental, geopolitical, and societal risks are top concerns, widespread cybercrime and cyber insecurity remain in the top ten for both short- and long-term horizons. Increased data collection (see Chapter 4, *Future outlook*) is leading to security concerns and potential abuse, which in turn is leading many jurisdictions to adopt data privacy and protection laws, including data localisation policies. This trend is also leading to tightened oversight of research collaborations, and even to the prohibition by some countries of some foreign-owned firms from operating on their territory, and this includes telecommunications, surveillance equipment, and mobile apps.

In our complex and evolving ecosystem, regulators and policy makers have a tough job balancing the promotion of innovation, the fostering of competition and inclusion, and the protection of ecosystems and individuals. **Successful innovation goes hand-in-hand with regulation**, and this is why we must be able to navigate the regulatory maze, where disparate financial, security, fraud, and privacy regulations intermingle and sometimes overlap.

The dynamics, mechanics, risks, and economics of payment ecosystems were covered in the previous chapters, and in this chapter I'll consolidate these elements, showing you how regulations aim to ensure ecosystem integrity and growth.

Europe has been at the forefront of extensive (and sometimes extra-territorial) regulations, starting with the impactful **General Data Protection Regulation (GDPR)** and the **Second Payment Services Directive (PSD2)**, both of which were passed in 2018. In the following sections, I will mostly cover European regulations, but I will also clearly define the common principles across all regulations and draw parallels with other geographies.

Payment services regulations

PSD2

The **Second Payment Services Directive (PSD2**, Directive 2015/2366/EU)[5] was created in 2015 and came into force in January 2018. As a "directive" (not a regulation), the PSD2 was enacted in each member state prior to the deadline. As the UK was still an EU member state in 2018, PSD2 was enacted as the **Payment Services Regulation 2017 (PSR)**.[6]

The aim of the directive is to promote open access and competition, strengthen the security of the payment ecosystem, and regulate previously unregulated firms. PSD2's main regulatory instruments will be explained in the following sections.

Strong Customer Authentication (SCA)

Strong Customer Authentication (SCA) aims to strengthen safeguards around the usage of payment accounts through two main authentication options: **Multi-Factor Authentication (MFA)** or an exemption called **Transaction Risk Analysis (TRA)**. SCA was enforced in the EU on 1 January 2021, but the UK delayed implementation until March 2022.

The requirements for SCA are specified in the **Regulatory Technical Standard (RTS)**[7] (Commission Delegated Regulation (EU) 2018/389), which was published by the **European Banking Authority (EBA)** and is amended by them from time to time.[8] For example, in the card payments ecosystem 3D Secure is an application of SCA, but in the banking world there is no equivalent industry standard other that what is specified in the RTS.

Apart from the regulatory obligations, card schemes have also "incentivised" the industry to behave more securely: in January 2021, Mastercard doubled the authentication fee in most EU countries for 3D Secure version 1; both Visa and Mastercard discontinued support for 3D Secure version 1.0.2 in October 2022 (see Chapter 1, 3D Secure).

MFA suggests the use of two or more factors for authenticating payment account holders and users. These factors must be independent of each other, which means that knowledge or possession of one factor shouldn't enable anyone to derive another factor, and the breach of one factor shouldn't compromise the integrity of the others. All factors must be secure, which

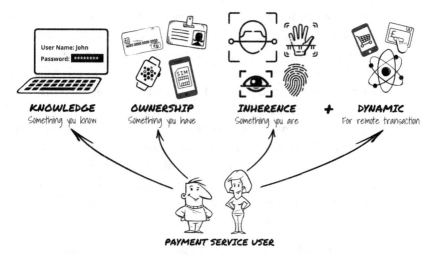

Figure 5.1 Multi-factor authentication (MFA).

Source: drawing by the author.

means that safeguards should be implemented to protect them. There are three types of authentication factor:

- **Knowledge**: something you know;
- **Ownership**: something you have; and
- **Inherence**: something you are.

In addition, a fourth factor is required for remote transactions (where the customer is not present), and it must be dynamic (i.e. can't be reused) and specific to that transaction, the payer, and the payee. This is illustrated in Figure 5.1.

TRANSACTION RISK ANALYSIS (TRA)

TRA is one of the allowed SCA exemptions under PSD2. It can be applied to low-risk remote payments instead of SCA and depends on fraud levels. TRA is defined in Article 18 of the EBA RTS, and businesses wishing to take advantage of this exemption must meet the following criteria:

- **The transaction is deemed low-risk**, and this means that *all* of the following conditions must be met:

- The fraud rate for that type of transaction is equivalent to or below the **Reference Fraud Rates** and the amount of the transaction must be below the relevant **Exemption Threshold Value (ETV)**. In addition, PSPs must calculate the overall fraud rate every 90 days, document it, and audit it. Table 5.1 gives the reference fraud rates and ETVs:
- **Real-time Transaction Risk Analysis must not identify any adverse risk factors** such as abnormal payer spending or abnormal behavioural pattern, unusual information about the payer's device/software access, malware infection in any session of the authentication process, known fraud scenarios, abnormal payer location, or high-risk payee location.

- **Transaction monitoring must be in place and in real time**, and PSPs must include at a minimum:
  - The payer's previous spending patterns;
  - The payment transaction history of each of the PSP's PSUs;
  - The payer's location at the time of the payment transaction and the payee's location at the time of the payment transaction if the PSP provides the access device or the software; and
  - Identification of PSU abnormal payment patterns in relation to their transaction history.

In order to assess whether a payment transaction should be allowed without SCA, PSPs must combine all these risk factors into **a risk score for each individual transaction**.

Table 5.1 TRA reference fraud rates and ETVs. Commission Delegated Regulation (EU) 2018/389.

Exemption Threshold Value (ETV)	Reference fraud rate (%)	
	Remote card-based payments	Credit transfers
€500	0.01	0.005
€250	0.06	0.01
€100	0.13	0.015

In the cards world, acquirers must apply for the TRA exemption with the regulator in order for their merchants to take advantage of it. In this highly competitive market, this can be a commercial differentiator for acquirers and PSPs alike (see Elavon[9]), and card schemes also offer guidance and products (see Mastercard[10]).

SCA EXEMPTIONS

Chapter 3 of the EBA RTS specifies several exemptions to SCA. TRA is one of them and was covered in detail earlier, given its significance to the customer experience. The other exemptions are specified in Table 5.2.

 Professionals should remember:

SCA exemptions add an additional dimension to the **Liability Shift** (see Chapter 2, Liability shift), in as much as if a merchant or acquirer requests an exemption and the request is accepted by the issuer, the liability stays with the merchant. If the exemption is applied by the issuer, the liability shifts to the issuer.

SCA exemptions aim to provide frictionless customer interactions for specific payment scenarios, and they may help with cart abandonment and declined transactions. As only acquirers can request exemptions, this may give acquirers a competitive advantage in getting merchants. For mainstream acquirers dealing with low- to medium-risk merchants, consistently meeting the fraud thresholds and abiding by the reporting requirements may be a tall order as tightly managing fraud risk has perhaps not been as stringent as for high-risk acquirers. This may, however, be achieved through the adoption of modern technologies (e.g. machine learning) which would enable acquirers to truly differentiate themselves by bringing "SCA-exempt" merchant services, showing their superior fraud detection talent in an increasingly commoditised market (this might mean that acquirers may have to clearly categorise their merchant portfolios into levels of risk for which these solutions may or may not be offered).

Table 5.2 SCA exemptions. Commission Delegated Regulation (EU) 2018/389.

SCA exemption	RTS article	Exemption applicability	When SCA should be conducted
Access to payment information	10	Account information services for balance and transaction history for the last 90 days.	For the first transaction and when 90 days have elapsed since the last SCA was performed. Note: the EBA is proposing to extend the 90-day period to 180 days at the time of writing. In the UK, AISPs were exempted from SCA from September 2022.
Contactless payments	11	Contactless transactions up to €50 with a maximum of €150 cumulative spend or five consecutive transactions.	The number of consecutive transactions since the last SCA was performed exceeds five. The cumulative value of transactions since the last SCA was performed exceeds €150.
Unattended terminals for transport fares and parking fees	12	Any.	SCA is not required, but PSPs must still implement transaction monitoring to detect unauthorised or fraudulent transactions.
Trusted beneficiaries	13	When the payer makes a payment to a payee included in a list or trusted beneficiaries they have created.	When the payer creates or amends their list of trusted beneficiaries.
Recurring transactions	14	Any.	When the recurring transaction is first initiated. When the payer amends the recurring transaction.
Credit transfers to self	15	When the payer sends a credit transfer to themselves or when both sending and receiving accounts are held by the same ASPSP.	SCA is not required.
Low-value remote transactions	16	Remote transactions up to €30 with a maximum of €100 cumulative spend or five consecutive transactions.	The number of consecutive transactions since the last SCA was performed exceeds five. The cumulative value of transactions since the last SCA was performed exceeds €100.
Secure corporate payments	17	For non-consumer payments.	SCA not required, but security requirements apply.
Transaction Risk Analysis	18	Low-risk transactions (as defined in the RTS).	Reference fraud rates and ETV apply, and transaction monitoring must be in place. Fraud rates must be ~~calculated every 90 days~~

AUTHENTICATION AT LARGE

PSD2 introduced the concept of "one-leg out" transactions, which is when a business based outside of the EU sells goods or services to customers within the EU. In this scenario, those businesses should apply SCA, but only on a "best endeavour" basis, and they are not required to do so in their own country.[11]

In the UK, since Brexit, the UK RTS diverged from the EBA RTS on SCA. For example, the EBA is of the opinion that inherence relates to physical, physiological, and behavioural characteristics related to the body. The UK adds to that definition behavioural characteristics that are not related to the body (e.g. shopping patterns). I think this definition is more flexible and could be particularly suited to vulnerable users.

In the US, there is no equivalent to the EU SCA, although the CFPB issued a circular pointing out that not protecting data could be "unfair practice" and recommending the use of multi-factor authentication (MFA) as prescribed by the **FIDO** Alliance.[12]

On the card rails, the industry is already doing it for itself, as the card schemes can unilaterally, and commercially, decide on the rules (within applicable regulations). We saw in Chapter 1 (*Card payments authentication*) how they give "incentives" to the market for deploying newer versions of 3D Secure. EMV also continues to develop their standards to make interactions more seamless and secure (e.g. EMV Secure Remote Commerce).

In the tech industry, it will be interesting to watch how the **WebAuthn** standard develops. In June 2023, the World Wide Web Consortium (W3C) released the new Secure Payment Confirmation (SPC) specification,[13] which is a web API that allows merchants, banks, and PSPs to streamline payment transaction authentication in line with FIDO 2 specifications.

Secure communications

PSD2 banned screen scraping (see Chapter 4, *What do we mean by open banking?*), and as it forced ASPSPs to give TPPs access to data, safeguards were introduced to preserve the integrity of payment interactions. This is covered in Chapter 4 of the EBA RTS ("Common and secure open standards of communication"), which gives two access options: the Dedicated Interface (open API; see Chapter 4, *Open vs private APIs*) and use of the PSU's interface (e.g. online banking facility) as a contingency mechanism when the dedicated interface is unavailable, as long as the TPP can be authenticated separately from the PSU.

 Professionals should remember:

- **ASPSPs (e.g. banks) should make sure that their APIs are available, performant, and non-discriminatory to TPPs.** ASPSPs also have reporting obligations to their competent authority.
- **APIs are subject to security requirements** listed in the EBA RTS.
- **ASPSPs must provide a fallback mechanism** when the APIs are not available. There are exemptions to this listed in the EBA RTS.
- To use any interface, **TPPs must be authorised by the PSU,** and they **must be securely authenticated** separately from the PSU (e.g. eIDAS certificate). PSUs can withdraw their authorisation at any time.

What's next for PSD2?

EUROPEAN COMMISSION REVIEW OF PSD2

The review concluded that PSD2 had a clear, positive impact on fraud prevention through the introduction of SCA and on consumers by increasing efficiency, transparency, and choice. However, the review noted that an **unlevel playing field between PSPs remains**, partly due to the lack of direct access by non-bank PSPs to settlement infrastructures and due to the challenges PSPs face in obtaining bank accounts to secure licences. TPPs still have data access challenges, and whilst cross-border payment services have increased, many payment schemes (especially debit card schemes) remain largely domestic across the EU block. In addition, **Open Banking has not gained the hoped-for traction**, and **new types of fraud** have emerged for which PSD2 is not equipped to address.

PSD3 PROPOSAL

The **Third Payment Services Directive (PSD3)** was proposed by the European Commission on 28 June 2023[14] alongside the new **Payment Services Regulation** (**PSR**). The new regulatory framework aims to bring a higher degree of harmonisation and consistent application of the regulation for both payment and eMoney institutions. Please note that the new EU PSR, whilst it has the same name, is different from the UK PSR 2017, which was the enactment of PSD2 in the UK.

Consequently, **most of the content in PSD2 will come under the new Payment Systems Regulation (PSR)**. This is a major change, as the PSR is a regulation, not a directive, meaning that it will be automatically enforced in all member states on a set date (just like the EU GDPR was), therefore ensuring harmonisation across the EU.

Elements of the **eMoney Directive** will also move into the PSR, and as a result, the eMoney Directive **will cease to exist and eMoney institutions (EMIs) will disappear**. Under the new regime, Payment institutions (PIs) can be authorised to offer eMoney services, which is a welcome simplification. As a result, PSD3 will focus on the licensing and authorisation of PIs and EMIs, which is a good thing, as it will give national competent authorities some leeway in the implementation of their licensing frameworks.

From the past history of EU regulatory cycles, the package is not expected to come into force until 2026, and it extends PSD2 in the following ways:

- *Improving competition and levelling the playing field*: PSD2 drove the growth in the numbers of both PIs and EMIs, but these continue to face challenges. To address this, PSD3 will require banks to clearly explain the reasons for refusing to open bank accounts, as well as for the withdrawal of services. Going forward, grounds for refusal or withdrawal must be on the basis of either "serious risk" or "illegal activity". PSPs that are refused access to banking services will be able to appeal to their regulator. In addition, central banks will be allowed to provide account services to non-bank PSPs (some, like the Bank of England, already do). PIs will potentially be allowed to access designated payment schemes. Currently, PIs are regulated under PSD2, and EMIs are regulated under the eMoney Directive, which means that a mature legal framework is already in place. However, governance and licensing arrangements are quite distinct (see Table 4.3), and PSD3 aims to harmonise the two.
- *Improving security and fraud prevention*: PSR/PSD3 extend the implementation of the **Confirmation of Payee (CoP)** overlay service (**IBAN/ name matching**) to all credit transfers, require PSPs to share threat intelligence, and strengthen transaction monitoring. PSPs also have an obligation to educate PSUs and staff on payment fraud. PSR/PSD3 will

    simplify the SCA process for AISPs and clarify the requirements for **Merchant-Initiated Transactions (MITs)** and digital wallets.

- *Improving open banking and towards open finance*: APSPs (e.g. banks) will no longer be required to permanently maintain two interfaces for access (i.e. dedicated interface and fallback mechanism), and they will have more flexibility in the way they ensure continuous data access for TPPs. Open banking providers will retain the right, in line with applicable laws, to claim damages from the ASPSPs for loss of business. On 28 June 2023, the European Commission also proposed the Financial Data Access (FIDA)[15] framework, which extends the obligation to provide financial data beyond payment account data (see Chapter 4, *Towards open finance* and Figure 4.8), and which is contingent on the development of the SEPA Payment Account Access (SPAA) scheme (see Chapter 3, *SEPA payments types*).

- *Consumer duty of care*: PSR/PSD3 will grant refund rights to victims if the fraud is caused by a failure of the IBAN/name verification service, or for impersonation fraud (see Chapter 3, *Types of APP scams*, and *SEPA payments types*). Victims would be able to claim 100% of the fraudulent amount from their PSP for authorised scams, but reimbursement conditions will apply (e.g. type of scam, gross negligence), but the proposal is unclear on the PSP liability models. In addition, PSPs will be required to provide more transparency.

For credit transfers and money remittance from the EU to third countries, PSPs must **inform consumers about currency conversion charges**. PSPs must **include unambiguous information that identifies the payee** (e.g. commercial trade name) **on payment account statements** (see Chapter 1, *Retrievals*), as well as providing open-banking consumers with a dashboard showing granted data access rights together with a withdrawal of consent functionality.

PSR/PSD3 also looks at access to cash: **merchants will be allowed to disburse cash without the transaction being associated with a purchase** (cashback), contingent on restrictions (e.g. amount cap to guarantee fair competition with ATMs). PSPs will be required to **provide PSUs with information on all applicable charges made by other ATM operators** in the same member state. PSR/PSD3 also proposes changes to **speed up the release of unused blocked funds for pre-authorised transactions**, with a requirement that the blocked amount be proportionate to the expected final amount. In addition, **ATM operators who don't service payment accounts will be allowed to operate ATMs without a licence**, subject to the transparency of fee requirements.

e-Money regulations

At the time of writing, the EU eMoney Directive[16] (Directive 2009/110/EC) regulates e-Money institutions in Europe (see Chapter 4, *eMoney*, and *Cash vs eMoney vs CBDC*), and it is a very short directive (11 pages). It specifies what EMIs can and can't do, as shown in the next section.

In the UK, the regulator for eMoney institutions is the **Financial Conduct Authority** (**FCA**), and they provide a register of authorised firms (see *Licences to operate a payment business*).

In the US, the **Federal Trade Commission** (**FTC**) has authority over non-bank fintech entities that provide a variety of financial services, including lending, payments, and cryptocurrency offerings.

There are similar bodies in other geographies.

Global context of payment services regulations

This book will not be enough to cover global regulations, which is why I chose to cover the main EU regulations in order to introduce the concepts. The way non-bank PSPs (e.g. eMoney businesses) are covered (or not) by regulations will depend on the country. The way these ecosystem actors are described will also vary: they may very well be called eMoney institutions (EMIs), payment institutions (PIs), payment banks, or even fintechs. How banks are covered by regulations will also depend on the country's laws, but unlike non-bank PSPs the regulations are somewhat similar worldwide because banks are of systemic importance. For those who want to delve further, please see the *Regulators* section in this chapter, which will give you an idea of the scope of the various competent authorities and enable you to find the applicable regulations.

In general, payment businesses will be able to offer **Payment Services**, and in order to enable those not operating within Europe or the UK to draw parallels, these will be defined as:

- Services enabling **cash to be placed on a payment account** as well as all the operations required for operating a payment account;

- Services enabling **cash withdrawals from a payment account** as well as all the operations required for operating a payment account;
- **Execution of payment transactions**, including transfers of funds on a payment account with the user's payment service provider or with another payment service provider:
  - Execution of Direct Debits, including one-off Direct Debits;
  - Execution of payment transactions through a payment card or a similar device; and
  - Execution of credit transfers, including standing orders;

- **Execution of payment transactions where the funds are covered by a credit line** for a payment service user:
  - Execution of Direct Debits, including one-off Direct Debits;
  - Execution of payment transactions through a payment card or a similar device; and
  - Execution of credit transfers, including standing orders;

- **Issuing of payment instruments** and/or **acquiring** of payment transactions; and
- **Money remittance**.
- In addition, payment businesses may be able to offer other services, as allowed by applicable laws:
- Account information services;
- Payment initiation services;
- eMoney issuance;
- The ability to conduct business on an agency basis; and
- Granting of credit related to payment services.

Licences to operate a payment business

Outside of Europe, other regulations will cover payment businesses, and the previous section aimed to enable readers to pinpoint specific aspects of interest in their own local regulations. Within this context, we'll examine what it takes to become a payment business.

Permissions give firms the right to operate a payment business. Because some entities are already heavily regulated under other regimes (e.g. prudential),[17] the following institutions don't require payment permissions:

credit unions, national savings banks, banks, building societies, and municipal banks. There may be some exceptions, such as when the organisation operates in a limited network (e.g. a gift card that can only be used in one shopping centre).

These permissions offer an access path to non-bank payment service providers. These organisations tend to be less regulated in advanced economies (because regulatory frameworks are more mature) than in emerging markets, where they might only be able to offer fewer services. However, in the majority of jurisdictions, non-bank PSPs are subject to Anti-Money Laundering (AML) and Counter Terrorism Financing (CTF) obligations, or at least safeguarding requirements.

Firms which fail to obtain the relevant permissions but carry on trading could, at worst, be subject to fines and supervisory enforcement actions from regulators or, at best, find it difficult to obtain bank accounts or have their accounts withdrawn (de-risking), which in turn prevents them from obtaining necessary permissions. It's a Catch-22.

This can all get very confusing, and Table 5.3 gives a quick recap.

The rows in Table 5.3 are listed in order of the risk that licensed businesses may pose to the payment ecosystem, from lowest to highest, and the regulatory requirements will therefore be more stringent as you move down the table. EMIs have attracted a lot of regulatory scrutiny in the last few years, especially after the Wirecard scandal.[18]

You may also have noticed that EMIs can do a lot of things, and they can be perceived to be very similar to banks. You know how the saying goes: "If it looks like a duck, swims like a duck, and quacks like a duck, it's probably a duck". Well, in this case, it's not a duck. (I have a thing about ducks ...). Arguably, most of the neo-banks, such as Monzo and Starling, started life as EMIs, and like many similar firms they called themselves "banks" for a long time. Regulators disliked this, as consumers could be misled with regard to compensation (see Figure 4.15), and several regulators issued warnings.[19,20] Some neo-banks eventually grew and became "proper" banks, such as, once again, Monzo and Starling. Some fintechs took another path: in the US, Moven, one of the first digital banks, closed its consumer business after nine years, and pivoted towards becoming a B2B business supplying technology to banks through their Banking-as-a-Service (BaaS) platform. In the meantime, Varo was successful in obtaining a US bank charter (becoming Varo Bank after starting as Varo Money) and

Table 5.3 Differences between payment licences. Examples given are related to the UK and EU markets and regulations applicable in July 2023.

	AIS	PIS	Payment services	eMoney issuance	Agency business	Examples
Registered AISP (RAISP)	Yes	No	No	No	No	Xero, Intuit (QuickBooks), Credit Kudos, ClearScore, Experian, Yodlee
Small Payment Institution (Registered SPI)	No	No	Yes	No	No	SimbaPay, Lemonade Finance, KogoPay, Salt Edge
Small Electronic Money Institution (Registered SEMI)	No	No	Yes	Yes	No	Billon, Shrap, Nochex, FinBlocks, Silicon Silk, Payver
Authorised Payment Institution (PI)	Yes	Yes	Yes	No	Yes	Visa, Mastercard, Worldpay, Amazon, American Express, Plaid, Verifone, Currensea, Western Union, Token.io, Moneygram, GoCardless
Authorised Electronic Money Institution (EMI)	Yes	Yes	Yes	Yes	Yes	Wise, Stripe, Curve, Google Pay, Revolut, WorldRemit, Sumup, Modulr, TrueLayer

is now a full-fledged digital bank, as well as the first neo-bank to join the Zelle network. In the meantime, in Germany, N26 is still struggling at the time of writing.[21]

The types of permissions required for businesses wanting to "get into payments" are listed in more detail in the following sections and apply to the European market. There will be similar permissions in other geographies (although they might not go by the same name or have the same structure). The Bank for International Settlements (BIS) provides a good global regulatory overview in their 2021 paper "Fintech and payments: regulating digital payment services and e-money".[22] The descriptions given here will help you translate the EU obligations into other regulatory frameworks.

Payment institution

> A **Payment Institution** is a regulated payment business which can offer payment services and may be able to offer other payment-related services but can't issue eMoney.

An acquirer is an example of a payment institution.

Relatively speaking, this is one of the easiest permissions to get. In general, firms applying for this licence need to have a good reputation, the appropriate knowledge to provide payment services, and meet thresholds for average monthly payment transactions. For new companies, having the appropriate knowledge may be difficult, and usually this is achieved through an advisory board or independent non-executive directors. With this licence, the types of payment services allowed may be limited.

In Europe, including the UK, there are two types of payment institution licences.

SMALL PAYMENT INSTITUTION (SPI)

A firm may apply for an **SPI** licence if their projected average monthly payment transactions don't exceed €3 million and their registered office is located in the country where they intend to provide payment services. SPIs are not allowed to provide payment initiation or account information services (see Chapter 3, *Bank ecosystem actors*). An SPI is required to register with their national competent authority and is referred to as a **registered entity**. At the time of writing, there are about 500 SPIs registered in the UK, mostly small money transfer businesses.

AUTHORISED PAYMENT INSTITUTION (PI)

A firm may apply for a **PI** licence when their projected average monthly payment transactions exceed €3 million and they plan to offer payment services in other EU countries where they don't have a registered office. This is called a **Passport Arrangement**. When Brexit happened and the UK left the EU, firms benefitting from a passport arrangement to and from the UK lost this ability. As a result, many companies established registered offices on either side of the Channel (there was a relatively long runway through temporary permission regimes allowing firms to cater for this). A PI is required to be authorised by their national competent authority and is recognised as an **authorised entity** in their home country and all other EU states (this is called a **Passporting Arrangement**). At the time of writing, there are less than 500 authorised PIs in the UK.

eMoney institution

An **eMoney Institution (EMI)** is a regulated payment business which can offer payment services and issue eMoney, and which may be able to offer other payment-related services.

Wise, Stripe, and Revolut are examples of eMoney institutions.

This is a harder permission to get, and firms wishing to apply for this type of licence will face more stringent requirements. In Europe, including the UK, there are two types of eMoney institutions, the small eMoney institution (SEMI) and the authorised eMoney institution (EMI).

SMALL ELECTRONIC MONEY INSTITUTION (SEMI)

A firm may apply for a **SEMI** licence if their projected monthly average outstanding eMoney doesn't exceed €5 million and their registered office is in the country where they intend to provide payment services. SEMIs can also provide payment services unrelated to eMoney if their average monthly turnover in payment transactions doesn't exceed €3 million. Whilst SEMIs don't have to comply with the full might of AML regulations, they are subject to **safeguarding** requirements for customer funds, which means they have to keep clients' funds completely separate from their own operational funds (see Figure 4.15). Unfortunately, eMoney institutions often fail in this obligation,[23] and with the difficulties that some experience in obtaining bank accounts, this may be a vicious circle.

SEMIs are not allowed to provide payment initiation or account information services (see Chapter 3, *New bank ecosystem actors*). A SEMI is required to register with their national competent authority and is referred to as a **registered entity**. At the time of writing, there are about 30 registered SEMIs in the UK.

AUTHORISED ELECTRONIC MONEY INSTITUTION (EMI)

A firm may apply for an **EMI** licence when their projected monthly average outstanding eMoney exceeds €5 million and they plan to offer payment services in other EU countries through the passport arrangement. EMIs can also provide payment services unrelated to eMoney. An EMI must comply with AML regulations and must be authorised by their national competent authority. An authorised EMI is recognised as an **authorised entity** in their home country and all other EU states (via the passporting arrangement). At the time of writing, there are less than 130 EMIs authorised in the UK.

TPP PERMISSIONS

A TPP wishing *only* to provide account information services must be **registered** with their national regulator, and there is no need for them to be authorised. Such a TPP is known as a **Registered AISP** (**RAISP**) and is subject to less-stringent requirements. Indeed, whilst this in not the case in the EU under PSD2, the UK Financial Conduct Authority (FCA) released RAISPs from the AML obligations applicable to TPPs[24] (which makes absolute sense since they are not involved in the movement of funds).

Conversely, a TPP wishing to offer payment initiation services must be authorised as either an authorised PI or an authorised EMI.

AGENCY BUSINESS

Both authorised PIs and EMIs can conduct business on an "agency basis", and this means that they can allow other businesses (their agents) to conduct business on their behalf.

The agent of an authorised payment institution (**the Principal**) is called a **PSD Agent**, and the agent of an authorised eMoney institution (**the Principal**) is called an **EMD Agent**.

PSD Agents and **EMD Agents** can conduct business on behalf of one or more **Principal** firms. This is similar to the card scheme membership model (see Chapter 2, *Scheme membership*).

PSD agents will generally be small organisations, and in the UK, for example, there are in excess of 23,000 PSD agents at the time of writing.

If EMD agents are only distributing the eMoney of the principal, they are classed as "distributors" and don't require to be registered with the regulator (i.e. they are only reselling the eMoney of their principal). However, if EMD agents provide unrelated payment services on behalf of a principal, they need to be registered as an agent with the regulator, which is a more difficult permission to obtain than for a PSD agent. For example, in the UK there are less than 250 EMD agents registered with the FCA at the time of writing.

As a generic principle, a principal firm using the agency model must take responsibility for the actions of its agent(s) as if it had carried out that business itself.

 Professionals should remember:

- An EMI can offer digital payment accounts that look and feel like a bank account.
- EMIs generally don't or are not allowed to (depending on the jurisdiction) pay interest on customer balances.
- EMIs are not credit institutions and therefore can't engage in lending activities in the way banks do.
- In general, EMI customers are not protected under banking compensation schemes, but this is dependent on the jurisdiction. For example, in the US EMIs can partner with banks for the supply of underlying products which may be covered by existing banking compensation schemes.

Open banking registrations

Depending on the country, and how the regulators approach open banking, providers of open-banking services must register with the implementation entity. In the UK, this is the Open Banking Implementation Entity[25] (OBIE), and ASPSPs, TPPs, vendors, and Technical Services Providers (TSPs) will find the necessary tools to enter this world, such as conformance services (e.g. with API specifications). In Chapter 3, we covered the Confirmation of Payee (CoP) overlay service. Both ASPSPs and smaller PSPs can register with the governance entity (e.g. Pay.UK in the UK) for participation, and they would need to be regulator-approved (e.g. "registered entities" in the EU and UK).

There will be similar regimes in other geographies, depending on the national open-banking framework (see Figure 4.6).

Phone paid services

In some geographies, such as the UK, businesses that sell content, goods, or services that are charged to a phone bill (e.g. through direct carrier billing services) will be subject to additional requirements. Originally, these regulations were introduced to control the provision of premium rate services (e.g. phone competitions, voting), but as the industry evolved, this now includes the provision of other services (see Chapter 4, *Mobile money*).

In the UK, the regulator is the Phone-Paid Services Authority (PSA), and the applicable law is **Code 15**.[26] As a UK example, Microsoft (the merchant) is registered with the PSA for the provision of carrier billing over the EE network (the carrier) on the Microsoft Store for purchases of games (the products), and EE uses Boku as the Direct Carrier Billing (DCB) provider in the UK, which is also registered with the PSA (see Figure 4.11). As a testimony to the evolution of the payments industry, merchants can also be crypto providers.

Crypto and virtual asset providers

In the UK, a crypto business must be registered with the FCA for AML purposes, and those in scope are:

- Crypto-asset exchange providers, including crypto-asset ATMs;
- Peer-to-peer providers;

- Crypto-asset issuers;
- Initial Exchange Offerings (ICOs); and
- Custodian wallet providers.

The FCA maintains a list of registered crypto-asset businesses,[27] as well as a list of unregistered crypto businesses[28] (which are therefore acting illegally). At the time of writing, there were 42 registered crypto businesses and 76 illegal ones in the UK.

A firm should apply for a crypto licence in the UK, even if it is a bank, investment firm, or a company with a UK eMoney or payment institution licence. In addition, UK banks are not required to provide bank accounts to crypto-asset providers unless the latter are regulated PSPs. Therefore, the ease of accessing a bank account will vary depending on the bank and crypto-asset provider, and most UK banks are banning transfers to crypto exchanges.

Anti-Money Laundering (AML)

Main concepts

Most countries have Anti-Money Laundering and Counter-Terrorism Financing (AML/CTF) laws applying to financial services institutions, albeit to varying degrees of effectiveness. Increasingly, AML regulations may also apply to businesses outside the financial services sector (e.g. art galleries, jewellers, estate agents, solicitors). AML/CTF regulations globally will use the same definitions and concepts, and the trends are similar:

- Increased due diligence;
- Increased risk assessment and governance;
- Increased transparency (e.g. beneficial ownership, thresholds on anonymous prepaid instruments, ban on anonymous bank and savings accounts and safe deposit boxes);
- Increased focus on tax crimes (which may be included as predicate offences for money-laundering and terrorism-financing activities);
- Increased security (e.g. by the inclusion of data protection policies in AML policies);

- Increased accountability (i.e. personal and legal entity accountability); and
- Increased focus on virtual asset and service providers (e.g. cryptocurrencies, fiat-to-crypto providers, and custodian wallet providers).

Please also note that this chapter doesn't constitute legal advice, and only aims to give you an appreciation of the regulatory obligations that payment ecosystem actors may have. Individual country regulations may not include all of the elements listed in this section, and therefore, regulatory enforcement and applicability may differ across jurisdictions. To understand what applies to a given business in a particular country or region, readers have to understand the specific laws.

The fundamental AML concepts are explained in the following sections.

Customer Due Diligence

> **Customer Due Diligence (CDD)** is the process by which businesses verify that their customers are who they say they are, and is usually conducted at the underwriting stage or when creating a new business relationship. CDD allows businesses to the assess money-laundering and terrorism-financing risks to which customers may potentially expose them.

Figure 5.2 shows when businesses should conduct CDD.

When money laundering or terrorism financing is suspected

When the circumstances of an existing customer **change**

When carrying out a transaction that exceeds the amount specified by the law

When establishing a new business relationship

When the accuracy or adequacy of the information provided is in doubt

WHEN SHOULD I CONDUCT CDD?

Figure 5.2 Customer Due Diligence (CDD).

Source: drawing by the author.

Usually, businesses must conduct CDD in the following situations:

- **When establishing a new business relationship.**
- **When the circumstances of an existing customer change.** In practical terms, this could mean a change in the customer's business activity, a significant change in business volumes, or a change in ownership structure.
- **When carrying out an occasional transaction that exceeds the amount specified by the law.** Typically, the thresholds for eMoney institutions will be lower than for banks, and these thresholds may also vary depending on the type of business (e.g. high-value vs low-value business).
- **When money laundering or terrorism financing is suspected.**
- **When the accuracy or adequacy of the information provided is in doubt** (e.g. when there are discrepancies between the information provided and that held by official bodies for the customer).

If a customer or transaction fails the CDD risk assessment, the business should act appropriately, and they should report the suspicious activity as soon as they know or suspect that a person or business is engaged in money laundering or terrorism financing. The various laws will specify the time period within which suspicious activity should be reported. Organisations, large or small, often fail to meet this obligation.

When establishing a new business relationship, firms conducting their CDD risk assessment should:

- **Verify the customer's identity** through an independent, reliable source. In practice, this means verifying the customer's name, having sight of a photograph on an official document, and collecting the residential address and date of birth. It may also mean obtaining details of the customer's business or employment. This step is generally referred to as **Know-Your-Customer (KYC)**, and can be conducted manually or digitally (eKYC). People often confuse KYC and CDD, using the terms interchangeably, but they are not the same thing: KYC happens when setting up a business relationship (and can be supported by technology providers), whilst CDD is a continuous assurance process throughout the relationship (and can also be supported by technology providers).

- Establish **beneficial ownership** for business customers (i.e. the relationship between the signatory and any underlying beneficial owners, especially if they have significant control over the business).
- **Define the purpose of the relationship** when it is expected to be ongoing. This will typically mean understanding the type of business, activity, and volumes expected throughout the relationship.
- **Determine the source and origin of funds.** Typically, this will involve obtaining copies of recent and current financial statements.

When the circumstances of an existing customer change, firms conducting their CDD risk assessment should:

- **Keep customer information up-to-date** and amend the risk assessment accordingly.
- **Carry out further due diligence measures if necessary.**

When carrying out occasional transactions – transactions that aren't within the ongoing business relationship – firms conducting their CDD risk assessment should:

- **Apply CDD if the occasional single transaction exceeds the threshold value** specified by the applicable national law.
- **Identify potentially linked transactions** to determine whether a transaction has been deliberately split to remain below the applicable thresholds set by the law. Potential indicators may be that a number of payments have been made by the same customer in a short span, or that a number of customers have made transactions on behalf of the same person, or that a number of customers have made credit transfers to the same person. **When a linked transaction is identified, businesses should conduct CDD.**

CDD should also be conducted on occasional transactions that are below the legal thresholds if there is a suspicion of money laundering.

Enhanced Due Diligence

Enhanced Due Diligence (EDD) is the process by which businesses perform more stringent Customer Due Diligence (CDD) on customers at the underwriting stage or during the course of a business relationship. EDD is usually performed when the customer is not present when KYC is performed, when Politically Exposed Persons (PEPs) are involved, where the nature of the customer's business changes, when there is a high risk of money laundering or terrorism financing, or when the customer is in a high-risk country.

Enhanced Due Diligence (EDD) is more stringent than CDD, and the scenarios for which this should be conducted are shown in Figure 5.3.

In any situation involving a high risk of money laundering

When the customer is not physically present when KYC is performed

When the transaction involves a high risk third country

When entering into a business relationship with a Politically Exposed Person (PEP)

WHEN SHOULD I CONDUCT EDD?

Figure 5.3 Enhanced Due Diligence (EDD).

Source: drawing by the author.

 The EDD risk assessment should be carried out when:

- The **customer is not physically present when KYC is performed**.
- Entering in into a business relationship with a **Politically Exposed Person (PEP)**. In practical terms, this usually means members of government, Parliament, etc., their family members, and known close associates. The exact way PEPs should be treated will depend on the regulation and can be a controversial matter, as seen in the UK.[29]

- **The transaction involves a high-risk third country** as classified by the jurisdiction. This can get complicated: whilst the **Financial Action Task Force (FATF)** publishes lists of high-risk countries (see Figure 5.5), each jurisdiction is free to publish their own list, such as the EU,[30] which added countries to the FATF list, and the US,[31] which follows the FATF list.
- **Any situation that involves a high risk of money laundering.** In practical terms, this may apply if the customer is a money transmitter, currency exchange, or crypto firm, and should also involve checking whether the business has the appropriate credentials from their regulator.

If a customer or transaction fails the EDD risk assessment, the business should act appropriately, and they should report the suspicious activity as soon as they know or suspect that a person or business is engaged in money laundering or terrorism financing.

Suspicious Activity Reporting (SAR) and governance

CDD and EDD help businesses to identify money-laundering and terrorism-financing crimes. When such financial crimes are detected or suspected, businesses should report them (through a nominated officer) to the regulator via the **Suspicious Activity Reporting (SAR)** process, which is part of the internal governance and monitoring a firm should have in place. Payment businesses often fail to adequately file SARs, and regulators have been enforcing this through heavy fines,[32] such as with the $12 million fine issued to Merrill Lynch by the SEC in July 2023. In addition, larger organisations may have a regulatory requirement to appoint a **Money Laundering Reporting Officer (MLRO)** who may act as the nominated officer. AML/CTF governance is a serious matter for regulators, and enforcement has been noticeable, such as with the UK FCA £107.8 million fine on Santander in December 2022.[33]

Recordkeeping

Businesses should provide evidence that they are doing the right thing. This means keeping records of all due diligence measures they carry out, including customer identification records, risk assessments, policies, controls, and procedures, as well as staff training records. In addition, transactional records should also be kept, and this may include daily transactions, receipts, cheques, and correspondence. Generally, the formats in which the information can be kept consist of originals, photocopies, scanned documents, microfiche, and electronic forms.

The records' **retention period** is usually five years, as in the EU, the UK, and the US. Some may get confused with this requirement when compared with applicable data protection regulations (such as the EU GDPR, or the California Consumer Privacy Rights Act (CPRA)), which may impose different data retention regimes. The two sets of regulations are not incompatible, as retaining data for legal purposes is usually a valid reason.

Policy statement

Increasingly, with financial services regulations, it is not sufficient for businesses to comply; they also have to demonstrate how they comply. With AML/CTF regulations, businesses should produce a policy statement that includes their AML policies, procedures, and controls. This document provides a framework as evidence of how the business is prepared to face the threat of money laundering. The exact content of the statement depends on the nature of the business, but it should at least detail the approach and the responsibilities of named individuals, the KYC, CDD, and SAR processes, as well as the monitoring activities and controls in place to ensure the policies are followed. In addition, it should include a description of staff training activities.

Enforcement

Enforcement of AML regulations may include:

- **Public reprimand**: this can take the form of cease-and-desist orders, suspension of authorisation, or a ban from managerial functions.
- **Fines**: these are generally proportionate to the severity of the offence and size of the company. In the EU, the pecuniary sanction should be at least €5 million or 10% of the global annual turnover and at least €5 million for a natural person. For non-financial institutions, penalties can amount to twice the amount of benefit derived from the breach, or at least €1 million.

- **Prison sentences**, which may also be given for aiding, abetting, inciting, or attempting to commit the crime. In the UK, individual and legal entities can both be prosecuted.
- **Additional sanctions**: this may include exclusion from entitlement to public benefits, aid, access to public funding (including tendering, grants, and concessions); disqualification from carrying out commercial activities, judicial supervision, or winding-up orders; the closure of premises used for committing the offence; and the freezing or confiscating of the property concerned.

PREDICATE OFFENCES

Increasingly, AML regulations include **Predicate Offences**, which are crimes forming part of a larger crime. In a financial context, the predicate crime would be any crime that generates monetary proceeds, and the larger crime would be money laundering or the financing of terrorism. Predicate offences are well defined in the EU Directive (EU) 2018/1673 on combatting money laundering by criminal law,[34] and they are illustrated in Figure 5.4.

Figure 5.4 aims to illustrate how other crimes can lead to money laundering and terrorism financing, but this is not an exhaustive list, and it doesn't in any way constitute legal advice. I have categorised the various

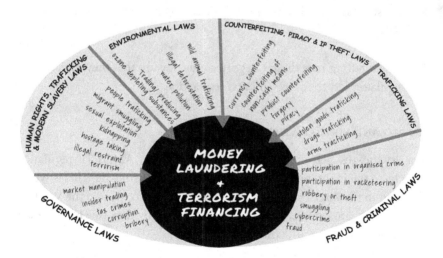

Figure 5.4 Money-laundering and terrorism-financing predicate offences.
Source: drawing by the author.

types of laws under which predicate offences may be prosecuted to give you an idea of this complex regulatory landscape and how regulatory enforcement can hit from multiple fronts.

Special cases

MONEY TRANSMITTERS

Money transmitters come in all sizes, and usually large businesses will be regulated by the main financial services regulator(s), but smaller businesses may not. This is the case in the UK, where if a money transmitter is not already regulated by the FCA, they should register with HRMC for AML purposes. Such businesses include:

- *Bureaux de change* or currency exchange offices;
- Those who transmit money, or any representation of money, including businesses with an exemption certificate from the FCA to be a small eMoney issuer (just collecting and delivering money as a cash courier is not transmitting money);
- Those who cash cheques that are payable to their customers;
- Those who take payments on telecommunications, digital, and IT devices, and act as an intermediary between a payer and supplier; and
- Those who provide a payment service for utility and other household bills.

Businesses falling into these categories must ensure that they register with the regulator, lest they face enforcement action.

CRYPTO AND VIRTUAL ASSET PROVIDERS

Due to the absence of specific crypto regulation, AML/CTF regulations have been the main instrument to control crypto businesses. This is well illustrated in the 2021 Baker McKenzie report, "Crypto Around the World".[35]

In the UK, in-scope crypto and virtual asset providers (see *Licences to operate a payment business*), must conduct CDD when:

- They establish a business relationship;
- They suspect money laundering;

- They doubt the veracity of any documents or information previously obtained;
- They carry out an occasional transaction that amounts to a transfer of funds (in the definition of the Wire Transfer Regulation (EU) 2015/847) exceeding €1,000; or
- They carry out other occasional transactions amounting to €15,000 or more.

The UK FCA has been very active in enforcing the rules, and total fines to crypto firms and their employees surged 92% to $193 million in 2022.[36] In addition, since 8 October 2023, all firms **marketing crypto assets to UK consumers**, including firms based overseas, **must comply with the FCA's rules on financial promotions**.[37] Breach of the rules is a criminal offence punishable by up to two years imprisonment, an unlimited fine, or both.

Financial Action Task Force

The Financial Action Task Force (**FATF**) is an independent intergovernmental body that develops and promotes policies to protect the global financial system against money laundering, terrorist financing, and the financing of the proliferation of weapons of mass destruction. The FATF is also known as **GAFI** (Groupe d'Action Financière), as it is headquartered in Paris.

The **FATF Recommendations** are recognised as the global Anti-Money Laundering and Counter-Terrorist Financing standard. At the time of writing, the FATF had 26 member countries, and Russia's membership was suspended on 24 February 2023,[38] but the FATF fell short of blacklisting Russia.[39]

Examples of FATF guidance include "Digital Identity,"[40] "Virtual Assets and Virtual Asset Providers" (2021),[41] the more recent (June 2023) "Targeted Update on Implementation of the FATF Standards on Virtual Assets and Virtual Asset Service Providers",[42] and "Countering Ransomware Financing".[43]

Black and grey lists

The FATF identifies countries with weak AML/CFT controls and lists them in two public documents that are published three times a year.

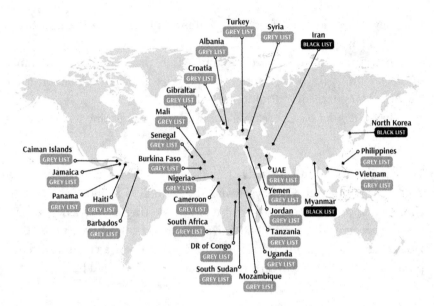

Figure 5.5 FATF black and grey lists.

Source: drawing by the author. Source data: FATF website, July 2023.

The **black list** contains countries that have serious deficiencies when it comes to countering money laundering and terrorism financing. For these countries, the FATF urges all members to apply EDD and countermeasures to protect the international financial ecosystem (e.g. sanctions). At the time of writing, there are three countries on this list: the Democratic People's Republic of Korea, Iran, and Myanmar.

The grey list contains countries subject to increased monitoring which are actively working with the FATF to address their AML/CTF deficiencies and are committed to resolving these within agreed time frames. At the time of writing, 27 countries are on the grey list. The FATF doesn't call for the application of EDD for these countries, and therefore doesn't envisage de-risking or cutting off entire swathes of customers, but members should deploy risk-based approaches when dealing with them.

Figure 5.5 gives a global map of the FATF black and grey lists.

Travel Rule

The **Travel Rule**[44] (aka FATF Recommendation 16), published in June 2022, is an important recommendation from the FATF, and applies to virtual asset transfers and crypto companies, which are referred to as **VASPs (Virtual Asset Service Providers)**. As the market develops, illicit financing risks associated with DeFi, NFTs, and decentralised wallets are growing (covered in *Beyond Payments*). The Travel Rule requires VASPs and other financial services institutions to share accurate payer and payee information (e.g. KYC). In their June 2023 progress update, the FATF highlights that countries continue to struggle, with 75% of jurisdictions partially or not at all compliant, and that the lack of regulation creates significant criminal opportunities (only 35 countries out of 135 have passed regulations for the travel rule).

The FATF, however, acknowledges that there is collaboration in the private sector, and a good example is the Travel Rule Universal Solution Technology (TRUST),[45] an initiative led by Coinbase and counting 57 members at the time of writing. TRUST is an industry-driven solution designed and built collaboratively by leading crypto exchanges to comply with the Travel Rule while protecting the security and privacy of their customers. Meanwhile, in Spain, Banco Santander, BBVA, and CaixaBank formed a joint venture in July 2023, FrauDfense, to tackle financial crime and share threat intelligence.[46]

EU, US, and UK Regulations

Now that you understand the fundamental principles of AML/CTF obligations, you can determine how various regulations deploy these principles, and some of these are listed here.

In **Europe**, the **5th Anti-Money Laundering Directive (EU) 2015/849**[47] (5AMLD) is the applicable regulation, whilst a 6th Anti Money Laundering Directive[48] is in the late stages of the legislative process at the time of writing.

In the **UK**, the **Money Laundering and Terrorist Financing (Amendment) Regulations 2019**[49] (MLRs)[50] and the **Proceeds of Crime Act 2002**[51] are in force, and the **Financial Services and Markets Act 2023 (FSMA)**,[52] which received royal ascent on 29 June 2023, is the main law for financial services. The FSMA also establishes a framework to enable the eventual revocation of retained EU law relating to financial services and markets (although this will take time).[53]

In the **US**, the **Bank Secrecy Act (BSA)**[54] is the federal AML/CTF regulation, whilst the **US Patriot Act**[55] aims to deter and punish terrorist acts in the US and around the world.

Parallels can easily be drawn for other geographies.

Unauthorised fraud

Unauthorised fraud, as defined in Chapter 3, is well understood globally and covered by most regulations worldwide. I don't propose to cover this topic extensively here, but the various applicable regulations are listed below in *Cybersecurity, data protection, and data privacy*. I will make one point, however: it has always been my firm belief that **cyber / information security and fraud prevention are two sides of the same coin**. This has become more and more evident in a world that is becoming increasingly digital. There is so much value to be derived by understanding this point, and security teams should work very closely with fraud teams, but this only seems to happen in mature businesses which understand risk management. Many have challenged my assertion over the years, but I am glad that a recent Forbes article agrees with me.[56]

Authorised fraud

In as much as Authorised Push Payment (APP) fraud and fraud prevention best practices were covered in Chapter 3, the mechanics should be understood. Authorised fraud is largely unregulated around the world, except for the UK and perhaps Australia, with the ASIC and ACCC cross-industry code for reimbursement, and the EU, with the forthcoming EU PSR/PSD3 with Articles 16.a and 50.1 (Confirmation of Payee), and Articles 54 and 57 (authorised payments and impersonation fraud), but the latter have some way to go yet. For an excellent round-up of the global regulations for authorised fraud, see the 2023 Biocatch report entitled "Authorized Payment Fraud – A Global Guide to Customer Reimbursement Models for Financial Scams".[57] The global regulatory landscape for authorised fraud is shown in Figure 5.6.

In this section, we'll concentrate on what the UK has done, since fraud regulations and codes have been in force for a while.

In Chapter 3, *Fraud prevention best practice*, we examined the elements that businesses should put in place to combat fraud, and the UK Payment Systems Regulator (PSR) began to keep a closer eye on APP scams in 2016 after the Super-Complaint from Which?[58] (a consumer trade association) on behalf of the UK population. The new regulation, which will take effect in 2024, aims to address authorised fraud, and covers the FPS payment scheme

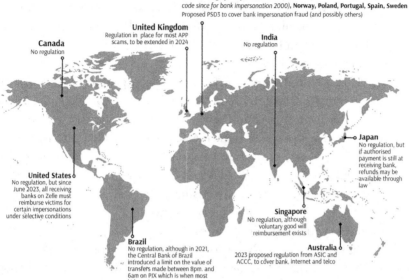

Figure 5.6 Global regulatory landscape for authorised fraud, including voluntary codes.

Source: Drawing by the author. Source Data: Biocatch, "Authorized Payment Fraud – A Global Guide to Customer Reimbursement Models for Financial Scams, 2023".

(see Chapter 3, *Bank payments schemes worldwide*), and its provisions will carry over into the New Payments Architecture (NPA). It implements a number of measures to combat authorised fraud from which other geographies may learn.

Industry cooperation

The UK regulation covers **all PSPs sending and receiving payments** that are either direct or indirect participants in the FPS scheme, and it also includes PISPs. It implements greater accountability across the board. Elements of the strategy are listed below:

- Directed firms already have to publish balanced scorecards.
- Big Tech is also rendered accountable through the proposed Online Safety Bill,[59] where financial crime, fraud, and illegal online advertising

are priority offences, and through the proposed Economic Crime and Corporate Transparency Bill,[60] which unlocks information sharing.

- Pay.UK, the operator of FPS, is developing the Enhanced Fraud Data (EFD) standard and building an API which PSPs are expected to implement by the end of 2023.
- The Home Office is also working with tech platforms on consistent data reporting. There are various fraud charters between the Home Office and firms in accountancy, telcos, and retail banking, and existing fraud charters will be implemented with tech platforms by the end of 2023, with new charters to be agreed with the insurance sector and other sectors in 2024. The FCA and Google already have a voluntary agreement to change their advertising policies on investment products to only allow FCA-approved organisations.
- In addition, the **Confirmation of Payee** service (see Chapter 3, *Bank payment mechanics*), already deployed by a number of UK PSPs, is now mandated for the rest of the ecosystem, with a deadline of 31 October 2023 for a first wave of about 30 banks, building societies, eMoney institutions, and investment firms and 31 October 2024 for a second wave of 400 more PSPs.

Customer care

Contingent reimbursement

Since 2020, a voluntary contingent reimbursement model (CRM Code)[61] has been in place in the UK, although it has been patchy in its deployment. This code has evolved to establish accountability on receiving ASPSPs (i.e. entities who hold the fraudster's accounts), and by December 2023 these firms must monitor received payments to help them **identify suspicious inbound payments and accounts** that might be being used by scammers.

The UK Payment Systems Regulator (PSR) issued their policy statement[62] entitled "Fighting authorised push payment fraud: a new reimbursement requirement" in June 2023, and it is about **customer aftercare**: consumers, micro-enterprises, and charities will be covered, with special provisions being made for vulnerable customers.

The new regulation **implements a mandatory reimbursement model** where the **liability is equally split between the sending and receiving**

PSPs, and it applies to the 1,500+ PSPs using the FPS rails. Whilst author-ised fraud reimbursement will become mandatory, there will be some exceptions:

- Payments across another payment system (e.g. bank account to crypto wallet/exchange);
- International payments;
- Civil disputes; and
- Unauthorised fraud (already covered by existing regulations), fraud committed by the account holder (i.e. first party fraud), or gross negli-gence from the account holder.

There are also discussions taking place between regulators with respect to "on us" payments (i.e. where the payer's account is held by the same ASPSP as the fraudster's account), which are therefore not taking place over a bank payment scheme but through the ASPSP's internal systems. In addition, the Bank of England, which operates the CHAPS scheme, is committed to achieving comparable levels of protection for this scheme.

The regulation doesn't come into effect until 2024, and consultations are still taking place at the time of writing (e.g. maximum reimbursement, definition of "gross negligence").

Communications and duty of care

As part of the UK Home Office Strategy, a National Fraud Squad will be established with 400 new officers,[63] and the City of London Police will be overhauling Action Fraud, the much-maligned fraud and cybercrime reporting service.[64]

End user education is also important in the new regulation, as PSPs are mandated to communicate clearly and explain the processes to victims of authorised fraud.

In addition, the FCA's **Consumer Duty Bill**[65] implements standards of caution to ensure fair outcomes for consumers. This bill has been in place since 31 July 2023 for new and existing products or for services that are open to sale or renewal, and it comes into force on 31 July 2024 for closed products or services.

UK regulators will continue to monitor the implementation of the various laws in this space, and this approach will evolve over time. Other jurisdictions may learn from this example.[66] In the US, total losses from online scams and identity theft reported to the US Federal Bureau of Investigation (FBI) increased to $10.3 billion in 2022 from $6.9 billion in 2021.[67]

Cybersecurity, Data Protection, and Data Privacy

With ever-increasing digitisation and hyperconnectivity, these regulations are becoming even more crucial, especially in financial services. Frameworks vary across jurisdictions, but I will mention a few of them here.

Europe

The **Directive on Security of Network and Information Systems (NIS)** was introduced in 2016 and updated by the **NIS2**[68] Directive, which came into force in 2023 with a deadline for compliance set to October 2024. NIS2 expands the reach of its cybersecurity rules to new sectors and entities, including search engines, cloud computing services, and marketplaces.

The **Cybersecurity Act**[69] came into force in April 2019 and has been applicable in full since June 2021 for all member states. It establishes the EU **Agency for Network and Information Security (ENISA)**[70] as the competent authority and a pan-European framework for certification of information and communication technology.

The EU **Cyber Resilience Act**[71] came into force in June 2019 and introduced a framework to protect consumers from unsafe and non-compliant products containing digital elements as well as market surveillance, and it aims to provide a level playing field for economic operators. This regulation will be amended to cater for changing market conditions, and this was proposed in September 2022.[72]

The EU **General Data Protection Regulation (GDPR)**[73] had a worldwide impact when it launched in May 2018. The GDPR applies to personal information processing carried out by organisations within the EU and to organisations outside the EU which offer goods and services to individuals in the EU. It gave individuals more rights than those offered in the previous directive and introduced more accountability for data controllers and processors. Its extra-territorial nature conferred it much media attention, and several jurisdictions have followed in the GDPR's footsteps.

The UK enacted most of these laws: for example, the GDPR was enacted as the **UK Data Protection Act 2018** (**DPA**, aka the UK GDPR).[74] But since Brexit, UK businesses have no longer been bound by the EU GDPR (unless they operate in or trade with the EU). However, the UK has secured adequacy with the EU until 2025 for both the GDPR and the EU Law Enforcement Directive (which protects citizens' fundamental right to data protection whenever personal data is used by criminal law enforcement authorities for law enforcement purposes), which means that data transfers are unrestricted between the UK and the EU until then. Important regulations with relation to cybercrime and fraud prevention are the **Computer Misuse Act 1990**[75] and the **Anti-Terrorism, Crime and Security Act 2001**.[76]

The US

There are numerous laws at the federal level, including:

- The FTC **Gramm–Leach–Bliley Act** (**GLBA**)[77] has been in force since 1999 and is the main federal cybersecurity regulation affecting financial services in the US;
- The **US Code Title 15**[78] (Sections 7001 to 7006) on "Electronic Records and Signatures in eCommerce" makes provisions for consumer data protection;
- The **Public Law 109–455**[79] on "Undertaking Spam, Spyware, and Fraud Enforcement with Enforcers beyond Borders Act of 2006", also known as the "**US SAFE WEB Act of 2006**";
- The **Computer Fraud and Abuse Act** of 1986; and
- The **Privacy Act**[80] of 1974 (2020 Edition).

In addition, following in the footsteps of the EU GDPR, a number of US states have implemented data privacy laws. This legislation includes the:

- California Privacy Rights Act (2020);
- Colorado Privacy Act (2023);
- Connecticut Personal Data Privacy and Online Monitoring Act;
- Maryland Online Consumer Protection Act;
- Massachusetts Data Privacy Law;
- New York Privacy Act; and
- Virginia Consumer Data Protection Act (2023).

In conclusion, the US has numerous federal and state laws offering varying degrees of consumer data protection; however, most laws share the requirement of obtaining customer consent before processing personal data as well as an obligation to keep that data safe. The applicability of the various laws for payment businesses will depend on the type of business and where they operate.

On 10 July 2023, the EU Commission adopted a new adequacy decision for safe and trusted data transfers between the EU and certified organisations in the US. This is referred to as the **EU–US Data Privacy Framework**,[81] and you may have heard of previous invalidated iterations such as Privacy Shield or Safe Harbour.

Rest of the world

UNCTAD (the United Nations Conference on Trade and Development), a permanent intergovernmental body established by the United Nations General Assembly in 1964, provides a good website with an interactive map[82] listing the status of data protection and privacy regulations around the world, and it is an excellent source of information. At the time of writing, UNCTAD shows that out of 194 countries 137 (71%) have data protection / privacy regulations in place, whilst a few others have draft regulations, including Ethiopia, Honduras, Iraq, Jordan, Malawi, Myanmar, Namibia, Pakistan, Saudi Arabia, Tanzania, and the United Arab Emirates.

Big Tech regulations worldwide

Globally, there is a noticeable trend to bring more accountability into the technology space, especially for systemically important platforms.

Over the past few years, the EU tightened control over Big Tech, with warnings and/or enforcement actions against Meta, Twitter (now X), Google, Apple, and Microsoft, and in late 2022 they approved the **Digital Services Act (DSA)**[83] for digital services including online marketplaces, social networks, content-sharing platforms, app stores, and online travel and accommodation platforms. They also introduced the **Digital Markets Act (DMA)**[84] to control systemically important platforms (i.e. "gatekeepers"). Both regulations come into force in early 2024.

The UK is behind its EU neighbours, but the government plans to give the **Competition and Markets Authority (CMA)**, through its **Digital Markets Unit (DMU)**, regulatory power over Big Tech, and to introduce a new

Digital Markets, Competition and Consumers Bill,[85] which is, at the time of writing, in the early stages of the legislative process. The FCA issued a feedback statement in July 2023 on potential competition impacts of Big Tech entry and expansion in retail financial services, and by the end of 2023 it will issue a call for input[86] on Big Tech firms as "gatekeepers". In the meantime, the CMA has been considering an April 2023 Google settlement offer over unfair practice towards app developers on the Play Store.[87]

In **India**, the regulators have also been active. In 2021, the Google Play store was forced to end auto-renewals, and Amazon had to stop Amazon Prime monthly subscription auto-renewals and free trials to meet the Reserve Bank of India's rules. At the time of writing, Amazon offers one-off yearly, three-monthly, and monthly memberships without auto-renewal.[88] In addition, at the time of writing, India is set to release the **Digital India Act**[89] to regulate Big Tech, replacing the **Information Technology Act, 2000**,[90] and introducing controls over data localisation, social media, online gaming, cyberbullying, e-commerce, Artificial Intelligence, and internet platforms.

In the **US**, Big Tech is unlikely to see any kind of regulation anytime soon, at least not in 2023.[91] In the meantime, after filing a complaint against Microsoft's Activision deal in 2022, the FTC put their challenge on hold for the foreseeable future in July 2023.[92]

China has always exerted tight control over Big Tech, as we observed with the corporate dismemberment of Ant Group in 2020[93] (the company behind Alipay). Since then, the regulatory crackdown has wiped $1.1 trillion off Chinese Big Tech,[94] but the Chinese government is showing signs of relaxation in 2023.[95]

In 2021, **Russia** tightened control over Big Tech by effectively banning international companies from operating without a Russian entity or domestic representation.[96]

The **Milken Institute**[97] provides a good tracker on global tech regulations, as well good insight reports.

Artificial Intelligence

Artificial Intelligence (**AI**), more specifically **Machine Learning**, has been used in financial services for a long time, and applications include fraud prevention, transaction monitoring, automated decision-making, forecast modelling, voice commerce, segmentation, and regulatory compliance. Currently, in financial services, machine learning is primarily used to predict outcomes, generate insights, and make decisions. The launch of Open AI's ChatGPT in November 2022 conferred upon AI renewed media interest. ChatGPT's underlying technology is generative AI, but what is it all about? Figure 5.7 gives provides important contextual information.

As shown in Figure 5.7, **Generative AI**, as used by ChatGPT, is a subset of **Deep Learning**, which in turn is a subset of machine learning. Each subset enhances the previous layer, which means that, as an example, risk-scoring services may use machine learning, but if they add deep learning, they can enhance the data models with different types of data, which can in turn be enhanced by generative AI.

We know that the financial services industry, and payments in particular, continuously generates a lot of data. Consolidating all this data into something useful and trustworthy, from numerous, disparate, and potentially incompatible sources, is beyond human capability. This makes machine learning particularly useful, as it is good at making sense of vast amounts of data.

This in turn generates its own set of risks, particularly when machine learning is applied to individuals. Before AI, decisioning processes were largely based on human intervention and predefined rules (supported by technology). Solutions using machine learning, and subsequent AI technologies, are independently able to make increasingly complex decisions.

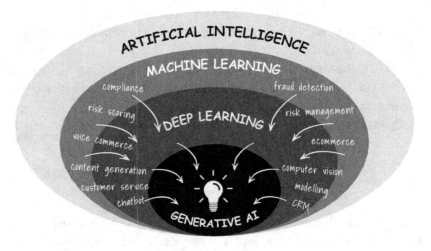

Figure 5.7 Artificial Intelligence, machine learning, deep learning, and generative AI in context.

Source: drawing by the author.

This ability in turn creates its own set of risks: bias, ethics, accuracy, transparency, explainability, security, intellectual property, privacy, data provenance, etc. These are explained very well in two *Harvard Business Review* articles: "When Machine Learning Goes Off the Rails"[98] (2021) and "Managing the Risks of Generative AI"[99] (2023).

Consequently, it is no wonder that regulators worldwide are getting worried, and again, Europe is at the forefront in proposing the first ever regulatory framework for Artificial Intelligence, the **AI Act**,[100] which was enacted on 14 June 2023 and is expected to reach final agreement at the end of 2023.

The **UK**'s approach is different from the EU's and is more "industry-friendly", as shown in their "**A pro-innovation approach to AI regulation**"[101] policy paper of June 2023. The UK GDPR is already principles-based and aligns with the AI governance approach, making the UK GDPR a powerful AI governance tool. Indeed, the UK Information Commissioner's Office has released significant AI guidelines.[102]

In **China**, the government continues to exert tight control, and from August 2023, in a world first, their AI regulation came into force,[103] specifically affecting generative AI.

In the **US**, AI regulation is in its early stages, although guidelines have been issued, such as the "**Blueprint for an AI Bill of Rights**".[104] Existing regulations may implement control elements around AI, such as those around privacy, security, and discrimination. Despite the lack of overarching law, it is expected that the FTC will be active in this space going forward, as seen with their enforcement action against Facebook (now Meta) in 2019.[105] A number of states have implemented regulations around bias and/or transparency, such as New York, Illinois, and Colorado. The January 2023 report from Holistic AI, "**The State of Global AI Regulations in 2023**",[106] gives a good roundup.

Crypto

As examined in the AML section, Virtual Asset Service Providers (VASPs) are primarily regulated through AML frameworks worldwide. Again here, the EU is at the forefront with a new legal framework to support market integrity and financial stability: the **Markets in Crypto Assets Regulation (MiCA)**,[107] which was adopted in June 2023 and is, at the time of writing, in the final stages of the legislative process. It creates pan-European rules for crypto assets not currently regulated by existing laws, and it institutes key provisions for those issuing and trading crypto assets. It covers the transparency, disclosure, authorisation, and supervision of transactions, and will also regulate public offers of crypto assets to ensure consumers are better informed about the risks. It is expected to come into force at the end of 2024.

In the **UK**, the government published their "**Factsheet: cryptoassets technical**"[108] policy paper in June 2023. In my opinion, it's not really a "policy", as it just states that crypto firms have AML and transparency (e.g. advertising, promotions) obligations under existing regulations. However, the new **Financial Services and Markets Act** (**FSMA**) will regulate the crypto space more comprehensively, although additional regulations are not expected to come into force until late 2023 and thereafter[109] (most likely through a variety of legal instruments).

In the **US**, the situation, as of July 2023, is still fluid, and most regulators are talking about it, as detailed in the Thomson Reuters June 2023 article "The (somewhat lively) state of crypto regulation".[110] However, the New York Attorney General proposed a new comprehensive bill in May 2023, the **Crypto Regulation, Protection, Transparency, and Oversight (CRPTO) Act**[111] in a bid to "eliminate conflicts of interest, increase transparency, and impose commonsense measures to protect investors".

The **PwC Global Crypto Regulation Report 2023**[112] gives a good global roundup.

Regulators

In Europe, the main legislators are the **European Parliament** and the **Council of the European Union**, and the main supra-national regulator is the **European Commission** alongside its directorates such as the Directorate General for Competition (DG Comp), which enforces EU competition rules in cooperation with national competition authorities (DG Comp is the equivalent of the US FTC and the Antitrust Division of the Department of Justice). When you hear that a proposed EU regulation is entering the "trilogue" stage, it means that informal discussions are taking place between these three entities as part of the legislative process. Each EU state also has their own national competent authorities.

In the UK, the **Financial Conduct Authority (FCA)**, the **Payment Systems Regulator (PSR)**, the **Competition and Markets Authority (CMA)**, and **His Majesty's Revenue and Customs (HMRC)** are the main regulators for payment services and AML obligations, whilst the **National Crime Agency (NCA)** is where businesses should send their SARs.

In the US, the **Federal Trade Commission (FTC)**, the **Financial Crimes Enforcement Network (FinCen)**, the **Securities and Exchange Commission (SEC)**, the **Commodity Futures Trading Commission (CFTC)**, the **Office of the Comptroller of the Currency (OCC)**, the **Federal Deposit Insurance Corporation (FDIC)**, the **Federal Financial Institutions Examination Council (FFIEC)**, the **Consumer Financial Protection Bureau (CFPB)**, the **Federal Communications Commission (FCC)**, and the **Financial Industry Regulatory Authority (FINRA)** are relevant authorities involved in protecting consumers and investors. In addition, the **US Secret Service** also has responsibilities for investigating financial crimes including counterfeit currency, forgery or theft of US treasury checks and bonds, and credit card fraud. Each US state also has their own competent authorities.

Regulatory sandboxes

In our fast-moving environment, regulators and policy makers want to promote safe innovation, and the concept of regulatory sandboxes, where innovators can test their solutions in regulator-supported "safe places", is gaining popularity.

> A **Regulatory Sandbox** is a safe environment enabling the testing of new, innovative technologies, services, or approaches which are not fully compliant with the existing legal and regulatory frameworks. This can take place using near-real-life (synthetic) data or real-life data.

In my opinion, regulatory sandboxes can be a win–win scenario for both innovators and regulators. They foster innovation by enabling new solutions to be tested in real-life (or near-real-life) conditions, and they enable regulators to acquire the necessary knowledge to create future-proof regulations or amend existing ones.

The **UK Financial Conduct Authority** (FCA) has a successful programme,[113] and so has Australia with the **Australian Securities and Investments Commission (ASIC)** programme.[114] The **European Commission** launched a regulatory sandbox for blockchain technology[115] in February 2023, and started a pilot for an AI regulatory sandbox[116] in June 2022, with results expected in the second half of 2023. In the **US**, regulatory sandboxes, at the time of writing, only exist at the state level.[117]

Lessons learnt

A modern business conundrum

The law is for the lawful. As technology advances, behaviours change and consumers adopt new technologies and share more data whilst demanding safety and expecting their trust not to be broken. Fraudsters, on the other hand, are given more opportunities to commit crime. Tech-savvy criminals study new developments and processes. They "follow the money", innovate, cooperate, and are not affected by long regulatory cycles like the rest of us. As a result, fraudsters are always a few steps ahead, and we constantly play catch up as customers want more services and businesses need more data to offer them.

Figure 5.8 A modern business conundrum.

Source: drawing by the author.

Organisations of all types are faced with a business conundrum: how can they ensure that customers are genuine through the implementation of mechanisms that may introduce friction whilst delivering exciting, seamless, and safe experiences for which they need to collect more data, which they have to protect? This is illustrated in Figure 5.8.

 Avoiding regulatory silos

All the regulations and industry standards (e.g. EMV, PCI DSS) covered in this chapter have three main things in common:

- **They all specify identity verification obligations**: whether we look at CDD, KYC, identity and access management, authentication, or pattern identification, these elements have the common objective of ensuring that the user is the genuine article.
- **They all specify fraud information-sharing requirements**: whether we look at threat intelligence, incident response, disclosure, or transaction monitoring, these elements have the common objective of stopping the attackers in their tracks.
- **They all specify data security requirements**: whether we look at data privacy, data protection, information security, or cybersecurity, these elements have the common objective of protecting users and businesses to ensure the integrity of the ecosystem. Payment businesses must have a security strategy, not just a payment one.

All too often, businesses will have separate regulatory compliance programmes to deal with each set of regulations (e.g. a team for PSD2 compliance, a different team for AML compliance, a team responsible for the PCI DSS). From an organisational and operational stance, this is perfectly acceptable. However, businesses may be in danger of creating uneconomical regulatory silos, where technology investments are made multiple times to address a common issue.

In addition, processes risk becoming inefficient and overly complicated. For example, incident response obligations are common to all regulations and standards covered in this book, and they all have different triggers, thresholds, and reporting mechanisms. In practice, resources from different teams will be responsible for those processes, but at a fundamental level the process is the same, albeit with different stakeholders and parameters. Resource savings could be achieved by creating a single, modular, and parameterisable incident response process, which would have the added benefit of being future-proofed against new regulatory requirements as they arise.

There are many other examples where avoiding regulatory silos could be beneficial. This was highlighted by American Banker in May 2023[118] ("The costs of compliance – when will investment in risk technology start paying off for banks?"), which noted that technology investments made by banks for financial crime compliance costs amount to more than 50% of all financial crime compliance costs. These investments are made to increase operational efficiency by reducing manual tasks through automation and should ultimately reduce operational costs. Yet, the report notes, FCC costs rose by 19% since 2020 and are expected to rise by 8% over the next three years, suggesting that banks are not seeing a return on their investment. American Banker comes to the same conclusion as mine: avoid overspending on technology that will ultimately be underused in each silo, take a holistic approach on compliance by improving communications and cooperation across multidisciplinary teams, and share technology. Mic drop.

Putting customers at the centre

I am not trying to teach anyone to suck eggs, but this is worthy of signposting. All the regulations I covered in this chapter include provisions to protect individuals, and some are even dedicated to that task (e.g. Consumer Duty Bill). The fact that organisations have been trying to become "customer-centric" for the past few decades is a sign that it's not an easy task, and some have been more successful than others. Digital transformation is key to customer-centricity, and those who haven't had to transform (e.g. Amazon, because they were born technology-led) have been more successful than those hampered by legacy environments. Data is key to digital transformation, and how we collect it, classify it, process it, modify it, aggregate it, protect it, discard it, and generally use it is the key to success.

Regtech

Automation is necessary, as evidenced by the booming regtech market. This relatively new industry has become fundamental to payment ecosystems, and a good source of information is the Deloitte Regtech Universe[119] report, which is updated regularly. At the time of writing, Deloitte list a total of 524 regtech companies covering regulatory reporting, risk management, identity management and control, compliance, and transaction monitoring. When I first looked at this report a few years back, it only had 88 regtech companies listed.

The term **Regtech** refers to any business that **uses technology** to improve, digitise, automate, or provide enablers to **help organisations manage their increasing regulatory compliance commitments**. It is most usefully applied to heavily regulated sectors such as financial services, healthcare, and gaming.

Combining ever-increasing digitisation, the complexity of financial services regulations and associated compliance costs, and growing financial crime and fraud makes a good case for regtech.

Payments regulations and licences – conclusion

This was perhaps the most difficult chapter to write. Everyone who knows me is aware that I am a fan of regulations and standards (I know, I'm a sad person). Not everyone is. My challenge was to write a chapter on regulations that people will want to read or at least find useful. I hope I have achieved this through drawing parallels and through giving real-life examples, references, and illustrations. Any suggestions for future editions are welcome.

When we look ahead at the regulatory landscape, we notice that the **regulations are becoming clearer** as regulators and policy makers acquire more and more digital knowledge. Definitions that were vague in previous regulations are getting tighter, simplifying enforcement. More guidelines are issued. That's good. If you want to regulate something, you have to define it clearly first. Vagueness leads to interpretation and loopholes, and only serves to keep lawyers and criminals in business. However, at the same time, **regulations are becoming more complex** because their scope in payments is extending as the ecosystems themselves become wider and their boundaries more blurred. As a result, automation has become necessary and **the regtech market will continue to expand**.

Businesses will continue to wait until the last minute to comply with regulations. Given the length of regulatory cycles, we know that organisations have plenty of time to, at least, think about their regulatory compliance plans. But everything is always just about ready on deadline day. As a personal anecdote, I was unwittingly at the receiving end of this phenomenon. In the UK, there is an organisation that awards a Crystal Mark for "Plain English" to various types of publications. I wanted to obtain the mark for this book and contacted them in mid-July 2023. They replied straight away to let me know that they wouldn't be able to help me for at least the next six months, as they were far too busy reviewing publications, policies, and other documents from financial services institutions needing to comply with the transparency and clarity requirement of the Consumer Duty Bill that came into force on 31 July 2023. That bill was proposed in May 2021. Writing in plain English is probably, in my opinion, the least onerous compliance requirement in the bill. And yet ...

If you think this book is gobbledegook and jibber-jabber (as American icon Mr. T would say),[120] then blame the banks.

Seriously, this is not a good thing, as regulations are there for a number of reasons, and they ultimately impact society. An example is where, in the UK, APP fraud was first identified in 2014. It took until 2019/2020 for regulations to arrive, and in 2023 we're finally seeing a fraud victim compensation model that might just work. It took nearly ten years to address a serious problem. I wish businesses would "do the right thing" much earlier, instead of waiting for regulations to be "done unto them". Of course, this is much easier to achieve in "self-regulating" ecosystems such as the card rails (within applicable regulations, of course). More cooperation between the public and private sectors should be sought, and increasingly this is happening.

Technology-led businesses will continue to grab pieces of the payments (and banking) pie and will become more regulated as a result (yes, the Regulations at the Edges Principle strikes again!). How will this happen in practice? Your guess is a good as mine. Big Tech has the resources to expand and defend its positions, and of course it can always partner with or acquire regulated entities. In August 2023, the Apple Card savings account hit $10 billion in deposits and 97% of users chose to have their daily cash automatically deposited into their account.[121] At the time of writing, this is a partnership between Apple and Goldman Sachs, which is currently making noises about exiting the partnership and passing it on to American Express (because they want to exit the B2C market). What Apple will do remains to be seen: they may partner with American Express, or they may take some of the Goldman Sachs functions in house (e.g. underwriting, fraud prevention, and customer service) and partner with a less-well-known lender for the regulatory part. In any instance, payments, and banking, are changing.

There is also a **global aspiration towards standardisation**, or at least interoperability. Even with centralised systems, this is difficult to achieve, but most jurisdictions are trying. It will be a completely different ball game when we start looking at decentralised systems seriously. We have covered upcoming regulations in the crypto space in this section, and they are a stake in the ground. BUT. If we accept that the decentralised world is boundary-less, how can you ensure boundary-less governance across jurisdictions? In our traditional world, we have examples of boundary-less enforcement with intergovernmental bodies such as Interpol. The Metaverse will increasingly see payments crossing between virtual and real worlds, and notwithstanding the Regulations at the Edges Principle (Box 3.6), perhaps the Metaverse will also need its own Interpol,[122] a kind of Decentralised Autonomous Organisation (DAO) of like-minded law enforcers. You'll have to read *Beyond Payments* for my musings on the topic.

And we're now nearly at the end of our journey!

Notes

1   "Mind the gap: we need better oversight of crypto activities", European Central Bank, 5 April 2023. Available at: https://www.bankingsupervision. europa.eu/press/blog/2023/html/ssm.blog230405~03fd3d664f. en.html (Accessed 20 July 2023).

2   "One-fifth of UK businesses hit by fraud, Home Office survey shows", The Financial Times, 11 May 2023. Available at: https://www.ft.com/content/c249a73e-5c84-4135-81ff-8c3563ff71ee (Accessed 20 July 2023).

3   "Risks for merchants in cross-border BNPL transactions", The Paypers, 14 April 2022. Available at: https://thepaypers.com/expert-opinion/risks-for-merchants-in-cross-border-bnpl-transactions--1255751 (Accessed 20 July 2023).

4   "The Global Risks Report 2023, 18th Edition", World Economic Forum, January 2023. Available at: https://www3.weforum.org/docs/WEF_Global_Risks_Report_2023.pdf (Accessed 20 July 2023).

5   "Directive (EU) 2015/2366 of The European Parliament and of The Council", Official Journal of the European Union, 25 November 2015. Available at: https://eur-lex.europa.eu/legal-content/EN/TXT/PDF/?uri=CELEX:32015L2366 (Accessed 20 July 2023).

6   "The Payment Services Regulations 2017", legislation.gov.uk website. Available at: https://www.legislation.gov.uk/uksi/2017/752/contents/made (Accessed 20 July 2023).

7   "Commission Delegated Regulation (EU) 2018/389 of 27 November 2017 supplementing Directive (EU) 2015/2366 of the European Parliament and of the Council with regard to regulatory technical standards for strong customer authentication and common and secure open standards of communication (Text with EEA relevance)", EUR-Lex, 27 November 2017. Available at: https://eur-lex.europa.eu/legal-content/EN/TXT/?uri=CELEX%3A32018R0389 (Accessed 20 July 2023).

8   "EBA/RTS/2022/03", European Banking Authority, 5 April 2022. Available at: https://www.eba.europa.eu/sites/default/documents/files/document_library/Publications/Draft%20Technical%20Standards/2022/EBA-RTS-2022-03%20RTS%20on%20SCA%26CSC/1029858/Final%20Report%20on%20the%20amendment%20of%20the%20RTS%20on%20SCA%26CSC.pdf (Accessed 20 July 2023).

9   "Elavon's transaction risk analysis", Elavon website, 7 September 2022. Available at: https://www.elavon.co.uk/insights/news/elavons-transaction-risk-analysis.html (Accessed 20 July 2023).

10 "Identity Check™", Mastercard website. Available at: https://www.mastercard.co.uk/en-gb/business/overview/safety-and-security/identity-check.html (Accessed 20 July 2023).

11 "Question 2018_4233", EBA Single Rule Book, 6 September 2019. Available at: https://www.eba.europa.eu/single-rule-book-qa/-/qna/view/publicId/2018_4233 (Accessed 21 July 2023).

12 "Consumer Financial Protection Circular 2022–04", CFPB, April 2022. Available at: https://www.consumerfinance.gov/compliance/circulars/circular-2022–04-insufficient-data-protection-or-security-for-sensitive-consumer-information/ (Accessed 21 July 2023).

13 "Secure Payment Confirmation", W3C, 21 June 2023. Available at: https://www.w3.org/TR/secure-payment-confirmation/ (Accessed 21 July 2023).

14 "Modernising payment services and opening financial services data: new opportunities for consumers and businesses", European Com-

mission, 28 June 2023. Available at: https://ec.europa.eu/commission/presscorner/detail/en/ip_23_3543 (Accessed 21 July 2023).

15 "Financial data access and payments package", European Commission, 28 June 2023. Available at: https://finance.ec.europa.eu/publications/financial-data-access-and-payments-package_en (Accessed 21 July 2023).

16 "Directive 2009/110/EC of The European Parliament and of The Council" EUR-Lex", 16 September 2009. Available at: https://eur-lex.europa.eu/legal-content/en/TXT/?uri=CELEX%3A32009L0110 (Accessed 21 July 2023).

17 "What is the Prudential Regulation Authority (PRA)?" Bank of England website. Available at: https://www.bankofengland.co.uk/explainers/what-is-the-prudential-regulation-authority-pra (Accessed 10 October 2023).

18 "German regulator's top official dismissed over Wirecard wrongdoing", Pymnts, 29 January 2021. Available at: https://www.pymnts.com/news/international/2021/german-regulators-top-official-dismissed-over-wirecard-wrongdoing/ (Accessed 7 July 2023).

19 "UK's FCA To FinTechs: You're Not Banks", Pymnts, 19 May 2021. Available at: https://www.pymnts.com/news/regulation/2021/uks-fca-to-fintechs-youre-not-banks/ (Accessed 8 July 2023).

20 "California regulator orders Chime to stop calling itself a bank", BankingDive, 6 May 2021. Available at: https://www.bankingdive.com/news/california-regulator-orders-chime-to-stop-calling-itself-a-bank/599710/ (Accessed 8 July 2023).

21 "N26 appoints chief risk officer to fix ongoing AML and compliance concerns", Finextra, 26 July 2023. Available at: https://www.finextra.com/newsarticle/42698/n26-appoints-chief-risk-officer-to-fix-ongoing-aml-and-compliance-concerns (Accessed 26 July 2023).

22 "Fintech and payments: regulating digital payment services and e-money", Financial Stability Institute, Bank for International Settlements, July 2021. Available at: https://www.bis.org/fsi/publ/insights33.pdf (Accessed 8 July 2023).

23 "Most EMIs fail to use their safeguarding account properly, here's why", PSP Labs, 13 October 2021. Available at: https://psplab.com/most-emis-fail-to-use-safeguarding-account-properly/ (Accessed 9 July 2023).

24 "UK removes AISPs from AML regulation", Finextra, 16 June 2022. Available at: https://www.finextra.com/newsarticle/40464/uk-removes-aisps-from-aml-regulation (Accessed 8 July 2023).

25 "About Us", Open Banking Implementation Entity website. Available at: https://www.openbanking.org.uk/about-us/ (Accessed 22 June 2023).

26 "Code of Practice", PSA website. Available at: https://psauthority.org.uk/For-Business/Code-15 (Accessed 22 July 2023).

27 "Registered cryptoasset firms", FCA Register. Available at: https://register.fca.org.uk/s/search?predefined=CA (Accessed 23 July 2023).

28 "Unregistered Cryptoasset Businesses", FCA Register. Available at: https://register.fca.org.uk/s/search?predefined=U (Accessed 23 July 2023).

29 "UK banks make free speech commitment after NatWest-Farage row", Reuters, 26 July 2023. Available at: https://www.reuters.com/world/uk/uk-banks-make-free-speech-commitment-after-natwest-farage-row-2023-07-26/ (Accessed 27 July 2023).

30 "High risk third countries and the international context content of anti-money laundering and countering the financing of terrorism", European Commission, 17 May 2023. Available at: https://finance.ec.europa.eu/financial-crime/high-risk-third-countries-and-international-context-content-anti-money-laundering-and-countering_en (Accessed 22 July 2023).

31 "Financial Action Task Force identifies jurisdictions with Anti-Money Laundering and combating the financing of terrorism and counter-proliferation deficiencies", FINCEN, 31 October 2022. Available at: https://www.fincen.gov/news/news-releases/financial-action-task-force-identifies-jurisdictions-anti-money-laundering-and-3 (Accessed 22 July 2023).

32 "Merrill Fined $12 Million over failure to file Suspicious Activity Reports", NAPA, 11 July 2023. Available at: https://www.napa-net.org/news-info/daily-news/merrill-fined-12-million-over-failure-file-suspicious-activity-reports (Accessed 22 July 2023).

33 "Final Notice to Santander UK Plc, Reference Number 106054", FCA, 8 December 2022. Available at: https://www.fca.org.uk/publication/final-notices/santander-uk-plc-2022.pdf (Accessed 22 July 2023).

34 "Directive (EU) 2018/1673 on combating money laundering by criminal law", EUR-Lex, 3 February 2022. Available at: https://eur-lex.europa.eu/EN/legal-content/summary/combating-money-laundering-by-criminal-law.html (Accessed 23 July 2023).

35 "Crypto around the world", Baker McKenzie, 2021. Available at: https://www.bakermckenzie.com/en/-/media/files/insight/guides/2021/baker_mckenzie_crypto_around_the-world.pdf (Accessed 23 July 2023).

36 "Financial crime: Anti-Money Laundering and crypto fines surge to £4bn in regulatory crackdown", City AM, 22 January 2023. https://www.cityam.com/financial-crime-anti-money-laundering-and-crypto-fines-surge-to-4bn-in-regulatory-crackdown/ (Accessed 23 July 2023).

37 "Cryptoasset firms marketing to UK consumers must get ready for the financial promotions regime by 8 October 2023", FCA, 4 July 2023. https://www.fca.org.uk/publication/correspondence/letter-to-cryptoasset-firms-financial-promotions-regime.pdf (Accessed 23 July 2023).

38 "FATF Statement on the Russian Federation", FATF website, 24 February 2023. Available at: https://www.fatf-gafi.org/en/publications/Fatfgeneral/fatf-statement-russian-federation.html (Accessed 22 July 2023).

39 "No reason for financial crime watchdog to blacklist Russia, says central bank", Reuters, 21 June 2023. Available at: https://www.reuters.com/world/europe/nabiullina-says-adding-moscow-fatf-blacklist-would-be-politically-motivated-2023–06–21/ (Accessed 22 July 2023).

40 "Guidance on Digital ID", FATF website, 6 March 2020. Available at: https://www.fatf-gafi.org/en/publications/Financialinclusionandnpoissues/Digital-identity-guidance.html (Accessed 22 July 2023).

41 "Updated Guidance for a Risk-Based Approach to Virtual Assets and Virtual Asset Service Providers", FATF website, 28 October 2021. Available at: https://www.fatf-gafi.org/en/publications/Fatfrecommendations/Guidance-rba-virtual-assets-2021.html (Accessed 22 July 2023).

42 "Targeted Update on Implementation of the FATF Standards on Virtual Assets and Virtual Asset Service Providers", FATF website, 20 June 2023. Available at: https://www.fatf-gafi.org/en/publications/Fatfrecommendations/targeted-update-virtual-assets-vasps-2023.html (Accessed 22 July 2023).

43 "Countering Ransomware Financing", FATF website, 14 March 2023. Available at: https://www.fatf-gafi.org/en/publications/Methodsandtrends/countering-ransomware-financing.html (Accessed 22 July 2023).

44 "Updated Guidance for a Risk-Based Approach to Virtual Assets and Virtual Asset Service Providers" FATF, October 2021. Available at: https://www.fatf-gafi.org/en/publications/Fatfrecommendations/Guidance-rba-virtual-assets-2021.html (Accessed 23 July 2023).

45 "The standard for Travel Rule compliance – Travel Rule Universal Solution Technology (TRUST)", Coinbase website. Available at: https://www.coinbase.com/travelrule (Accessed 23 July 2023).

46 "Banco Santander, BBVA and CaixaBank join forces to fight fraud", Santander website, 24 July 2023. Available at: https://www.santander.com/en/press-room/press-releases/2023/07/banco-santander-bbva-and-caixabank-join-forces-to-fight-fraud (Accessed 25 July 2023).

47 "Directive (EU) 2015/849 of The European Parliament and of The Council on the prevention of the use of the financial system for the purposes of money laundering or terrorist financing, amending Regulation

(EU) No 648/2012 of the European Parliament and of the Council, and repealing Directive 2005/60/EC of the European Parliament and of the Council and Commission Directive 2006/70/EC", EUR-Lex, 20 May 2015. Available at: https://eur-lex.europa.eu/legal-content/EN/TXT/?uri=celex%3A32015L0849 (Accessed 24 July 2023).

48   "Proposal for a Directive of The European Parliament and of The Council on the mechanisms to be put in place by the Member States for the prevention of the use of the financial system for the purposes of money laundering or terrorist financing and repealing Directive (EU) 2015/849", European Commission, 20 July 2021. Available at: https://eur-lex.europa.eu/legal-content/EN/TXT/?uri=celex%3A52021PC0423 (Accessed 24 July 2023).

49   "Money laundering and terrorist financing (amendment) regulations 2019", HM Revenue & Customs, 10 January 2020. Available at: https://www.gov.uk/government/publications/money-laundering-and-terrorist-financing-amendment-regulations-2019/money-laundering-and-terrorist-financing-amendment-regulations-2019 (Accessed 24 July 2023).

50   "Money Laundering Regulations", Financial Conduct Authority, 21 February 2022. Available at: https://www.fca.org.uk/firms/financial-crime/money-laundering-regulations#revisions (Accessed 24 July 2023).

51   "Proceeds of Crime Act 2002", legislation.gov.uk website. Available at: https://www.legislation.gov.uk/ukpga/2002/29/contents (Accessed 21 August 2023).

52   "Financial Services and Markets Act 2023", legislation.go.uk, 29 June 2023. Available at: https://www.legislation.gov.uk/ukpga/2023/29/enacted (Accessed 24 July 2023).

53   "Financial Services and Markets Act 2023: Building a Smarter Regulatory Framework in the UK?", Travers Smith, 14 July 2023. Available at: https://www.traverssmith.com/knowledge/knowledge-container/financial-services-and-markets-act-2023-building-a-smarter-regulatory-framework-in-the-uk/ (Accessed 24 July 2023).

54   "Bank Secrecy Act (BSA)", Office of the Comptroller of the Currency website. Available at: https://www.occ.treas.gov/topics/supervision-and-examination/bsa/index-bsa.html (Accessed 24 July 2023).

55   "USA Patriot Act", FINCEN website. Available at: https://www.fincen.gov/resources/statutes-regulations/usa-patriot-act (Accessed 7 August 2023).

56   "Better together: Cybersecurity and fraud prevention", Forbes, 2 March 2023. Available at: https://www.forbes.com/sites/forbestechcouncil/2023/03/02/better-together-cybersecurity-and-fraud-prevention/ (Accessed 21 August 2023).

57 "Authorized Payment Fraud – A Global Guide to Customer Reimbursement Models for Financial Scams" Biocatch, August 2023. Availableat:https://www.biocatch.com/resources/white-paper/customer-reimbursement-models-for-financial-scams (Accessed 6 August 2023).

58 "Which? makes scams super-complaint", Which? Website, 23 September 2016. Available at: https://www.which.co.uk/news/article/which-makes-scams-super-complaint-453196-aoJnj6T9a66H (Accessed 24 July 2023).

59 "Online Safety Bill", UK Parliament website. Available at: https://bills.parliament.uk/bills/3137 (Accessed 24 July 2023).

60 "Economic Crime and Corporate Transparency Bill", UK Parliament website. Available at: https://bills.parliament.uk/bills/3339 (Accessed 24 July 2023).

61 "The Contingent Reimbursement Model Code (CRM Code)", Lending Standards Board website. Available at: https://www.lendingstandardsboard.org.uk/crm-code/ (Accessed 24 July 2023).

62 "Fighting authorised push payment fraud: a new reimbursement requirement", Payment Systems Regulator, June 2023. Available at: https://www.psr.org.uk/media/iolpbwou/ps23-3-app-fraud-reimbursement-policy-statement-final-june-2023.pdf (Accessed 24 July 2023).

63 "Government announces £400m anti-fraud push, including 400 additional investigators", London Post, 3 May 2023. Available at: https://london-post.co.uk/government-announces-400m-anti-fraud-push-including-400-additional-investigators/ (Accessed 25 July 2023).

64 "New suppliers appointed for Action Fraud service replacement", City of London Police, 13 June 2023. Available at: https://www.cityoflondon.police.uk/news/city-of-london/news/2023/june/new-suppliers-appointed-for-action-fraud-service-replacement/ (Accessed 25 July 2023).

65 "Consumer Duty", FCA website. Available at: https://www.fca.org.uk/firms/consumer-duty (Accessed 24 July 2023).

66 "Will the US embrace the UK Contingent Reimbursement Model to fight online scam losses?", Reuters, 10 April 2023. Available at: https://www.thomsonreuters.com/en-us/posts/investigation-fraud-and-risk/us-embrace-contingent-reimbursement/ (Accessed 24 July 2023).

67 "Internet Crime Report 2022", Federal Bureau of Investigation, Internet Crime Complaint Center, 2023. Available at: https://www.ic3.gov/Media/PDF/AnnualReport/2022_IC3Report.pdf (Accessed 24 July 2023).

68 "Directive (EU) 2022/2555 of The European Parliament and of The Council on measures for a high common level of cybersecurity across

the Union, amending Regulation (EU) No 910/2014 and Directive (EU) 2018/1972, and repealing Directive (EU) 2016/1148 (NIS 2 Directive)", EUR-Lex, 14 December 2022. Available at: https://eur-lex.europa.eu/eli/dir/2022/2555 (Accessed 24 July 2023).

69 "Regulation (EU) 2019/881 of The European Parliament and of The Council on ENISA (the European Union Agency for Cybersecurity) and on information and communications technology cybersecurity certification and repealing Regulation (EU) No 526/2013 (Cybersecurity Act)", EUR-Lex, 17 April 2019. Available at: https://eur-lex.europa.eu/eli/reg/2019/881/oj (Accessed 24 July 2023).

70 ENISA website. Available at: https://www.enisa.europa.eu/ (Accessed 24 July 2023).

71 "Regulation (EU) 2019/1020 of The European Parliament and of The Council on market surveillance and compliance of products and amending Directive 2004/42/EC and Regulations (EC) No 765/2008 and (EU) No 305/2011", EUR-Lex, 20 June 2019. Available at: https://eur-lex.europa.eu/eli/reg/2019/1020 (Accessed 24 July 2023).

72 "Proposal for a Regulation of The European Parliament and of The Council on horizontal cybersecurity requirements for products with digital elements and amending Regulation (EU) 2019/1020", European Commission, 15 September 2022. Available at: https://eur-lex.europa.eu/legal-content/EN/TXT/?uri=celex:52022PC0454 (Accessed 24 July 2023).

73 "Regulation (EU) 2016/679 of The European Parliament and of The Council on the protection of natural persons with regard to the processing of personal data and on the free movement of such data, and repealing Directive 95/46/EC (General Data Protection Regulation)", EUR-Lex, 27 April 2016. Available at: https://eur-lex.europa.eu/eli/reg/2016/679/oj (Accessed 24 July 2023).

74 "The Data Protection Act" legislation.gov.uk website. Available at: https://www.legislation.gov.uk/ukpga/2018/12/contents/enacted (Accessed 24 July 2023).

75 "Computer Misuse Act 1990", legislation.gov.uk website. Available at: https://www.legislation.gov.uk/ukpga/1990/18/contents (Accessed 21 August 2023).

76 "Anti-terrorism, Crime and Security Act 2001", legislation.gov.uk website. Available at: https://www.legislation.gov.uk/ukpga/2001/24/contents (Accessed 21 August 2023).

77 "Gramm-Leach-Bliley Act", Federal Trade Commission website. Available at: https://www.ftc.gov/business-guidance/privacy-security/gramm-leach-bliley-act (Accessed 24 July 2023).

78 "15 U.S.C. I - Electronic Records And Signatures In Commerce", GovInfo website. Available at: https://www.govinfo.gov/app/details/USCODE-2021-title15/USCODE-2021-title15-chap96-subchapI/summary (Accessed 24 July 2023).

79 "Public Law 109 - 455 – Undertaking Spam, Spyware, And Fraud Enforcement with Enforcers beyond Borders Act of 2006", or the "U.S. SAFE WEB Act of 2006", GovInfo website. Available at: https://www.govinfo.gov/app/details/PLAW-109publ455/summary (Accessed 24 July 2023).

80 "Overview of The Privacy Act of 1974 (2020 Edition)", Office of Privacy and Civil Liberties website. Available at: https://www.justice.gov/opcl/overview-privacy-act-1974–2020-edition (Accessed 24 July 2023).

81 "Commission Implementing Decision pursuant to Regulation (EU) 2016/679 of the European Parliament and of the Council on the adequate level of protection of personal data under the EU-US Data Privacy Framework", European Commission, 10 July 2023. Available at: https://commission.europa.eu/system/files/2023–07/Adequacy%20decision%20EU-US%20Data%20Privacy%20Framework_en.pdf (Accessed 24 July 2023).

82 "Data Protection and Privacy Legislation Worldwide", UNCTAD website. Available at: https://unctad.org/page/data-protection-and-privacy-legislation-worldwide (Accessed 24 July 2023).

83 "Regulation (EU) 2022/2065 of The European Parliament and of The Council on a Single Market for Digital Services and amending Directive 2000/31/EC (Digital Services Act)", Official Journal of the European Union, 19 October 2022. Available at: https://eur-lex.europa.eu/legal-content/EN/TXT/?uri=celex%3A32022R2065 (Accessed 26 July 2023).

84 "Regulation (EU) 2022/1925 of The European Parliament and of The Council on contestable and fair markets in the digital sector and amending Directives (EU) 2019/1937 and (EU) 2020/1828 (Digital Markets Act)", EUR-Lex, 14 September 2022. Available at: https://eur-lex.europa.eu/legal-content/EN/TXT/?toc=OJ%3AL%3A2022%3A265%3ATOC&uri=uriserv%3AOJ.L_.2022.265.01.0001.01.ENG (Accessed 26 July 2023).

85 "Digital Markets, Competition and Consumers Bill", UK Parliament website, 21 July 2023. Available at: https://bills.parliament.uk/bills/3453 (Accessed 26 July 2023).

86 "FS23/4: Potential competition impacts of Big Tech entry and expansion in retail financial services", Financial Conduct Authority website, 12 July 2023. Available at: https://www.fca.org.uk/publications/feedback-statements/fs23–4-potential-competition-impacts-big-tech-entry-and-expansion-retail-financial-services (Accessed 26 July 2023).

87 "App developers on Google Play store offered payment choices following CMA probe", Gov.UK website, 19 April 2023. Available at: https://www.gov.uk/government/news/app-developers-on-google-play-store-offered-payment-choices-following-cma-probe (Accessed 26 July 2023).

88 "Amazon Prime Terms and Conditions", Amazon Website, update 12 January 2023. Available at: https://www.amazon.in/gp/help/customer/display.html/ref=pc_tc?nodeId=202042460&tag=kp-web-inline-21 (Accessed 26 July 2023).

89 "India to introduce new Digital India Act to regulate Big Tech", The Hindu Business Line, 1 May 2023. Available at: https://www.thehindubusinessline.com/info-tech/india-to-introduce-new-digital-india-act-to-regulate-big-tech/article66799883.ece (Accessed 26 July 2023).

90 "The Information Technology Act, 2000", Ministry of Law, Justice and Company Affairs, 9 June 2000. Available at: kbadqkdlcswfjdelrquehwuxcfmijmuixngudufgbuubgubfugbububjxcgfvsbdihbgfGhdfgFHytyh RtMjk4NzY= (eprocure.gov.in) (Accessed 26 July 2023).

91 "Big Tech unlikely to face major US legislation in 2023, but EU threats loom", S&P Global, Market Intelligence, 12 January 2023. Available at: https://www.spglobal.com/marketintelligence/en/news-insights/latest-news-headlines/big-tech-unlikely-to-face-major-us-legislation-in-2023-but-eu-threats-loom-73689665 (Accessed 26 July 2023).

92 "FTC Puts Challenge to Microsoft, Activision Deal on Hold", techdirt, 24 July 2023. https://www.techdirt.com/2023/07/24/ftc-puts-challenge-to-microsoft-activision-deal-on-hold/ (Accessed 26 July 2023).

93 "Ant's miserable Christmas and unhappy new year", Euromoney, 4 January 2021. Available at: https://www.euromoney.com/article/27yz6pbfifkgvp1oivf28/capital-markets/ants-miserable-christmas-and-unhappy-new-year (Accessed 26 July 2023).

94 "Beijing's regulatory crackdown wipes $1.1 trillion off Chinese Big Tech", Reuters, 12 July 2023. Available at: https://www.reuters.com/technology/beijings-regulatory-crackdown-wipes-11-trln-off-chinese-big-tech-2023-07-12/ (Accessed 26 July 2023).

95 "Is China's 'tech crackdown' over? Our 2023 regulatory outlook for the sector", China Briefing, 22 February 2023. Available at: https://www.china-briefing.com/news/is-chinas-tech-crackdown-over-our-2023-regulatory-outlook-for-the-sector/ (Accessed 26 July 2023).

96 "Russia: new rules tighten the central bank's control over payments", Finance Magnates, 4 May 2021. Available at: https://www.financemagnates.com/fintech/payments/russia-new-rules-tighten-the-central-banks-control-over-payments/ (Accessed 26 July 2023).

97 "Tech Regulation Tracker and Digest", Milken Institute website. Available at: https://milkeninstitute.org/research-department/regional-economics/tech-regulation-tracker-digest (Accessed 26 July 2023).

98 "When machine learning goes off the rails", Harvard Business Review, January–February 2021. Available at: https://hbr.org/2021/01/when-machine-learning-goes-off-the-rails (Accessed 27 July 2023).

99 "Managing the risks of generative AI", Harvard Business Review, 6 June 2023. Available at: https://hbr.org/2023/06/managing-the-risks-of-generative-ai (Accessed 27 July 2023).

100 "EU AI Act: first regulation on Artificial Intelligence", European Parliament, 14 June 2023. Available at: https://www.europarl.europa.eu/news/en/headlines/society/20230601STO93804/eu-ai-act-first-regulation-on-artificial-intelligence (Accessed 27 July 2023).

101 "A pro-innovation approach to AI regulation", Gov.UK website, 22 June 2023. Available at: https://www.gov.uk/government/publications/ai-regulation-a-pro-innovation-approach/white-paper (Accessed 27 July 2023).

102 "Our work on Artificial Intelligence", ICO website. Available at: https://ico.org.uk/about-the-ico/what-we-do/our-work-on-artificial-intelligence/ (Accessed 27 July 2023).

103 "How China is staying ahead of the AI race amidst a global ChatGPT rush", Techwire Asia, 31 July 2023. Available at: https://techwireasia.com/2023/07/generative-ai-is-progressing-well-in-china/ (Accessed 2 August 2023).

104 "Blueprint for an AI Bill of Rights", White House website. Available at: https://www.whitehouse.gov/ostp/ai-bill-of-rights/ (Accessed 27 July 2023).

105 "UNITED STATES OF AMERICA, Plaintiff v. FACEBOOK, Inc., a corporation, Defendant. Case No. 19-cv-2184 Complaint for Civil Penalties, Injunction, and Other Relief", Available at: https://www.ftc.gov/system/files/documents/cases/182_3109_facebook_complaint_filed_7-24-19.pdf (Accessed 27 July 2023).

106 "The state of AI regulations in 2023", Holistic AI, 16 January 2023. Available at: https://www.holisticai.com/papers/the-state-of-ai-regulations-in-2023 (Accessed 27 July 2023).

107 "Regulation (EU) 2023/1114 of The European Parliament and of The Council on markets in crypto-assets and amending Regulations (EU) No 1093/2010 and (EU) No 1095/2010 and Directives 2013/36/EU and (EU) 2019/1937", Official Journal of the European Union, 31 May 2023. Available at: https://eur-lex.europa.eu/legal-content/EN/TXT/?uri=CELEX%3A32023R1114 (Accessed 27 July 2023).

108   "Policy paper: Factsheet: cryptoassets technical", Gov.UK website, 20 June 2023. Available at: https://www.gov.uk/government/publications/ economic-crime-and-corporate-transparency-bill-2022-factsheets/ fact-sheet-cryptoassets-technical (Accessed 27 July 2023).

109   "Building a Smarter Financial Services Regulatory Framework for the UK: HM Treasury's Plan for Delivery", HM Treasury, July 2023. Available at: https://assets.publishing.service.gov.uk/government/uploads/ system/uploads/attachment_data/file/1168648/Building_a_Smarter_ Financial_Services_Regulatory_Framework_for_the_UK_Plan_for_ delivery.pdf (Accessed 27 July 2023).

110   "The (somewhat lively) state of crypto regulation", Thomson Reuters, 1 June 2023. Available at: https://www.thomsonreuters.com/en-us/posts/ investigation-fraud-and-risk/crypto-regulation/ (Accessed 27 July 2023).

111   "Crypto Regulation, Protection, Transparency, and Oversight (CRPTO) Act", New York State Attorney General website, 5 May 2023. Available at: https://ag.ny.gov/press-release/2023/attorney-general-james- proposes-nation-leading-regulations-cryptocurrency (Accessed 27 July 2023).

112   "PwC Global Crypto Regulation Report 2023", PwC, 19 December 2022 (updated). Available at: https://www.pwc.com/gx/en/new-ventures/ cryptocurrency-assets/pwc-global-crypto-regulation-report-2023.pdf (Accessed 27 July 2023).

113   "Regulatory Sandbox accepted firms", Financial Conduct Authority web- site, updated 7 July 2023. Available at: https://www.fca.org.uk/firms/ innovation/regulatory-sandbox/accepted-firms (Accessed 27 July 2023).

114   "Innovation Hub", ASIC website. Available at: https://asic.gov.au/for- business/innovation-hub/enhanced-regulatory-sandbox/ (Accessed 27 July 2023).

115   "Launch of the European blockchain regulatory sandbox", European Commission, February 2023. Available at: https://digital-strategy.ec. europa.eu/en/news/launch-european-blockchain-regulatory-sandbox (Accessed 27 July 2023).

116   "First regulatory sandbox on Artificial Intelligence presented", European Commission website, 22 June 2022. Available at: https://digital-strategy. ec.europa.eu/en/news/first-regulatory-sandbox-artificial-intelligence- presented (Accessed 27 July 2023).

117   "EU and U.S. regulatory sandboxes: groundbreaking tools for fostering innovation and shaping applicable regulations", JD Supra, 2 May 2023. Available at: https://www.jdsupra.com/legalnews/eu-and-u-s-regulatory- sandboxes-2759128/ (Accessed 27 July 2023).

118 "The costs of compliance – when will investment in risk technology start paying off for banks?" American Banker, 3 May 2023. Available at: https://internationalbanker.com/finance/the-costs-of-compliance-when-will-investment-in-risk-technology-start-paying-off-for-banks/ (Accessed 25 July 2023).

119 "Deloitte Regtech Universe", Deloitte website. Available at: https://www2.deloitte.com/lu/en/pages/technology/articles/regtech-companies-compliance.html (Accessed 25 July 2023).

120 "Quit your jibber jabber says Mr. T! I Pity The Fool", YouTube, 6 August, 2010. Available at: https://www.youtube.com/watch?v=GydAcTk5s5E (Accessed 16 October 2023).

121 "Apple Card savings account hits $10bn in deposits", Finextra, 3 August 2023. Available at: https://www.finextra.com/newsarticle/42729/apple-card-savings-account-hits-10bn-in-deposits (Accessed 3 August 2023).

122 "The Metaverse will need its own INTERPOL to police payments crossing between virtual, real worlds", Pymnts, 30 November 2021. Available at: https://www.pymnts.com/safety-and-security/2021/metaverse-will-need-its-own-interpol-police-payments-crossing-virtual-real-worlds/ (Accessed 27 July 2023).

CONCLUSION (IS THIS THE END?)

Three months have passed since I started writing this book, and I have hardly slept. In that time, I constantly had to revisit every chapter because a payment ecosystem actor did something interesting that I wanted to include, or because a regulation changed or came into effect, or because a new type of fraud emerged. I had to stop somewhere, and this is my somewhere. Did I answer all your questions? I hope I managed to answer at least some of them. But if you, like me, are curious about why some questions remain, I hope I have equipped you to go and find the answers. I also attempted to provide a comprehensive glossary, because I haven't seen one like it in the industry and I always wanted one. I hope it will be useful.

I remain deeply passionate about the payments industry, and I hope I have managed to instil some of that interest in you, Dear Reader. I also hope the ducks will achieve some level of serenity as a result, and that they now feel able to maximise their paddling efforts! As for those of you who are new to payments, I'll be glad if you now find the industry less mystifying.

DOI: 10.4324/9781032631394-7

I am sure I will be compelled to update this edition in a couple of years from now, when I will look at it fondly as some sort of historical document. Although, the fundamental mechanisms for centralised payments will remain the same, what happens around them will invariably evolve, sometimes in unexpected ways.

I hope I have managed to do what I set out to do – namely, to write a book about payments that isn't boring and that would appeal not only to those needing a refresher or wanting to understand parts of the industry with which they are unfamiliar, but also to those new to the industry wanting to "get into payments".

This book wouldn't have been possible without the lovely people in my life. To all my industry friends, especially those who took the time to read the book and endorse it, namely, Flavia Alzetta, Otto Benz, David Birch, Tom Blomfield, Simon Burrows, Stuart Campbell, Tony Craddock, John Davies, Janusz Diemko, Alison Donnelly, Dr Mark Goldspink, Adrian Hausser, Paul Horlock, Sir Ron Kalifa, Ken Lipton, Andy McDonald, Mark McMurtrie, Jeremy Nicholds, Ken Palla, Chris Skinner, Stanley Skoglund, Soteris Vasili, Jim Wadsworth, Charles White, Gary Yamamura, and Angela Yore, I am honoured to be in your crowd and grateful for your support. Special thanks and gratitude are due to Roger Alexander, my friend and mentor for so many years. He pushed me to write this book, and I ignored his advice for a while before I finally took the plunge. Roger, I hope I made you proud. My gratitude goes to the Routledge team, especially to Rebecca Marsh for taking a chance on my first book, to Lauren Whelan for being so efficient in making this book the best it can be, and to my copyeditor Michael Helfield for his sense of humour and excellent taste in music.

My thanks also go to Jonathan Davies for showing me the perfect paddling and to my good friend Andrew Billing-Giles for making "the duck" real; it really makes me smile each time I see it. Ayup me duck! I thank as well my friends and loved ones for their encouragement, especially Paul Merricks for teaching me how to write a glossary: the good things in it are the result of his advice, and all the mistakes therein are solely mine. I thank Pauline and Mac Millington for their love and support over the years, for taking the time to read this book and comment on it, and for questioning my assertions, listening to my ramblings, and cheering me on. A special dedication goes out to Frank and Anne Andrew, Kirsty and Ali, with my love always. And I thank my sister, Aida Keehner, for never once looking bored with my daily (and long) payment stories and for actually reading everything I sent her. Sis, you're the one in that Jess Glynne song. To my husband David for his unwavering love and patience, you're my anchor.

Finally, I thank you, Dear Reader, for accompanying me on this whistle-stop tour into the fascinating world of centralised payments. I hope it wasn't a bumpy ride!

All that remains for me to say is: "Mind the gap" as you leave this train, and, hopefully, you'll join me on the next platform for the next book, *Beyond Payments: From Centralised to Decentralised and Everything in Between*.

I UNDERSTAND PAYMENTS!

(It would look nice on a T-shirt, don't you think?)

GLOSSARY

3D Secure (3DS)   An EMV standard for the authentication of e-commerce transactions. Deployments include Mastercard's "SecureCode" and "Identity Check", Visa's "Visa Secure", and American Express' "SafeKey". 3D Secure stands for "3 Domain Secure" and refers to the three ecosystem domains involved in the process: the acquirer domain (acquirer and merchant), the issuer domain, and the interoperability domain (the card scheme).

3D Secure Server (3DSS)   3D Secure infrastructure deployed by a merchant. Used to be known as the merchant plug-in (MPI). This technology is usually provided by the merchant's PSP, usually a payment gateway provider, but some Access Control Server (ACS) providers also supply the 3D Secure Server technology. This functionality provides the bridge between the cardholder (e.g. a pop-up window) and the acquirer during the authorisation process.

3DSS   See *3D Secure Server*.

A2A Payment   See *Account-to-Account Payment*.

Aadhaar   A digital identity framework developed by the Unique Identification Authority of India (UIDAI) on behalf of the Government of India. It consists of a 12-digit individual identification number and a set of rules governing the framework The Aadhaar number serves as proof of identity and residence for any Indian resident, irrespective of age, and is valid for life. Through the Aadhaar deployment, the Indian government intends to promote financial inclusion for a largely rural and underbanked population, by facilitating access to banking, mobile phone connections, and other government and non-government services. In March 2023, Aadhaar authentication transactions climbed to 2.31 billion, and UIDAI claims that its digital KYC (eKYC) deployment has significantly reduced customer acquisition costs for financial services institutions, telcos, and others.

ABA Routing Number   An ABA (American Bankers Association) Routing Number is a nine-digit code used to identify banks in America. Similar to a UK sort code, it is sometimes referred to as a "check routing number", ABA number, routing transit number (RTN), or Fedwire number.

Access to Account (XS2A)   A term widely used in the early days of the EU Second Payment Services Directive (PSD2), but not so much now, where the concept has generally been replaced with "open banking".

Access Control Server (ACS)   3D Secure infrastructure deployed by an issuer. Most issuers outsource this to an independent software vendor (ISV).

Account Information Service Provider (AISP)   A Third Party PSP (TPP) that accesses information from a payment account (card account or bank account) on behalf of a Payment System User (PSU) on a read-only basis.

Account Servicing PSP (ASPSP)   The ecosystem actor who manages the Payment System User's (PSU) account throughout its lifecycle, from creation to closure. This can be a bank, an issuer, or a non-bank payment service provider (PSP).

Account-to-Account Payment (A2A Payment)   A type of payment that allows a payer to move money from their bank account to a payee's bank account.

Accredited Scanning Vendor (ASV)   A third party that provides e-commerce merchants with network vulnerability scans (aka ASV scans), as dictated by the PCI DSS validation requirements for that merchant. The PCI SSC maintains a list of ASVs on their website.

ACH   See *Automated Clearing House*.

ACH Scheme   A legacy bank payment scheme or payment system. An ACH Scheme is a network that enables payers to send money to payees on the bank rails with longer settlement times than modern real-time payment systems. Also referred to as an "ACH System".

ACH System   See *ACH Scheme*.

Acquirer   A payment service provider (PSP) that enables a merchant to connect to a card scheme. Commonly referred to as an "acquiring bank", "merchant bank" (if they are also a bank), "merchant services provider (MSP)", "merchant acquirer", "acquiring PSP", or "processor". Acquiring services are also referred to as "merchant services".

Acquirer Margin   A fee levied by an acquirer on a merchant for each card transaction and is supposed to cover the credit risk and overheads that the acquirer has, as well as the profit that the acquirer makes.

Acquiring   The process of acquiring card transactions from merchants to enable those merchants to take card payments for cards issued on a given card scheme (e.g. Visa, Mastercard). Acquiring connects merchants with card schemes.

Acquiring Bank   An acquiring PSP that is also a bank.

Acquiring Clearing Files   Contains all the acquirer's card transactions for that day. Each acquirer will produce as many acquiring clearing files as the number of card schemes of which they are members (e.g. one for Visa, one for Mastercard, etc.). Acquirers submit their clearing files to the schemes in batch usually at the end of the day in line with the card scheme clearing cycle, and these files are specified in the card scheme operating regulations.

Acquiring PSP   See *Acquirer*.

ACS   See *Access Control Server*.

Address Verification Service (AVS)   A fraud prevention feature available to merchants to verify that the address given by the cardholder matches the billing address associated with the cardholder's account. Can be used in the Card Present (CP) and Card Not Present (CNP) channels.

AI   See *Artificial Intelligence*.

AISP   See *Account Information Service Provider*.

Alternative Finance (AltFi)   A catch-all term for almost any source of business funding other than traditional bank loans and overdrafts.

Alternative Payments   A term coined by the cards industry that is generally used to describe non-card payments.

AltFi   See *Alternative Finance*.

American Express   A card scheme that operates according to the Three Party Model.

AML   See *Anti-Money Laundering*.

AML/CFT   See *Anti-Money Laundering*.

AML/CTF   See *Anti-Money Laundering*.

Anti-Money Laundering (AML)   The collection of laws, processes, and regulations that prevent illegally obtained money from entering the financial system. Increasingly, AML frameworks include Counter-Terrorism Financing (CTF) provisions, as well as tax-related offences. Also referred to as AML/CFT or AML/CTF.

API   See *Application Programming Interface*.

API Aggregator   A Third Party Provider (TPP) which enables businesses to operate across ecosystem participants and regions by taking the interfacing work unto themselves and offering their client one set of APIs to operate across standards (and therefore geographies).

APP Fraud   See *Authorised Push Payment (APP) Fraud*.

Application Programming Interface (API)   A software interface allowing parties to communicate with each other through an agreed set of definitions and protocols. The document or standard that describes how to build or use such an interface is called an "API specification".

Artificial Intelligence (AI)   A branch of computer science concerned with building smart machines capable of performing tasks that typically require human intelligence.

ASPSP   See *Account Servicing PSP*.

ASV   See *Accredited Scanning Vendor*.

ASV Scan   See *Network Vulnerability Scan*.

ATM   See *Automated Teller Machine*.

ATV   See *Average Transaction Value*.

Authentication   The method by which a cardholder is authenticated. There are various authentication factors, such as a PIN, a signature, and biometrics.

Authentify®   In April 2022, Early Warning, the consortium of seven of the largest banks behind Zelle, launched Authentify®, an identity verification service for consumers and businesses that leverages trusted bank data. This enables merchants to reduce cart abandonment and fraud ratios whilst streamlining the identity verification process for consumers. It also gives financial services institutions the ability to provide value-added services to their customers outside of the banking experience.

Authorisation   A process by which an Account Servicing PSP (ASPSP) is asked to verify that a payer is genuine and allowed to make a payment transaction. The process is different for card rails and bank rails, but generally involves an authorisation request made to the ASPSP, which will return their authorisation decision.

Authorisation Decision   The second step of the payment account holder authorisation process.

Authorisation Request   The first step of the payment account holder authorisation process.

Authorised Fraud   A term used to describe a type of fraud where the payment transaction has been authorised by the payer but the payee is a fraudulent account. See *Authorised Push Payment (APP) Fraud*.

Authorised Push Payment (APP) Fraud   A type of fraud that happens on the bank rails where a fraudster impersonates a payee and tricks a payer into sending funds to a fraudulent bank account. This type of attack generally starts through phishing via an attack called Business Email Compromise (BEC). A type of authorised fraud.

Automated Banking Machine (ABM)   See *Automated Teller Machine*.

Automated Clearing House (ACH)   Used to describe legacy bank payment schemes with longer settlement cycles (i.e. a few days) when compared to more modern bank payments systems, which settle in real time or near real time. The first ACH System in the world, BACS, was launched in the UK in 1968. The first ACH System in the US, Fed-ACH, was launched in 1972 and was operated by the Federal Reserve Bank of San Francisco.

Automated Teller Machine (ATM)   A self-service card terminal which allows cardholders to withdraw or deposit money, check their balances, transfer funds between accounts, pay bills, etc. Whilst all ATMs will allow cardholders to withdraw cash, not all ATMs will offer additional functionality. Sometimes referred to as an Automated Banking Machine (ABM).

Average Transaction Value (ATV)   A measure of the average amount that customers spend on each purchase over a period of time (e.g. a month). The ATV is a valuable metric that can help merchants inform their product and pricing strategy. For example, if a merchant generates

£20,000 over 100 transactions in a month, the ATV for that month will be £200.

AVS   See *Address Verification Service.*

B2B   See *Business-to-Business.*

B2C   See *Business-to-Consumer.*

B2G   See *Business-to-Government.*

BaaP   See *Banking-as-a-Platform.*

BaaS   See *Banking-as-a-Service.*

BACS   See *Bankers Automated Clearing Services.*

Bancomat   An Italian domestic card scheme.

Bancontact   A Belgian domestic card scheme.

Bank   A financial services institution. In a payments context, a bank can be an Account Servicing PSP (ASPSP) on the bank rails, or an issuer on the card rails.

Bank Identification Number (BIN)   The first six or first eight digits of a card number. The modern term is Issuer Identification Number (IIN), which was supposed to replace the original term of BIN to reflect the fact that issuers don't have to be banks (e.g. eMoney institutions). But the term BIN is so well established that the industry still sticks with it. The BIN identifies a number of elements, including the card scheme (e.g. Visa), the issuer (e.g. Santander), the type of card (e.g. credit, debit, purchasing), and the country (e.g. UK). Both six- and eight-digit BINs exist.

Bank Rails   Used to describe the bank (ACH) payments ecosystem, its operating procedures and infrastructure.

Bank Transfer   A payment method by which the funding mechanism is a bank account.

BankAxept   A Norwegian domestic card scheme.

BANKART (BIPS)   A Slovenian domestic ACH Scheme.

Bankers Automated Clearing Services (BACS)   A domestic UK ACH Scheme used for regular bulk credit transfers and Direct Debits (DDs). BACS is managed by Pay.UK and was the first ACH Scheme in the world, launched in 1968.

BankID   A digital identity framework in Sweden and Norway. Whilst the name is the same, they are separate frameworks.

Banking-as-a-Platform (BaaP)   Where banks integrate technology provided by fintech firms allowing them to provide innovative services to their customers. This can kick-start digital transformation for banks.

Banking-as-a-Service (BaaS)   Technology provided by regulated institutions to non-bank payment services providers (PSPs) to enable them to provide financial services to their customers. Also see *Embedded Finance*.

Banknet   The Mastercard network.

BEC   See *Business Email Compromise*.

Beneficial Ownership   A concept describing the relationship between a business signatory and any underlying beneficial owners, especially if they have significant control over the business.

Berlin Group   The German open banking standard.

Big Tech   A collective term used to describe large technology companies and platforms.

BIN   See *Bank Identification Number*.

BIN Rental   See *BIN Sponsorship*.

BIN Sponsorship   The process by which BIN sponsors, which can be acquirers or issuers, enable other eligible organisations to issue cards by allowing them to use BIN ranges that they control (this is sometimes described as "BIN rental"). Working with a principal scheme member allows these eligible organisations to issue cards and adhere to the card scheme rules and regulatory requirements, giving them quick time to market. This is traditionally associated with the prepaid and eMoney markets. Also see *Scheme Membership*.

Black List   See *Financial Action Task Force*.

Blended Pricing   A pricing model by which a merchant only sees one rate on their merchant service charge (MSC), and this rate has no contractual link to interchange. This is the least transparent pricing model and will be typically used for small to medium-sized merchants. Independent Sales Organisations (ISOs) and payment service providers (PSPs) may favour this model, although acquirers will generally try to use it for smaller merchants if applicable regulations don't prevent them from doing so.

Blockchain   A type of Distributed Ledger Technology (DLT) that uses cryptographic approaches to create and share transactions (the data blocks) across participants for validation. Time-stamped "blocks" of data are strung together (chain), and these blocks are intermittently validated (consensus protocol) by users of the network.

Blockchain Settlement   A blockchain mechanism by which transactions are settled. This mechanism is decentralised and relies on a consensus protocol.

Blockchain Trilemma   A concept coined by Ethereum's co-founder Vitalik Buterin describing the challenge faced by blockchain developers stating that optimal levels of decentralisation, security, and scalability are hard to achieve, as one of the three elements must be sacrificed in favour of the other two.

BNPL   See *Buy-Now-Pay-Later*.

Business Email Compromise (BEC)   A type of phishing attack where a fraudster compromises the email environment of a business so they can impersonate that business and trick victims into, for example, sending funds to accounts they own. See also *Authorised Push Payment (APP) Fraud*.

Business-to-Business (B2B)   A term used to describe a business model where one business makes a commercial transaction with another business.

Business-to-Consumer (B2C)   A term used to describe the business model of selling products directly to customers and thereby bypassing any third party (e.g. wholesalers, distributors, intermediaries).

Business-to-Government (B2G)   A term used to describe the trade between the business sector as a supplier and a government body as a customer.

Buy-Now-Pay-Later (BNPL)   A payment method where consumers can pay for goods by instalments after delivery, interest free. It is a form of credit that is rapidly gaining popularity and increasingly attracting regulatory scrutiny. BNPL is a value-added service that can be offered to merchants for integration into their payment facilities. Sometimes called "e-invoices".

Card Absent   An attempt from Visa to rename Card Not Present (CNP). This has not caught on.

Card Acceptance   The process by which merchants take payments by card. Also referred to as "payment acceptance".

Card Authorisation Value (CAV)   What JCB calls the card verification value (CVV).

Card-Based Payment Instrument Issuer (CBPII)   A Third Party PSP (TPP) that issues card-based payment instruments (physical or virtual) that can be used to initiate a payment transaction from a payment account (e.g. a bank account) held with an Account Servicing Payment Service Provider (ASPSP) other than the issuer. Essentially, a CBPII is a combination of an Account Information Service Provider (AISP), Payment Initiation Service Provider (PISP), issuer, and money remittance. This is a form of decoupled debit. CBPIIs come in two forms: closed loop (don't involve a card scheme) and open loop (involve a card scheme). See also *Closed Loop* and *Closed Loop Card*.

Card Brand   A card scheme.

Card Identification Number (CID)   What American Express calls the card verification value (CVV).

Card Imprinting Machine   A manual card reader that takes the imprint of a card. The card must have embossed elements if it is to be processed with a card imprinting machine, which has metal plates for taking the imprint. Also known as a zip-zap machine or knuckle-buster (for obvious reasons).

Card Issuing   See *Issuing*.

Card Network   A term generally used to describe a card scheme, but it sometimes may only refer to the infrastructure provided by a card scheme, such as VisaNet for Visa, or Banknet for Mastercard.

Card Not Present (CNP)   The terminology used to describe remote card payment transactions. This falls into two categories: e-commerce and mail order telephone order (MOTO). Also referred to as Customer Not Present.

Card Number   See *Primary Account Number*.

Card On File   A type of transaction where a cardholder authorises a merchant to store their card information securely and bill the cardholder's account for future purchases without the cardholder's intervention. A form a merchant-initiated transaction (MIT).

Card on File Transaction   See *Recurring Transaction*.

Card Optimisation   See *Payments Optimisation*.

Card Payment Channel   A term used to describe the cardholder mode of interaction with the merchant. It can be Card Present (face-to-face) or Card Not Present (e-commerce, telephone, mail order, etc.).

Card Payments Value Chain   The set of activities performed by its stakeholders to deliver valuable products and services to the card payments market.

Card Present   The terminology used to describe physical face-to-face card payment transactions. Also referred to as Card Present.

Card Rails   The term used to describe the card payments ecosystem, its operating procedures, and its infrastructure.

Card Scheme   A payment scheme (or payment system) that provides an ecosystem for card payments.

Card Scheme Fee   Any fee that that is paid to a card scheme for their contribution to the ecosystem (e.g. authorisation fee, chargeback fee, retrieval fee).

Card Scheme Rails   See *Card Rails*.

Card Skimmer   See *Skimmer*.

Card Swipe   A term used to describe a card transaction using the magnetic stripe (aka magstripe).

Card Terminal Manufacturer   A type of payee's PSP (aka merchant's PSP) on the card rails. They supply card payment terminals to merchants to enable them to accept physical card payments.

Card Verification Code (CVC)   What Mastercard calls the card verification value (CVV).

Card Verification Value (CVV)   Whilst this is a generic term to describe all card verification values, in common language it refers to the CVV2. The CVV2 is a three-digit code found on the signature panel for most cards (e.g. Visa, Mastercard) but for American Express it has four digits and is printed on the front of the card. The CVV2 is used to authenticate remote transactions (e.g. e-commerce or telephone) to verify that the cardholder has the card in their possession. See also *CVV1, iCVV, Dynamic CVV (dCVV)*.

Cardholder   A consumer or business that has a card account. A type of payer or payment service user (PSU).

Cardholder Account Number   The part of the Primary Account Number (PAN) that identifies the cardholder and is the next nine digits after the BIN for six-digit BINs, or the next seven digits after the BIN for eight-digit BINs.

Cardholder Data   In PCI DSS terms, cardholder data consists of the Primary Account Number (PAN), cardholder name, expiry date, and service code.

Cardholder Data Environment (CDE)   Consists of the people, processes, and technologies that store, process, or transmit cardholder data or sensitive cardholder data. The PCI DSS security requirements apply to all system components that are included in or connected to the CDE.

Cardholder Settlement   Part of the commercial arrangement between the cardholder and the issuer. With debit cards, this is usually a "banking" arrangement. With credit cards, it is a "lending" arrangement.

Cardholder Verification Method (CVM) Limit   The contactless payment limit. This can be either for a single transaction (e.g. £100 in the UK), or for consecutive transactions (e.g. £300 in the UK). If this threshold is reached, the cardholder has to be authenticated to reset the counter (e.g. PIN).

Carte Bancaire   A French domestic card scheme.

Cash Advance   See *Merchant Financing*.

Cashback   A facility which can be either a payment incentive offered by issuers to cardholders by which a percentage of purchases is offered back to credit card holders, or a facility by which a physical merchant can give a cardholder cash back within agreed limits. The amount of the cash given back to the cardholder is added to the transaction amount. This is useful to maintain access to cash where ATMs are not available.

Cash on Delivery (CoD)   A transaction in which a payment for goods is made at the time of delivery. Specific to countries and suppliers. Very popular in some regions, such as Central Europe. A form of delayed payment. Sometimes referred to as "collect on delivery", since delivery may allow for cash, cheque, or electronic payments to be used.

CAV   See *Card Authorisation Value*.

CBDC   See *Central Bank Digital Currency*.

CBPII   See *Card-Based Payment Instrument Issuer*.

CDD   See *Customer Due Diligence*.

CDE   See *Cardholder Data Environment*.

CEC   Belgium's domestic ACH Scheme.

Central Bank Digital Currency (CBDC)   A type of virtual asset. It is different from a cryptocurrency or virtual currency, as it is issued by a state/central bank and has legal tender status. CBDC implementations may use Distributed Ledger Technology (DLT), but they don't have to. Essentially the digital equivalent of notes and coins.

CENTRO   Lithuania's domestic ACH Scheme.

CHAPS   See *Clearing House Automated Payment System*.

Chargeback   A cardholder can invoke the chargeback process through their issuer to get the transaction amount back from the merchant for a disputed purchase, or it can be invoked directly by the card issuer when they suspect fraud. For merchants, the chargeback is the most painful of the exceptions. It is generally triggered by fraudulent activity, but not always.

Chargeback Activism A type of first party fraud where activists raise chargebacks to punish a company for ideological differences or disagreements.

Chargeback Category Chargeback reason codes are classified into categories, and although these will differ in their description depending on the card scheme, the industry broadly agrees on four categories: authorisation, fraud, consumer disputes, and processing errors.

Chargeback Defence The process by which a merchant defends a chargeback. If a merchant fails to defend a chargeback within the period specified by the card scheme, their account will be automatically debited for the amount of the disputed transaction. Also called "chargeback representment".

Chargeback Process Outsourcing Chargeback process outsourcing service providers are independent software vendors (ISVs) which manage the whole chargeback process on behalf of merchants and other card ecosystem stakeholders. Some providers have evolved into full-blown fraud prevention service providers.

Chargeback Ratio This represents the number of chargebacks filed against a merchant in a given month against their total number of transactions in a month. And because each card scheme has their own operating regulations, there is a different chargeback ratio for each scheme.

Chargeback Reason Code A code associated with a description that must be presented as part of the chargeback request to allow the merchant to provide the correct information in defence. These codes are specified by each card scheme in their operating regulations.

Chargeback Representment See *Chargeback Defence*.

Checksum The last digit in a Primary Account Number (PAN). It is calculated by applying a mathematical formula called the Luhn Algorithm (aka Modulus 10) to the BIN and Cardholder Account Number. The checksum is not part of the account number itself but is essential for the validation of card numbers (e.g. typos, missed digits, etc.).

Chip and PIN   A deployment of EMV chip where a personal identification number (PIN) – a four-digit code selected and managed by the cardholder – is used to authenticate face-to-face transactions at the physical point of sale (POS) (e.g. UK, Europe).

Chip and Signature   A deployment of EMV chip where a signature is used to authenticate face-to-face transactions at the physical point of sale (POS) (e.g. United States).

Chip Card   A credit or debit card that follows the EMV chip standard. Also called an "EMV card" and historically a "smart card".

CHIPS   See *Clearing House Interbank Payment System*.

CID   See *Card Identification Number*.

Clearing   The non-monetary exchange of transaction information. On the card rails, clearing is the process by which merchant transactions are reconciled with cardholder transactions. Merchant transactions are managed by the acquirer, and cardholder transactions are managed by the issuer, and the clearing process is orchestrated by the card scheme. On the bank rails, clearing is the process by which banking transactions are reconciled between banks. The banking transactions are managed by the sender's and receiver's banks, and the clearing process is orchestrated by the bank payment scheme for transaction reconciliation.

Clearing Cycle   In theory, this describes how long it takes for the clearing of funds to complete. In practice, the term "clearing cycle" is generally associated with cheques (as it takes a few days for cheques to clear). For digital payments (card or bank accounts), the term "settlement cycle" is used.

Clearing File   A file produced by a payment scheme direct participant for submission to the payment scheme so they can perform the clearing process.

Clearing House Automated Payment System (CHAPS)   A UK bank payment scheme that launched in 1984 and is used for same-day high-value wholesale payments as well as time-critical high-value retail payments. CHAPS uses the SWIFT messaging network for cross-border payments. CHAPS is managed and operated by the Bank of England.

Clearing House Interbank Payment System (CHIPS)   A US large-value payment system (LVPS) privately operated by The Clearing House.

Closed Loop   Any system that is limited in its scope.

Closed Loop Card   A payment card that is limited in its scope. Examples are gift cards, fuel cards, and some store cards. These are not generally run on card scheme networks.

CNP   See *Card Not Present.*

Co-branded Card   A type of card where a merchant partners with a card scheme for a card product. These are typically open loop store cards, airline cards, etc.

CoD   See *Cash on Delivery.*

Collect on Delivery (CoD)   See *Cash on Delivery.*

Confirmation of Payee   An overlay service implemented on top of a bank payment scheme. Confirmation of Payee (CoP) enables payers to check the name and sort code/bank account number before they complete a bank payment. CoP is intended to help with reducing Authorised Push Payment (APP) fraud.

Consensus Protocol   The blockchain trust framework by which transactions are validated. Nodes "listen" to the network and gather valid transactions (i.e. legal, not double spending, etc.) to fit in a block. These nodes are called "miners" or "validators", and they add valid transactions to their blocks. Not all valid blocks will be added to the chain, as this is determined by the consensus protocol. The consensus (Proof of Work (PoW), Proof of Stake (PoS), etc.) determines the ordering of validated blocks and is what enables the blockchain network to be trustless. When the validated winning block is added to the chain, the transaction becomes irreversible. This is the equivalent of the settlement process on centralised payment systems.

Consortium Blockchain   A type of permissioned blockchain controlled by a group.

Contactless Payment   A method of payment where a cardholder pays for something by tapping or waiving their contactless card or contactless-enabled device (smart phone, card, key fob, etc.) over a card terminal.

Contingent Reimbursement   A reimbursement model used in the context of authorised fraud by which victims of scams may be reimbursed under certain conditions.

Continuous Payment Authority (CPA)   See *Recurring Transaction.*

CoP   See *Confirmation of Payee.*

Correspondent Banking   An arrangement under which one bank holds funds owned by another bank (the respondent bank) and provides payment and other services to that respondent bank.

Counter-Terrorist Financing (CTF)   The collection of laws, processes, and regulations that prevent the financing of terrorism. Also referred to as Combatting the Financing of Terrorism.

CP   See *Card Present*.

CPA   See *Continuous Payment Authority* and *Recurring Transaction*.

Credit Transfer   A payment instruction from the bank account holder to their bank to transfer funds to a payee. The payee can be the same person as the instructing bank account holder (e.g. a bank account holder moving funds between their own accounts), and this includes single ad hoc payments, or different (e.g. a bank account holder moving funds to another person's account). For retail payments, these generally have lower-value thresholds than credit transfers on large-value payment systems (LVPS) and are mostly associated with consumer transactions. Credit transfers can also be submitted in batch by the account holder's bank to the bank payment scheme (e.g. salaries, pension contributions, etc.), but in this case, each fund transfer in the batch counts as a single transaction. This latter type of payment usually has high-value minimum thresholds (not necessarily by the scheme rules, but mostly due to economics) and is not supported by all bank payment schemes.

Cross-Border   International.

Crypto Asset   At a high level, a crypto asset is a type of virtual asset that lives on a blockchain, is secured by cryptography, and comes in five types: cryptocurrency, Non-Fungible Token (NFT), utility token, stablecoin, and security token. There is no formally accepted definition or classification of crypto assets. This book offers a classification of crypto assets according to their primary purpose, as listed in the white paper for that particular crypto asset.

Cryptocurrency   A type of crypto asset intended to be used as a medium of exchange. This was the original purpose of Bitcoin BTC, but over the years, it has morphed into a store of value used for speculative purposes. Some even refer to Bitcoin as "digital gold", which is a misnomer since gold is a stable asset and cryptocurrencies are highly volatile and unregulated. To this day, no cryptocurrency can claim to be a true medium of exchange.

Crypto Wallet   A facility used to store the user's public and private keys which act as a certificate of ownership for crypto assets that are stored on Distributed Ledger Technology (DLT), usually a blockchain.

CTF   See *Counter-Terrorist Financing.*

Customer Due Diligence (CDD)   The process by which businesses verify that their customers are who they say they are, and is usually conducted at the underwriting stage, or when creating a new business relationship. CDD allows businesses to assess money-laundering and terrorism-financing risks to which customers may potentially expose them.

Customer Not Present   See *Card Not Present.*

Customer Present   See *Card Present.*

CVC   See *Card Verification Code.*

CVM   See *Cardholder Verification Limit.*

CVV   See *Card Verification Value.*

CVV1   A static card verification value stored on Tracks 1 and 2 of the magnetic stripe (magstripe). The CVV1 is used to authenticate magstripe transactions (this process takes place between the magstripe, the physical card payment terminal, and the issuer during the authorisation process).

CVV2   The static card verification value printed on a card.

CVV3   See *iCVV.*

Dankort   A Danish domestic card scheme.

DAO   See *Decentralised Autonomous Organisation.*

Data Subject Access Request (DSAR)   A request that can be made by an individual to a business whereby the business must provide all of the information they hold about that individual within a specified time frame. These requests are associated with data protection regulations.

DCB   See *Direct Carrier Billing.*

DCC   See *Dynamic Currency Conversion.*

dCVV   See *Dynamic CVV.*

DD   See *Direct Debit.*

Decentralised Autonomous Organisation (DAO)   A group of people without a central leader or company dictating any of the decisions. Built on a blockchain using smart contracts. Members of DAOs often buy their way in by purchasing governance tokens specifically for the DAO.

Decoupled Authentication   Decoupled authentication is different from the standard authentication process. Here, cardholder authentication happens outside of their payment interaction with the merchant, at a different time, even if the cardholder is offline. Merchants can set a time limit (e.g. one minute, a week) for the cardholder to complete the authentication process, and this can take place on a device different to that used by the cardholder during the transaction.

Decoupled Debit A concept by which non-bank issuers could issue debit cards that are not tied to a specific bank account. Early examples are associated with retailers (e.g. Target REDcard™ Debit) and can only be used at that retailer (closed loop). Newer examples include cards provided by Card-Based Payment Instrument Issuers (CBPIIs).

Deep Learning A subset of machine learning.

Deferred Net Settlement See *Settlement Cycle*.

Deferred Settlement See *Settlement Cycle*.

DeFi A generic term for decentralised applications providing financial services on a blockchain settlement layer. Examples of DeFi services include investments, insurance, asset management, payments, lending, and trading.

Delayed Payment A type of payment where an agreement between a payer and a payee is made for the purchase of goods or services and there is an agreed delay for the payment, in part or in full, from the time of purchase.

Delegated Authentication This is where issuers delegate the authentication process to a third party (e.g. merchant, acquirer, digital wallet provider). For example, if a merchant can perform the cardholder authentication through a card-scheme-approved method, information can be passed on to the issuer to confirm the cardholder's identity, and there will be no need for the issuer to authenticate the transaction. This means a lot less friction for cardholders (e.g. one-click payments).

DIAS Greece's domestic ACH Scheme.

Digital Currency A broad term used to describe any currency, money, or money-like asset that exists purely in a digital form. There are several types of digital currencies and many ways of defining the subsets, sometimes conflicting. They can be regulated or unregulated, and some can be secured by cryptography. See *CBCD*, *Crypto Asset*, and *Virtual Currency*.

Digital Identity Refers to information used digitally to represent external identities, including individuals, organisations, applications, and devices. Digital identity can be used for a range of purposes and may offer benefits, ranging from authentication and authorisation of users for access to information and resources, to facilitating e-commerce and personalised digital experiences.

Digital Wallet   A digital payment facility that enables digital transactions.

Direct Carrier Billing (DCB)   An online payment method by which users can make purchases by charging the payment to their mobile phone bill for single or recurring payments. DCB is usually confined to digital goods, and spending limits may apply, but this will depend on the geography, mobile carrier, and applicable regulations.

Direct Debit (DD)   A type of payment on the bank rails that is used to make regular payments without needing to reauthorise once the Direct Debit is set up (e.g. utility bills, subscriptions). This is a type of recurring transaction.

Direct Participant   A term used to describe bank payment scheme participants that are directly connected to the bank payment scheme. See also *Directly Connected Settling Participant* and *Directly Connected Non-Settling Participant*.

Direct Payment Instruction   See *Payment Instruction*.

Directly Connected Non-Settling Participant   A bank payment scheme participant that can connect to the payment scheme but cannot settle funds directly with the payment scheme. These participants will settle funds through directly connected settling participants.

Directly Connected Settling Participant   A bank payment scheme participant directly connected to the scheme and able to settle directly through the settlement agent for that scheme (a central bank) through their settlement account. See also *RTGS Account*.

Discover   A card scheme operating according to the Three Party Model.

Discretionary Data   The discretionary data is the balance of digits available on Track 1 (79 digits), Track 2 (40 digits), and the chip (40 digits) after the Primary Account Number (PAN), cardholder name, and service code. It is used by issuers pretty much as they see fit. For example, they may use the discretionary data to create new card products with specific characteristics (e.g. a student card) or for security. On Tracks 1 and 2, it may include PIN verification elements like the CVV1. On the Chip, it will contain the iCVV.

Distributed Ledger Technology (DLT)   A type of distributed database enabling the storage, recording, and sharing of digital information between consenting parties, without the need for a central authority. DLT is based on the principle of peer-to-peer networking.

DLT   See *Distributed Ledger Technology*.

Domestic Card Scheme   A card scheme which operates only in one geography. Issuers can issue cards that are cobranded between a domestic card scheme and an open loop scheme (see *Cobranded Card*), in which case, these cards can be used domestically (through the domestic card scheme) and internationally (through the open loop card scheme, such as Visa or Mastercard).

DSAR   See *Data Subject Access Request*.

DTMF Masking   See *Dual Tone Multi-Frequency (DTMF) Masking*.

Dual Tone Multi-Frequency (DTMF) Masking   A technology deployed in telephone operations where the consumer enters their card number, expiry date, and security code using their telephone keypad during a telephone payment transaction, rather than speaking their payment card data. The telephone agent will not hear the phone tones (as these could be used to derive digits and therefore card numbers), helping with security and PCI DSS compliance.

Due Diligence   The process of conducting the relevant checks that a business or person should perform before entering into an agreement or contract with another party.

Durbin Amendment   A US regulation that caps interchange fees on debit cards.

Dynamic Currency Conversion   A value-added service that can be sold to merchants by payment service providers (PSPs) or independent software vendors (ISVs). It enables cardholders to see the amount of their transaction displayed in either their home currency or the local currency when using their card abroad. This service relies on a pricing structure involving exchange rates, conversion fees, and transaction fees.

Dynamic CVV   An enhancement to the card verification process whereby an issuer supplies the cardholder with a little device as well as a card. The little device calculates a dynamic CVV (dCVV) each time a remote transaction is initiated by the cardholder, and this is the three-digit number that the cardholder would use on an e-commerce website or over the telephone. This can also be achieved through the card itself, where a small electronic screen is embedded directly onto the back of the card to perform the same function. It is meant to replace the static CVV2. The cost of production of these cards/devices is such that deployments are quite rare.

EBA   See *European Banking Authority*.

EBA Clearing (STEP2 & RT1)   A bank payment scheme provided by EBA clearing and used in SEPA countries such as Germany, which doesn't have its own domestic bank payment scheme.

Ecosystem   A business ecosystem is an arrangement by which participants will create value for a common set of customers and share the benefits of value creation. Every business ecosystem has participants, and at least one member acts as the orchestrator of the participants. The most famous ecosystem is Amazon. A notable difference between an ecosystem and a value chain is that an ecosystem is not necessarily built around a fixed chain of processes and is all about seizing opportunities and innovating. The payments industry is at various stages of transitioning between value chains and ecosystems.

ECP   See *Excessive Chargebacks Program*.

EDD   See *Enhanced Due Diligence*.

eID   A generic term to describe electronic identification to ensure secure access to online services or carry out payment transactions.

EKS   Latvia's domestic bank payment scheme.

Electronic Money Institution   A regulated payment business allowed to manage eMoney on behalf of its users. In Europe, there are two types of eMoney institutions, the small eMoney institution (SEMI) and the authorised eMoney institution (EMI).

Electronic Payments Network (EPN)   A US ACH retail payment system (RPS) operated by TCH and governed by NACHA.

Electronic Point of Sale (EPOS)   A combination of hardware and software designed to help merchants accept card payments and run their business more effectively. Some providers specialise in specific industries and provide turnkey solutions (e.g. hospitality, retail, etc.). Their functionality may include features such as sales management, accounting, data collection, product, and stock management, as well as the capability to accept payments. Modern EPOS systems may include technologies such as touchscreen and apps. A type of point of sale (POS) system.

Embedded Finance   Describes services that integrate financial services like lending, payment processing, or insurance into non-financial business infrastructures, processes, or customer journeys.

EMD Agent   A small business that acts as an agent of an authorised eMoney institution (EMI), the latter being referred to as the "principal".

EMI   See *Electronic Money Institution*.

eMoney   A type of virtual asset. It is an electronic store of value that acts as a cash substitute and is issued by a regulated entity called an eMoney institution (EMI). It may be used for making payments to entities other than the issuer (unlike a virtual currency). Types of eMoney include prepaid cards, electronic prepaid accounts, and virtual payment accounts for use online.

EMV   The set of standards for cards.

EMV Card   A credit or debit card that follows the EMV chip standard. Also called a "chip card" and historically a "smart card".

EMV Chip   An EMV standard for chip cards. The EMV chip itself is an integrated circuit consisting of a microprocessor and a memory constructed according to ISO/IEC 7816 (contact) and ISO/IEC 14443 (contactless). The chip contains the data required for EMV transactions at the point of sale (POS).

EMVCo   A consortium controlled equally by Visa, Mastercard, American Express, UnionPay, and Discover. EMVCo is responsible for developing and maintaining EMV card standards. EMV takes its initials from Eurocard, Mastercard and Visa, the original founders in 1999. In 2002, Mastercard merged with Europay International SA, the owners of the Eurocard brand. Whilst the Europay name disappeared, the EMV name remains.

Enhanced Due Diligence (EDD)   The process by which businesses perform more stringent Customer Due Diligence (CDD) on customers at underwriting stage, or during the course of a business relationship. EDD is usually performed where the customer is not present when KYC is performed, when Politically Exposed Persons (PEPs) are involved, where the nature of the customer's business changes, where there is a high risk of money laundering or terrorism financing, or where the customer is in a high-risk country.

EPC Payment Scheme   The European Payments Council (EPC) Payment Scheme is used by thousands of payment service providers (PSPs) across Europe. To the EPC, a payment scheme represents the set of rules which PSPs have agreed upon to execute transactions through a specific instrument (e.g. credit transfer) and doesn't include the infrastructure to deliver them. What we generally call a "payment scheme" (i.e. card scheme, bank payment scheme) refers to the set of governing rules as well as the technical infrastructure that processes transactions (the EPC refers to these as "payment systems").

EPI   See *European Payments Initiative*.

EPOS   See *Electronic Point of Sale*.

EPN   See *Electronic Payments Network*.

Equens Worldline   The Netherlands' domestic bank payment scheme.

European Banking Authority (EBA)   An independent EU authority which works to ensure effective and consistent prudential regulation and supervision across the European banking sector.

European Payments Initiative (EPI)   In February 2021, 31 major European banks created a joint venture with acquirers Worldline and Nets (now owned by Nexi), aiming to build this pan-European network to rival Visa and Mastercard. In March 2022, the EPI seemingly disbanded, but in April 2023, at the time P27 collapsed, in a surprising move, the EPI acquired Dutch payment scheme iDeal and Belgian mobile payments App Payconiq, progress which was welcomed by the European Central Bank. Watch this space, as this may very well become the EU equivalent of the American Zelle.

E-Wallet   A web application that can be accessed from any connected device and is used to make payments, usually with several funding options (e.g. cards, bank accounts, etc.). PayPal is an example of an e-wallet.

Exceptions   Exceptions is a term to describe what happens when a card transaction is questioned or doesn't go as expected. Exceptions can lead to customer disputes. Types of exceptions include retrievals, refunds, and chargebacks.

Excessive Chargebacks Program (ECP)   A Mastercard merchant-monitoring programme to control fraud. In general, merchants will be included in a card scheme chargeback-monitoring programme if their chargeback ratio exceeds the card scheme limit. See *Merchant Monitoring Programme*.

Exchange Token   A type of utility token which is only used in a specific crypto exchange.

Exemption Threshold Value (ETV)   An indicator used in the context of the PSD2 Transaction Risk Analysis (TRA) exemption to Strong Customer Authentication (SCA). A transaction may qualify for the TRA exemption if its value is below the relevant ETV for that transaction type and the business complies with the reference fraud rate for that transaction type.

Factoring   See *Merchant Financing.*

Fast IDentity Online (FIDO)   A set of standards for authentication protocols ultimately aimed at eliminating passwords. The standards (e.g. WebAuthn) are managed by the FIDO Alliance, an open industry association with members from across the globe, including Amazon, Apple, Bank of America, American Express, Google, Intel, Idemia, Meta, PayPal, and many others.

Faster Payments System (FPS)   A UK domestic ACH Scheme. The FPS launched in 2008 and is the UK real-time payment system for payments up to £1 million. It allows customers to make electronic payments almost instantaneously, 7 days/week, 24h/day. FPS is managed by Pay.UK.

FATF   See *Financial Action Task Force.*

FedACH   A US ACH retail payment system (RPS) operated by the Federal Reserve Bank and governed by NACHA. An ACH Scheme.

FedNow   A US real-time retail payment system (RPS) operated by the Federal Reserve Bank and governed by NACHA. A bank payment scheme that launched in July 2023.

Fedwire   A US large-value payment system (LVPS) governed by NACHA and operated by the Federal Reserve Bank. A bank payment scheme.

Fedwire Number   See *ABA Routing Number.*

Fiat Money   Government-issued currency that is not backed by a physical commodity, such as gold or silver, but rather by the government that issued it. It derives its value from supply and demand, and the stability of the issuing government. Fiat money gives central banks greater control over the economy, as they can control how much money is printed. Fiat money has therefore no intrinsic value, and it is often referred to as "paper money". Governments have to make it legal tender by setting it as the standard for debt repayment. Most modern currencies are fiat money.

FIDO   See *Fast IDentity Online.*

Financial Action Task Force (FATF)   An independent intergovernmental body that develops and promotes policies to protect the global financial system against money laundering, terrorist financing, and the financing of the proliferation of weapons of mass destruction. The FATF is also known as GAFI (Groupe d'Action Financière), as it is headquartered in Paris. The FATF identifies countries with weak AML/CFT controls and lists them in two public documents that are published three times a year: the black list and the grey list.

Fintech   A very broad term used to describe any business that uses technology to improve, digitise, automate, or provide enablers to financial services aimed at businesses or consumers.

First Party Fraud   This happens when a payment account holder knowingly commits fraud. Sometimes referred to as "friendly fraud".

Form Factor   The medium with which a payment is made. It can be a plastic card, a mobile phone, or a wearable item (e.g. smartwatch, ring, etc.).

Four Party Model   A two-sided economic model by which there is a separation between acquirers and issuers. This promotes competition, as commercial terms can be set on either side (merchant and cardholder) to the benefit of merchants and cardholders. This model is also referred to as "open loop". Examples of card schemes operating on this model are Visa and Mastercard. The four parties referred to are the cardholder, the merchant, the acquirer, and the issuer.

FPS   See *Faster Payments System*.

Friendly Fraud   A term used to describe first party fraud. For example, when a cardholder tries to get money back on a purchase they made and for which they have received the goods. Nothing friendly about it. Sometimes called "cyber-shoplifting".

G2C   See *Government-to-Consumer*.

GAFI   See *Financial Action Task Force*.

GDPR   The EU General Data Protection Regulation.

Generative AI   A subset of deep learning, which itself is a subset of machine learning, the latter being an application of Artificial Intelligence (AI).

Girocard   A German domestic card scheme.

Governance Token   An upgraded version of a utility token which gives more rights to their holders (e.g. voting).

Government-to-Consumer (G2C)   A term used to describe a business model where a government entity provides services directly to consumers (e.g. tax, registration, educational services, employment help).

Grey List   See *Financial Action Task Force.*

High-Risk Acquirer   An acquirer which specialises in high-risk merchants. They typically charge higher fees.

High-Risk MCC   Merchants with a high-risk MCC will usually belong to industries that generate the highest levels of cardholder disputes, and represent higher levels of financial risk, or create additional brand risk for the card schemes (e.g. online pharmaceuticals, online gambling/gaming, online dating, etc.). In addition, card schemes may impose additional requirements for certain Card-Not-Present merchants within MCCs not necessarily classified as high risk (e.g. online tobacco sales vs retail tobacco sales). High-risk MCCs are subject to additional requirements from the card schemes.

High Risk Merchant   A merchant belonging to a high-risk sector.

High Risk Sector   When an industry or business sector experiences higher levels of chargebacks or fraud, the card schemes tend to classify them as "high risk". These will include travel, online pharmaceuticals, adult, dating, gaming, health and wellness, gambling, jewellery, and legal services. They can be subject to additional rules and/or permissions.

Hologram   A card security feature present on a physical credit or debit card originally designed to prevent fraudsters from cloning cards, as it is difficult to reproduce.

Hybrid Blockchain   A combination of permissioned and permissionless blockchains controlled by a central authority but also offering some permissionless elements. The controlling entity can make the blockchain accessible to everyone (through a public blockchain) whilst a permissioned blockchain controls ledger updates.

IBAN   See *International Bank Account Number.*

Iberpay   Spain's domestic bank payment scheme.

iCVV   See *Integrated Chip Card Verification Value.*

International Electrotechnical Commission (IEC)   An international standards organisation that prepares and publishes international standards for all electrical, electronic and related technologies. The standards collection addresses product development, performance, compatibility and related topics in order to ensure product compatibility and environmental safety.

IIN   See *Issuer Identification Number.*

Independent Sales Organisation (ISO)   Prepares and publishes international standards intended to ensure that products and services are safe, reliable, and of good quality. ISO standards cover a broad range of topics, unlike IEC standards, which are specific to electrical and electronic technologies.

Independent Software Vendor (ISV)   A technology provider that supplies technology enablers.

Indirect Payment Instruction   See *Payment Instruction*.

Indirectly Connected Participant   A bank payment scheme participant that is not directly connected to the payment scheme nor able to settle directly through the settlement agent. These participants will connect and settle funds through directly connected settling participants.

Integrated Chip Card Verification Value (iCVV)   An alternative card verification value (CVV) found on EMV cards, stored on the EMV chip. The iCVV is generated by the chip and the card payment terminal for each transaction (i.e. it is dynamic) using a different calculation from the one used for the CVV1 on the magstripe. Issuers use the iCVV to identify fraudulent use of chip cards in magstripe-read transactions. Also known as the CVV3.

Interac   Interac Corp. is a Canadian financial services business that serves multiple purposes. They operate the domestic debit card scheme Interac Debit (for which most Canadian banks are issuers) and ATM network throughout Canada, and through their partnership with NYCE terminals, Canadian Interac Debit cardholders can use their cards at 2 million US retailers. Interac is also the operator of three bank payment schemes: Interac e-Transfer for consumers and businesses, Interac e-Transfer Bulk (payables and receivables) for businesses, and Interac Bulk Disbursements, also for businesses. Interac also provides identity verification services, such as "Interac sign-in" for access to government services, "Interac verification services" for access to financial services, and the "Interac document verification" service for personal information verification using government-issued photo ID and advanced biometrics from participating service providers, eliminating the need for in-person visits to access online services that require proof of identity. Interac has also been selected by Payments Canada to provide the infrastructure for Canada's real-time payments rails.

Interbank Settlement   A centralised function coordinated by the payment scheme. On the card rails, interbank settlement is the process of moving funds between issuers and acquirers and is managed by the card scheme through their settlement agents. This is the first step of the settlement process for card payments. On the bank rails, interbank settlement happens between banks through the settlement agent (a central bank) for a given bank payment scheme.

Interchange   An ecosystem funding mechanism specific to the card rails. It is a percentage of the card transaction value. In the Four Party Model, this amount flows from the acquirer to the issuer. In some countries, such as the EU, interchange is regulated, but the interchange rules are specified by the card schemes (within applicable regulations).

Interchange +   A pricing model by which a merchant will be able to see the merchant service charge (MSC) split between the interchange and the rest, but both card scheme fees and acquirer margin will be amalgamated into a fixed percentage on top on the interchange fee. This model offers less transparency than Interchange++, but the merchant still sees the interchange. This is typically used for larger merchants.

Interchange ++   A pricing model by which a merchant will be able to see the merchant service charge (MSC) split between interchange, card scheme fees, and acquirer margin. This is the most transparent of pricing model. This is typically used by acquirers for larger merchants, although regulations in some geographies may force acquirers (and others) to use this pricing model for all merchants.

Interchange Fee Regulation (IFR)   A European regulation that caps interchange fees on some cards.

Internal Security Assessor (ISA)   A qualified security professional who can be used as an alternative to a Qualified Security Assessor (QSA) for validating PCI compliance. ISAs are listed on the PCI SSC web site and must renew their certification annually. ISAs are generally used by larger companies.

International Bank Account Number (IBAN)   An internationally agreed-upon system of identifying bank accounts across national borders to facilitate the communication and processing of cross-border transactions with a reduced risk of transcription errors.

Internet of Things (IoT)   Describes the network of physical objects – things – that contain sensors, software, and other technologies enabling them to connect and exchange data with other devices and systems over the internet.

Invoice Factoring   See *Factoring*.

IoT   See *Internet of Things*.

ISA   See *Internal Security Assessor*.

ISO   See *International Organization for Standardization* or *Independent Sales Organisation*.

ISO 13616   A standard by which an IBAN is constructed.

ISO/IEC 14443   A standard for contactless card transactions. Applied as an EMV standard for the EMV chip structure for contactless transactions.

ISO 18092   A standard for Near Field Communication (NFC). Information Technology – Telecommunications and Information Exchange between Systems – Near Field Communication – Interface and Protocol (NFCIP-1). 2013.

ISO 18245   A standard for Merchant Category Codes (MCCs).

ISO 20022   A modern messaging standard for data interchange between financial institutions, and prior to its release in 2004, large-value payment systems (LVPS) used SWIFT messaging, and retail payment systems (RPSs) used ISO 8583. Unlike ISO 8583, ISO 20022 data is machine readable (not sequential) and uses XML (Extensible Markup Language) and ASN.1 (Abstract Syntax Notation). It can significantly streamline payment messaging by providing richer data, more transparency, better interoperability (e.g. standardising non-Latin alphabets), and adapting to changing needs and business models. ISO 20022 involves the processing of much larger data volumes, and payment ecosystem actors need to update their infrastructures to manage the additional information, which means substantial investment. ISO 20022 is particularly fundamental to modern real-time payments (RTP) infrastructures.

ISO 21481   A standard for Near Field Communication (NFC). Information Technology – Telecommunications and Information Exchange between Systems – Near Field Communication Interface and Protocol 2 (NFCIP-2). 2021.

ISO/IEC 7812   The standard by which a Primary Account Number (PAN) is constructed for six-digit BIN cards. ISO 7812-2 is the standard for eight-digit BIN cards.

ISO 7813   The standard by which the magnetic stripe on a payment card is constructed. A magnetic stripe contains two tracks commonly referred to as "Track 1" and "Track 2".

ISO/IEC 7816   A standard for contact card transactions. Applied as an EMV standard for the EMV chip structure for contact transactions.

ISO 8583   The payment messaging standard used to communicate between card payment ecosystem actors. This legacy messaging standard is also used by other payments ecosystems (bank payment schemes). ISO 8583 is an old standard and uses a bitmap format where each data element is assigned a specific position and is processed sequentially (i.e. as it is being read). It has been used since 1987 and is now on its third version (2003). ISO 8583 is now considered a legacy standard, although card schemes use this protocol and there is no evidence that they are planning to move away from it.

Issuer   An Account Servicing PSP (ASPSP) on the card rails. They provide and manage the cardholder account. An issuer can be a bank, or a non-bank payment service provider (PSP).

Issuer Identification Number   See *Bank Identification Number*.

Issuer Processor   An ecosystem actor which connects issuers to card schemes. The issuer processor is not a bank or an issuer. In a similar fashion to a bank wanting to provide acquiring services and outsourcing the processes to a non-bank acquirer (hence the term "processor" sometimes being used for these entities). Issuer processors are an important part of the ecosystem, and they have facilitated quick time to market for many fintechs and new entrants, as well as incumbent issuers plagued by old technology.

Issuing   The process of creating and managing card products for cardholders. These products can be physical or virtual, and may take many forms, including consumer credit cards, commercial cards, and debit cards.

Issuing Bank   An issuer that is also a bank.

Issuing Clearing File   A card scheme collects all the acquiring clearing files from their acquiring members for that day, in line with their clearing and settlement processes. They will then collate and reconcile them to produce the issuing clearing files. A card scheme will produce as many issuing clearing files as there are issuing members for that scheme. Issuers will use these files to settle their positions with the settlement agent.

ISV   See *Independent Software Vendor*.

itsme app   A privately led digital identity service in Belgium.

JCB   A card scheme operating on the Three Party Model.

Know Your Customer (KYC)   A process to verify a customer's identity through an independent, reliable source.

KYC   See *Know Your Customer.*

Large-Value Payment System (LVPS)   A bank payment scheme that is designed for high-value payments.

Level 1   The first data level for card transactions. Level 1 data is typically associated with consumer transactions and provides limited purchase data. All merchants will be able to accept these transactions, physically or virtually, and all cards (e.g. consumer, commercial, corporate, government, etc.) can be accepted that way.

Level 2   The second data level for card transactions. Level 2 data adds more information to benefit the corporate/government/industrial buyer. Commercial, corporate, purchasing, and government cards are eligible for Level 2 processing, but not consumer cards (which can only be processed at Level 1). Historically, the amount of extra data transmitted in a card transaction by a merchant has been limited only by the capabilities of hardware point of sale (POS) terminals.

Level 3   The third data level for card transactions. Level 3 data provides line-item detail equivalent to the information found on an itemised invoice. Historically, these transactions could only be accepted virtually (i.e. through a payment gateway) and often integrated with enterprise resource planning (ERP) platforms such as SAP or Oracle NetSuite. This is because they were beyond the capabilities of traditional hardware POS terminals (as many of the data elements require text input, and standard card terminals have basic numeric keypads). Increasingly, modern card payment terminals offer Level 3 capability through touchscreen technology (see *Smart POS*).

Liability Shift   The process by which a liability is shifted from one party to the other. In the card payments industry, when fraud happens in the Card Present channel, the liability is shifted from the merchant to the issuer. When fraud happens in the e-commerce channel, liability will be shifted from the merchant to the issuer if the merchant has authenticated the transaction using 3D Secure. There is no liability shift for the MOTO channel at the time of writing, although this may change with newer versions of 3D Secure.

Load Balancing   Usually refers to the practice of merchants sourcing acquiring services from multiple acquirers so as to reduce their chargeback ratio. Using load balancing to reduce the chargeback ratio is not good practice and could lead to merchants being blacklisted, but load balancing may be used for legitimate purposes (e.g. not putting all your acquiring eggs in one basket).

Luhn Algorithm   Also known as Modulus 10. A mathematical formula used to validate a card number.

LVPS   See *Large-Value Payment System.*

Machine Learning (ML)   A subset of Artificial Intelligence (AI).

Magnetic Stripe   A data container in a physical card constructed in accordance with ISO/IEC 7813 and embodied in two magnetic tracks used for data storage: Track 1 and Track 2. Also known as magstripe.

Magstripe   See *Magnetic Stripe.*

Mail Order Telephone Order (MOTO)   The term used to describe card payment transactions conducted over the telephone or via mail order.

Major Industry Identifier (MII)   The first digit in the card number. It identifies the industry or type of card (e.g. 1 = airlines).

Marketplace   Traditionally, a marketplace is a trading environment, such as eBay, Amazon, or Etsy, which connects buyers with multiple sellers and maintains complete control over the payment transactions, their fulfilment, and the end-to-end customer experience. With a marketplace, a cardholder intends to buy a product or service, and the marketplace will offer these products or services from multiple sellers. Marketplaces also come in other forms on different infrastructures (e.g. Web 3.0), such as NFT marketplaces.

Master Merchant   See *Merchant of Record.*

Mastercard   A card scheme operating on the Four Party Model.

MCC   See *Merchant Category Code.*

Merchant   A term generally describing an entity that provides goods or services and is able to accept card payments. A merchant can be virtual (e.g. e-commerce) or physical (e.g. a brick-and-mortar shop). Increasingly, this term is also used to describe businesses that accept bank payments.

Merchant Acquirer   See *Acquirer.*

Merchant Aggregator   See *Payment Aggregator.*

Merchant Bank   See *Acquirer.*

Merchant Category Code (MCC)   Used to classify a business by the types of goods or services they provide. Good News! In an attempt to provide consistency across the card payments ecosystem, an international standard (ISO 18245) is used for this four-digit identifier, but there will be variations across card schemes.

Merchant Financing   A value-added service that has seen a resurgence of popularity during the pandemic and can be offered to merchants on the card rails. There are two forms of merchant financing. A merchant cash advance is a form of debt financing that involves a merchant borrowing money based on their projected sales. Providers of such services include YouLend, 365 Business Finance, Nucleus Commercial Finance, and Liberis Ltd, to name but a few. Factoring (aka invoice factoring) is another form of merchant financing, and it involves the sale of unpaid invoices to a third party at a discount. Merchant financing is a form of alternative finance or embedded finance.

Merchant ID (MID)   Given to a business when they are onboarded directly by an acquirer or by an ISO. This is, in effect, their customer number and is a unique code linked with the merchant's bank account. The MID identifies a merchant to their acquirer (either directly, or indirectly through their partner ISO).

Merchant-Initiated Transaction (MIT)   A payment that is initiated by the merchant, according to the agreement they have with the cardholder, which allows them to initiate a payment on the cardholder's behalf.

Merchant Level   This term is generally used in the context of PCI DSS, and there are three merchant levels:

- Level 1: those who process more than 6 million transactions annually per card scheme
- Level 2: those who process between 1 and 6 million transactions annually per card scheme
- Level 3: e-commerce merchants who process between 20,000 and 6 million transactions per card scheme
- Level 4: those who process less than 20,000 transactions annually per card scheme and all other merchants

There are different PCI DSS validation requirements (e.g. SAQ, ROC), depending on the merchant level.

Merchant Loyalty   A value-added service that can be offered to merchants by payment service providers (PSPs) or independent software vendors (ISVs). The benefits offered to consumers through the merchant loyalty programme can either be funded by the merchant or the partner, or the consumer (i.e. via membership).

Merchant Monitoring Programme   A card scheme programme to monitor merchant compliance with operating regulations. Generally associated with fraud monitoring.

Merchant of Record   A payment aggregation model targeting smaller merchants which want to accept card payments but may not be able to afford (or be approved to get) payment services directly from and acquirer or an ISO. Also referred to as "master merchant".

Merchant Onboarding   A process involving assessing merchant risk and contracting with the merchant. This step is about ascertaining whether the merchant's potential value is worth the risk, and therefore the cost.

Merchant Plug In   See *3D Secure Server*.

Merchant Service Charge (MSC)   What a merchant pays an acquirer.

MSC = interchange + card scheme fees + acquirer margin

There are various ways of presenting the MSC to merchants, depending on a number of factors (e.g. size, risk), some more transparent than others (see *Interchange+*, *Interchange++* and *Blended Pricing*).

Merchant Services   A generic term used to describe services provided to merchants to enable them to connect to a card scheme.

Merchant Services Provider (MSP)   A generic term that describes an organisation that provides merchant services, such as an ISO or a payfac.

Merchant Settlement   The second and final step of the settlement process on the card rails, by which the acquirer will credit the merchant account according to their commercial contract. Acquirers may decide to defer merchant settlement as a risk management tool for certain industries (e.g. airlines, hospitality).

Merchant's PSP   A payment services provider (PSP) that provides technology to merchants to enable them to connect to a card scheme. See *Payee's PSP*.

Metaverse   A virtual reality space in which users can interact with a computer-generated environment and other users.

MFA   See *Multi-Factor Authentication*.

MID   See *Merchant ID*.

MII   See *Major Industry Identifier*.

MIT   See *Merchant-Initiated Transaction*.

MitID   A digital identity framework in Denmark which replaced the NemID framework in June 2023.

ML   See *Machine Learning*.

MLRO   See *Money Laundering Reporting Officer*.

MNO   See *Mobile Network Operator*.

Mobiilivarmenne   A digital identity framework in Finland which is a partnership between telcos.

Mobile Money   A way to store and manage money in an account linked to a mobile phone, similar to a bank account. Most mobile money services allow users to purchase items in shops or online, pay bills and school fees, and top-up mobile airtime. Cash withdrawals can also be carried out at authorised agents. Most mobile money services are offered by local mobile telecom operators. A type of mobile payment that doesn't rely on a formal financial services infrastructure (e.g. bank accounts).

Mobile Network Operator (MNO)   A telecommunications services provider that supplies wireless voice and data communication to its subscribed mobile users. Also referred to as a "carrier service provider", "mobile phone operator", "mobile network carrier", "mobile carrier", or, simply, "carrier".

Mobile Payment   A broad term to describe payment facilities that have a mobile element. It encompasses mobile banking, mobile wallets, mobile money, and even mobile payment acceptance. Mobile payments can be classified in two categories: those that necessitate a formal payment instrument as the underlying payment mechanism (e.g. card or bank account), and those that don't (e.g. use of cash).

Mobile Point of Sale (mPOS)   A physical device, usually proprietary to its manufacturer, which can be either attached to a standard mobile phone (e.g. a dongle) or used on its own by a merchant to enable mobility (e.g. market traders) at a relatively low cost. mPOS solutions have evolved in recent years and may take many forms: tablet-based systems, mobile-phone-based systems, terminal-based systems, etc.

Mobile Wallet   A payment facility tied to a mobile hardware device that usually uses cards as the funding option.

Modulus 10   See *Luhn Algorithm*.

Money Laundering   Concealing the origin of money obtained from illegal activities such as drug trafficking, corruption, embezzlement, or gambling, by converting it into a legitimate source. There are three stages of money laundering – placement, layering, and integration – that allow illicit funds to enter the legitimate financial system, obfuscate their origins, and then to reintegrate them so as to appear as legal tender. A form of financial crime.

Money Laundering Reporting Officer (MLRO)   An employee appointed to oversee a firm's compliance with Anti-Money Laundering (AML) regulations and to alert the company where there is knowledge or suspicion of money laundering.

Money Remittance   A payment service by which funds are sent by a payer to a payee where no payment account needs to be opened in the name of either the payer or payee.

Money Transfer Operator (MTO)   A financial company (usually not a bank) engaged in money remittance including cross-border transfer of funds. MTOs use their internal systems and/or access to banking networks. The MTO will use their own banking relationships and each country's bank payment capabilities where they can.

MOTO   See *Mail Order Telephone Order*.

Merchant Plug-In (MPI)   See *3D Secure Server*.

mPOS   See *Mobile Point of Sale*.

MSC   See *Merchant Service Charge*.

MSP   See *Merchant Services Provider*.

MT Message   A legacy SWIFT message type (i.e. prior to ISO 2002).

MTO   See *Money Transfer Operator*.

Multi-Factor Authentication (MFA)   The use of two or more authentication factors when authenticating payment account holders and users.

MX Message   A SWIFT message type that complies with ISO 2002.

myID.be   A government-issued digital identity in Belgium.

NACHA   See *National Automated Clearing House Association*.

National Automated Clearing House Association (NACHA)   The US governance body for some US bank payment schemes. NACHA is also an accreditation body.

National Citizen ID   A government issued digital identity in Finland.

Near Field Communication (NFC)   A contactless interface. Contactless-enabled cards and contactless-enabled card payment terminals use this interface.

NemID   A digital identity framework in Denmark.

Network Vulnerability Scan   A software facility provided by ASVs which inspects the potential points of exploit on a computer or network to identify security holes. A vulnerability scan detects and classifies system weaknesses in computers, networks, and communications equipment and predicts the effectiveness of countermeasures. Also referred to as an "ASV scan".

Nexi (formerly Sia)   Italy's domestic bank payment scheme.

NextGenPSD2 An open banking standard originally proposed by the Berlin Group, and on which all national EU open banking standards are based.

NFC See *Near Field Communication*.

NFT See *Non-Fungible Token*.

Non-Fungible Token (NFT) A type of crypto asset that has been tokenised on a blockchain and assigned a unique identification. Non-fungible means "unique", and therefore can't be replicated. An NFT is different from other crypto assets, or fiat currencies, which are interchangeable. NFTs are largely unregulated, unless they come in scope of securities regulations.

Offline Bank Transfer A payment method that breaks the payment process into two stages. First, the user would complete a transaction on the platform used and will be given the destination bank account details and other information, including a transaction identifier. Second, the user will make a payment through their bank to the platform with the details provided. They could also pay cash later at an affiliated outlet or store. Once the second stage is completed, the transaction would be considered complete on the platform. This is a form of "delayed payment". Many PSPs offer this payment method to merchants, and it is popular in some geographies.

Open API A communication interface that follows a public standard or set of standards that are available for developers to use.

Open Banking Refers to the use of open APIs that enable Third Party PSPs (TPPs) to build and provide account information or payment initiation services through data access to payment accounts managed by Account Servicing PSPs (ASPSPs).

Open Banking Payment A subset of A2A payments that follow agreed standards of interoperability, such as open APIs.

Open Finance An evolution of open banking where data sharing extends beyond payment account data into wider financial services data.

Open Loop See *Four Party Model*.

Operating Regulations This usually refers to the rules set by a card scheme for the operation and governance of their network.

Operating Rules See *Operating Regulations*.

Overlay Service A term generally used in the bank payment context, but also applies to the card rails. These are services implemented on top of an existing payment scheme. Some bank payment examples are Confirmation of Payee, request-to-pay, and Variable Recurring Payments. On the card rails, 3D Secure can be considered and overlay service.

P27   The P27 cross-border real-time A2A payment system aimed to combine eight bank payment schemes across the Nordics into one integrated real-time bank scheme, but it collapsed in April 2023 due to a lack of political alignment and critical mass, as well as conflicts of interest.

P2P   See *Peer-to-Peer*.

PAN   See *Primary Account Number*.

PAN Key Entry   A Card Not Present (CNP) payment transaction by which a merchant enters the cardholder details into a payment terminal. This is a type of merchant-initiated transaction (MIT) usually associated with MOTO. These transactions are not authenticated, and therefore expensive to process for merchants.

Passport Arrangement   See *Passporting Arrangement*.

Passporting Arrangement   A term used in Europe to describe the process by which a payment firm authorised to conduct business by one country's regulator is able to conduct business in all countries in the EU block without having to be authorised by the other regulators.

Pay-by-Link   A payment method by which a customer is able to make a payment through a web payment link sent to them whilst they're on the phone, chat, or social media channel. This means that card details don't have to be shared during the interaction. Pay-by-link is a value-added service that can be offered by a payment service provider (PSP) or independent software vendor (ISV) for merchants to integrate within their environment.

Payee   The entity or person that gets paid. See *Payment Service User*.

Payee's PSP   The ecosystem actor which enables a payee to accept payments. On the card rails, they provide merchants with the connectivity to the acquirer. They can be either physical (e.g. payment terminal provider) or virtual (e.g. e-commerce payment gateway). Sometimes, these are also referred to as payment service providers (PSPs) or managed service providers (MSPs), which can be a bit confusing! Context is important. On the bank rails, it can be any entity that provides payment functionality enabling a business to accept bank payments.

Payer   The entity or person who pays. See *Payment Service User*.

Payer's PSP   A payment service provider (PSP) that provides a payer with a payment account. Also referred to as an Account Servicing PSP (ASPSP). On the card rails, they provide the payer with a card account and are also referred to as an "issuer". On the bank rails, this entity is a bank, and they provide a payer with a bank account.

Payfac   See *Payment Facilitator*.

Payment Acceptance   The process by which merchants take payments by card. Also referred to as card acceptance.

Payment Aggregator   An aggregator of payment services. This is a generic term, and to understand its nuances you need to look at specific models, such as merchants of record, payment facilitator, ISO, etc.

Payment Card Industry Data Security Standard (PCI DSS)   A data security standard developed and maintained by the PCI SSC. It applies to all organisations which store, process, or transmit cardholder information, either electronically or manually. Card schemes include PCI DSS compliance in their operating regulations and may levy penalties on their members and stakeholders for non-compliance. Acquirers are responsible for ensuring the PCI compliance of their merchant portfolios. Card schemes manage the compliance of service providers directly.

Payment Card Industry Standards Security Council (PCI SSC)   A council founded by American Express, Discover, JCB International, Mastercard, and Visa, and UnionPay is a strategic member. The PCI SCC is a body similar to EMVCo and is responsible for the development and maintenance of PCI standards. It encourages industry participation through various programmes, including "Participating Organisations", "Affiliate Members", and "Special Interest Groups".

Payment Facilitator   A type of payment aggregator. A payment facilitator, such as Stripe or PayPal, connects one buyer with one seller. The cardholder intends to buy from the seller and may not even know that a payfac is involved, as they only facilitate the payment. With a payfac, the seller is responsible for the fulfilment and end-to-end customer experience. This is a payment aggregation model that offers merchant services on a sub-merchant platform. Those sub-merchants then no longer have to get their own merchant ID (MID) and can instead be boarded under the master MID of the payment facilitator.

Payment Gateway   A type of merchant PSP on the card rails. They supply merchants with the technology to enable them to accept online card payments on their websites. See *Payee's PSP*.

Payment Initiation Service Provider (PISP)   A Third Party PSP (TPP) which initiates payments on behalf of a payer.

Payment Institution (PI)   A regulated payment business that is able to receive payments, remit money, issue cards, but can't store value. In Europe, there are two types of payment institutions, the small payment institution (SPI) and the authorised payment institution (PI).

Payment Instruction   The process by which a payer instructs their Account Servicing PSP (ASPSP), such as a bank, to perform a payment. A payment instruction can be direct (e.g. the bank account holder makes a payment through their online banking facility), or indirect (the bank account holder makes a payment through a digital wallet). Sometimes called "Payment Order".

Payment Method   A facility that a payer (e.g. cardholder or bank account holder) will use to make payments.

Payment Page   The customer-facing part of a virtual terminal that is integrated into a merchant's environment (e.g. online shop). For telephone sales, a virtual terminal can be used by the merchant, and this is where they would enter the cardholder's details as supplied by the cardholder over the phone. See *Payee's PSP*.

Payment Scheme   Generally, this refers to the ecosystem actor which provides the centralised payments infrastructure and operating rules. For the card rails, examples of payment schemes are Visa, Mastercard, American Express, etc., and these are also referred to as "card schemes", "card networks", or "card brands". For the bank rails, examples of payment schemes are UK FPS, US FedACH, etc. In Europe, however, a SEPA payment scheme only refers to the operating rules and technical specifications for the scheme (e.g. SEPA credit transfer). SEPA refers to the payment schemes mentioned above as "payment systems".

Payment Service User (PSU)   The ecosystem actor which uses payment services. If the actor makes a payment, they are referred to as a "payer", and if they receive a payment, they are referred to as a "payee". On the card rails, the PSU can be the actor which pays with a card, referred to as a "cardholder", or the PSU who gets paid with a card, referred to as a "merchant". On the bank rails, the PSUs are bank account holders.

Payment System   A card scheme or bank payment scheme.

Payment Terminal   A payment facility to enable merchants to accept card payments. Payment terminals can be physical (hardware) or virtual (digital). See also POS, EPOS, mPOS, SoftPOS, Payment Page, Virtual Terminal, and Unattended Payment Terminal.

Payments Optimisation   The process by which a merchant optimises their card payment acceptance fees. Acquirers, merchant PSPs, and professional services firms can offer this service.

Payment Services Provider (PSP)   Any entity providing a payment service in a payments ecosystem.

Paytech   A term used to describe technology used in the payments ecosystem. A subset of fintech.

PCI DSS   See Payment Card Industry Data Security Standard.

PCI SSC   See Payment Card Industry Standards Security Council.

Peer-to-Peer (P2P)   A generic term used to describe services, platforms, or facilities that seemingly enable interactions between peers. It is used interchangeably with person-to-person, a term I have also used in this book (based on the sources).

Peer-to-Peer Money Exchange   A type of fintech company challenging traditional Money Transfer Operators (MTOs) and bank wire transfers. Instead of using correspondent banking and cross-border transactions, they "crowd-source" fund transfer matches in each of the countries involved in a fund transfer. And then, theoretically, they only need to perform domestic bank transactions at each end, making them cheaper.

Peer-to-Peer Networking   A principle by which peers communicate with each other without the need for a central authority or intermediary.

Peer-to-Peer Payments   A misnomer. Used to describe digital payment apps such as Venmo or Zelle. To the users, it looks like they're making a payment directly to their friend (or supplier, etc.) without intermediaries (hence peer-to-peer). This is not the case. Regardless of the rails used (i.e. card or bank), these payments still need to go through the existing mechanisms (i.e. authorisation, clearing and settlement), and therefore through intermediaries.

PEP   See Politically Exposed Person.

Permissioned Blockchain A blockchain controlled by a central entity where access is restricted to certain nodes, and rights also can be restricted.

Permissionless Blockchain A blockchain where any user can join (i.e. become a node).

Personal Identification Number (PIN) This is an authentication factor consisting of a number of digits that only a payment account holder should know.

PI See *Payment Institution.*

PIN See *Personal Identification Number.*

PISP See *Payment Initiation Service Provider.*

Pix A domestic real-time retail payment system (RPS) in Brazil.

Point of Sale (POS) A system used by businesses to manage sales transactions. In the past, a POS in a shop would consist of a cash register and a ledger to record purchases and sales. Today, we have dedicated electronic terminals and solutions to automate the processes – from customer purchases to inventory management. In the payments world, the term "POS" is used interchangeably with "POS terminal".

PolishAPI The Polish open banking standard.

Politically Exposed Person (PEP) Usually a member of government, parliament, etc., their family members, and known close associates. The exact way PEPs should be treated with regard to Anti-Money Laundering (AML) regulation will depend on the specific regulation.

PoS See *Proof of Stake.*

POS See *Point of Sale.*

Post Pay A payment method by which consumers order goods online and pay for them later at affiliated outlets or stores. The delay between the initial order and the payment means that this isn't suited for perishable goods and time-sensitive purchases. A form of delayed payment.

PoW See *Proof of Work.*

Predicate Offence A crime that forms part of a larger crime.

Prepaid Card Generally refers to open loop prepaid cards which run on card scheme networks. They can be used in the same way as a debit card or credit cards. The key difference is that they need to be loaded up with funds in advance.

Prepay Card Cards which are not run on card scheme networks and are usually authorised immediately. Consumers need to buy a card or voucher before starting a transaction. These can be referred to as "stored value cards" and will be denominated in the currency in use for the specified amount. Increasingly, these are delivered as virtual cards.

Primary Account Number (PAN)   The card number, which is constructed according to the ISO/IEC 7812 (identification cards) standard. Usually 16 digits but can be up to 19 digits.

Private API   A communication interface specific to one organisation. Its use can only be granted by that organisation.

Private Blockchain   A type of permissioned blockchain controlled by one authority.

Programme Manager   Generally associated with the prepaid card industry. A programme manager acts as an aggregator between the different parties in the card payments value chain through "BIN sponsorship" agreements with an Issuer. Programme managers bring quick time to market for their clients as they bring market knowledge. A programme manager is different from an Issuer Processor as they build the card programme functionality and technology that will exist on the Issuer Processor platform. Some programme managers are also Issuer Processors.

Proof of Stake (PoS)   A blockchain consensus protocol by which validators stake their own funds. A coin/token is picked randomly from all staked funds. The owner of the "winning" coin gets to add their block to the chain.

Proof of Work (PoW)   A blockchain consensus protocol by which miners compete to solve a cryptographic puzzle. Whomever solves the puzzle first gets to add their block to the chain.

PSD Agent   A small business that acts as an agent of an authorised payment institution (PI), the latter being referred to as the "principal".

PSD2   See *Second Payment Services Directive*.

PSD3   The EU Third Payment Services Directive.

PSP   See *Payment Services Provider*.

Payment Services Regulator (PSR)   Also referred to as Payment Services Regulation.

PSU   See *Payment Service User*.

Public Blockchain   A type of permissionless blockchain.

QR Code   An authentication method for payments. Particularly popular in Asia but gaining popularity in other parts of the world.

QSA   See *Qualified Security Assessor.*

QSAC   See *Qualified Security Assessor Company.*

Qualified Security Assessor   An individual employed by a Qualified Security Assessor Company (QSAC) who is certified by the PCI SSC as a PCI compliance assessor. They need to have specific information security knowledge, and their certification must be renewed annually with the PCI SSC. QSAs are used by businesses to validate their compliance with the PCI standards.

Qualified Security Assessor Company (QSAC)   An independent security company that meets specific requirements and has been qualified by the PCI SSC to employ QSAs. QSACs are listed on the PCI SSC website.

RAISP   An Account Information Service Provider (AISP) that has registered with their regulator.

Real-Time Bank Transfer   A payment method that allows users to make online payments in real time using the bank rails. Usually for online and mobile banking.

Real-Time Gross Settlement   See *Settlement Cycle.*

Real-Time Gross Settlement Account (RTGS Account)   An account held by a bank or authorised non-bank institution at a central bank or central monetary authority.

Real-Time Payment System   A bank payment scheme where settlement happens in real time or near real time.

Recurring Transaction   A type of payment transaction where the payment account holder gives a payee (e.g. merchant) their payment account details (e.g. card account details), so they can take regular payments from them. The payment will be made at a regular frequency, for example, once a year or once a month, without account holder intervention. On the card rails, recurring transactions are also known as "card on file" transactions, subscription transactions and continuous payment authority (CPA) transactions. For this type of transaction, the merchant stores the card details on their system. A type of merchant-initiated transaction (MIT). On the bank rails, Direct Debits, standing orders, and Variable Recurring Payments can be considered recurring transactions.

Refund   A type of payment transaction and is a relatively simple process, as it is a purchase process in reverse. This process is invoked by the payer. After clearing and settlement, the amount of the refund is credited to the payer's account and a corresponding debit will be made to the payee's account.

Reference Fraud Rate   An indicator used in the context of the PSD2 Transaction Risk Analysis (TRA) exemption to Strong Customer Authentication (SCA). A transaction may qualify for the TRA exemption if the business can demonstrate, for that transaction type, that they maintain an overall quarterly fraud rate as specified by the reference fraud rate for the exemption threshold value, as set by the PSD2 regulations.

Regtech   Refers to any business that uses technology to improve, digitise, automate, or provide enablers to help organisations manage their increasing regulatory compliance commitments. It is most usefully applied to heavily regulated sectors such as financial services, healthcare, or gaming.

Regulatory Sandbox   A safe environment provided by regulators to enable the testing of new, innovative technologies, services, or approaches which are not fully compliant with the existing legal and regulatory frameworks. This can take place using near-real-life data (synthetic) or real-life data.

Regulatory Technical Standard (RTS)   Technical standard specifications published by the European Banking Authority in support of the deployment of European regulations.

Report on Compliance (ROC)   Produced by a Qualified Security Assessor (QSA) or an Internal Security Assessor (ISA) when they validate the PCI DSS compliance of a business. A ROC must be renewed annually for businesses in scope (see *Merchant Level*). ROC templates can be found on the PCI SSC website.

Request for Information   See *Retrieval*.

Request-to-Pay (RtP)   An overlay service on the bank rails; it is similar in intent to sending an invoice. RtP involves a payee (e.g. a supplier of goods or services) initiating a digital payment request from a payer, without having to send an invoice. It caters for modern behaviours. For example, the payer can receive the request through their mobile device, or their banking app, or via a Third Party PSP (TPP). But RtP is not just about digital invoicing: it gives more flexibility to payers. For each payment request, a payer may choose to pay in full, in part (asking for more time), or decline to pay altogether. A payer can also communicate with the payee through this service. Because of this flexibility, and the hoped-for outcome that it would help people avoid falling into debt, it could save money at a national level. Not all bank payment schemes can support RtP, and of course banks and other payment service providers (PSPs) need to deploy it for it to be available to bank account holders.

Retail CBDC A type of central bank digital currency (CBDC) for general-purpose domestic use, including B2C, B2B, P2P, and G2C.

Retail Payment System (RPS) A term used to describe ACH Schemes that typically handle high volumes of low-value retail payments.

Retail Settlement A term used on the bank rails to describe how funds will be moved to a consumer's bank account. This is the equivalent of merchant settlement on the card rails and happens after interbank settlement. However, whereas merchant settlement is contingent to contractual arrangements, retail settlement times apply to everyone in the same way according to the bank payment scheme rules.

Retrieval A process on the card rails to request information about a transaction. This process can be invoked by a cardholder when they don't recognise a transaction on their card statement. The process can also be invoked directly by the issuer of the card if a transaction is flagged by their fraud prevention systems. Sometimes called a "request for information" or "retrieval request".

Retrieval Request See *Retrieval*.

ROC See *Report on Compliance*.

Routing Transit Number See *ABA Routing Number*.

RPS See *Retail Payment System*.

RTGS See *Real-Time Gross Settlement*.

RTGS Account See *Real-Time Gross Settlement Account*.

RTN See *ABA Routing Number*.

RtP See *Request-to-Pay*.

RTP® A US real-time payment scheme privately operated by The Clearing House and governed by NACHA.

RTS See *Regulatory Technical Standard*.

Safeguarding A requirement on regulated firms to keep clients' funds completely separate from their operational funds. The bank account where customer funds are kept is referred to as a "safeguarding account".

SAQ   See *Self-Assessment Questionnaire.*

SAR   See *Suspicious Activity Reporting.*

SCA   See *Strong Customer Authentication.*

sCBDC   See *Synthetic CBDC.*

Scheme Membership   The permissions necessary for a payment service provider (PSP) or Account Servicing PSP (ASPSP) to participate in a given card scheme. There are two types of memberships: principal (settling) and affiliate (non-settling). Affiliate members must be sponsored by principal members. Prospective members must have the appropriate regulatory credentials from their competent authority.

Screen Scraping   A method of accessing data by which an account holder shares their account login credentials with a Third Party PSP (TPP). The TPP then uses the account holder's credentials to access the account and copies or "scrapes" the data for use outside of the account holder's account facility (e.g. online banking portal). This is, outside of Europe, still a popular method. Apart from the fact that bank account holders would most probably be in breach of their bank's terms and conditions (i.e. sharing of credentials with outside parties), this method is not very secure, especially in financial services. In Europe, PSD2 banned screen scraping. Screen scraping is sometimes referred to as "direct access".

SCT   See *SEPA Credit Transfer.*

SCT Inst   See *SEPA Instant Credit Transfer.*

SDD B2B   See *SEPA Direct Debit B2B.*

SDD Core   See *SEPA Direct Debit.*

SDK   See *Software Development Kit.*

Second Payment Services Directive   The EU Second Payment Services Directive (PSD2) is a regulatory framework that came into force in 2018 and was the catalyst for open banking worldwide.

Security Token   A type of crypto asset that is an investment contract representing the legal ownership of a digital, physical, or intangible asset. Security token investors aim to generate a profit (e.g. dividend payments, interest, profit share, residual rights). Security tokens are regulated under applicable securities regulations and can only be traded on regulated platforms.

Self-Assessment Questionnaire (SAQ)   A form that businesses may use to self-validate PCI DSS compliance, and there are several options depending on the type and size of the merchant (see *Merchant Level*). SAQs are found in the PCI SSC Document Library. Not all merchants are allowed to self-validate.

Semantic Web   See *Web 3.0.*

SEMI   See *Electronic Money Institution.*

Sensitive Authentication Data   In PCI DSS terms, sensitive authentication data consists of the CVV1, CVV2, CVV3, PIN/PIN block and the other data elements contained in the discretionary data on the magnetic stripe or chip.

SEPA   See *Single Euro Payment Area.*

SEPA Credit Transfer (SCT)   An EPC payment scheme.

SEPA Direct Debit (SDD Core)   An EPC payment scheme.

SEPA Direct Debit B2B (SDD B2B)   An EPC payment scheme.

SEPA Instant Credit Transfer (SCT Inst)   An EPC payment scheme.

SEPA One-Leg-Out Instant Credit Transfer (OCT Inst)   An EPC payment scheme for transfers between SEPA and non-SEPA countries.

SEPA Payment Account Access (SPAA)   An EPC payment scheme that specifies a service giving Account Servicing PSPs (ASPSPs) the ability to offer value-added services to Third Party PSPs (TPPs) by capitalising on the account data they hold (Proxy Lookup scheme). This could potentially lead to a new surge of open finance services based on data sharing.

SEPA Proxy Lookup (SPL)   An EPC payment scheme that provides a data look-up function to be used before initiating a payment, and it covers mobile payments where the mobile number or associated email address is used as a proxy to an IBAN. This scheme may evolve over time to include additional proxy types and identifiers. This may lead to the development of a Confirmation of Payee (CoP) service.

SEPA Request-to-Pay (SRTP)   An EPC payment scheme that provides a request-to-pay (RtP) functionality.

Service Code   A three-digit number contained in the magnetic stripe or the chip. It is used by issuers to tell merchants about the usage characteristics of the card (i.e. how the card can and can't be used) – for example, whether the card is for international use or domestic only, or whether a PIN is required for all transactions, or whether it's only to be used at ATMs and the applicable interchange.

Service Provider Level   This term is used in the context of PCI standards and dictates the obligations and compliance validation requirements of service providers. Service providers have two levels:
- Level 1: those who process and/or transmit more than 300,000 transactions annually per scheme.
- Level 2: those who process and/or transmit less than 300,000 transactions annually per scheme.

Settlement   The last step in the transfer of value between a payer and a payee. After settlement, the obligations of all the parties are fulfilled and the transaction is considered complete.

Settlement Agent   A bank which orchestrates the finality of the transfer of value between parties that hold accounts with them. On the card rails, settlement agents are usually commercial banks chosen by the card schemes according to their reputation, size, and geographic coverage. On the bank rails, the settlement agent is a central bank.

Settlement Cycle   Refers to the time it takes for payment transactions to be settled. On the bank rails, the settlement cycle is dependent on the bank payment scheme and can be performed in three ways:
- In real time: real-time gross settlement (RTGS) where each payment is presented and settled immediately (this is used by most large-value payment systems (LVPS); or
- In near real time: deferred net settlement several times a day where banks batch their transactions at several points during the day and submit the batch each time. This is used by most real-time retail bank payment schemes (retail payment systems). To a payer, the settlement process is transparent, as the payments take place within seconds and look as though in "real time"; or
- In batch at the end of the day: deferred net settlement, where banks batch their transactions at the end of the day and submit them in one go, and this is used by (older) retail ACH Schemes, and it usually takes a few days.

On the card rails, the clearing and settlement processes are described in the card scheme operating regulations, and the settlement cycle is contingent to the contractual arrangements between parties. Merchant settlement can be deferred by the acquirer as a risk management tool for specific industries (e.g. airline, hospitality).

Shim   See Shimmer.

Shimmer (Shim)   A device used by fraudsters to capture data from the EMV chip. A shimmer fits inside the card payment terminal, unattended payment terminal, or ATM, directly between the card and the card reader, and is therefore difficult to detect (and needs to be less than 0.1 mm thick to enable the card reader to accommodate a card).

Shopping Cart   A software facility on a merchant's e-commerce website that enables customers to make purchases. A virtual terminal should be capable of supporting multiple shopping carts.

SIBS   Portugal's domestic bank payment scheme.

Signature Panel   An area on the back of a card containing two elements: the cardholder signature and a printed three-digit code. On some modern cards, you may also find the whole PAN printed on the signature strip, just before the three-digit code. This acts as a visual reminder for the cardholder when the PAN is not present on the front of the card. The cardholder's signature is used to authenticate the cardholder for face-to-face transactions in chip and signature or non-EMV markets. Also called "signature strip".

Signature Strip   See *Signature Panel*.

Single Euro Payment Area (SEPA)   An initiative that aims to enable payers anywhere in the EU (as well as in a number of other countries) to make fast, safe, and efficient cashless Euro credit transfers (introduced in 2008) and Direct Debits (introduced in 2009) to anywhere within the area, just like national payments.

Skimmer   A device used by fraudsters to read information from the magnetic stripe. Skimmers are most often found at ATMs and petrol stations and other unattended terminals, but shops and restaurants are not immune (although more difficult to compromise, unless the merchant colludes with the fraudster or is negligent). Skimmers are devices overlayed on top of the card payment terminals, and sometimes combined with small cameras to capture cardholder PINs.

Smart Card   A historical term for a chip card.

Smart POS   A type of electronic point of sale (EPOS). Smart POS terminals support standard card payments but also a range of applications to support the merchant's business. They are usually cloud-based and use operating systems such as Android (making them much more flexible) but are still proprietary to their manufacturers.

Society for Worldwide Interbank Financial Telecommunications (SWIFT)   Specifies a set of standard messages and formats that the industry agrees on, thus minimising translation and counterparty verification costs, as well as improving security. SWIFT doesn't actually move funds; the bank payment schemes do that.

SoftPOS   A modern iteration of mobile point of sale (mPOS) which doesn't rely on additional hardware and allows merchants to accept card payments directly on a standard consumer smart phone or tablet (i.e. Android or iOS).

Software Development Kit (SDK)   A collection of software development tools provided in one installable package. An example is SoftPOS virtual card terminals which can be deployed on a merchant's own device (e.g. smart phone or tablet).

Sort Code   A six-digit number used to identity banks in the UK. It's usually split in pairs (e.g. 01-02-03): the first two digits identify the bank and the last four identify the bank branch. Similar to the ABA Routing Number in the US.

SPI   See *Payment Institution*.

Stablecoin   A type of crypto asset with the intended purpose to facilitate trades on crypto exchanges. Stablecoins were created to address the volatility risks associated with cryptocurrencies and can be either pegged to a collateral (e.g. fiat currency, commodity, another cryptocurrency), or rely on a "mint and burn" stabilising mechanism to control the supply. The former is referred to as a "collateralised stablecoin" and the latter as "non-collateralised" or "algorithmic". Stablecoins are becoming increasingly regulated.

Stand-In Processing (STIP)   A process by which a card scheme would step in on behalf of an issuer when that issuer is unable to provide a real-time response during the authorisation process. An issuer may face this situation during planned or unplanned outages or network problems. The card scheme would "stand in" on behalf of the issuer to approve or decline a transaction using pre-defined rules set by the issuer. Whilst this type of service has long been established, card schemes continue to innovate by incorporating new technologies, such as Artificial Intelligence or deep learning models, into the STIP mechanism.

Standing Order   A payment instruction from the bank account holder to their bank to transfer funds to a payee for a fixed amount at a fixed frequency. The payee can be the same person as the instructing bank account holder (e.g. a bank account holder moving funds between their own accounts) or a different person. This is a type of recurring transaction, albeit completely controlled by the payer, unlike Direct Debit. Examples would be when a bank account holder transfers a fixed sum from their bank account to their savings account at the end of every month, or when they transfer money to their children every month. This type of payment is not supported by all bank payment schemes.

STET   France's domestic bank payment scheme.

STET Standard   The French open banking standard.

STIP   See *Stand-In-Processing*.

STP   See *Straight-Through Processing*.

Straight-Through Processing (STP)   A process by which automation is used to process electronic transfers with as little manual intervention as possible. STP applications are in payment processing as well as securities trading. Any company involved with STP must have the necessary infrastructure in place to facilitate STP efficiency.

Strong Customer Authentication (SCA)   An EU regulatory requirement brought by the Second Payment Services Directive (PSD2). It mandates the implementation of two or more authentication factors when authenticating payment transactions. Specific requirements and characteristics apply to the authentication factors. A form of multi-factor authentication (MFA).

Sub-Merchant   A generic term used on the card rails to refer to a small business that uses the services of a merchant aggregator such as a payfac to accept card payments.

Subscription Transaction   Another term for recurring transaction.

Suspicious Activity Reporting   The process by which financial crimes are reported to the regulator.

Sweeping   A process on the bank rails by which funds from one bank account can be moved to another account according to a set of rules set by the bank account holder. For example, covering a short-term deficit in a bank account with funds from another account with a positive balance, or moving surplus funds from an account to another offering higher savings interest.

SWIFT   See *Society for Worldwide Interbank Financial Telecommunications*.

Synthetic CBDC (sCBDC)   A model by which the central bank digital currency (CBDC) is issued by a central bank and private issuers issue, which is then used for retail purposes. This is similar to how eMoney works.

TARGET Instant Payment Settlement (TIPS)   A SEPA messaging system specific to the EU. Essentially the EU equivalent to SWIFT for Euro-denominated payments. Domestic schemes in the EU completed their migration to TIPS in 2022.

TCH   See *The Clearing House.*

Terminal ID (TID)   An identifier issued to a merchant by an acquirer or ISO, usually one per physical or virtual device. The TID ensures that all payment transactions can be linked back to a specific merchant and a specific location for the merchant and, in some cases, a specific device at the specific location. The TID combined with the merchant ID (MID) ensures that the card payment can be traced back to its source.

Terrorist Financing   The provision of funds or financial support to terrorists. A form of financial crime.

The Clearing House (TCH)   A banking association and payments company owned by the largest commercial banks in the US. It is the operator of the RTP® and EPN bank payment schemes.

Third Party Provider (TPP)   A payment ecosystem actor which provides payment service users (PSUs) with access services to payment accounts.

Three Party Model   An economic model by which there is no separation between card acquiring and card issuing. This doesn't promote competition, as commercial terms are set unilaterally by the payment scheme, which also operates as an acquirer and an issuer. This model is also referred to as "closed loop". Examples of payment schemes operating in this model are American Express and Discover. The three parties referred to are the cardholder, the merchant, and the card scheme.

TID   See *Terminal ID.*

TIPS   See *TARGET Instant Payment Settlement.*

TPP   See *Third Party PSP.*

TRA   See *Transaction Risk Analysis.*

Track 1   One of the magnetic tracks contained on a card's magnetic stripe. A data container.

Track 2   One of the magnetic tracks contained on a card's magnetic stripe. A data container.

Transaction Risk Analysis (TRA)   An exemption to Strong Customer Authentication (SCA) that can be applied by PSPs instead of SCA as directed by the EU Second Payment Services Directive (PSD2).

Travel Rule A Financial Action Task Force (FATF) recommendation by which Virtual Asset Service Providers (VASPs) and other financial services institutions are required to share accurate payer and payee information.

TUPAS A digital identity framework in Finland which is a partnership between all Finnish banks.

Two Party Model An economic model in which the merchant is both the issuer and the acquirer. Cardholders for these schemes can only use the card for payments at the issuer, which in this case is the merchant itself. Examples include some store cards (e.g. Target REDcard™ Debit), some fuel cards (e.g. Shell Fuel Card), some public transport cards (e.g. Oyster for Transport for London), and gift cards. These are true closed loop networks.

UK Open Banking The UK open banking standard.

Unattended Payment Terminal (UPT) A self-service payment terminal where the customer interacts directly with the device to obtain goods or services. Examples are self-service terminals at petrol stations, toll booths, vending machines, etc.

Unauthorised Fraud A type of fraud where the account holder hasn't provided authorisation for the payment and the transaction is carried out by a criminal (e.g. the victim's card details are used without their knowledge or consent), or when the account holder acts fraudulently (e.g. a mule account).

UnionPay A card scheme operating on the Four Party Model.

UPT See *Unattended Payment Terminal*.

Utility Token A type of crypto asset with the intended purpose of giving crypto-project developers the ability to raise interest in their project, encourage developers to create applications, and generally create value in a blockchain ecosystem. These tokens can be used to redeem a special service or receive special treatment, and are often given out for free to promote the project (airdrop). Utility tokens are unregulated.

Value Chain A business model describing the steps involved in bringing a product or service to market, from design to distribution, and everything in between.

Valued-Added Reseller (VAR) A business that enhances the value of other companies' products by adding customised products or services to the core product for resale to their customers.

VAR   See *Valued-Added Reseller*.

Variable Recurring Payment (VRP)   A payment instruction issued by a bank account holder to their bank authorising a biller (e.g. a subscription service) to collect payments from their account at regular intervals (e.g. weekly, monthly, yearly), within agreed limits, without the bank account holder's intervention after the first instruction. It is a bank payment scheme overlay service and is a type of recurring transaction, but it offers more flexibility and transparency than alternatives such as Direct Debit and card recurring transactions, as the bank account holder remains in control of the payment limits and the payment instruction's end date is agreed upfront. At any point up to clearing and settlement, the bank account holder can change any of the agreed parameters, enabling them to respond to changes in circumstances as they happen.

VASP   See *Virtual Asset Service Provider*.

VDMP   The Visa Dispute Monitoring Program. See *Merchant Monitoring Programme*.

Virtual Asset   The term "virtual asset" refers to any digital representation of value that can be digitally traded, transferred, or used for payment or investment purposes.

Virtual Asset Service Provider (VASP)   Defined by the Financial Action Task Force (FATF) as a business that conducts one or more of the following actions on behalf of its clients:
- Exchange between virtual assets and fiat currencies;
- Exchange between one or more forms of virtual assets;
- Transfer of virtual assets;
- Safekeeping and/or administration or virtual assets or instruments enabling control over virtual assets; or
- Participating in and provision of financial services related to an issuer's offer and/or sale of a virtual asset.

This encompasses a range of crypto businesses, including exchanges, ATM operators, wallet custodians, and hedge funds

Virtual Currency   A type of virtual asset that is issued, managed, and controlled by private issuers, developers, or the founding organisation. A virtual currency is used in a specific community and relies on a system of trust defined by the private issuer. As such, it is a form of a closed loop medium of exchange.

Virtual Terminal A payment facility that enables e-commerce and other virtual transactions. It is the digital equivalent of a physical card payment terminal.

Visa A card scheme operating on the Four Party Model.

Visa Dispute Monitoring Program A programme to control fraud. In general, merchants will be included in a card scheme's chargeback-monitoring programme if their chargeback ratio exceeds the card scheme limit.

VisaNet The Visa network.

Vocalink A technology provider specialising in bank payment systems. Vocalink provides the infrastructure for the UK retail bank payment schemes (FPS, BACS) as well as the ATM network. Vocalink also provides bank payment infrastructures in other geographies. Acquired by Mastercard in 2017.

VRP See *Variable Recurring Payment*.

Web 2.0 The current version of the internet.

Web 3.0 The next version of the internet. It is a decentralised infrastructure built on blockchain technologies and applications. Also referred to as the "semantic web".

WebAuthn See *FIDO*.

Wholesale CBDC A type of central bank digital currency (CBDC) aimed at financial firms holding reserve deposits with a central bank and using interbank settlement and other financial market transactions.

Wire Transfer A term used to describe a large-value payment system (LVPS) that generally operates on a real-time gross settlement (RTGS) basis.

XS2A See *Access to Account*.

Zip-Zap Machine See *Card Imprinting Machine*.

INDEX

Note: References to boxes, figures and tables are indicated by an italic *b*, *f* or *t* after the page number. References to items in the Glossary are indicated by page numbers in **bold** type.

Printed in the United States
by Baker & Taylor Publisher Services